T0366551

The Canterbury and York Society

VOLUME LXXXVI

GENERAL EDITOR: PROFESSOR R. L. STOREY
ISSN 0262–995X

THE PUBLICATIONS OF THE

Lincoln Record Society

VOLUME 86

ISSN 0267–2634

ROYAL WRITS ADDRESSED TO JOHN BUCKINGHAM

Royal Writs addressed to

John Buckingham

BISHOP OF LINCOLN

1363–1398

LINCOLN REGISTER 12B
A Calendar

EDITED BY

A. K. McHARDY

The Canterbury and York Society and
The Lincoln Record Society

The Boydell Press
1997

First published 1997

A joint publication of
the Canterbury and York Society and
the Lincoln Record Society
published by The Boydell Press
an imprint of Boydell and Brewer Ltd
PO Box 9, Woodbridge, Suffolk IP12 3DF, UK
and of Boydell and Brewer Inc.
PO Box 41026, Rochester, NY 14604–4126, USA

Canterbury and York Society
ISBN 0 907239 58 7

Lincoln Record Society
ISBN 0 901503 63 0

A catalogue record for this book is available
from the British Library

Details of previous volumes of both societies available
from Boydell and Brewer Ltd

This publication is printed on acid-free paper

Printed in Great Britain by
St Edmundsbury Press Ltd, Bury St Edmunds, Suffolk

CONTENTS

To
PAT CRIMMIN
for twenty years of supportive friendship

ABBREVIATIONS

BRUC	A.B. Emden, *A Biographical Register of the University of Cambridge to 1500* (Cambridge, 1963)
BRUO	A.B. Emden, *A Biographical Register of the University of Oxford to 1500*, 3 volumes (Oxford, 1957–59)
CCR	*Calendar of Close Rolls*
CFR	*Calendar of Fine Rolls*
CPR	*Calendar of Patent Rolls*
Complete Peerage	G.E. Cockayne, *The Complete Peerage*, ed. V. Gibbs *et al.*, 12 volumes (London, 1910–59)
C&Y	Canterbury and York Society
Fasti	John Le Neve, *Fasti Ecclesiae Anglicanae 1300–1541*, 12 volumes, revised and expanded edition (London 1962–67); most references are to volume I, ed. H.P.F. King (1962)
Foedera	Thomas Rymer, *Foedera, Conventiones, Littera*, 17 vols. (London, 1704–17)
HBC	*Handbook of British Chronology*, ed. E.B. Fryde, D.E. Greenway, S. Porter and I. Roy, 3rd ed. (London, 1986)
LAO	Lincolnshire Archives Office
LAO Index	Alphabetical Index of Entries in the Institutions Registers of the Bishops of Lincoln: typescript
LRS	Lincoln Record Society
LRS 81	*Clerical Poll-Taxes of the Diocese of Lincoln 1377–1381*, ed. A.K. McHardy, LRS 81 (1992)
McHardy, *SCH* 18	A.K. McHardy, 'Liturgy and Propaganda in the Diocese of Lincoln during the Hundred Years War', *Religion and National Identity*, ed. Stuart Mews, Studies in Church History 18 (1982)
Martival	*The Registers of Roger Martival, Bishop of Salisbury 1315–1330, vol. III: Royal Writs*, ed. Susan Reynolds, C&Y LIX (1965)
PRO	Public Record Office
RDP	*Reports from Lords' Committees touching the Dignity of a Peer of the Realm*, vol. IV (London, 1829)
Reg. 9	LAO, Register of John Gynewell (Institutions)
Reg. 9C	LAO, Register of John Gynewell (Royal Writs)
Reg. 10	LAO, Register of John Buckingham (Institutions I)
Reg. 11	LAO, Register of John Buckingham (Institutions II)
Reg. 12	LAO, Register of John Buckingham (Memoranda)
Reg. 12B	LAO, Register of John Buckingham (Royal Writs)
Rot. Gravesend	*Rotuli Ricardi Gravesend, diocesis Lincolniensis*, ed. F.N. Davis, C&Y XXXI (1925)

Rot. Wells	*Rotuli Hugonis de Welles, episcopi Lincolniensis*, ed. F.N. Davis, W.P.W. Phillimore, H.E. Salter, 3 volumes, C&Y I, III, IV (1907–9)
SCH	Studies in Church History
Smith, *Guide*	David M. Smith, *Guide to Bishops' Registers of England and Wales* (London: Royal Historical Society, 1981)
Sutton	*The Rolls and Register of Bishop Oliver Sutton 1280–1299*, ed. Rosalind M.T. Hill, 8 volumes, LRS 39, 43, 48, 52, 60, 64, 69, 76 (1948–86)
Tout, *Chapters*	T.F. Tout, *Chapters in the Administrative History of Mediaeval England*, 6 volumes (Manchester, 1920–33)
VCH	*Victoria History of the Counties of England* (London, 1900–)
Wilkinson, *Chancery*	B. Wilkinson, *The Chancery under Edward III* (Manchester, 1929)

INTRODUCTION

(i) THE PURPOSE OF THIS EDITION

There are three purposes behind the publication of this edition of Lincoln Register 12B. The first is to place in the public domain a manuscript which has already been lost once and which seemed in danger of being overlooked a second time; the second is to demonstrate the variety and importance of the material contained in this register and in similar collections; and the third is to show how these writs relate to material kept elsewhere, both in other registers of Bishop Buckingham and among the public records, so that the subjects contained here can be pursued more fully.

Lincoln Register 12B is composed of sheets about 34 cm. high and between 23 and 25 cm. wide. It is unbound and unsewn but there are two pairs of sewing holes, one towards the top and another towards the bottom of each sheet, and some traces of a greenish sewing string in a few of these.

This register, which contains most of the royal writs addressed to Bishop Buckingham, was one of a small group of Lincoln episcopal registers which at some time became separated from the rest. Perhaps the separation took place around 1600, for it was 'about James I's time' that the first twenty-nine Lincoln registers were bound, 'in undressed brown calf with clasps'.[1] Several registers, including Register 12B, were not bound at this time and still remain in limp parchment covers. This register at least did not remain unknown, for in 1887 A.R. Maddison (1843–1912), a canon of Lincoln and distinguished local historian, published one of the writs (**210** in the present edition) in the *Archaeological Journal*.[2] However, these unbound registers were, with one exception, unknown to Canon Foster who gave the first systematic description of the Lincoln episcopal registers in a paper delivered to the Canterbury and York Society and which was subsequently printed in 1935.[3] In the same year, though, the Pilgrim Trust gave a grant of £2,000 to set up the Lincoln Diocesan Record Office, and it was the archivist first appointed to take charge of this office, Miss Kathleen Major, who described and numbered six more bishops' registers. Her description of this exciting time was set out in a paper read to the Royal Historical Society on 8 December 1938, and is characteristically

---

[1] C.W. Foster, 'The Lincoln Episcopal Registers, being the substance of an address delivered to the Canterbury and York Society', *Reports and Papers of the Associated Architectural and Archaeological Societies* vol. xli, pt. II (1935), 155–68b. The exception was Reg. 5B which Canon Foster described on p. 159.

[2] 'Original Documents: from a volume of "brevia regia" issued during the episcopate of John Bokingham, Bishop of Lincoln', *Archaeological Journal* XLIV, pp. 403–4. To the transcript of the writ is appended a history of the Moigne family until 1578, with a conjectural family tree. See further, Nicholas Bennett, 'A.R. Maddison and the Development of Local History in Lincolnshire', in Christopher Sturman, ed., *Some Historians of Lincolnshire*, Society for Lincolnshire History and Archaeology: Occasional Papers 9 (1992), pp. 27–31.

[3] Foster, 'Lincoln Episcopal Registers', 155–68b.

modest and brief: '. . . in the last two years a few supplementary registers have been assembled from various boxes and placed with the main series'.[4]

The registers discovered by Miss Major were 7B (Thomas Bek, Ordinations), 9B, C, and D (John Gynewell, Royal Writs, Licences and Dispensations, and Ordinations), 12B (John Buckingham, Royal Writs), and 15B (Philip Repingdon, Royal Writs). The inadvertent omission of 12B from the Royal Historical Society's invaluable *Guide to Bishops' Registers of England and Wales*[5] suggested to the present editor that a calendar of this register, made some years earlier in the course of postgraduate research, might usefully become the basis of an edition.[6] In the course of arranging the newly-discovered registers, a gathering of writs addressed to Bishop John Gynewell (1347–62) was placed with those addressed to Bucking-ham.[7] Conversely, a gathering of writs addressed to Buckingham was mistakenly placed among the licences and dispensations issued by Gynewell, Register 9C. The former properly belong with a future edition of 9B (Gynewell, Royal Writs) and have been omitted, but the latter are included in this edition as **145–185**.[8]

(ii) ROYAL WRITS ADDRESSED TO BISHOPS: A HISTORY OF REGISTRATION

The earliest royal writs to be recorded in a Lincoln register occur during the episcopate of Oliver Sutton (1280–99). These were all entered into the sections of the register, mainly institutions, where they applied. Thus we have one writ, 1282, in the archdeaconry of Lincoln section of the institutions.[9] The equivalent section for the archdeaconry of Northampton and the deanery of Rutland yields twenty-three writs, the earliest of 1281, the latest 1299, nearly all being mandates to admit a particular candidate to a benefice following a lawsuit.[10] The *memoranda* section contains two writs, but only one, a *certiorari* concerning the validity of a marriage, was addressed to Sutton; the other was directed to collectors of a clerical tax.[11]

After Sutton's death royal writs received during the vacancy were copied onto a separate roll by those responsible for record-keeping;[12] the impetus may well have come from John de Schalby, for eighteen years the registrar of Bishop Sutton, probably the registrar of his successor, and from 1299 to 1333 a canon of Lincoln.[13] During the episcopate of John Dalderby (1300–20) another collection of royal writs

4   Kathleen Major, 'The Lincoln Diocesan Records', *Transactions of the Royal Historical Society*, 4th series XXII (1940), 39–66, esp. p. 40.
5   By David M. Smith (London, 1981). Ironically an article on 12B appeared in the same year: A.K. McHardy, 'Notes on a Neglected Source: a Register of Royal Writs in the Lincoln Diocesan Archives', *Lincolnshire History and Archaeology* 16 (1981), 25–7.
6   'The Crown and the Diocese of Lincoln during the Episcopate of John Buckingham 1363–98', D.Phil. thesis (Oxford, 1972).
7   Reg. 12B, ff. 1–5v.
8   Reg. 9C, pp. 21–32 (there is no ancient foliation). See Smith, *Guide*, p. 114. I am grateful to Dr. Nicholas Bennett for drawing my attention to these 41 writs.
9   An *admittatis* concerning a moiety of Kirkby Laythorpe, Sutton, I.31. Professor Smith points out that the probable response to a writ, if not the writ itself, is to be found in *Rot. Wells*, II.204 (1223).
10   *Sutton*, II.9–10, 15–16, 29–31, 35–40, 56, 72, 77, 79–80, 85, 88, 97, 100–101, 109, 132–3, 142, 144–5, 164.
11   *Ibid.*, V.49, 131–2.
12   LAO, Records of the Dean and Chapter of Lincoln, D&C A/4/7/2.
13   *The Book of John de Schalby concerning the Bishops of Lincoln and their Acts*, ed. and trans. J.H. Srawley, Lincoln Minster Pamphlets 2 (1966), p. 3. The identification of Schalby's hand was made by

was apparently made, of which the part covering the years 1308–9 survives as a fragment.[14]

For the next century copies of writs were more systematically made and preserved, and at the end of a long episcopate they were numerous enough to form a separate register, while after a short one they formed a section of a composite register and were often bound next to the *memoranda*. Thus we have a register, 5B (213 ff.) from the time of Henry Burghersh (1320–40), 50 folios of writs (Reg. 7B, ff. 17–67) from the time of Thomas Bek (1342–47), and a complete register, 9C (104 ff.), plus a detached section (ff. 1–4) of 12B from Gynewell's episcopate (1347–62).

After Buckingham's time the short tenure of the see by Henry Beaufort (1398–1404) yields only 10 folios of writs in his single register (Reg. 13), while Philip Repingdon, who succeeded Beaufort in 1405, kept enough writs between then and his resignation in 1419 to yield a slim register of 20 folios (Reg. 15B). The steep decline in the volume of surviving writs continues thereafter; Richard Fleming's interrupted tenure of Lincoln is covered by writs dated during only four years of the first part of his episcopate.[15] The five years of William Gray's time at Lincoln show a more systematic keeping of royal writs (Reg. 17, ff. 189–95, Sept. 1431 – July 1435), but during the years of William Alnwick (1437–49) and Marmaduke Lumley (1450) no separate writ collections survive. After a two-year vacancy John Chedworth became bishop of Lincoln in 1452 but early zeal was not maintained in the registry and only writs dated June 1452 are now extant (Reg. 20, f. 323).

Just as Lincoln had taken the lead in registering ecclesiastical business at the beginning of the thirteenth century,[16] so it seems to have taken the lead in forming collections of royal writs at the end of it. However, a number of other dioceses followed suit: Winchester,[17] Exeter,[18] Canterbury,[19] Worcester[20] and Hereford.[21] At Salisbury the earliest extant collection of royal writs dates from the episcopate of Roger Martival, but the manuscript is such a model of efficiency – with the date of receipt and the content of the return that was made recorded so meticulously – that it is hard to imagine that this was a first attempt to keep such a register by the Salisbury chancery.[22] Interestingly, before becoming bishop of Salisbury Roger

---

Canon Foster, and his conclusions followed by Professor Hill, *The Registrum Antiquissimum of the Cathedral Church of Lincoln*, ed. C.W. Foster, vol. I, LRS 27 (1931), pp. xxviii–xxxv.

[14] LAO, D&C A/7/2a-c. This and the subsequent information about writs in registers is derived from Smith, *Guide*.

[15] 1420–23 inclusive. Richard Fleming was bishop 1420–24 and 1425–31, see Smith, *Guide*, p. 117 and n.

[16] Smith, *Guide*, p. vii.

[17] *Registrum Henrici Woodlock, diocesis Wintoniensis, A.D.1305–1316*, ed. A.W. Goodman, 2 vols., C&Y 43, 44 (1940–41).

[18] Devon Record Office, Reg. Walter Stapledon (1308–26), ff. 185–216v.

[19] Lambeth Palace Library, Reg. Walter Reynolds (1313–27), ff. 296–313.

[20] Hereford and Worcester Record Office, Thomas Cobham (1317–27), royal writs *temp.* Cobham 1317–21 are bound in Reg. Walter Maidstone, pp. 111–14.

[21] *Registrum Thome Charlton, episcopi Herefordensis, A.D. MCCCXXVII–MCCCXLIV*, ed. W.W. Capes, Cantilupe Society (1912) and C&Y 9 (1913). 'Charlton's register . . . is the first Hereford register to be subdivided into category sections, firstly a section (without a heading) chiefly devoted to commissions (ff. 1–11v), followed by sections containing royal writs (ff. 12–23)', Smith, *Guide*, p. 97.

[22] 1315–30, *Martival*.

Martival was dean of Lincoln from 1310, where for five years he kept greater residence, along with John de Schalby who played an important part in a jurisdictional dispute between Martival and the canons.[23]

The registering of writs by the Lincoln chancery declined and disappeared in the first half of the fifteenth century, and the presence of a distinctive collection of writs disappeared from registers of other dioceses in the southern province. At Canterbury Henry Chichele (1414–43) was the last archbishop in whose register a section devoted exclusively to royal writs can be discerned.[24] The same is true of the registers of Nicholas Bubwith (1406–7) of London, of Robert Hallum (1407–17) of Salisbury, and of Robert Mascall (1404–16) of Hereford.[25] Only at Winchester, during the long episcopate of William Waynflete (1447–86), was the old tradition maintained,[26] but then Waynflete was a meticulous administrator and, moreover, a man drawn into the highest level of government service only in middle life.[27]

It is probably no coincidence that bishops' chanceries began to make distinctive records of royal writs during, and shortly after, the reign of Edward I. This was a period in which crown-church relations occupied a higher profile than at any point since Henry II, witnessing as it did such important legislation at the statute known as *mortmain (de viris religiosis)* (1279), and the ecclesiastical clauses (numbers 1, 2 and 28) of the statutes of Westminster I (1275) and (numbers 5, 19, 32, 33, 41 and 43) of Westminster II (1285), and the issuing of the writ or so-called statute of *circumspecte agatis* in the summer of 1286.[28] Later, outbreak of a war on two fronts, against France and Scotland, led to greatly increased financial demands on the church. The pan-European dispute over kings' rights to tax their clerical subjects, which in England took the form of a dispute between Edward I and Archbishop Winchelsey, had a direct result on the number of writs addressed to prelates,[29] while the treatment of alien priories throughout the Anglo-French wars of the fourteenth century followed closely the measures devised for their custody and exploitation in 1295.[30] The many writs addressed to Bishop Buckingham on the subjects of debts arising from direct taxation of the clergy and from the crown's custody of alien

[23] Kathleen Edwards, *The English Secular Cathedrals in the Middle Ages* (Manchester, 1967), pp. 332–3; *The Book of John de Schalby*, ed. Srawley, p. 3.

[24] Lambeth Palace Library, Reg. Chichele II, ff. 373–8, printed, *The Register of Henry Chichele, Archbishop of Canterbury 1414–1443*, ed. E.F. Jacob, vol. IV (Oxford, 1947), pp. 303–14.

[25] His register was edited by J.H. Parry, Cantilupe Society 8 (1916).

[26] Hampshire Record Office, A1/13, ff. 1–24v (second series); A1/14, ff. 1–24v (second series). This information is derived from Smith, *Guide*, p. 208.

[27] Virginia Davis, *William Waynflete: Bishop and Educationalist* (Woodbridge, 1993), pp. 22–34.

[28] Sandra Raban, *Mortmain Legislation and the English Church 1279–1500* (Cambridge, 1982), esp. chap. 1; *Statutes of the Realm* vol. I (Record Commission, 1810), pp. 26–39, 71–95. These texts may conveniently be consulted in translation in Harry Rothwell, ed. and trans., *English Historical Documents vol. III, 1189–1327* (London, 1975), pp. 419–20, 397–410, 428–57.

[29] Brian Tierney, *The Crisis of Church and State 1050–1300* (Englewood Cliffs, New Jersey, 1964), chaps. 3 and 4, prints in translation, with references, the most important texts generated by the quarrels between Philip IV and Boniface VIII. The English aspect of the dispute is the subject of J.H. Denton, *Robert Winchelsey and the Crown 1294–1313: a Study in the Defence of Ecclesiastical Liberty* (Cambridge, 1980).

[30] *CFR 1272–1307*, pp. 362–6; see also Alison McHardy, 'The Effects of War on the Church: the Case of the Alien Priories in the Fourteenth Century', in Michael Jones and Malcolm Vale, eds., *England and her Neighbours 1066–1453: Essays in honour of Pierre Chaplais* (London, 1989), pp. 277–95, and references.

priories in times of war thus stemmed directly from the international politics of the 1290s.

Similarly, the changes in the content, quality and size of bishops' registers in the first half of the fifteenth century were probably also the result of the shifting pattern of the English church's relationship with the crown. For not only did the practice of creating separate collections of royal writs gradually cease but the character of bishops' registers, especially the *memoranda* sections, changed in those years; in general they became shorter and, for historians' purposes, less diverse and interesting. The records of institutions became, by the mid- to late-fifteenth century, the pre-eminent concern of bishops' chanceries, just as they had been for much of the thirteenth century.

We may speculate on why this change took place. The start of the making of bishops' rolls and registers coincided with advances in record-keeping in the royal chancery during the reign of King John (1199–1216), a fact to which Canon Foster long ago drew attention.[31] It was during the first half of the fifteenth century that the very strong links between royal government and the clergy became weakened.[32] So it is surely reasonable to infer that the gradual decline in the standard of eccesiastical record-keeping was the result of a loosening of the links between the clergy and royal government which were such a feature of earlier centuries.

In fact, the number of writs registered by the Lincoln episcopal chancery had already begun to fall by the time of Bishop Buckingham. The total number of writs in Reg. 12B, just over 500, which over an episcopate of thirty-five years represents an average of only fourteen a year, is recorded on seventy-five folios. By contrast the twenty-year episcopate of Henry Burghersh has left us a register (5B) which is 213 folios long. A calendar of a little under half this register (the first ninety-three folios) reveals 715 writs.[33] In fact, Burghersh's chancery practice has much more in common with that of his Salisbury contemporary Roger Martival (1315–30) than with that of his successor Buckingham; not only did the fifteen years of Martival's episcopate generate a writ register of 327 folios containing over 870 writs (fifty-eight a year), but Martival's registrar, like Burghersh's, was meticulous in recording the date of receipt and the return or execution which a writ prompted.[34]

A number of suggestions may be advanced to explain the proportionally much smaller number of writs surviving from John Buckingham's long episcopate. In the first place, it is clear that a number of enregistered writs have been lost; the first quire of writs addressed to him ends with **25** which is dated 12 December 1364, but **26** is dated 14 October 1365, so that almost a year's worth of writs has failed to survive. A similar loss has occurred for the year 1375, from which only one writ, **186**, has survived.

It is also clear that when the bishop was bombarded with writs on a particular

[31] In 1935, *loc. cit.*, p. 156.
[32] J.L. Kirby, 'The Rise of the Under-Treasurer of the Exchequer', *EHR* 72 (1957), pp. 666–77; J.C. Sainty, 'The Tenure of Offices in the Exchequer', *ibid.* 116 (1965), pp. 449–57; R.L. Storey, 'Gentleman-bureaucrats', in Cecil H. Clough, ed., *Profession, Vocation and Culture in Later Medieval England: Essays dedicated to the memory of A.R. Myers* (Liverpool, 1982), pp. 90–129, esp. the Appendix, pp. 110–29.
[33] Prepared by Miss Judith Cripps while an assistant archivist at LAO. Her manuscript calendar has the reference MCD 997, and her description of Reg. 5B is in the *LAO Archivists' Report* 26 (1975–77), pp. 42–4. Thanks are due to Professor Smith for a copy of this lively description.
[34] *Martival, passim.*

subject not all were copied onto the parchment sheets which would later form the register. To take but one example, the flurry of writs concerning the status of Maud Huntercombe (**416–20**) were not the only ones on the subject; another, which was not entered, survives along with its return in the public records and is noted in **Appendix A, no. 17**.

It was also the case that a number of writs were registered among the *memoranda*, and even more with the institutions, as will be clear from **Appendix B**; in particular, writs of consultation and prohibition, issued in the course of advowson suits in the royal court, were more likely to be registered among the institutions than with other royal writs. It is also true, as we shall see further in section iv, that writs on particular subjects, especially those of national importance such as summonses to parliament, or mandates to organise special prayers, might be entered either among other writs, or in the *memoranda*, with no apparent principle behind the decision.

However, it is clear that between the episcopate of Henry Burghersh and that of John Buckingham a change of policy had taken place, and we may illustrate this by analysing a sample of the writs addressed to Burghersh. During the first four years of Burghersh's episcopate 300 writs were received.[35] They may be divided into the following groups: papal taxes (9 writs), enquiries (9), debts to the crown, including taxation (42), debts to religious houses (17), patronage (1), miscellaneous (3), crime – mainly theft but including two cases each of assault and trespass – (25 writs, all issued by the court of King's Bench), and debts to individuals (193).

We can see from this sample that what made the greatest difference between the size of the two writ registers was the exclusion from Register 12B of two classes of business. One was criminal matters, save in those cases, to be discussed below, which had financial implications for the crown. Anyone wishing to pursue this subject in Lincoln diocese in the later fourteenth century must do so in the Public Record Office in the class KB 145. The second, and more important, exclusion was of private debts. In our register only two cases of debts to private individuals occur: one involved a John Yarborough, an associate of the bishop (**434, 440**);[36] in the other case (**207**) the bishop was himself the creditor. In Burghersh's register, on the other hand, private debts accounted for nearly two-thirds of the first 300 writs received.

(iii) THE SUBJECT MATTER OF THE WRITS

The royal writs addressed to medieval English bishops and preserved in their archives have been neglected by scholars; ecclesiastical historians see writs as too worldly to be worth their attention, while historians of politics, government and law tend to regard any material in episcopal registers as too far from the real and

[35] Reg. 5B. The first ninety-three folios were calendared by Miss Judith Cripps while an assistant archivist at LAO, and the conclusions arrived at here are based on her calendar, LAO, MCD.997. See also 'The Writ Register of Bishop Burghersh (Register 5B)', *LAO, Archivists' Report* 26 (1975–77), pp. 42–4.
[36] There were two prominent men of this name, the receiver-general of the duke of Lancaster, and his brother, *John of Gaunt's Register*, ed. S. Armitage Smith, Camden Third Series XXI (1911), II.321. The man named in these writs is probably to be identified with the John Yarborough who was associated with Buckingham in making a grant to Louth Park abbey, who was a joint keeper of Haugham alien priory, *CPR 1381–5*, p. 343; *CFR 1377–83*, p. 286.

mainstream world of public life to concern them. Yet this class of material has much to offer both classes of enquirer, as this edition should show. Above all, these documents enable historians of government and administration to see how royal and episcopal authority worked in practice, and what were the limitations on their power. If this collection has a moral it is a cheering one: that administration, especially government administration, was fallible and inefficient then as now, and that its ability to get its own way was extremely uneven.

It should be emphasised at the outset that most of the writs in this volume were not issued at the personal command of the monarchs reigning in the second half of the fourteenth century: Edward III and Richard II. On the contrary, these were writs 'of course', that is, mandates in standard form, which were issued on routine business; this applies even to those issued by Chancery, with their apparent attestation by the king himself, 'Myself as witness' (*Teste me ipso*). The routine and uncontentious nature of so many of these writs enables us to see behind the rhetoric and posturing of chronicles and parliamentary proceedings to the reality of government, if not for the peasantry, then at least for some of the middling and lesser ranks of society, and the many writs arising from actions before the court of Common Pleas give us some perspective on the operation of law from the viewpoint of the consumer.

The changing history of the spiritual life of later fourteenth-century England is represented here by the enquiry (**446**) concerning the activities of Amia Palmer, a writ of *venire faciatis*, and not, as one might have expected, of *corpus cum causa*. The long return to this writ tells us much about a radical group of lollards active in Northampton in the middle 1390s, tells us how changed the ideas of Wyclife had become by this time, and also provides a list of lollard beliefs which are precisely dated. The Latin text of these opinions has already been printed, and at least some of them subjected to detailed scrutiny.[37] John Wyclife himself was the subject of **227**, but this concerned not his ideas but his brief employment on a diplomatic mission for which he had failed to return overpaid expenses.[38] Tangential to these are **437–9** issued on behalf of Wyclife's former follower Philip Repingdon. A canon of Leicester abbey as well as an Oxford graduate, Repingdon abjured his heretical beliefs in October 1382 and eleven years later was elected abbot of Leicester.[39]

Repingdon became abbot under somewhat unusual circumstances. William Kereby, abbot since 1378, resigned in May 1393, but before doing so arranged for himself a corrody of exceptional generosity.[40] Kereby was probably infirm at the time of his resignation – he died within a year – and his apparent incapacity, the

---

[37] A.K. McHardy, 'Bishop Buckingham and the Lollards of Lincoln Diocese', in *Schism, Heresy and Religious Protest*, ed. Derek Baker, SCH 9 (1972), 131–46; see also Margaret Aston, ' "Caim's Castles": Poverty, Politics and Disendowment', in *The Church, Politics and Patronage*, ed. R.B. Dobson (Gloucester, 1984), pp. 45–67, esp. 48–9.

[38] A.K. McHardy, 'John Wycliffe's Mission to Bruges: a Financial Footnote', *Journal of Theological Studies* 26 (1973), 521–2.

[39] *BRUO*, III.1565–67 gives a succinct account of his career, with references; his *memoranda* register has been edited by Margaret Archer for the Lincoln Record Society, vols. 57 (1963), 58 (1963) and 74 (1982). The introduction to volume I gives a full account of Repingdon's episcopate.

[40] Printed in translation, with comment, by A. Hamilton Thompson, 'A Corrody from Leicester Abbey, A.D. 1393–4, with Some Notes on Corrodies', *Transactions of the Leicestershire Archaeological Society* xiv (1926), 114–34.

expenses of a recent archiepiscopal visitation, and the generous corrody all probably contributed to presenting his successor with difficult financial circumstances,[41] and the new abbot responded by pursuing a number of the abbey's ecclesiastical debtors. During his time Repingdon played several parts, but that of 'astute financier' is one that has not hitherto been recognised. Sir John Clanvowe, another person with lollard tendencies, also makes appearances (**286, 295, 326**), again in a financial context.[42]

Although not theological, a number of writs were directed to the bishop because of the church's jurisdiction over matters of Christian life which had worldly, especially financial, implications. Matrimonial matters formed one such category. In every instance these enquiries were generated by cases of dispute over property which were being heard in the royal courts. All seem to have have arisen from allegations made late in the case: the other party cannot inherit because he or she is a bastard, or because a marriage was invalid (**410, 412**), or a divorce had taken place (**225, 503, 505**) so leading to loss of dower rights. The suspicion is that these allegations were made by the party which was in the wrong and was casting about for desperate means by which to delay the loss of their case. This was certainly true of the case of Katherine Hebden (**506–9**), for her adversary, Sir John la Warre, had first alleged that her supposed mother died without issue. At stake was land in south Lincolnshire, in five parishes including Gosberton, which was disputed between la Warre and Katherine and her husband Sir Nicholas Hebden, and a minor called John Verdon. Buckingham's commission of enquiry found that Katherine was not a bastard, and the Hebdens evidently won their case, for the house of Nicholas Hebden, knight, of Gosberton, is mentioned in 1408.[43]

Of some dozen allegations of bastardy the most interesting case concerned the legitimacy of Bernard Brocas junior (**287**). The Brocas family, who were of Gascon origin, were of considerable prominence by the mid-fourteenth century, and the varied activities of this clan are well-documented and have received considerable attention.[44] The writ in Register 12B arose from a dispute between Bernard Brocas junior and his stepfather, Sir Henry Langfield. The elder Brocas, Sir Bernard, knight, was married three times, his first wife, and the mother of Bernard junior, being Agnes Vavasour, daughter of Mauger Vavasour of Denton, Yorkshire, and of Weekley, Northamptonshire. If the witnesses called in support of the younger Bernard were correct, the marriage took place when the groom was aged no more than fifteen. After the birth of three children – Bernard junior, and two daughters, Margaret and Joanna, whose existence has not been otherwise recorded – the couple were divorced before May 1360. An unusual feature of this divorce was that both parties were permitted to remarry, but Agnes' second husband, Henry Langfield, did not benefit to the extent he might have expected from this match since much of her property was settled on the son of her first marriage. On Agnes' death, which

---

[41] A. Hamilton Thompson, *Leicester Abbey* (Leicestershire Archaeological Society, 1949), pp. 51–4.

[42] K.B. McFarlane, *Lancastrian Kings and Lollard Knights*, part two, chap. V and appendix B.

[43] *The Register of Philip Repingdon*, ed. Margaret Archer, LRS 58 (1963), II.268.

[44] The latest and most reliable account, with references, is the biography of Sir Bernard Brocas MP (c.1330–95), by Linda Woodger, now Clark, in J.S. Roskell, Linda Clark, Carole Rawcliffe, *The Commons 1386–1421*, History of Parliament (Stroud, 1992), I.359–62. The information in the following paragraph is derived from this unless otherwise stated.

took place before 26 January 1385, the inquisition *post mortem* on her property in Northamptonshire found that she had no lands in the county.[45]

The four witnesses who testified to Bernard junior's legitimacy included a relative, Arnold Brocas, who was a prominent king's clerk,[46] and most interestingly, William Hermite who had been the parochial chaplain of Clewer, in Berkshire, at the time when the marriage took place there. After an interval of forty years his vivid recollections included the names of some of the wedding guests and the wording of the ceremony itself, and his testimony forms an interesting comparison to the wedding service recorded in **308**. The account of the Brocas wedding adds to discussion of the importance of the church porch in marriage ceremonies found in Professor Brooke's survey of medieval marriage.[47] In the extensive testimony on this case no mention was made of the divorce of the elder Bernard Brocas and Agnes Vavasour, though this is documented. Contrariwise, in Katherine Hebden's case, in which a previous marriage of her mother also allowed her adversary to make an allegation of bastardy, the fact of her mother's divorce (though the word itself is not used) was the main element in Katherine's testimony.

Related to these questions of marital status and bastardy were two cases which enquired whether a particular woman was a nun. The first case was **43, 44 (Appendix A, no. 1)** dated 20 May 1367 asking whether Alice (Alesia, Aleisa) daugther of John de Everingham was a nun of Haverholme priory (Lincs.: Gilbertine) as William Prestwold master of the order of Sempringham alleged, and the second **416–20 and Appendix A, no. 17** dated from the early 1390s and asked whether Maud Huntercombe was a professed nun of Burnham abbey (Bucks.: Augustinian). It should perhaps not surprise us that the question of whether a particular woman was a nun should arise. Many religious houses for women included a number who were neither professed nuns nor novices nor *conversae*; young girls of good family might be sent to nunneries for some of their upbringing, while it was a common practice for widows to retire to a religious house as a 'paying guest'. The problem of the status of such women had long been a matter of concern.

Our evidence in the first case, though it was clearly not the start of the business, begins on 21 January 1366 when Buckingham issued a letter to the dean and chapter of Lincoln cathedral, and to abbots, priors, rectors, vicars and parochial chaplains throughout the diocese; he had written earlier, he said, to denounce Alice, daughter of John Everingham, who was, it was alleged, an excommunicate nun of Haverholme. Her friends, however, maintained that she had been excommunicated by the malice of William Prestwold, master of the order of Sempringham, and she herself had lodged an appeal with the court of Canterbury where her case was pending; therefore sentence was to be stayed until the outcome was known.[48]

The master still pressed his suit against her and signified her as being excommunicate and an apostate on 17 November 1366, a royal mandate for her arrest

---

[45] *Calendar of Inquisitions Post Mortem XVI (7–15 Richard II)*, no. 155. No inquisition was held into her former property in Yorkshire.

[46] Clerk of the king's works, an office he resigned on becoming chamberlain of the Exchequer, appointed 6 Jan. 1388, Tout, *Chapters*, III.430 n. 3, 451–2.

[47] Christopher Brooke, *The Medieval Idea of Marriage* (Oxford, 1989), chap. 10, 'The Church Porch: Marriage and Architecture', pp. 248–57, and references.

[48] Reg. 12, f. 26.

being issued on 12 December.[49] She then lodged a document in Chancery explaining that she had appealed to the pope for the redress of her grievance and to the court of Canterbury for defence. She and Prestwold were ordered to appear in Chancery a month after Easter 1367, and on 13 February a mandate to stay execution of the order against Alice was issued.[50] A writ was therefore despatched on 20 May 1367 to Buckingham ordering an enquiry to be made into Alice's status, but both this and a subsequent writ, referred to but not entered in the register, arrived too late for the bishop to take action (**43**). A third writ, which with its return survives both in the orignal (**Appendix A, no. 1**) and in the register copy (**44**), elicited the return that after enquiry it was found that Alice was not a nun. The answer was made on 8 February 1368 and as a result, on the 12th of the month, the crown mandate for her arrest was cancelled, an action repeated two days later when the bishop's return was enrolled.[51] This was not the end of the matter, for the master then appealed to Rome, but the rest of the story eludes us.[52]

A quarter of a century later, in 1391–92, Buckingham received a flurry of writs on the subject of Maud Huntercombe (**416, 417**). These asked on what day and year Maud had assumed the religious habit at Burnham abbey and whether or not she was professed in the order. Meanwhile, on 10 July the abbess of Burnham reported Maud as a religious apostate, a vagabond in secular habit who was likely to be found in the counties of London and Berkshire, among other places.[53] Stay of execution of the first two writs was ordered on 6 November 1391, but a year later the process started again, with writs issued through the winter of 1392–93 (**418–20**, and **Appendix A, no. 17**). Buckingham had set up a commission of enquiry in July 1392 and sent his return to the final writ on 20 April 1393. By then the matter had come not only before Chancery but even before parliament as a petition.

This was high profile territory for the Huntercombes, a minor Buckinghamshire family of which three successive heads were called John. John I, always called Sir John, had three sisters (Elizabeth, Agnes and Margaret) and was the father of John II and of two daughters, Maud (the subject of the writs) and Elizabeth (who married). John II was survived only by one child, John III. It was the deaths in quick succession of John III, a childless minor, and of his aunt Elizabeth, a married woman, on 12 August 1390 and 10 January 1391, respectively, which provoked the crisis.[54] For the temptation to better himself was too much for Giles Frensh, a local man who claimed that Maud was his wife and that as Elizabeth's heiress the property at issue, two-thirds of the manor of Huntercombe, should be hers. To make good his claim he seems to have abducted Maud.

Frensh was described as a servant of the king, and was indeed a yeoman of the household.[55] He was evidently also a hard taskmaster, taking legal action against William Skynner of Maidenhead for leaving his service in quest of better wages,

---

[49] PRO, Significations of Religious Apostates, C81/179.1791 (Sempringham), no. 2; *CPR 1364–7*, p. 369.

[50] *CPR 1367–70*, p. 83; *CPR 1364–7*, p. 428.

[51] *CPR 1367–70*, p. 83.

[52] F. Donald Logan, *Runaway Religious in Medieval England c.1240–1540* (Cambridge, 1996), p. 24.

[53] PRO, C81, File 1789 (Augustinian), no. 3.

[54] *Calendar of Inquisitions Post Mortem, vol. XVI, 7–17 Richard II*, pp. 404–5.

[55] I am informed of this by Ms. Shelagh Mitchell who is writing a thesis on the household of Richard II. His relationship to Giles Frensshe, yeoman of the king's chamber who in 1386 received a corrody at Evesham abbey, is unclear. They may have been father and son, or perhaps the same person since the corrody may not have been effective, *CCR 1385–8*, p. 272.

'contrary to the ordinance'.[56] Since the manor of Huntercombe as well as Burnham abbey and the place of Frensh's residence all lay within the parish of Burnham we might view this as a little local difficulty. But a powerful spectator to the proceedings was Elizabeth's widower, Sir Robert Cherlton (**Appendix C**), then chief justice of Common Pleas, and it is hard to imagine that he was not consulted about the decision of Maud and Elizabeth's three aunts and their husbands to sue Giles Frensh in Chancery.

The episode was apparently ended by Buckingham's return of 29 April 1393 which reported that his enquiry had shown that Maud was indeed a nun. Maud's aunts duly won their case and it was from the descendants of two of them, Elizabeth and Margaret, that in 1440 Henry VI was to acquire the manor of Huntercombe along with the crucial advowson of Eton parish church for his new foundation of Eton College.[57]

In addition to questions about the status of individuals the church also had jurisdiction over testamentary matters and these gave rise to one interesting case among our writs which, like the legitimacy of Bernard Brocas, spilled over into the bishop's *memoranda* register (**451–3**). The will was that of Richard Cary who had died in the Black Death, in June 1349.[58] Cary was a prominent citizen of Oxford; he was already a leading member of the city council in December 1324 when he witnessed the foundation of what was later called The Queen's College.[59] He married Alice, daughter of William Bicester, a former mayor (1311), and himself was mayor in 1328. From then until his death he was either mayor or an alderman in every year but two (1329 and 1336). Cary became involved with the pious benefactions of his father-in-law, as did his brother-in-law Nicholas and his own son John, and the complications of these chantries, spread over more than five decades, rather than any family dispute, seem to have been behind the three writs addressed to Buckingham.[60] What is notable here is that the lay power was deciding which of two wills was the genuine one, and making a direct impact on the contents of the bishop's register as a result.

If the dispute over Cary's will arose from the confusion resulting from a life cut short by the Black Death, a number of writs arose, either directy or indirectly out of dramatic political events. Thus the *coup* of 19–20 October 1330, in which Roger Mortimer, earl of March, was toppled from power by the young Edward III and his associates, had financial results which were still unresolved decades later (**112, 126, 149**). The downfall of another political figure, Michael de la Pole, earl of Suffolk, was the subject of two writs (**361, 362**) addressed to his former receiver; the first was the result of Pole's impeachment in the 'Wonderful Parliament' of 1386, the second the consequence of the appeal against him in the 'Merciless Parliament' of 1388.

Edward III's attempts to manipulate the wool market to pay for his continental war during the earlier years of his reign also generated a number of writs. Three

---

[56] *CCR 1389–92*, p. 497.
[57] Eton College Records, 38/194, 54/3, 36/85. Thanks are due to Mrs. Hatfield, the archivist of Eton College, for identifying these items and sending me copies of the catalogue calendars.
[58] For what follows see *VCH Oxfordshire* vol. IV (1979). His biography can be constructed from pp. 19, 43, 59, 67–8, 283.
[59] By Adam de Broom, *CPR 1324–7*, p. 63.
[60] See *VCH Oxfordshire*, IV.384, and K.L. Wood-Legh, *Perpetual Chantries in Britain* (Cambridge, 1965), pp. 32–3.

series of writs – (**21, 29, 59**), (**36, 138**) and (**25, 139**) – arose directly out of the wool scheme of 1337 in which the king and his associates intervened directly in the wool market, their plan being to push up prices artificially. These were the long-term results of a policy whose failure is well known and has received considerable attention,[61] though perhaps the crown's tenacity in pursuing defaulters at every level for so many years has not hitherto been appreciated. In the early 1340s Edward III turned for the first time to English financiers to raise the loans necessary for sending expeditions abroad, and in 1343 a company was formed, headed by Thomas Melchebourne of Lynn (**135**), which first collected the customs on wool, and then farmed them.[62] Politics also obtruded in a number of less dramatic ways. Summonses to parliament are one example of this. The writs calendared here have been both printed and calendared elsewhere,[63] but worthy of attention is the action which they provoked and, in particular, the evidence that the *praemunientes* clause to summon representatives of the lower clergy continued to be taken seriously by the bishop (**157, 186, 213, 236, 253, 257, 267, 274, 293, 341, 394, 415, 432, 490, 496**).[64]

Above all, politics in the fourteenth century meant 'war', and this is strongly reflected in the subject matter of the writs. There was a summons to the bishop to appear in the field with the feudal service which he owed (**288**), and there were five requests for prayers, either for particular expeditions, or for the war effort (often disguised as prayers for peace) in general (**214, 275, 323, 353, 395**).[65]

The greatest impact of the war on the church was financial and the imposition and collection of direct taxation on the clergy forms the largest single item of subject-matter of this collection. Every aspect of this subject is covered: mandates to collect taxes and to appoint the local collectors who would actually do the work (**133, 197, 208, 216, 254, 263, 282, 289, 296, 317, 349, 357, 403, 422, 450, 462**), assessment of taxation (**219, 235**) and exemption from taxes on account of poverty (**457**). The greatest number of writs on this subject concerned arrears of taxation, sometimes dating back for decades (*passim*; see subject index). A very small number of writs recorded the payment of overdue taxes and ordered the sequestration of the subjects' property to be relaxed (**40, 67, 81, 103**). The large number of mandates about taxation forms another of the contrasts between the writ register of Buckingham and that of Burghersh; we may speculate that it was the large number of writs about debts to the crown which had forced those about private debts out of the register.

It was not only the crown which could tax the English clergy; the papacy had a similar and more ancient right. It was, however, little exercised in the fourteenth century, and such impositions of papal taxation as took place were shared with the crown, which took the major share.[66] Papal taxation is the subject of a small number

---

[61] Notably from Professor E.B. Fryde, many of whose papers are printed in *Studies in Medieval Trade and Finance* (London, 1983).
[62] G.O. Sayles, 'The "English Company" of 1343 and a Merchant's Oath', *Speculum* VI (1931), pp. 177–205; E.B. Fryde, 'The English Farmers of the Customs, 1343–51', in *Studies in Medieval Trade and Finance* (London, 1983); T.H. Lloyd, *The English Wool Trade in the Middle Ages* (Cambridge, 1977), pp. 194, 198–9. I owe thanks to Professor Mark Ormrod for directing me to these references.
[63] *RDP* and *CCR*.
[64] For some discussion see McHardy, 'The Representation of the English Lower Clergy in Parliament during the Later Fourteenth Century', in *Sanctity and Secularity: the Church and the World*, SCH 10 (1973), pp. 97–108.
[65] Discussed in McHardy, SCH 18.
[66] W.E. Lunt, *Financial Relations of the Papacy with England 1327–1534. Studies in Anglo-Papal*

of items in the register; two (**6, 204**) were about the first fruits of benefices, the latter being one of the few non-writs in this collection. Numbers **19** and **94** concerned the quadrennial tenth levied by the pope between 1330 and 1333 and whose profits were shared with Edward III, 'who was in the enviable position of receiving the money without incurring the opprobrium of imposing the tax'.[67] However, after the outbreak of the French war in 1337 the English crown was able, as a matter of routine, to impose taxes upon the English clergy and to keep the entire profits for itself. Hence the prohibition against collecting a papal tax, issued in 1389 (**363**).

Allied to the imposition and collection of direct taxation on the clergy was the treatment of the alien priories, which were taken into the king's hand in time of war against the French. These were then farmed out, often to the priors themselves, especially in the earlier phases of the war, but increasingly to king's clerks, and the profits of this process went to the Exchequer, or to prominent courtiers.[68]

The result was that the crown took a certain interest in the financial health of these small houses, for it was especially concerned that debts to them were paid so that the farmers would be able to meet their obligations at the Exchequer. Hence those who owed money to alien priories found that during periods of war, when these were taken into the king's hands, the crown became their creditor (*passim*; see subject index under Aliens, priories, debts to). The line between a private debt and a debt to the crown could thus be crossed very easily.

Another instance of the way this could happen was when a creditor died leaving an heir in royal wardship. This was the case when the earl of Pembroke died leaving his three-year-old son a royal ward, so that debts to the dead earl became debts to the crown (**262, 270, 291, 304**). Less surprising was that debts to Queen Philippa also became debts to the crown on her death (**93, 113, 124, 141, 368, 377, 408**). More unusual were those instances in which the creditor had his property confiscated so that his debtors found themselves being pursued by the royal administration (**112, 126, 149**).

Much more usual were the cases in which a royal official had demitted office leaving his financial obligations to the crown in some disarray. The case of Wycliffe, a 'temporary contract worker', has already been mentioned, but career officials like John Stretele the former constable of Bordeaux (**7**) and William Sleaford clerk of works at Westminster and the Tower (**367**) were also involved. Noteworthy in these cases are the wide geographical implications of these writs, from the shipping routes round Brittany in the west, *via* diplomatic discussions in Bruges, to timber shipped from Riga in the east.

Akin to these were the writs concerning the executors and successors of royal officials or agents for money owed on crown business. It was because clerics were often appointed as executors that the diocesan administration was drawn into these testamentary cases involving, for example, the profits of the customs (**135**), the

---

Relations in the Middle Ages II (Cambridge, Mass., 1962) is the classic exposition of this subject. However, it suffers greatly from the lack of an index. A recent clear analysis of papal revenues from England, with references to this and other work by Lunt, is to be found in A.D.M. Barrell, *The Papacy, Scotland and Northern England, 1342–1378* (Cambridge, 1996), chap. 1.

[67] *Ibid.*, p. 22.

[68] McHardy, 'The Effects of War on the Church', pp. 277–95.

repair of Oakham castle (**260**) and allied to this, the administration of the manor of Berkhamstead, a detached part of the duchy of Cornwall (**381**, **448**, **466**, **474**, **497**).

A bishop might also be involved with the inception of an individual's period of public office. Thus Buckingham was ordered to receive the oaths of a customs collector (**294**), a constable of the staple (**383**), two sheriffs (**247**, **489**) and two escheators (**382**, **456**). More unusually, Buckingham was permitted to receive the attorneys of a man about to go overseas (**203**), an interesting departure from the common practice – recorded in the close rolls _passim_ – by which attorneys were received by chancery clerks.

A considerable number of writs concerned court actions between clerks for the recovery of debts (_passim_; see 'Debts, to religious houses', in the subject index). Debt had been confirmed as a lay plea by the Constitutions of Clarendon in 1164, though clerks had the privilege that they could not be imprisoned for debt.[69] The commonest type of case was that in which the plaintiff was a religious house and the defendant an incumbent who owed money arising from his benefice. The sum outstanding was usually arrears of rent, though it was occasionally a pension. Most of these debts were of cash but in three cases of debt to Leicester abbey involved wax as well (**223**, **283**, **437**). The great majority of these debt cases arose from the mesne process, the stage between the issuing of the original writ and the defendant's appearance in court. Fifty years ago Margaret Hastings called for more work to be done on this stage of cases before this court, and it is hoped that these writs will assist such enquiry.[70]

Though the criminal side of diocesan life made little impact on the contents of this register, a few writs concerned crime, broadly defined, in some way. One asked if a particular individual, convicted in the lay courts and delivered into episcopal custody, was dead (**2**). Individuals sought for 'crimes and excesses' (**37**) and even for kidnapping (**137**, **143**) were being pursued by the Exchequer, as was a suicide (**259**, **266**) in the person of his executor. Enquiries by the court of King's Bench sought to discover when a particular man was married to a widow, in which case he would be considered a bigamist and so unable to claim benefit of clergy (**39**, **58**, **218**).[71] The concept of a guilty animal, in this case a horse who had killed a man, is found in three writs issued by the Exchequer; an animal (or even inanimate object) would in this case be forfeit, through the crown to the church as a gift to God (**372**, **374**, **385**).

Indeed, the crown's financial interest in its subjects is the overriding impression which this collection of writs conveys, and allied to this was a willingness in turn to support lesser property-owners against their debtors. Yet, as we have seen, debts to private individuals could easily become, through accident or royal policy, debts to the crown. The majority of the writs here were generated, either directly or indirectly, by the war with France and show that this war affected all sections of the clerical estate in every part of the diocese.

Finally, it is pertinent to enquire to what extent this collection illuminates the state of relations between the lay and ecclesiastical jurisdictions. The 'grass roots'

---

[69] T.F.T. Plucknett, _A Concise History of the Common Law_, 5th ed. (London, 1956), p. 17; L.C. Gabel, _Benefit of Clergy in England in the Later Middle Ages_, Smith College Studies in History XIV, 1–4 (1928–29), p. 59.

[70] M. Hastings, _The Court of Common Pleas in Fifteenth Century England_ (Ithaca, N.Y., 1947), chap. XII: 'Mesne Process'.

[71] Gabel, _Benefit of Clergy_, pp. 87–90.

view of crown-church relations evident in the writs addressed to Bishop Bucking-ham contrasts with the matters of high policy and the drama of conflict, especially when these involved Anglo-Papal relations, which have traditionally caught the attention of historians of the fourteenth century.[72] Little of this is to be found in Register 12B, though one writ forbade the bishop to collect a papal subsidy in which the crown had no share (**363**). A small number of writs and their returns illustrate the interaction of lay and ecclesiastical courts. In two writs reference was made to the statutes of provisors (**483, 492**). Two other writs, both about disputed advow-sons, were prohibitions against proceeding with cases in the ecclesiastical courts (**339, 460**). Another *ne teneatis* (**284**), issued by the Exchequer, was aimed not at preventing the hearing of a case but at postponing it. Buckingham had caused a summons to be served on John Dautre, rector of Leckhampstead (Bucks.) and clerk of John Hermesthorp a chamberlain of the Exchequer, citing him to appear at Lidington on the morrow of Hilary 1383, a day when he would be busy at the Exchequer. The bishop was not to punish Dautre for non-appearance on that day, since the king's business should take precedence over the bishop's. It was doubtless a sentiment with which Buckingham, himself a king's clerk for sixteen years, would not have disagreed.[73]

There is also evidence about attempts to impede cases by having them trans-ferred to the wrong court, in each instance the defendant falsely claiming that the case came within the jurisdiction of the lay court, and so effecting the issue of a prohibition. In one instance the defendant pretended that the case was one of chattels and debt (**248**), but a consultation was subsequently issued when it was discovered that the issue was one of adultery (**249**). In another, the prohibition (**240**) alleged that a plea of trespass had been brought by the rector of Wheathampstead against one of his parishioners. The consultation (**241**), however, acknowledged that the charge was one of violence to the rector, which, as the defendant well knew, lay within the jurisdiction of the court Christian. This last writ may be discerned as stemming from the so-called statute of *circumspecte agatis*, which had confirmed that violence to clerks was a plea which pertained to church courts.

The influence of *circumspecte agatis* may also be detected in the writs arising from cases involving tithes, for it had stated that tithe cases belonged to ecclesias-tical jurisdiction where they formed not more than a quarter of the benefice's total value. Only the consultation (**331**) was entered in the case of the prior of Beaulieu v. Walter Alnthorp about tithes in Clophill, in which the defendant had maliciously alleged that he was being sued for debt.

Two other tithe cases are represented by writs of *certiorari*. The first concerned the yearly value of St. Andrew's church, Sawtry; the annual value of two parts of its tithes; and the question whether the two parts constituted a quarter of the value of the church (**358**). Buckingham replied that the tithes' annual value was estimated to be 20 shillings, less than a quarter of the church's total value, 12 marks. Another dispute, between two Lincolnshire rectors, those of West Keal and Bolingbroke, was delayed by the rector of Bolingbroke's assertion that the dispute concerned an advowson. When the true nature of the case was made known a mandate was

---

[72] The most recent account, with references, is to be found in Robert C. Palmer, *English Law in the Age of the Black Death 1348–1381* (Chapel Hill, N.C., 1993), chap. 4: 'Regulating the Church'.
[73] Buckingham was a king's clerk from 1347 to 1363. Most of his offices can be ascertained from the references in Tout, *Chapters*, VI.171.

directed to Buckingham to discover the value of the tithes in question (**371**), though it is not known what action he took.

This small group of writs shows both clergy[74] and laymen obtaining writs of prohibition against the church courts, sometimes with malicious intent. Little is known, however, about the church courts of the diocese in this period,[75] and it is ironical that the whole series of Lincoln registers of royal writs, which are chiefly records arising from business in royal courts, should have been carefully preserved, while records of the ecclesiastical courts are almost totally lacking before the sixteenth century.[76]

(iv) LINKS BETWEEN REGISTER 12B AND OTHER SOURCES

The writs entered by Buckingham's clerks into what would become a separate register cannot be viewed in isolation. Not only is this collection incomplete, as we have seen, but anyone wishing to pursue particular subjects will find that the trail of evidence leads into other registers and other archives. In the first place, the Public Record Office offers rich rewards, and as more work is done on the legal records the reader's task will become easier. This is an exciting area in which to work. The class of Chancery *certiorari* (ecclesiastical), C 269 shows what can be gleaned from one class. A related class is C 243 Chancery: *levari facias*; these are mostly addressed to sheriffs but clerks were often the subject of the mandates. However, this class does contain a few writs addressed to bishops; C 243/65/12 is a case in point, being the original writ and return of **3** in the register. One file of C 269 is concerned with gathering information about aliens beneficed in England (**Appendix 1, no. 30**), and the introduction to the new standard list set for C 269 directs readers to C 145 (Chancery: Miscellaneous Inquisitions), for similar enquiries but addressed to sheriffs. Another class connected to C 269 is E 179, the Clerical Series, where may be found the original and return to **116**.

Numerous writs include helpful cross-references to the voluminous records of the Exchequer, especially the *Memoranda* Rolls – though it it not immediately apparent whether these refer to the King's Remembrancer series (E 159) or the Lord Treasurer's Remembrancer series (E 368) – and to the Pipe Rolls (E 372). However, the cases arising from Common Pleas may be pursued by the stout-hearted into the massive plea rolls (CP 40). Other, less daunting, classes of documents arising from this court are in preparation; Dr. Crook hopes soon to start work on the unsorted Common Pleas files of writs (CP 52).

As far as the bishop's own registers went, it is clear that the demarcation lines between them were far from absolute. Indeed, osmosis seems to characterise the four registers which survive from this episcopate. As a rough rule we can say that lengthy enquiries generated by writs were, when enregistered, noted in the bishop's memoranda (for example, **287**, **308**, **451–3**, **506–9**), though a notable exception is

---

[74] G.B. Flahiff, 'The Use of Prohibitions by Clerics against Ecclesiastical Courts in England', *Medieval Studies* III (1941), 101–16.

[75] C. Morris, 'The Commissary of the Bishop in the Diocese of Lincoln', *Journal of Ecclesiastical History* X (1959); 'A Consistory Court in the Middle Ages', *ibid.* XIV (1963).

[76] K. Major, *A Handlist of the Records of the Bishops of Lincoln and the Archdeacons of Lincoln and Stow* (Oxford, 1953), p. 55.

446. It is also true that writs addressed to the bishops as a group – for example, summonses to parliament[77] and mandates to proceed against heretics[78] – were as likely to be entered in the memoranda as among the writs. Letters patent can also be found in both the memoranda and institutions registers. Among the memoranda are to be found *mortmain* licences,[79] and among the institutions not only presentations to benefices,[80] and revocations of the same,[81] but also permissions to elect new heads of religious houses, and the ratification of such elections,[82] all subjects which can also be found, and more speedily pursued, in the printed calendars of Chancery rolls. Disputes over advowsons might leave their mark on more than one register, but were likely to involve the institutions rather than memoranda. An example is the Bedfordshire parish of Wilden. Writs of *certiorari* were entered in the collection of writs (**145, 175**), while two consultations arising from the disputed advowson were entered among the institutions (**Appendix B**). Another Bedfordshire benefice, Marston Moretaine, generated even more documentation which was enregistered in a similar pattern (**449, 454, 455** and **Appendix B**).

Surpassing both these was the archdeaconry of Buckingham. The dignity was the subject of disputes for almost forty years, from the early 1350s until the early 1390s, and though the outline of the story is already known[83] more details can be filled in by recourse to references drawn from Lincoln Registers 10, 11, 12 and 12B. There are four writs on this subject in the writ register (**388, 390, 391, 396**), and another in the second institutions register (**Appendix B**). References in Buckingham's first register of institutions refer enquirers to the memoranda,[84] and material on that subject may certainly be found there.[85] Buckingham's registers do not provide the whole story of this contested benefice, which, as the references in Le Neve's *Fasti* show, also spilled out into both royal and papal records.

On some subjects, however, the enregistering of writs seems to have been somewhat haphazard. One writ and its execution was duplicated in Register 12, f. 420, and 12B (**456**). Most summonses to parliament were entered in the writ collection (for the twenty-six writs of summons, and prorogations, see the subject index). Two, however, were entered among the *memoranda*.[86] In the case of taxation there seem to have been changes of policy; mandates to levy clerical taxes were almost always recorded in the memoranda register[87] until 1381 when they were entered among the writs, a practice which continued until the last two grants made during the episcopate (1397 and 1398)[88] when the orders to appoint collectors and

---

77 Reg. 12, ff. 29v, 69v.
78 'Breve Regium contra T. Compworth', Reg. 12, f. 311. This was part of a provincial drive against Compworth, and the entry began with a commission from Archbishop Courtenay (f. 310v), and ended with a commission of Buckingham, 30 Aug. 1385. The most recent discussion of Compworth's career is by Maureen Jurkowski, 'Lawyers and Lollardy in the Early 15th Century', in Margaret Aston and Colin Richmond, eds., *Lollardy and Gentry in the Later Middle Ages* (Stroud, 1997), pp. 155–82.
79 *Ibid.*, ff. 335v–336, 386, 394v.
80 Reg. 10, f. 45v; Reg. 11, f. 160, for example.
81 Reg. 11, f. 160; Reg. 12, f. 166v.
82 Reg. 11, ff. 301v, 385v.
83 See *Fasti*, I.15.
84 Reg. 10, ff. 410v, 450v.
85 Reg. 12, ff. 99–99v.
86 Reg. 12, ff. 29v, 69v.
87 Reg. 12, f. 118 (1370/72), ff. 134–5 (1371), f. 145 (1377), ff. 182–183v (1979), f. 196v (1380).
88 Following the meeting of convocation in April 1397, at which a moiety of a tenth was granted, no

the subsequent commissions were again entered in the memoranda register. Why these changes should have been made is not clear, but convocation material – the summonses and choosing of proctors – was entered in the memoranda, and the granting of taxation was of course the chief business of that body. Also, in the 1370s much of the taxation was of a new and experimental kind and the instructions of successive archbishops of Canterbury for the organisation of these new taxes were crucial; the memoranda register was clearly the appropriate place for archiepiscopal letters. At the end of the episcopate there was clearly considerable confusion; politically there was turmoil, with Archbishop Arundel exiled in the summer of 1397. The Lincoln episcopal administration may also have become more lax as the bishop aged, for Buckingham, whose career can be traced back to 1346,[89] can scarcely have been less than eighty years old by 1397.

(v) EDITORIAL METHOD

The calendar printed here follows the style and nomenclature adopted by Miss Susan Reynolds in her edition of *The Registers of Roger Martival Bishop of Salisbury 1315–1330, volume III: Royal Writs* (C&Y LIX, 1965), and those wishing to discover the Latin of the writs in this edition are referred to the formulary to be found on pages xiv–xxxiii of that volume. Where the language of the present material seemed especially unusual, important or even puzzling a transcript (in brackets) has been given so that readers may evaluate it for themselves. Occasionally a writ, execution, or return has merited a full transcript; in these cases an English summary is printed first.

Editorial insertions are printed in square brackets. Margin flags or headings are underlined.

No attempt has been made to convert old money into decimal equivalents. Women's Christian names have been partially and selectively modernised.

Where possible place-names have been identified and given in their modern spelling, with the help of Eilert Eckwall, *The Concise Oxford Dictionary of English Place-Names*, 4th ed. (Oxford, 1960). In the calendar entries the modern forms of place-names are given first, with the manuscript form following in round brackets. The counties referred to are the ancient counties of England.

Where dates are related to moveable feasts I have converted these into modern calendar equivalents. However, I have not converted the fixed dates which were such important landmarks in the administrative year: Michaelmas 29 September (octave 6 October, quindene 13 October), Martinmas 11 November (octave 18 November, quindene 25 November), Hilary 13 January (octave 20 January, quindene 27 January), the Nativity of St. John the Baptist 24 June (octave 1 July, quindene 8 July).

---

writ ordering collection appears to have been sent out by the crown, but instead instructions were issued by Archbishop Arundel, Reg. 12, f. 460–460v; ff. 460v–461 (1398).
[89] He was ordained as a priest 15 April 1346, *The Register of Wolstan de Bransford*, ed. R.M. Haines, Worcestershire Historical Society, N.S. IV (1966), p. 249.

(vi) ACKNOWLEDGEMENTS

This volume was completed during a period of study leave. I am most grateful to the Trustees of the Leverhulme Foundation for granting me a Fellowship which made this completion possible earlier than would otherwise have been the case, and provided valuable thinking time.

I am greatly indebted to Professor M.C.E. Jones for his help with the Anglo-Norman material in this volume. Thanks are also due to those who have answered queries about particular matters, especially Professor Mark Ormrod and Professor David Smith. Both Professor Smith and Dr. David Crook of the Public Record Office kindly read a draft of the introduction and portions of the text, and made helpful suggestions for additions and improvements. I was particularly fortunate in being able to call on the unique combination of ecclesiastical and legal expertise possessed by the general editor, and have availed myself of this freely. The errors and defects remaining are all my own work. Finally, thanks are due to Val Idoine, chiropractor, and to Kathleen Morison, teacher of Alexander Technique, for enabling me to complete this work in comfort.

ROYAL WRITS ADDRESSED TO
THE BISHOP OF LINCOLN
1363–1398

LAO, Register 12B (John Buckingham, Writs)

1. [f. 5] <u>Monicio pro parliamento</u>[1]
Summons to attend parliament at Westminster on the octave of Michaelmas [6 Oct.]. Order to summon the dean of Lincoln and all the archdeacons to be there in person, with *praemunientes* clause (to warn the chapter to elect one proctor, and the clergy of the diocese to elect two).
Teste me ipso 18 June 1363.
[EXECUTION]. The writ is contained in a mandate of the bishop to the official of archdeacon Lincoln ordering execution and the return of a written report by the feast of St. Faith [6 Oct.].
Woburn, 9 July 1363.[2]

    [1] See *CCR 1360–4*, pp. 536–7, and *RDP*, IV.634.
    [2] See Reg. 12, f. 10v for the appointment of Buckingham's own proctor.

2. Inquisicio pro Ricardo de Elianore de Brokhole
Chancery *certiorari* to know whether Richard Elianore de Brokhole, who was indicted before John Moubray and Thomas de Ingelby, justices of gaol delivery at Northampton, and who was then delivered to the bishop's prison under clerical privilege, is dead.
Teste me ipso 28 June 1363.
RETURN. After diligent enquiry we found that Richard Elianore de Brokhole died in our prison at Banbury on 4 August 1362.

3. Bloxham
Chancery *levari faciatis de bonis ecclesiasticis*, returnable on the quindene of Michaelmas, against Lambert de Trikyngham rector of Bloxholm (Bloxham), for £20 which he received as a loan from the hanaper of Chancery, and whose term for repayment has now elapsed, as Richard de Ravenser, keeper of the hanaper of Chancery has testified.
Teste me ipso, Clipston, 15 Aug. 1363.
RETURN. No ecclesiastical goods of Lambert could be found in the diocese at the time of the reception of the writ, as the official of the archdeacon of Lincoln in whose archdeaconry Bloxholm church is, has certified; therefore we could not levy the money.[1]

    [1] The original writ, with the return on the dorse, is PRO, Chancery: *Levari facias* C243/65/12. The only addition is the name Burstall beside the dating clause.

4. [f. 5v] <u>Breve contra Talerand' cardinalem prebend' de Thame</u>[1]
Exchequer *certiorari (scrutatis registris)* to know whether Talleyrand, cardinal of Perigord, is now prebendary of Thame. We know that he was so in 20 Edward III, but, if he is not, we wish to know the day and year of his death, and the name of the present holder and the date of his institution; and *leviari faciatis* returnable at the Exchequer on the quindene of Michaelmas against Talleyrand, for 112 shillings being the tax on the first moiety of a tenth granted by the clergy in 20 Edward III and 112 shillings for the second moiety.
Teste William de Skypwyth, 4 July 1363.
Return. This writ arrived on 10 October and therefore on account of the shortness of time we could not execute it.

    [1] For Talleyrand's intermittent tenure of the prebend of Thame from 3 July 1335 until his death on 17 Jan. 1364 see *Fasti*, I.116, XII.40. His ecclesiastical and diplomatic careers are fully

charted in Norman P. Zacour, 'Cardinal Talleyrand de Perigord', *Transactions of the American Philosophical Society*, N.S. vol. 50, part 7 (1960).

5.   Breve de certiorando quis extitit prebendarius prebende de Thame
Exchequer *certiorari (scrutatis registris et aliis memorandis vestris)*, returnable on the quindene of St. Martin [25 Nov.], to know who was prebendary of Thame at the time of the grant of a clerical tenth in 20 Edward III, as 112 shillings are in debt to us for the first and 112 shillings for the second moiety of that grant.
Teste William de Skypwyth, 15 Oct. 1363. By the great (Pipe) roll for the 37th year in Oxfordshire.

6.   [ff. 5v–6] Breve de levando 1 libros de decano Wellen'
Exchequer *venire faciatis*, returnable on the quindene of Hilary, against William Hemyngton, rector of Pytchley (Pyghtesleye), executor of the will of Richard de Drury [*sic, rectius* Bury], deceased, lately dean of Wells,[1] to answer for the first fruits due to Pope John XXII for four years, half of which were granted to the king for urgent business, and for £50 arrears of the second year of the said reservation. Note of return of no lay fee by the sheriff of Northamptonshire on the morrow of Michaelmas, 36 Edward III.
Teste William de Skypwyth, 23 Nov. 1363. From the Easter Memoranda Roll (*Recorda*) 22 Edward III and the Memoranda Roll of Easter 34 Edward III (*Brevia Retornabilia)* and a writ returned to the Exchequer on the morrow of Michaelmas as above.
    [1]   1333; subsequently bishop of Durham, 1333–45, *Fasti*, VI.107; for his biography see *BRUO*, I.323–6.

7A.   Breve contra Magistrum Johannem Stretele
Exchequer *distringi faciatis* against all the goods, lands and chattels of Master John de Stretele lately constable of Bordeaux, and mandate to have his person before the Exchequer barons at Westminster on the morrow of the close of Easter [1 April 1364] to render account for the issue of our Breton *brefs* at our town of Bordeaux ('de exitis de brevibus nostris Brytanum apud civitatem nostram Burdeg')[1] from the time of the death of William de Wakefield, as Master John has not submitted his account. Note of return of no lay fee by John de Boys sheriff of Lincolnshire at the Exchequer on the morrow of Hilary.
Teste William de Skypwyth, 10 Dec. 1363, from the *originalia* roll of 35 Edward III and the Memoranda Roll of Michaelmas 38 Edward III (*Brevia Retornabilia.*)
    [1]   *Brefs* were safe-conducts for ships sailing round the coast of Brittany, and a valuable source of revenue for the administrations of Brittany and Gascony. See Michael Jones, *Ducal Brittany 1364–1399* (Oxford, 1970), p. 5, for definition, and the index s.v. *brefs de mer* for their importance.

7B.   [f. 6v]. Another copy of **7A**
RETURN. We could find no ecclesiastical goods of the said Master John Stretele in our diocese at the time of the receipt of the writ, and John is said to tarry in parts across the sea, so we could not in any way execute the writ.[1]
    [1]   Stretele (or Stretley) was dean of Lincoln cathedral from 17 Jan. 1361 until his death in 1368 or 1369, *Fasti*, I.4, XII.1. His arms, *Gyronny of eight or and sable, on a canton gules a covered cup of the first*, are carved on the dean's stall in the choir stalls of Lincoln cathedral, M.D. Anderson, *The Choir Stalls of Lincoln Minster* 2nd ed. (Lincoln, 1967), p. 47. His career can be

followed in *BRUO*, III.1804, in Tout, *Chapters*, see VI.408 for refs., esp to V.376 n. 5, and in P. Chaplais, 'The Chancery of Guyenne 1289–1453, pt. II, 1337–1453', in J. Conway Davies, ed., *Studies Presented to Sir Hilary Jenkinson* (Oxford, 1957), pp. 81–96. See *CPR 1367–70*, p. 161, for the pardon of his debts to the Crown, 30 Oct. 1365.

8.   [f. 6] Breve contra Rectorem ecclesie de Clopton'
Common Pleas *venire faciatis*, returnable on the quindene of Hilary, against John, rector of Clopton to answer the prior of St. Neots about a plea of debt of £20 15s 8d being arrears of a rent of 24s 8d p.a. Note of return of no lay fee by the sheriff of Northamptonshire on the octave of Martinmas [18 Nov.].
Teste Robert de Thorp 25 Nov. 1363.

9.   Breve contra Petrum de Dyngle Rectorem de Brampton
Common Pleas *venire faciatis*, returnable on the quindene of Hilary, against Peter rector of Brampton near Dyngle to answer the prior of St. Neots about a plea of debt of £40 being arrears of a rent of £5 p.a. Note of return of no lay fee by the sheriff of Northamptonshire at Westminster on the octave of Martinmas [18 Nov.].
Teste Robert de Thorp, 25 Nov. 1363.
RETURN. The writ came too late ('Tarde venit'.)

10.   Breve contra Abbatem Sancti Jacobi Northampton' nuper collectorem decime Regis
Exchequer *fieri faciatis de bonis et beneficiis ecclesiasticis*, returnable on the quindene of St. Hilary, for 5s from Finedon (Thyngedon) church, 20s from Bray-brook (Braybrok) church, 4s from the pension of the prior of Daventry in the same church, 10s from 'Mungewell' church, 5s from 'Grafton'[1] church, 5s from Alvescot (Alvescote) church, 36s 8d from the prebend of Empingham (Empyngham), 4s from Swalcliffe (Swalclive) church, with which the abbot of St. James, Northampton, collector of the last tenth granted to us in the archdeaconries of Northampton, Buckingham, Oxford, Huntingdon and the deanery of Rutland is charged, as appears by inspection of the rolls of the Exchequer; the money is to be given to the collector, and your actions in this matter signified to the Exchequer.
Teste William de Skypwyth, 22 Oct. 1363, from the account rolls of the said tax and the assessment roll of the spiritualities of Northampton archdeaconry.

    1   Either Grafton Regis or Grafton Underwood, Northants., or Grafton, Oxon.

[There are no margin notes from here until **64** f. 16v.]

11.   [f. 6v] Exchequer *certiorari (scrutatis registris et aliis memorandis vestris)* and *sequestrari faciatis*, returnable at the Exchequer on the quindene of Easter [7 April], against the prebendary of Lidington. We see by inspection of the rolls of the Exchequer that the prebendary of Lidington owes us 64s for the second tenth granted 25 Edward III and 32s for the second term of the tenth granted 30 Edward III and we know that the present holder was not the holder then. Mandate to find out the name of the then holder, if he is still alive, and if not, the day and year of his death, and to sequester the amounts from him or from his goods and chattels in the hands of his executors; also to find out who is the present holder and when he was installed.
Teste William de Skypwyth, 6 Feb. 1364.
Execution: we have caused the registers and other memoranda to be searched and

we find that John de Provana[1] was prebendary of Lidington in the years 25 and 30, and still is, it is said, but we could find no ecclesiastical goods of that prebend at the time of the receipt of the writ, so could not levy the money.

  [1] John de Provane held Liddington from 1348 until 1369 (?), *Fasti*, I.85.

12. Common Pleas *fieri faciatis de bonis ecclesiasticis sicut pluries*, returnable within three weeks of Easter [14 April], against Robert, rector of Langley (near Stevenage) (Langeleye Chenduyt), for 41 marks being arrears of a pension of 2 marks p.a. owed to the prior of Nostell (St. Oswald's), and 2 marks recovered against the said rector by the prior in Common Pleas in 28 Edward III. Note of return of no lay fee by the sheriff of Hertfordshire.
Teste Robert de Thorp', 6 Feb. 1364.

13. [f. 6v] Common Pleas *venire faciatis sicut alias*, returnable within three weeks from Easter [14 April], against Roger de Sutton rector of Glatton church, to answer the abbot of Missenden about a plea of debt of £20 being arrears of a rent of £4 p.a. Note of return of no lay fee by the sheriff of Huntingdonshire.
Teste Robert de Thorp, 10 Feb. 1364. Roll 309.

14. Exchequer *venire faciatis*, returnable within a month of Easter [21 April], against John rector of Clopton church[1] to show cause why he should not pay clerical tenths on his benefice which is valued at 20s, as the prior of St. Mary, Huntingdon, has told us. Note of return of no lay fee by the sheriff of Northamptonshire on the octave of St. Martin [18 Nov.].
Teste William de Skypwyth, 12 Feb. 1364.

  [1] See **8** for another charge against the rector.

15. [f. 7] Exchequer *certiorari (scrutato registro)* concerning the holder of the prebend of Milton [Ecclesia] in Lincoln cathedral for the years 11, 18, 10, 30 Edward III, as he owes:
£4 for the third year of the triennial tenth granted 11 Edward III;
£4 for his spiritualities for the first year of the triennial tenth granted 18 Edward III;
£4 for the second tenth of the biennial tenth granted granted 10 Edward III;
£4 for the first tenth of that same grant;
£4 for the first year of the triennial tenth granted in 11 Edward III;
£4 for the seond year of the same tenth;
40s from the church of Milton for the first term of the tenth granted 30 Edward III whether the holder is now dead, and who is now the prebendary and when he was installed.
Teste Henry de Greystock, 6 June 1364.
RETURN. Gaillard de la Motte (Gayllardus de Mota) cardinal deacon of St. Lucy (Santa Lucia) in Cilite was archdeacon of Oxford and prebendary of Milton in 11, 18, 10 and 30 Edward III and for many years before the said year 10, and Peter Aquens' cardinal priest of the Crowns of Four Saints is now prebendary of Milton prebend and was installed in 1362 but we do not know on which day.[1]

  [1] Gaillard de la Motte, cardinal deacon of Santa Lucia in Orthea, was archdeacon of Oxford and prebendary of both Aylesbury and Milton Ecclesia from 1312 until his death on 20 Dec. 1356, though his tenure of those prebends did not go unchallenged, *Fasti*, I.14, 25, 91; XII.33.

Peter de St. Martial occurs as prebendary of Milton Ecclesia in the Lincoln chapter accounts for the financial year 1364–65, and apparently succeeded Motte after a period when there was no holder of this benefice, *ibid.*, I.91.

16. [*Inquiratis de bastardia*], returnable before the justices of assize in Buckinghamshire at Wycombe on Thursday after Valentine's Day [20 Feb. 1365] by letter patent. William de Leicester and Agnes his wife brought in the king's court before the justices of assize in Buckinghamshire at [High] Wycombe an assize of *mort d'ancestor* against John de Broughton for two messuages with appurtenances in Stony Stratford formerly belonging to Thomas le Forster father of the said Agnes whose nearest heir she was, and she said that she was in possession from the day he died. But the said John objected that the said Agnes could not be an heir as she is a bastard, and William and Agnes say she is legitimate and not a bastard. Mandate[1] to convene an enquiry.
Teste Robert de Thorp, Wycombe, the Tuesday before the feast of St. Margaret the Virgin 38 Edward III [18 July 1364].

> [1]   In intention this writ is the same as *inquiratis de bastardia*, though this form of words does not occur; see Martival, p. xxxii.

17. [ff. 7–7v] [*Inquiratis de bastardia*], returnable before the justices of assize at Northampton on the Monday after St. Peter in Cathedra [24 Feb. 1365] by letters patent. Margaret Baudewyne of Thrapston in the king's court before Thomas de Ingelby and Illard de Usflet justices of assize in Northamptonshire at Northampton, brought an assize of *novel disseisin* against Oliver son of Isabel de Tolthorp, Alice de Veer, John Mayheu and John Hawe for two messuages, forty-four acres of land and five acres of meadow with appurtenances in Thrapston, claiming that she was the daughter and heir of one John Baudewyne, and had been disseised of the property by Oliver and others. Then Oliver said that John de Baudwyne had married one Isabel de Tolthorp by whom he had issue Margaret, and after some years Oliver, born of the same marriage, and that if Margaret was bringing the assize against her own brother he ought to be the heir. Margaret alleged that Oliver was altogether a bastard, and Oliver said he was legitimate and not a bastard. Mandate[1] to convene an enquiry on this matter
[f. 7v] *Teste* Thomas de Ingelby, North[ampton], 24 July 1364.

> [1]   See note to **16**.

18.   Exchequer *venire faciatis*, returnable on the morrow of Michaelmas, against Hugh Betoigne clerk, to answer the king, along with Richard de Melbourne, concerning £684 13s 4½d which John de Beaumont[1] owed to the Exchequer, and Hugh and Richard are his debtors,[2] as appears by inquisition taken before Saier de Rocheford lately sheriff of Lincolnshire and returned to the Exchequer.
Teste Henry de Greystock, 12 July 1364.

> [1]   John Beaumont kt. died 10 x 25 May 1342; his widow married, in 1345, Richard earl of Arundel 'with whom she had intrigued in her husband's lifetime', *Complete Peerage*, II.61.
> [2]   Licence for John Beaumont to enfeoff Richard de Melburn and Hugh de Betayne, rector of Linwood (Lyndewode), Lincs., of the manors of Folkingham and Barton on Humber, and the reversion of Hynton manor (unidentified; possibly Hinton, Northants.), and for them to re-grant them to John Beaumont, his wife and heirs, 10 May 1342, *CPR 1340–3*, p. 428. John died before the grant was executed, *CPR 1361–4*, p. 217.

19. Exchequer *fieri faciatis de bonis et beneficiis ecclesiasticis sicut pluries*, returnable on the morrow of Michaelmas, against Master Icher de Concoreto[1] late collector in England of the first fruits for John late supreme pontiff [John XXII] and of the quadrennial tenth imposed on the clergy of England by the said supreme pontiff[2] of which half is due to us, for £600 of a certain debt of £1,127 0s 6¼d, identified by a certain view of account at the Exchequer as being the half due to us of that tenth, as appears by inspection of the rolls of our Exchequer.
Teste Henry de Greystock, 20 June 1364.

> [1]   Itier de Concoreto was papal collector in England from 22 Aug. 1328, the date of his commission, until 13 Sept. 1335, when his successor was appointed, W.E. Lunt, *Accounts Rendered by Papal Collectors in England, 1317–1378*, Memoirs of the American Philosophical Society 70 (Philadelphia, 1968), pp. xxiii–xxviii. Details of this debt are described on p. xxviii.
> [2]   The mandatory quadrennial tenth 1330–33 was imposed at Edward III's request, and the profits shared equally between pope and king, W.E. Lunt, *Financial Relations of the Papacy with England 1327–1534* (Cambridge, Mass., 1962), pp. 75–88. See also C270 (Ecclesiastical Miscellanea)/15/7 for the view of Concoreto's account of the moiety of the first three years of this grant, 1333.

20. Chancery *levari faciatis de bonis ecclesiasticis*, returnable on the quindene of Michaelmas, against Brother Oliver prior of Ravendale for £11 15s 2d of the king's money lent to him by Richard de Ravenser keeper of the hanaper of Chancery, which he has not repaid by the appointed day, as the said clerk [Richard] has testified in Chancery.
Teste me ipso, 10 July 1364.

21. [ff. 7v–8] Exchequer *distringatis per omnia bona et beneficia sua ecclesiastica*, and *habeatis corpus*, returnable on the morrow of Hilary, against Robert Horn, chaplain, executor of Simon de Daventry,[1] to answer the king, along with Thomas, Simon's son and heir and Thomas Bayllif of Daventry holder of Simon's lands and tenements who have also been summoned. A certain indenture was made between the king and certain merchants in 11 Edward III for 30,000 sacks of wool to be provided by the said merchants and then transported to Bordeaux and there delivered by the hard work of William de la Pole and Reginald de Conducto [de Conduit] so that no merchant, native or alien, should export wool from the kingdom until the said 30,000 sacks were sold. The said Simon exported 64 sacks from the port of London in 12 Edward III and handed over 35 to William and Reginald so that 29 were exported contrary to the said convention and in contempt and retardation of the king's business. Note of return of no lay fee by the sheriff of Northamptonshire on the morrow of Michaelmas last.
Teste William de Skypwyth, 12 October 1364.

> [1]   For the execution of the ordinance that 30,000 sacks of wool be bought for the king's use, 26 July 1337, see *CPR 1334–8*, p. 480 where Simon Daventry is named as one of seven buyers in Northants. of 1,200 sacks @ 8½ marks. The whole episode may be explored further in the works of E.B. Fryde, *Studies in Medieval Trade and Finance* (London, 1983), chaps. 6–9, and *William de la Pole* (London, 1988).

22. [f. 8] Common Pleas *fieri faciatis de bonis et beneficiis ecclesiasticis sicut pluries*, returnable on the octave of Hilary, against Robert rector of Langley near Stevenage (Laneleye Cheynduyt), for 41 marks being arrears of a pension of 2 marks p.a. owed to the prior of St. Oswald's, and 2 marks recovered against the said rector by the prior in Common Pleas in 28 Edward III. Note of return of no lay fee by the sheriff of Hertfordshire.

Teste Robert de Thorp, 28 Nov. 1364.

23. [ff. 8–8v] Exchequer *certiorari (scrutatis registris)* concerning the holder of the prebend of Leicester St. Margaret in 11 Edward III and 18 Edward III as 61s 4d and £6 2s 8d is owing for the clerical taxes granted in those years, and if he is dead to certify the name of the present holder; and *levari faciatis de bonis et catallis*, returnable on the quindene of Hilary, for the said sums from the goods of the deceased prebendary in the hands of his executors.

Teste William de Skypwyth, 10 Dec. 1364.

Return:[1] after looking in the registers and memoranda we find that John Covenarum, cardinal, was prebendary of Leicester St. Margaret in 11 and 18 Edward III and enjoyed the fruits; he has been dead a long time and Master John de Edington (Edyngton) is now prebendary but we do not know what day and year he was installed. We can find no goods of the said John, deceased cardinal, in our diocese, and therefore could not levy the sums.[2]

> 1   This return was added later; there was insufficient space for it between this and the next writ and the note of return was finished in the margin.
> 2   Adam Limbergh occurs as prebendary in the chapter accounts during the financial years from 1327–28 until 1338–39. It therefore seems unlikely that John Raymond de Comminges cardinal bishop of Porto could have been prebendary during 11 Edward III [1337], but could have been in possession in 18 Edward III [1344]. He certainly held the dignity by February 1345, but died in Nov. 1348. Master John Edington held the prebend 1349–66, *Fasti*, I. 78.

24. Exchequer *certiorari* concerning the holder of the prebend of Cropredy (Croprith) in 10, 11, 12, 13, and 16 Edward III as the clerical taxes granted in those years have not been paid by the holder; the sums owing are £6 13s 4d for the second year of the biennial tenth granted in 10 Edward III, and 10 marks for the second year of the triennial tenth granted in 11 Edward III, and £6 13s 4d for the same tenth granted the same year, and £6 13s 4d for the third year of the same tenth, and 10 marks for the tenth granted 7 October 16 Edward III, and £13 6s 8d for the biennial tenth granted 12 Edward III, and £26 15s for divers years for the said prebend; and now we understand that there is a great quarrel about this prebend and that the prebendary at those times and years when the grants were made and [should have been] paid is not alive by whom those sums ought to be paid, and that same prebendary ought to be severely destrained for the sums owed to us; and if he is dead *levari faciatis*, returnable on the octave of Hilary, concerning those sums, from his executors or others, and certfiy when he died and the date of the installation of the present holder.

Teste the venerable Bishop John [Barnet], bishop of Bath and Wells, our Treasurer, 26 October 1364.

RETURN. After scrutinizing the registers we find that Bertrand de Pouget (Bertram' de Pocheto) [cardinal priest of SS. Marcellinus et Petrus] was prebendary of Cropredy in 10, 11, 12, 13 and 16 Edward III but he has been dead a long time, and Master Thomas de Paxton is now the prebendary but on what day or year he was installed our registers do not say.[1] We could find no goods of the said Bertrand in our diocese and so could not levy the money.

> 1   The Chapter Accounts, however, show that he succeeded during the financial year Sept. 1361 – Sept. 1362, *Fasti*, I.58.

25. Exchequer *venire faciatis*, returnable on the morrow of the Purification [3 Feb. 1365], against John le Longe chaplain, executor of the will of William de Bergham of Bridgnorth (Briggnenorth) to answer for William for £35 2s 7½d for the price of 2½ sacks 11 stones 4 pounds of wool on which customs have not been paid and which were removed ('transduct') by William in 11 Edward III [1337–38]. Note of return of no lay fee by Roger Cheyne sheriff of Shropshire on the morrow of Trinity 38 Edward III [20 May 1364].
Teste William de Skypwyth, 12 Dec. 1364.

[This is the end of the first quire of writs dating from Buckingham's episcopate; clearly material has been lost which covered the first nine months of 1365.]

26. [f. 9] Exchequer *levari faciatis de bonis et beneficiis ecclesiasticis*, returnable on the morrow of Hilary, against:
John Henry rector of Welton Ryval[1] for 33s 4d for the first term of the tenth granted 30 Edward III;
[the incumbents of]: Luddington in the Brook (Ludington) church 64s for the second tenth of the biennial tenth granted 35 Edward III;
Liddington (Lidington) church 32s for the second term of the tenth granted 30 Edward III;
the rector of Uppingham for 48s for the tenth granted 19 Edward III.
Return of no lay fees by William Beauson deputy of the earl of Hereford sheriff of Rutland ('subvic' Comitis Hereford vic' nostr' Com' Rotel') on the quindene of Michaelmas.
Teste William de Skypwyth, 14 Oct. 1365.
RETURN. John Hervy (*sic*) is dead nor are there any of his ecclesiastical goods in the diocese; no ecclesiastical goods of Luddington could be found; we caused the fruits of Liddington to the value of 32s and of Uppingham to the value of 48s to be sequestered and put up for sale but because we have no buyers we cannot raise the money.

[1] Welton Ryval was a prebend in Lincoln cathedral, its revenue derived in part from Welton near Lincoln. See also **31** and n.

27. Exchequer *levari faciatis de bonis et beneficiis ecclesiasticis*, returnable on the morrow of Hilary, against:
the rectors of Deddington and Datchet, for 106s 8d for the first year of the biennial tenth granted 35 Edward III;
the prioress of Clairruissel (Claro Rivulo) for £6 13s 4d for the arrears of the administration of Mapledurham church from 24 Edward III onwards;[1]
the prebendary of Sonning (Sonnings)[2] for £10 for the first year of the biennial tenth granted 20 Edward III;
portion of Hendred[3] (Henreth) church 6s 8d for the second year of the same grant;
Milton church for 40s for the first term of the tenth of 30 Edward III;
Iffley (Ziftele) church for 13s 8d for the same term of the same grant;
portion of Hendred church 3s 4d for the first moiety of the tenth of 30 Edward III;
Harwell (Harewell) church 26s 8d for the first moiety of the tenth granted 30 Edward III.
Note of return of no lay fees by Roger de Cotesford sheriff of Oxfordshire and Berkshire.

Teste William de Skypwyth, 16 Oct. 1365.
RETURN. The present writ arrived too late for us to execute it.

    1   See A.H. Cooke, *The Early History of Mapledurham*, Oxfordshire Record Society, Oxford-
shire Record Series 7 (1925).
    2   Berks., and therefore in Salisbury diocese. Sonning was not a prebend of any cathedral.
    3   Either West or East Hendred, Berks.

28.   Exchequer *levari faciatis de bonis et beneficiis ecclesiasticis*, returnable on
the morrow of Hilary, against the prioress of Clairruissel (Claro Rivulo) for £6 13s
4d for the arrears of the administration of the fruits of Mapledurham church from
38 Edward III. Note of return of no lay fee in Oxfordshire and Berkshire by Roger
Cotesford sheriff of those counties.
Teste Thomas de Lodelowe, 10 Dec. 1365.
RETURN. The present writ arrived too late for us to execute it.

29.   [ff. 9–9v] Exchequer *venire faciatis sicut pluries*, returnable on the quindene
of Hilary, against Robert Horn, chaplain, executor of Simon de Daventry, to answer
the king, along with Thomas, Simon's son and heir and Thomas Bayliff of Daventry
holder of Simon's lands and tenements who have also been summoned. A certain
indenture was made between the king and certain merchants in 11 Edward III for
30,000 sacks of wool to be provided by the said merchants and then transported to
Bordeaux and there delivered by the hard work of William de la Pole and Reginald
de Conducto [de Conduit] so that no merchant, native or alien, should export wool
from the kingdom until the said 30,000 sacks were sold. The said Simon exported
64 sacks from the port of London in 12 Edward III and handed over 35 to William
and Reginald so that 29 were exported contrary to the said convention and in
contempt and retardation of the king's business. Note of return of no lay fee by the
sheriff of Northamptonshire on the morrow of Michaelmas last.
Teste Thomas de Lodelowe, 10 Nov. 1365.
[See **21**]

30.   [f. 9v] Exchequer *venire faciatis de bonis et beneficiis ecclesiasticis*, return-
able on the quindene of Hilary, against the prebendary of Leighton Buzzard
(Leghton Busard) for £4 15s 8d from the tenth granted 16 Edward III.
Teste Thomas de Lodelowe, 1 Dec. 1365.

31.   [ff. 9v–10] Exchequer *levari faciatis de bonis et beneficiis ecclesiasticiis sicut
pluries*, returnable on the morrow of the close of Easter [21 April], for the sums
and terms named:
Uffington (Uffyngton) church with pension, 79s 9½d for the annual tenth granted
16 Edward III;
Beckingham (Bekyngham) church, for £4 owed for each term of the biennial tenth
granted 35 Edward III;
Mere (Meere) church, for 40s for the tenth granted 35 Edward III;[1]
William de Tiddeswell clerk for 19s 4½d for loans at the receipt of the Exchequer
for his journeys;
John de Hale rector of 'Clifton'[2] for half a mark for having writs for *oyer* and
terminer;

Henry de Walton prebendary of Nassington (Nassyngton), for 100s from the first moiety of the tenth granted 35 Edward III;

Mere church, for 20s from the first and second moiety of the tenth granted 35 Edward III;

Wyville (Wywell) church, for 19s 4d from the tenth granted 35 Edward III;

'Norton'[3] church, for 66s 8d from each term of the tenth granted 35 Edward III;

Welton Ryval[4] church, for 33s 4d owed from the second moiety of the tenth granted 35 Edward III;

the rector of Saddington (Sadyngton) church, for 8d from the tenth granted 35 Edward III;

Swithland (Swetlond) church, for 7s 4d owed from each term of the tenth granted 35 Edward III;

Shangton (Skankton) church, for 10s 8d owed from each term of the tenth granted 35 Edward III;

Mere church, for 40s from the annual tenth granted 34 Edward III;

the vicar of South Cadeby (Cateby) church, for 16s for the tenth granted 34 Edward III;

Anibaldo [Gaetani] cardinal [bishop] of Tusculum (St. Roman) who was rector of Corringham (Coryngham) [prebendal] church with pension, for £12 13s 4d for the annual tenth granted 16 Edward III;[5]

Mere church, for 40s both for the biennial tenth granted 25 Edward III and for the tenth granted 30 Edward III;

St. Margaret Leicester church, for 61s for the tenth granted 16 Edward III;

Adam de Beauchamp rector of Mablethorpe [St. Peter][6] (Malberthorp), for £20 for his pledges because has not yet presented his bill against Thomas de Carleton and John atte Kirke for a plea of trespass;

John de Stretton rector of Risby (Riceby),[7] for 10s for having writs;

John de Fynchedon clerk, half a mark for writs of oyer and terminer;

[f. 10] the prebendary of Grantham Australis, for £4 6s 8d for each term of the biennial tenth granted 35 Edward III;

the prebendary of Grantham Borialis, for 106s 8d for each of the biennial tenths granted 35 Edward III.

Note of no lay fees by William Haulay sheriff of Lincolnshire in his account on the morrow of Michaelmas 39 Edward III.

Teste Thomas de Lodelowe, 27 Nov. 1365.

[1]   For Buckingham's request for Mere's exemption from taxation on account of poverty see Reg. 12, f. 19.
[2]   Unidentified; there is no Clifton in Lincs. or Leics. It is possible that this refers to the prebendal church of Clifton, Notts.
[3]   Unidentified; 'a very common name', Eilart Eckwall, *The Concise Oxford Dictionary of English Place-Names* 4th ed. (Oxford, 1960), p. 344. Norton Disney (Lincs.) was a vicarage; there are three Nortons in Leics., and two in Lincs. It is possible that this was Bishop Norton, the prebendal church of the Lincoln cathedral prebend of Norton Episcopi.
[4]   A prebend of Lincoln cathedral, see *The Registrum Antiquissimum of the Cathedral Church of Lincoln*, ed. C.W. Foster, vol. II, LRS 28 (1933), pp. 147, 193–9.
[5]   Anibaldus Gaetani de Ceccano cardinal bishop of Tusculum was prebendary of Corringham 1335–50, *Fasti*, I.54.
[6]   The benefice is identified from Reg. 9, f. 58, which recorded the institution of Beauchamp's successor on 21 May 1349 following his death.
[7]   The only Risby in Lincs. which was a benefice was in the archdeaconry of Stow, and was a vicarage.

32. Exchequer *levari faciatis de bonis et beneficiis ecclesiasticis sicut pluries,* returnable on the morrow of Michaelmas; see **31** which is identical except for Uffington, Welton Ryvall and Norton which are omitted.
Teste Thomas de Lodelowe, 21 Feb. 1367.
RETURN. The present writ arrived too late for us to execute it because of the shortness of the time.

33. Exchequer *levari faciatis de bonis et beneficiis ecclesiasticis sicut pluries* returnable on the morrow of Michaelmas, against the prebendary of Leighton Buzzard for £4 15s 8d owing for the tenth granted 16 Edward III.
Teste Thomas de Lodelowe, 10 July 1367. By the great roll for 38 Edward III in Bedfordshire and Buckinghamshire and by writ returned on the morrow of the close of Easter [26 April].
RETURN. The present writ arrived too late for us to be able to execute it.
[See **30**]

34. [ff. 10–10v] Exchequer *levari faciatis de bonis et beneficiis ecclesiasticis sicut alias,* returnable on the morrow of Michaelmas, against:
the prioress of Clairruissel for £6 13s 4d for the administration of the fruit of Mapledurham church, from 24 Edward III;
the prebendary of Sonning (Sonnings) for £10 from the first tenth of the biennial tenth granted 20 Edward III;
from the portion of Hendred church [f. 10v] 6s 8d for the second tenth of the same grant;
Iffley church 13s 8d for the same;
Hendred church 23s 4d for the first moiety of the tenth granted 20 Edward III;
Harwell church 26s 8d for the first moiety of the same.
Teste Thomas de Lodelowe, 15 July 1367. By the roll for Oxfordshire for several years and a schedule delivered to the court by Roger Cotefford lately sheriff of Oxfordshire for 38 Edward III and by writ returned on the morrow of the close of Easter [26 April].
RETURN. The present writ arrived too late to be executed.
[See **27, 28**]

35. [f. 10v] Exchequer *venire faciatis,* returnable on the morrow of Michaelmas, against John de Newton rector of Steeple Gidding (Stepelgyddyng), one of the executors of Thomas de Peek, clerk, deceased, to answer the king, along with the executors of Richard Trewelton 'chivaler' the other executor of the said Thomas, for £15 6s 8d for the price of divers goods and chattels formerly belonging to the said Thomas and which after his death came to John's hands as was shown by inquisition taken before Nicholas de Styuecle sheriff of Cambridgeshire; the said £15 6s 8d was owed to the king when Thomas died. Note of return of no lay fee by Nicholas de Styuecle sheriff of Cambridgeshire on the morrow of Trinity [14 June].
Teste Thomas de Lodelowe, 1 July 1367. By the great roll for the year 39 in Nottinghamshire and Derbyshire and by the said inquisition which is in the file of writs ('ligula brevium') for Hilary term 41 and by writ returned on the morrow of Trinity by the said sheriff of Cambridgeshire.
RETURN. We caused the said John to be warned to be in the place and day named in the writ. Memorandum that 19 Sept. 1367 at Buckden (Bukeden) the rector

appeared and swore to appear [at the Exchequer] under pain of a pledge of £20. N. Steucle'.

36.   Exchequer *scire faciatis sicut alias*, returnable on the morrow of Michaelmas, against Richard atte Hull clerk, executor of the will of William atte Hull deceased, to show why he should not answer for £154 18s 11½d being the price of 13 sacks 6 stones 7 pounds of wool which in 11 Edward III were exported ('transducte') by the said William and on which customs have not been paid.[1]
Teste Thomas de Lodelowe, 5 July 1367. By the memoranda roll of 36 Edward II Hilary term among *recorda* and by a return by the sheriff of Shropshire on the morrow of Michaelmas. Charwelton
RETURN. We could find no Richard Attehull in our diocese though we made diligent enquiry.

> [1]   For William de la Hill (Hulle) of Bridgenorth, Salop, see *CPR 1334–8*, p. 502. The contract for the sale of the 30,000 sacks of wool was made on 26 July 1337, *CCR 1337–7*, pp. 148–9. 'There is independent evidence of much smuggling, and trials of offenders, who included one of the collectors of customs at London, dragged on for many years', E.B. Fryde, 'Edward III's Wool Monopoly, 1337', *History*, N.S. 37 (1952), p. 16.

37.   Exchequer *levari faciatis de bonis et beneficiis ecclesiasticis*, returnable on the quindene of Michaelmas, against Gilbert Dirches of Mendham both at the rectory of Drayton Beauchamp and elsewhere in your diocese to the value of 20s being a fine owed to the king for excesses and crimes against the king and people, returnable on the quindene of Michaelmas.[1]
Teste Thomas de Lodelowe, 12 June 1367.
RETURN. We caused the fruits and income of the church of Drayton Beauchamp to be sequestered to the said amount and put them up for public sale, but because we could find no buyers we could in no way levy the money.

> [1]   Gilbert Dirches (Arches) was excommunicated 15 Oct. 1376, PRO, C85/107/22.

38.   [f. 11] Exchequer [*levari faciatis*] *de bonis et beneficiis ecclesiasticis sicut pluries*, returnable on the morrow of Michaelmas, against Master Itherius (Ither) de Concoreto.
Teste Thomas de Lodelowe, 3 June 1367.
RETURN. The said Itherius (Itherus) de Concoreto has been dead a long time and we can find neither ecclesiastical goods nor executors of his in our diocese and therefore we cannot levy the said sums.
[See **19**]

39.   King's Bench *certiorari sicut alias*, returnable before us on the octave of Michaelmas wherever we are in England, whether John Okele of Stony Stratford (Stoneystretford) clerk, married one Anabel, widow, who was formerly the wife of Richard Cole, and signify whether you are able to obey our mandates or not.
Teste John Knyvet, 10 July 1367.[1]

> [1]   A clerk married to a widow was deemed *bigamus* and so ineligible to claim benefit of clergy, Leona C. Gabel, *Benefit of Clergy in England in the Later Middle Ages*, Smith College Studies in History XIV, nos. 1–4 (1928–29), pp. 87–9.

40. Exchequer *supersedeatis et sequestrum relaxari faciatis* for the sums and terms named:

Uffington church with pension, 79s 9½d for the annual tenth granted 16 Edward III;

Beckingham church, for £4 owed for each term of the biennial tenth granted 35 Edward III;

Mere church, for 40s for the tenth granted 35 Edward III;

William de Tiddeswell clerk for 19s 4½d for loans at the receipt of the Exchequer for his journeys;

John Hale rector of 'Clifton' for half a mark for having writs for *oyer* and *terminer*;

Henry de Walton prebendary of Nassington (Nassyngton), for 100s from the first moiety of the tenth granted 35 Edward III;

Mere church, for 20s from the first and second moiety of the tenth granted 35 Edward III;

Wyville church, for 19s 4d from the tenth granted 35 Edward III;

'Norton' church, for 66s 8d from each term of the tenth granted 35 Edward III;

Welton church, for 33s 4d owed from the second moiety of the tenth granted 35 Edward III;

the rector of Saddington church, for 8d from the tenth granted 35 Edward III;

Swithland church, for 7s 4d owed from each term of the tenth granted 35 Edward III;

Shangton church, for 10s 8d owed from each term of the tenth granted 35 Edward III;

Mere church, for 40s from the annual tenth granted 34 Edward III;

the vicar of South Cadeby church, for 16s for the tenth granted 34 Edward III;

Anibaldo [Gaetani] cardinal [bishop] of Tusculum (St. Roman) who was rector of Corringham [prebendal] church with pension, for £12 13s 4d for the annual tenth granted 16 Edward III;

Mere church, for 40s both for the biennial tenth granted 25 Edward III and for the tenth granted 30 Edward III;

St. Margaret Leicester church, for 61s for the tenth granted 16 Edward III;

Adam de Beauchamp rector of Mablethorpe St. Peter for £20 for his pledges because has not yet presented his bill against Thomas de Carleton and John atte Kirke for a plea of trespass;

John de Stretton rector of Risby for 10s for having writs;

John de Fynchedon clerk, half a mark for writs of oyer and terminer;

[f. 10] the prebendary of Grantham Australis, for £4 6s 8d for each term of the biennial tenth granted 35 Edward III;

the prebendary of Grantham Borialis, for 106s 8d for each of the biennial tenths granted 35 Edward III, concerning 79s 9½d owed by Robert de Tynton now rector of Uffington for the clerical tenth granted 16 Edward III.

Teste Thomas de Lodelowe, 18 May 1367.

[See **31**]

41. King's Bench *certioriari*, returnable on the octave of St. John Baptist [1 July] wherever we are in England, whether John de Ocle of Stony Stratford married Anabilla widow of Richard Cole at Stony Stratford.

Teste John Knyvet, 20 May 1367.

[See **39**]

42. [ff. 11–11v] Common Pleas *fieri faciatis de bonis ecclesiasticis*, returnable a month from Michaelmas, against Robert rector of Langley near Stevenage (Langelays Chenduyt) both for 81 marks from 84 marks to answer the prior and convent of Nostell (St. Oswald's) for arrears of 2 marks p.a. which they recovered against the rector in the court at Westminster, and for 12 marks being arrears of the pension before 12 Feb. 40 Edward III [f. 11v]. We ordered you by [a writ of] *fieri faciatis* to produce him at Westminster on a day now past, and we ordered you to sequester the fruits of the rectory but you could not produce the money because you could not find a buyer for the goods; therefore we order you *sicut alias* to return the sequestered good and chattels to the justices at Westminster. And if more money is raised, have it there on the same day. Note of return of no lay fee by sheriff of Hertfordshire.

Teste Robert de Thorp', 24 May 1367.

RETURN. We caused the goods of the said Robert to be sequestered and put up for sale but because we could find no buyers we could not raise the money; the said Robert has died and we could find no other goods of his either in the rectory or in the diocese and therefore we could not execute the writ.

[See **12, 22**]

43. Mandate, returnable in Chancery before the quindene of Michaelmas,[1] to hold an enquiry to find out whether Alice (Alesia) daughter of John de Everingham is a nun. William, the master of the order of Sempringham alleges that she is a nun of the house of Haverholm (Haverholme), and she denies this.

Teste me ipso, 20 May 1367.

[RETURN.] No return was made to this writ because it arrived too late. Another writ, *sicut alias*, arrived and that also could not be executed because of lack of time.[2]

---

[1]   In intent, though not form, a *certiorari*.

[2]   The enquiry arose from the signification of apostasy of Alice by the master of the order on 17 Nov. 1366, PRO, C81, file 1971 (Sempringham), no. 2. See LAO Reg. 12, f. 26; *CPR 1364–7*, pp. 369, 428; *CPR 1367–70*, p. 83, and further references in **Appendix A, no. 1**. For discussion see F. Donald Logan, *Runaway Religious in Medieval England, c.1240–1540* (Cambridge, 1996), pp. 24, 115, 266. This case is discussed in the introduction, pp. xix–xx.

44. [ff. 11v–12] Mandate to discover whether Alice daughter of John de Everingham is a nun, returnable in Chancery before the octave of the Purification [9 Feb. 1368], or else the bishop is to appear in Chancery to show why he cannot execute the writ.

Teste me ipso, 1 Dec. 1367.

RETURN. Concerning the order to make enquiry by examining Alesia de Everingham and the brothers and sisters of Haverholm of the order of Sempringham, we have made diligent enquiry and we find that Alesia is not a nun of Haverholme nor professed in that house.

[The original writ and return are given in **Appendix A, no. 1**]

45. [f. 12v] Exchequer *levari faciatis sicut pluries*, returnable on the morrow of Hilary, against:

Beckingham church, for £4 owed for each term of the biennial tenth granted 35 Edward III;

William de Tiddeswell clerk for 19s 4½d for loans at the Receipt of the Exchequer for his journeys;

John Hale rector of 'Clifton', for half a mark for having writs of *oyer* and *terminer*;

Henry de Walton prebendary of Nassington, for 100s from the first moiety of the tenth granted 35 Edward III;

Wyville church, for 19s 4d from the tenth granted 35 Edward III;

the rector of Saddington church, for 8d from the tenth granted 35 Edward III;

Swithland church, for 7s 8d owed from each term of the tenth granted 35 Edward III;

Shangton church, for 10s 8d owed from each term of the tenth granted 35 Edward III;

the vicar of South Cadeby church, for 16s for the tenth granted 34 Edward III;

Anibaldo Gaetani Cardinal bishop of Tusculum (St. Roman) who was rector of Corringham church with pension, for 79s 9½d for the annual tenth granted 16 Edward III;

St. Margaret's church, Leicester, 61s for the tenth granted 16 Edward III;

Adam de Beauchamp rector of Mablethorpe St. Peter, for £20 for his pledges because he has not yet presented his bill against Thomas de Carleton and John atte Kirke for a plea of trespass;

John de Stretton rector of Risby, for 10s for having writs;

John de Fynchedon clerk, half a mark for writs of oyer and terminer;

the prebendary of Grantham Borialis, for 106s 8d for each of the bienial tenths granted 35 Edward III.

Note of no lay fees by William Haulay sheriff of Lincolnshire in his account on the morrow of Michaelmas 39 Edward III.

Teste Thomas de Lodelowe, 25 Oct. 1367. By the great roll of 38 [Edward III] in Lincolnshire, and by examining the rolls of several years, and by a schedule sent in by William Hauley sheriff of Lincolnshire which is among the replies of sheriffs for Michaelmas term 39, and by a writ returned on the morrow of Michaelmas.

RETURN.[1] William Tydewell has been dead a long time nor are any of his goods left in the diocese; John Hale is not beneficed in the diocese, nor could we find any of his goods there; we could find no fruits to be sequestered of the prebends of Nassington and Leicester[2] St. Margaret; nor could we find any goods to be sequestered from the churches of Wyville and Risby and the prebend of Grantham Borialis; we caused the fruits and issues of Saddington, Swithland and Shangton to be sequestered to the values named in the writ and the goods of Corringham the same, and of Mablethorpe St. Peter to the value of 100s, but because we could find no buyers we could not raise the money; we could do nothing about 'Cateby'[3] because the vicarage is not in our diocese; Adam de Beauchamp and John de Stretton are not beneficed in our diocese and have no ecclesiastical goods there; we could do nothing about the other things contained in the writ because it came too late.

[See **31, 40**]

[1]   This is written in a different ink.

[2]   From this point onwards the return was written in the margin, since sufficient space had not been left between this and the following writ.

[3]   The only possible place of this name which is not in Lincoln diocese is Cadeby, Yorks West Riding, a hamlet within the parish of Sprotborough. I am grateful to Professor D.M. Smith for this identification.

46.   Exchequer *scire faciatis sicut pluries*, returnable on the morrow of Hilary, against Richard atte Hull executor of the will of William atte Hull deceased, to show why he should not answer for £154 18s 11½d being the price of 13 sacks 6

stones 7 pounds of wool which in 11 Edward III were exported ('transducte') by the said William and on which customs have not been paid.
Teste Thomas de Lodelowe, 21 Oct. 1367.
[See **36**]

47. Exchequer *levari faciatis de bonis et catallis*, returnable on the morrow of Hilary, as it appears by inspection of the rolls of the Exchequer that the prebendary of Tervin (Treven)[1] owes 10 marks for both parts of the biennial tenth granted 25 Edward III; 5 marks for the first part of the biennial tenth of 20 Edward III; and 33s 4d for the second term of ths same, and we understand that Peter Gildesburgh was prebendary in those years and it is said that he has been dead a long time and that at his death there were goods and chattels of his at Biggleswade rectory by which these debts could be met.
Teste Thomas de Lodelowe, 3 Nov. 1367. By the great roll of year 40 in Shrewsbury.
RETURN. No goods of Peter Gildesburgh as named in the writ could be found either at Biggleswade rectory nor elsewhere in the diocese and therefore we could not execute the writ.

[1]   In Lichfield cathedral; Peter de Gildesburgh was the prebendary from 1349 to 1357, *Fasti*, X.59. The modern spelling of the place (and river) is Tarvin (Cheshire). I am indebted to Professor M.C.E. Jones for this information.

48A. [f. 13] [*Inquiratis de bastardia*], returnable to the justices of assize at Lincoln on the Thursday after St. Peter in Cathedra [23 Feb. 1367]. Alice Bussy relative and heir of John Bussy of Lavyngton, in our court before Thomas de Ingelby and John Cavendisch justices of assize in Lincolnshire, at Lincoln by our writ arrayed and brought an assize of *novel disseisin* against William Harop' and Lucy his wife for certain tenements in Lavington (Lavyngton), Baston and Carlby (Carleby), and the said William and Lucy said that Lucy was the nearest relative and heir of the said John Bussy and that Alice was more remotely related, so that Lucy, as being the nearer, should be the heir; to this Alice replied that Lucy was altogether a bastard, in no way the heir of John Bussy, and William and Lucy said that Lucy was not a bastard but legitimate. Mandate to convene an enquiry and return the result by letters patent.
Teste Thomas de Ingelby, 28 Oct. 1366.

48B. *Idem breve duplicatum fuit sub eisdem verb'*

49. Common Pleas *venire faciatis sicut alias*, returnable on quindene of Hilary, against Richard rector of Barton, clerk, to answer the prior of Kenilworth for a debt of 42 marks being arrears of rent of 7 marks p.a. We sent you a mandate, returnable on quindene of Michaelmas, but you made return that the writ arrived too late for execution. Return of no lay fee by the sheriff of Northamptonshire. And know that unless you execute this writ we will proceed against you.
Teste Robert de Thorp, 25 Oct. 1366.
RETURN. We caused Richard rector of Barton[1] to be warned to appear at the day and place named in the writ.

[1]   Either Earls Barton or Barton Seagrave, both Northants.

50. King's Bench *certiorari*, returnable on the octave of Hilary, whether John de Ocle of Stony Stratford married Anabilla widow of Richard Cole.
Teste John Knyvet, 12 Nov. 1366 [*sic*].
RETURN. This writ arrived so late that we could not any way execute it.
[See **39, 41**]

51. [f. 13v] Common Pleas *venire faciatis*, returnable on the quindene of Hilary, against Walter Norman rector of Dallington (Daylyngton), your clerk, to answer the prioress of St. Giles of Flamstead for a debt of 20 marks, being arrears of rent of 5 marks p.a. We sent a previous writ returnable on the octave of Martinmas [18 Nov.] but you made return that the writ came too late for you to be able to execute it. Return of no lay fee by the sheriff of Northamptonshire. We will proceed against you if you do not execute this writ.
Teste Robert de Thorp', 22 Nov. 1366.
RETURN. We caused the said Walter Norman to be warned to appear at the day and place name in the writ.

52. Exchequer *levari faciatis de bonis et beneficiis ecclesiasticis*, returnable on the morrow of Hilary, against:
the rectors of Deddington and Datchet, for 106s 8d for the first year of the biennial tenth granted 35 Edward III;
the prioress of Clairruissel for £6 13s 4d for the arrears of the administration of Mapledurham church from 24 Edward III onwards;
the prebendary of Sonning for £10 for the first year of the biennial tenth granted 20 Edward III;
portion of 'Hendred' church 6s 8d for the second year of the same grant;
Milton church for 40s for the first term of the tenth of 30 Edward III;
Iffley church for 13s 8d for the same term of the same grant;
portion of 'Hendred' church 3s 4d for the first moiety of the tenth of 30 Edward III;
Harwell church 26s 8d for the first moiety of the tenth granted 30 Edward III.
Note of return of no lay fees by Roger de Cotesford sheriff of Oxfordshire and Berkshire.
Teste Thomas de Lodelowe, 13 July 1366.
RETURN. The present writ arrived too late for us to be able to execute it.
[See **27, 34**]

53. Exchequer *levari faciatis de bonis et beneficiis ecclesiasticis sicut pluries*, returnable on the morrow of Hilary, against the prebendary of Leighton Buzzard, for £4 15s 8d from the tenth granted 16 Edward III.
Teste Thomas de Lodelowe, 7 Oct. 1366.
RETURN. The present writ arrived too late for execution.
[See **30, 33**]

54. [f. 14] Exchequer *levari faciatis de bonis et beneficiis ecclesiasticis*, returnable on the morrow of Hilary, against the rector of Welton ('Welton Ryvall')[1] for 34s 4d for the first term of the tenth granted 30 Edward III, and from Liddington church 64s for the second tenth of the biennial tenth of 25 Edward III. Note of return of no lay fee by William Beaufor' deputy sheriff of Rutland and his accounts to the Exchequer.

Teste Thomas de Lodelowe, 13 Nov. 1366.

RETURN. We could find no goods in the rectory of Welton therefore we could not raise the money; we sequestered the goods of Liddington rectory to the sum mentioned but because we could find no buyers we could not in any way raise the money.

    1   For this benefice see **26**, and note.

55. Exchequer *levari faciatis de bonis et beneficiis ecclesiasticis*, returnable on the morrow of All Souls [3 Nov.], against:

the rectors of Deddington and Datchet, for 106s 8d for the first year of the biennial tenth granted 35 Edward III;

the prioress of Clairruissel for £6 13s 4d for the arrears of the administration of Mapledurham church from 24 Edward III onwards;

the prebendary of Sonning for £10 for the first year of the biennial tenth granted 20 Edward III;

portion of 'Hendred' church 6s 8d for the second year of the same grant;

Milton church for 40s for the first term of the tenth of 30 Edward III;

Iffley church for 13s 8d for the same term of the same grant;

portion of Hendred church 3s 4d for the first moiety of the tenth of 30 Edward III;

Harwell church 26s 8d for the first moiety of the tenth granted 30 Edward III.

Note of return of no lay fees by Roger de Cotesford sheriff of Oxfordshire and Berkshire.

Teste Thomas de Lodelowe, 13 Nov. 1366.

[See **27, 34, 52**]

56. [ff. 14–14v] Exchequer *levari faciatis de bonis et beneficiis ecclesiasticis sicut alias*, returnable on the morrow of Hilary, against:

Uffington church with pension, 79s 9½d for the annual tenth granted 16 Edward III;

Beckingham church, for £4 owed for each term of the biennial tenth granted 35 Edward III;

Mere church, for 40s for the tenth granted 35 Edward III;

William de Tiddeswell clerk for 19s 4½d for loans at the Receipt of the Exchequer for his journeys;

John Hale rector of 'Clifton' for half a mark for having writs of oyer and terminer;

Henry de Walton prebendary of Nassington for 100s from the first moiety of the tenth granted 35 Edward III;

Mere church, for 20s from the first and second moiety of the tenth granted 35 Edward III;

Wyville church, for 19s 4d from the tenth granted 35 Edward III;

'Norton' church, for 66s 8d from each term of the tenth granted 35 Edward III;

Welton (Welton Ryvall) church, for 33s 4d owed from the second moiety of the tenth granted 35 Edward III;

the rector of Saddington church, for 8d from the tenth granted 35 Edward III;

Swithland church, for 7s 8d owed from each term of the tenth granted 35 Edward III;

Shangton church, for 10s 8d owed from each term of the tenth granted 35 Edward III;

Mere church, for 40s from the annual tenth granted 34 Edward III;

the vicar of Cadeby church, for 16s for the tenth granted 34 Edward III;

Anibaldo [Gaetani] cardinal [bishop] of Tusculum (St. Roman) who was rector of Corringham [prebendal] church with pension, for 79s 9½d for the annual tenth granted 16 Edward III;

Mere church, for 40s both for the biennial tenth granted 25 Edward III and for the tenth granted 30 Edward III;

St. Margaret's church, Leicester, for 61s for the tenth granted 16 Edward III;

Adam de Beauchamp rector of Mablethorpe St. Peter for £20 for his pledges because has not yet presented his bill against Thomas de Carleton and John atte Kirke for a plea of trespass;

John de Stretton rector of Risby for 10s for having writs;

John de Fynchedon clerk, half a mark for writs of oyer and terminer;

[f. 10] the prebendary of Grantham Australis, for £4 6s 8d for each term of the biennial tenth granted 35 Edward III;

the prebendary of Grantham Borialis, for 106s 8d for each of the biennial tenths granted 35 Edward III.

Note of no lay fees by William Haulay sheriff of Lincolnshire in his account on the morrow of Michaelmas 39 Edward III.

Teste Thomas de Lodelowe, 28 Oct. 1366.

RETURN: We sequestered the fruits of Uffington and Norton to the sums named but because we could find no buyers we could not raise the money; William de Tiddeswell, Henry de Walton, the prebendary of Nassington and Annibaldus cardinal of St. Roman are dead and we could find no goods of theirs in the diocese; as for the rest, the writ came too late for us to be able to execute it.

[See **31, 32, 45**]

57. [f. 14v] Exchequer *levari faciatis de bonis et beneficiis ecclesiasticis*, returnable on the quindene of Hilary, against the prebendary of Buckden for £8 owed for the second and third years of the triennial tenth granted 18 Edward III.

Teste Thomas de Lodelowe, 27 Nov. 1366.

58. King's Bench *inquiratis sicut pluries*, returnable to the justices of goal delivery at Leicester on the Friday before St. Peter in Cathedra [19 Feb. 1367], in the case of William Broun of Scaptoft who was arraigned in our court before Thomas de Ingelby and others, justices of gaol delivery at Leicester, at the suit of Alice who was the wife of Nicholas le Smyth of Burton on a charge of killing the said Nicholas, formerly her husband; and William said that he was a clerk and that he ought not to answer without the ecclesiastical ordinary ('sine ordinario suo ecclesiastico respondere non deberet'). But on our side it was testified that William was a bigamist, because he had married one Christian formerly the wife of Thomas Wolf now dead, for which reason he ought not to enjoy the privilege of benefit of clergy ('per quod clericali privilegio de iure gaudere non deberet'). Mandate to convene an enquiry to discover whether William is a bigamist and to certify what you do in this matter.

Teste Thomas de Ingelby, 27 Nov. 1366.

RETURN. We convened an enquiry and it was found by this that William Broun of Scraptoft is not bigamous.

59. [f. 15] Exchequer *venire faciatis sicut pluries*, returnable on the quindene of Hilary, against Robert Horn, chaplain, executor of Simon de Daventry, to answer the king, along with Thomas, Simon's son and heir and Thomas Bayllif of Daventry holder of Simon's lands and tenements who has also been summoned. A certain indenture was made between the king and certain merchants in 11 Edward III for 30,000 sacks of wool to be provided by the said merchants and then transported to Bordeaux and there delivered by the hard work of William de la Pole and Reginald de Conducto [de Conduit] so that no merchant, native or alien, should export wool from the kingdom until the said 30,000 sacks were sold. The said Simon exported 64 sacks from the port of London in 12 Edward III and handed over 35 to William and Reginald so that 29 were exported contrary to the said convention and in contempt and retardation of the king's business.
Teste Thomas de Lodelowe, 16 Nov. 1366.
RETURN. We caused Simon de Daventry to be warned to be before the Exchequer barons at the day and place mentioned as the writ requires.
[See **21, 29**]

60. [ff. 15–15v] Exchequer *levari faciatis de bonis et beneficiis ecclesiasticis*, returnable on the morrow of the close of Easter [26 April 1367], against the following who have no lay fee as William Haulay sheriff of Lincolnshire testified in his account at the Exchequer for 40 Edward III:
the rector [*sic*] of Corringham (Caryngham) for £12 13s 4d for the second tenth of the biennial tenth granted 10 Edward III;
the rector of 'Stapleford'[1] (Stapilford), for 38s 8d for the second tenth of the biennial tenth granted 10 Edward III;
the rector of Caister (Castre), for £4 10s 8d for the second tenth of the biennial tenth granted 10 Edward III;
the rector of Corringham, for £12 13s 4d, for the first tenth of the biennial tenth granted 10 Edward III;
the rector of South Kelsey (Kelleseye St. Mary),[2] for 26s 8d, for the first tenth of the biennial tenth granted 10 Edward III;
the rector of [Great] Limber (Lymbergh),[3] for 28s 6d for the first tenth of the biennial tenth granted 10 Edward III;
the rector of [Great] Limber, 28s 6d for the second tenth of the triennial tenth granted 11 Edward III;
the rector of South Kelsey for 26s 8d for the second tenth of the triennial tenth granted 11 Edward III;
the rector of Corringham, for 19 marks for the second tenth of the triennial tenth granted 11 Edward III;
the rector of Caister, for £4 10s 8d for the first tenth of the biennial tenth granted 10 Edward III;
the rector of Corringham, for £12 13s 4d for the same tenth;
the rector of Brantingham (Brantyngham), for £6 13s 4d for the same tenth;
the rector of 'Boruse', for 66s 8d for the same tenth;
Ralph Strubby rector of Tilney (Tinlee),[4] for 1 mark for a fine for trespass;

the rector of South Kelsey, 26s 8d for the third tenth of the triennial tenth granted 11 Edward III;

the rector of [Great] Limber, 28s 6d for the same tenth;

the rector of Corringham, for £12 13s 4d for the same tenth;

the rector of St. Margaret's, Leicester, for £6 2s 8d for the biennial tenth of 12 and 13 Edward III;

the rector of Hagworthingham (Hagworthyngham), for 24s for the tenth granted 16 Edward III;

the rector of Toft [by Newton][5] for 4s for fleeces and lambs ('vellorum et agnorum') granted 18 Edward III;

the rector of Gosberton (Gosberkirke), for 16s for the tenth granted 16 Edward III;

the rector of Hagworthingham, for 24s for the same tenth;

the rector of Louth (Lauda), for £4 13s 4d for the first tenth of the triennial tenth granted 17 Edward III;

the rector of Corringham, for £12 13s 4d for the same tenth;

the rector of Hagworthingham, for 24s for the same tenth;

William Swyne chaplain for 6 marks for his forfeitures;

William de Boseworth chaplain for 100s for his forfeitures;

[f. 15v] Master John de Ufford farmer of Carlton (Carleton) prebend[6] for 53s 4d for the first tenth of the triennial tenth granted 17 Edward III;

Ketton (Ketten) church, for £6 13s 4d for the same tenth;

Louth church, for £4 13s 4d for the same tenth;

St. Margaret's church, Leicester, for 61s 4d for the same tenth;

Carlton cum Thurlby[7] church, for 53s 4d for the same tenth;

the prebend of Stow, for £4 4s 8d for the third year of the triennial tenth granted 11 Edward III;

the rector of Rothwell, for £4 for the biennial tenth granted 12 and 13 Edward III;

Roger de Donyngton clerk, for £43 10s 1d for loans;

the chancellor of Lincoln, 8s for the third year of the triennial tenth granted 11 Edward III;

from the said chancellor, 16s for the biennial tenth granted 12 and 13 Edward III;

Uffington (Uffyngton) church, for £7 19s 7d for the same tenth;

South Kelsey church, for 66s 8d for the biennial tenth granted 12 Edward III, the tenth granted 14 Edward III, and the second tenth of the triennial tenth granted 18 Edward III when John Savage was the rector;

John de Carlton clerk of the works and provisioner of our castle of Dublin, for £61 5s 8d received from William de Bromley (Brumlegh) our treasurer of Ireland;[8]

'Norton' church which belongs to Magelen cardinal,[9] for 65s 8d for the tenth granted 34 Edward III.

Teste Thomas de Lodelowe, 29 Oct. 1366. By examination of a schedule sent by the sheriff to the Exchequer in year 41.

RETURN. Goods of the churches of [Great] Limber to the value of 10s and of Toft to the value of 2s 6d, of Rothwell to the value of 14s, Gosberton to the value of 6s 8d and Uffington to the value of 7s were sequestrated and put up for sale but because we could find no buyers we could not levy the money; we could find no goods of Corringham, Leicester St. Margaret, South Kelsey, Ketton (Keten), Louth, Stapleford, Caister, Carlton cum Strubby and Hagworthingham, Stow and Norton and the chancellor of Lincoln which could be sequestrated; Reginald de Donyngton, John de Carleton, William de Brumlegh, Ralph de Strubby and William de Boreworth cannot be found in our diocese; John de Ufford is dead and neither his executor nor his goods are in our diocese; the churches of Brantingham and 'Boruse' are not in our diocese,[10] and therefore we could not in any way execute the present writ.

1   Either in Leics. or Lincs.; both were appropriated.
2   This was one of two rectories, and settlements, within the same parish boundary.
3   Great Limber was a vicarage. It was appropriated to the prior and convent of St. Anne by Coventry, see *The Register of Richard Fleming, Bishop of Lincoln 1420–31*, ed. N.H. Bennett, vol. 1, C&Y LXXIII (1984), no. 159.
4   Tilney is in Norfolk.
5   Of the two places called Toft in Lincs. this was the only benefice.
6   Either Carlton Kyme or Carlton Paynell. The farmer in 1343 had almost certainly been the leading minister of Edward III who, when archbishop-elect of Canterbury, died of the plague in 1349; see *BRUO* II.1390–2, s.n. 'Offord'.
7   For Carlton-le-Moorland and Thurlby, both in Graffoe deanery, Lincs., see LRS 81, nos. 495, 498.
8   Thanks are due to Dr. Dorothy Johnston for this identification.
9   Possibly the prebendal church of Norton Episcopi, held by Audoen Aubert cardinal bishop of Ostia from 1357–58 until his death in 1363, *Fasti*, I.97.
10   Brantingham, Yorks., East Riding.

61.   Common Pleas *fieri faciatis de bonis ecclesiasticis*, returnable on the quindene of Easter [2 May 1367], against Robert rector of Langley (near Stevenage), for 41 marks being arrears of a pension of 2 marks p.a. owed to the prior of Nostell (St. Oswald's) and 2 marks recovered against the said rector by the prior in Common Pleas in 28 Edward III. Note of return of no lay fee by the sheriff of Huntingdonshire.
Teste Robert de Thorp, 8 Nov. 1366.
RETURN. The goods and chattels in the rectory of Langley (Cheyndut) found and sequestered by us were worth 13s 10d on the estimation of trustworthy men; we put the goods up for public sale but could find no buyers and the said Robert rector has no other goods in our diocese by which the said sums and arrears can be raised.
[See **12, 22, 42**]

62.   Exchequer *levari faciatis de bonis et beneficiis ecclesiasticis sicut pluries*, returnable on the morrow of the close of Easter [26 April], against the prebendary of Leighton Buzzard for £4 15s 8d from the tenth granted 16 Edward III.
Teste Thomas de Lodelowe, 8 Feb. 1367
RETURN. We could find no goods of the prebendary of Leighton Buzzard in our jurisdiction ('sub districtu nostro') and therefore we could not execute the writ.
[See **30, 33, 53**]

63.   [f. 16] Exchequer *levari faciatis de bonis et beneficiis ecclesiasticis*, returnable on the morrow of the close of Easter [26 April], against:
the rector of Deddington and Datchet, for 106s 8d for the first year of the biennial tenth granted 35 Edward III;
the prioress of Clairruissel for £6 13s 4d for the arrears of the administration of Mapledurham church from 24 Edward III onwards; the prebendary of Sonning for £10 for the first year of the biennial tenth granted 20 Edward III;
portion of Hendred church for 6s 8d for the second year of the same grant;
Milton church for 40s for the first term of the tenth of 30 Edward III;
Iffley church for 13s 8d for the same term of the same grant;

portion of Hendred church for 3s 4d for the first moiety of the tenth of 30 Edward III;

Harwell church for 26s 8d for the first moiety of the tenth granted 30 Edward III. Note of return of no lay fees by Roger de Cotesford sheriff of Oxfordshire and Berkshire.

Teste Thomas de Lodelowe, 4 Feb. 1367

RETURN. We sequestrated goods to the value of 23s from Deddington and Datchet but no buyers for goods of Mapledurham and Iffley could be found; the churches of Hendred, Harwell (Harewell) and the prebend of Sonning do not exist in our diocese therefore we could in no way execute the writ.

[See **27, 51, 55**]

64.   Braybrok

Common Pleas *venire faciatis*, returnable on the quindene of Easter [2 May], against John rector of Braybrook to answer the prior of Daventry for a debt of £26 arrears of rent of 44s p.a. Note of return of no lay fee by the sheriff of Northamptonshire. on the octave of Hilary.

Teste Robert de Thorp, 30 Jan 1367.

EXECUTION. 22 April 1367 at Buckden in the registry ('in registraria ibidem') before John de Londedon, the said rector was warned to appear before the justices on the day and place mentioned, and he swore on the gospels that he would obey on pain of £20. Present: John de Banbury and Robert de Harwedon and others.

RETURN. We caused the said rector to be warned to appear on the day and place required in the writ.

65.   [f. 16v] Breve de certiorando Bukeden'

Exchequer *certiorari (scrutatis registris)*, returnable on the octave of Trinity [13 June], concerning the holder of the prebend of Buckden in 18 Edward III and on what day he died, who now occupies the rectory and on which days he was inducted and instituted.

Teste Thomas de Lodelowe, 5 May 1367.

66.   Breve pro decima triennal'

Exchequer *certiorari (scrutatis registris)*, returnable on the octave of Trinity [13 June], concerning the holder of Corringham (Coringham) rectory [*rectius* prebend] in 11 Edward III, 18 Edward III, 10 Edward III, and 8 Edward III as clerical taxes granted in those years have not been paid; it is thought that Peter [Iterii] cardinal [bishop of] Albano (Aquensis) now holds it but that he did not hold it in the years 8, 10, 11, 18 and we wish to know when the then holder was installed, when he died and who now holds it.

Teste Thomas de Lodelowe, 21 May 1367.

67.   Exchequer *supersedeatis et sequestrum relaxari faciatis* concerning the tax arrears of Corringham [see **66**].

Teste Thomas de Lodelowe, 20 May 1367.

68.   Breve retorn' Buckden'

Exchequer *supersedeatis et sequestrum relaxetis*, until the quindene of Michaelmas, concerning a mandate to levy £8 from the prebendary of Buckden being due from the second and third years of the triennial tenth granted 18 Edward III. In answer to our mandate to sequestrate, returnable on the quindene of Hilary, you returned on that day that you had caused the fruits of the prebend to be sequestrated to the value of £8, viz. from the sheaves in his tithe barn; and now William de Navesby prebendary of Buckden has mainperned at the Exchequer, by Roger de Denford and William de Thame of London his mainpernors, that he will answer for the £8 at the Exchequer on the quindene of Michaelmas, which was the day we gave him.

Teste Thomas de Lodelowe, 21 May 1367.

69. [f. 17] <u>Pro non collectis medietatibus decimarum annualium</u>
Exchequer *levari faciatis*, returnable on the morrow of Hilary, against:
the rector of Deddington and Datchet, for 106s 8d for the first year of the biennial tenth granted 35 Edward III;
the prioress of Clairruissel for £6 13s 4d for the arrears of the administration of Mapledurham church from 24 Edward III onwards;
the prebendary of Sonning for £10 for the first year of the biennial tenth granted 20 Edward III;
portion of Hendred church for 6s 8d for the second year of the same grant;
Milton church for 40s for the first term of the tenth of 30 Edward III;
Iffley church for 13s 8d for the same term of the same grant;
portion of Hendred church for 3s 4d for the first moiety of the tenth of 30 Edward III;
Harwell church for 26s 8d for the first moiety of the tenth granted 30 Edward III.
Note of return of no lay fees by Roger de Cotesford sheriff of Oxfordshire and Berkshire.
Teste Thomas de Lodelowe, 20 Oct. 1367. By examining debts among the rolls for several years and by a schedule sent into the Exchequer by Roger Cotteford late sheriff of Oxfordshire which is among the sheriffs' replies for 38 Edward III, and by a writ returned on the morrow of Michaelmas.
RETURN. We could find no goods of the churches of Mapledurham and Iffley at the time of the receipt of the writ; the churches of Hendred, Harwell and the prebend of Sonning are not in our diocese.
[See **27, 34, 52, 55, 63**]

70. <u>Breve contra possessorem prebende de Legton Busard</u>
Exchequer *levari faciatis de bonis et beneficiis ecclesiasticis sicut pluries*, returnable on the morrow of Hilary, against the prebendary of Leighton Buzzard (Bussard) for £4 15s 8d owed from the clerical tenth granted 16 Edward III.
Teste Thomas de Lodelow, 19 Oct. 1367. Through the great roll of year 38 in Bedfordshire and Buckinghamshire, and by a writ returned on the morrow of Michaelmas.
RETURN. We caused the fruits to be sequestered to the value named but could find no buyers so could not execute the writ.
[See **30, 33, 53, 62**]

71. <u>Breve contra Rectorem de Willesford'</u>
Exchequer *venire faciatis*, returnable on the quindene of Hilary, against Thomas Proud rector of Wilsford (Willesford) to answer the prior of Wilsford, alien, for 25

marks which he is unjustly holding back from the farmer who cannot, as a result, pay his farm at the Exchequer for the priory which is in the king's hand because of the French war.
Teste Thomas de Lodelowe, 23 Oct. 1367.

72.   Breve contra Rectorem sancti Petri de Riston
Common Pleas *venire faciatis*, returnable three weeks after Easter [9 May], against William Bray rector of St. Peter's Rushton (Riston) to answer the abbot of St. Augustine's Grimsby [Wellow Abbey] for a debt of 100s being arrears of rent of 13s 4d p.a. Note of return of no lay fee by the sheriff of Northamptonshire on the quindene of Hilary.
Teste Robert de Thorp, 8 Feb. 1368.

73.   Breve pro parliamento
Summons to attend a parliament to be held at Westminster on the 1 May next, with *premunientes* clause.[1]
Teste me ipso, 24 Feb. 1368.

> [1]   Printed *RDP*, IV.641; see also *CCR 1364–68*, p. 467.

74.   [f. 17v] Exchequer *fieri faciatis de bonis ecclesiasticis sicut alias*, returnable on the quindene of Trinity [18 June], in the following matter. Inspection of the Exchequer rolls shows that the abbot of Kirkstead, lately collector of the biennial tenth granted 20 Edward III in the archdeaconries of Lincoln, Stow, Leicester and the deanery of Rutland is burdened with the following who have not paid all or part of their dues:
Skeffington (Skeftyngton) church and pension, for 26s 8d for the first and second tenths of that grant;
from the same abbot and convent collectors of the first and second years of the biennial tenth granted 25 Edward III:
Thorngate prebend, for 10s;
Liddington church, for 64s; for the vicarage of the same, for 32s;
Welton Ryval [prebend], for £6 13s 4d;
Gulehall Magister Salvatoris cum porcionibus Kirketon and Hibaldstow (Hybaldestowe), Orby (Orreby) church, for 13s 4d;
Buckingham (Bukyngham) church [*sic, rectius* archdeaconry] for £4;
Welton Brinkhall (Welton Bringhall) Banastre' [*sic*], for 20s;[1]
Wyville (Wiwell) church and pension, for 21s 4d;
Southorpe (Southorp) church, for 6s 8d;
unless the aforesaid rectors and prebendaries and vicars can show before you that they have satisfied the collector, and cause the said sums to be paid to the recent collector. With the proviso that if the said rectors etc. show you any tallies and acquittances you are to send these into the Exchequer on the quindene of Trinity [18 June] and supersede your demands. Certify the Exchequer before the same date.
Teste Thomas de Lodelowe, 12 Feb. 1368.

> [1]   Welton Brinkhall was a prebend in Lincoln cathedral, cf. Welton Ryval, **26**, **31** and nn.; Thomas Banastre was prebendary of Dunham and Newport 1361–80, *Fasti*, I.61.

75. Common Pleas *fieri faciatis de bonis ecclesiasticis sicut alias*, returnable on the quindene of Hilary, against John de Somerby rector of Donington on Bain (Donyngton super Bayn) for £20 being arrears of rent of 100s p.a. due from his church of All Saints Trentham by equal portions at Easter and Michaelmas, recovered against him by the prior of Trentham before the justices at Westminster last Easter term, and similar mandate concerning 33s 4d of the 40s awarded to the prior as damages on the occasion of the detention of the rent; with warning that the king will proceed against the bishop if the mandate is not executed.
Teste Robert de Thorp', 20 Oct. 1368.

76. Common Pleas *venire faciatis*, returnable on the octave of Hilary, against Roger de Slaytburn' vicar of Friskney (Friskenay) to answer the prior of Bullington for a debt of £10 being arrears of rent of 5 marks p.a. Note of return of no lay fee by the sheriff of Lincolnshire on the octave of Michaelmas.
Teste Robert de Thorp, 16 Oct. 1368.
RETURN. The writ came too late.

77. Common Pleas *venire faciatis sicut pluries*, returnable on the quindene of Hilary, against William Bray rector of St. Peter's Rushton to answer the abbot of St. Augustine's Grimsby [Wellow Abbey] for a debt of 100s being arrears of rent of 13s 4d p.a. Note of return of no lay fee by the sheriff of Northamptonshire on the quindene of Hilary.
Teste Robert de Thorp, 28 Oct. 1368.
RETURN. We caused him to be warned.
[See **72**]

78. [f. 18]. Exchequer *certiorari (scrutatis registris)*, returnable on the quindene of Easter [15 April], to know who were the rectors [*sic*] of Corringham in 8, 10, 11, 16 and 18 Edward III.
Teste Thomas de Lodelowe, 13 Feb. 1369. By the memoranda roll of 43 Edward III, *Recorda*.
RETURN. After looking in the registers and other memoranda we find that a certain William de Estaimato, alien, was prebendary of the prebend of Corringham in 8 Edward III, also 10, 11 and 16 Edward III; one Reginald de Cusancia was prebendary in 18 Edward III; and Anibaldus (Anybaldus) [Gaetani] Cardinal, now dead, was prebendary of Corringham.[1]

   [1]   The more correct dates of the holders of this prebend are William d'Estaing 1290–1325, Renaud de Cusancia 1326–35, Anibaldus Gaetani de Ceccano cardinal bishop of Tusculum 1335–50; he died July-Aug. 1350, *Fasti*, I.54.

79. Exchequer *levari faciatis*, returnable on the morrow of the close of Easter [9 April], against the goods of the late Peter de Gildesburgh' rector of Biggleswade and prebendary of Tervin (Treven).
Teste Thomas de Lodelowe, 26 Jan. 1369. By the great roll of 41 in county of Shrewsbury and the memoranda roll of Michaelmas 43 in *Brevia returnabilia* roll 48.
RETURN. No goods of Peter de Gildesburgh deceased, named in the writ, could be found in Biggleswade rectory or elsewhere in the diocese at the time of the receipt of the writ, and therefore we could not execute the writ.
[See **47**]

80. Claro Rivulo

Exchequer *levari faciatis de bonis et beneficiis ecclesiasticis sicut pluries*, returnable on the morrow of the close of Easter [9 April], against:

the prioress of Clairruissel for £6 13s 4d for the administration of the fruits of Mapledurham church from 24 Edward III;

the prebendary of Sonning for the £10 from the first tenth of the biennial tenth granted 20 Edward III;

from the portion of Hendred church for 6s 8d for the second tenth of the same grant; Iffley church for 13s 8d for the same;

Hendred church for 23s 4d for the first moiety of the tenth granted 20 Edward III;

Harwell church for 26s 8d for the first moiety of the same.

Teste Thomas de Lodelowe, 26 Jan. 1369. [John] Edenesovere.

RETURN. No goods of the church of Mapledurham could be found, therefore we could not execute the writ.

[See **27, 28, 34, 52, 55, 63, 69**]

81. [ff. 18–18v] Bekyngham Tudeswell

Exchequer *levari faciatis de bonis et beneficiis ecclesiasticis sicut pluries*, returnable on the morrow of the close of Easter [9 April], against:

Beckingham church, for £4 owed for each term of the biennial tenth granted 35 Edward III;

Mere church, for 40s for the tenth granted 35 Edward III;

William de Tiddeswell clerk, for 19s 4½d for loans at the Receipt of the Exchequer for his journeys;

John Hale rector of Clifton, for half a mark for having writs of oyer and terminer;

Henry de Walton prebendary of Nassington, for 100s from the first moiety of the tenth granted 35 Edward III;

Mere church, for 20s from the first and second moiety of the tenth granted 35 Edward III;

Wyville church, for 19s 4d from the tenth granted 35 Edward III;

[Bishop] Norton church, for 66s 8d from each term of the tenth granted 35 Edward III;

Welton Ryvall [prebend] church, for 33s 4d owed from the second moiety of the tenth granted 35 Edward III;

the rector of Saddington church, for 8d from the tenth granted 35 Edward III;

Swithland church, for 7s 8d owed from each term of the tenth granted 35 Edward III;

Shangton church, for 10s 8d owed from each term of the tenth granted 35 Edward III;

Mere church, for 40s from the annual tenth granted 34 Edward III;

the vicar of South Cadeby church, for 16s for the tenth granted 34 Edward III;

Anibaldo [Gaetani] cardinal [bishop of Tusculum] of St. Roman who was rector of Corringham [prebendal] church with pension, for 79s 9½d for the annual tenth granted 16 Edward III;

Mere church, for 40s both for the biennial tenth granted 25 Edward III and for the tenth granted 30 Edward III;

St. Margaret's church, Leicester, for 61s for the tenth granted 16 Edward III;

Adam de Beauchamp rector of Mablethorpe St. Peter for £20 for his pledges because he has not yet presented his bill against Thomas de Carleton and John atte Kirke for a plea of trespass;

John de Stretton rector of Risby for 10s for having writs;

John de Fynchedon clerk, half a mark for writs of oyer and terminer;

the prebendary of Grantham Australis, for £4 6s 8d for each term of the biennial tenth granted 35 Edward III;

the prebendary of Grantham Borialis, for 106s 8d for each of the biennial tenths granted 35 Edward III.

Note of no lay fees by William Haulay Sheriff of Lincolnshire in his account on the morrow of Michaelmas 39 Edward III.

Teste Thomas de Lodelowe, 28 Jan. 1369. From the memoranda roll of Michaelmas term 43 Edward III.

RETURN. William Tideswell is a long time dead; John Hale, Adam de Beauchamp and John de Sretton are not beneficed in our diocese; no ecclesiastical goods in the churches of Beckingham, Nassington, Wyville, South Cadeby, Leicester St. Margaret, or the prebend of Grantham Borealis could be found at the time of the receipt of the writ, and therefore we could not execute it.

82. Exchequer *supersedeatis*, until the quindene of the close of Easter [23 April], concerning the mandate to levy from Richard de Chesterfield prebendary of Norton [Episcopi] 67s 8d owed for the clerical tenth granted 30 Edward III.

Teste Thomas de Lodelowe, 6 Feb. 1369. By the treasurer and barons because the said bishop had respite until the said quindene. [John] Edenesovere.

83. Exchequer *supersedeatis et sequestrum relaxetis*, until the quindene of Easter [15 April], concerning the mandate to levy from the ecclesiastical goods of Corringham prebend £12 13s 4d owed for the clerical tenth granted 16 Edward III.

Teste Thomas de Lodelowe, 30 Jan. 1369. By the barons at the prosecution of William de Mirfield because it is testified that the said church was in the hand of a certain cardinal in the said year 16 and the said William, as farmer of the church was prosecuted in the meantime, but is exonerated from the debt. [John] Edenesovere.

84. Common Pleas *venire faciatis sicut pluries*, returnable one month from Easter [29 April], against William Bray rector of St. Peter's Rushton, with warning that unless the bishop executed the mandate the crown would proceed against him.

Teste Robert de Thorp', 10 Feb. 1369.

EXECUTION. Memorandum that on 16 April 1369 in Liddington (Lidington) before John de Longedon the rector appeared and swore on the gospels which he held that he would preserve the bishop unharmed in the matter of this writ. Present: Nicholas de Thornton and John Harold notary public.

RETURN. We caused him to be warned.

[See **72**, **77**]

85. Exchequer *certiorari (scrutatis registris)*, returnable on the quindene of Easter [15 April], who was prebendary of Norton [Episcopi] in 30 Edward III.

Teste Thomas de Lodelowe, 20 Feb. 1369.

RETURN. After looking at the registers we find that the prebend of Norton was

vacant in 30 Edward III[1] and the fruits for that year pertained to the apostolic see because there was no possessor.
[See **82**]

[1]   1356. The last known holder, Philip Beauchamp, occurred in May 1354, and the next, Audoen Aubert cardinal bishop of Ostia, in the financial year 1357–58, *Fasti*, I.97.

86.   [ff. 18v–19] Common Pleas *venire faciatis sicut alias*, returnable on the octave of Hilary, against Roger de Slaytburn vicar of Friskney to answer the prior of Bullington for a debt of £10 being arrears of rent of 5 marks p.a.
Teste Robert de Thorp', 24 Jan 1370.
RETURN. This writ arrived too late for us to be able to execute it.
[See **76**]

87.   Nassyngton'
Exchequer *certiorari (scrutatis registris)*, returnable on the quindene of Easter [15 April], who was prebendary of Nassington in 30 Edward III.
Teste Thomas de Lodelowe, 20 Feb. 1369.
RETURN. After looking at the registers and other memoranda we find that in 30 Edward III Henry de Walton was prebendary of Nassington.[1]

[1]   He held the prebend from 1351 to 1365, despite two challengers, *Fasti*, I.95.

88.   Fylingham
22 May 1369 at Liddington there were brought to the lord bishop of Lincoln two royal writs of which the tenor of the first is this:
Exchequer *venire faciatis* [unfinished], returnable on the quindene of Trinity [17 June], against the below named rectors of churches, to answer the king separately for sums owed to the alien priory of Willoughton while it was in the king's hands during the French war, viz. John Wythornwyk rector of Fillingham (Fylingham) for 16s for tithes of Simon de Taillour payable at Michaelmas; John de Wynstowe rector of Blyborough (Bliburgh) for 40s for the tithes of two parts of all the sheaves of the whole lordship of Blyborough and two parts of the whole tithe on all sheaves of the whole lordship of Hugh Chaunce in the territory of Blyborough, and of a third part of all the tithes of all sheaves of the whole lordship of Robert Bennet in the same territory of Blyborough payable on the Purification of the Virgin; William Beauchamp rector of Harpswell (Herpeswell) for 20s for the tithes of the fee of Geoffrey de Neville payable at Michaelmas; Thomas de Helynge rector of Healing (Helynge) for 6s 8d for tithes of beans ('benys') of the fee of Richard de Helynge payable at Michaelmas; and Thomas de Wilughby rector of Rippingale (Reping-hale) for 6s 8d for tithes arising from the fee of Robert Lennet payable at Michaelmas as Richard de Ravenser clerk [the writ breaks off here; see below **97** for a complete writ on this subject.]

89A.   Ketilthorp'
Exchequer *venire faciatis sicut alias*, returnable on the quindene of St. John Baptist [8 July], against Robert de Northwode rector of Kettlethorpe (Ketilthorp') to answer Walter, yeoman of Master William de Askeby chancellor of the [same] Exchequer, for divers goods and chattels to the value of £40 which he unjustly holds back from him. Note of return of no lay fee by the sheriff of Lincolnshire on the quindene of Hilary.

Teste Thomas de Lodelowe, 7 June 1369.

89B. Ketilthorp
Identical writ to the one above.

90. Askeby
Chancery *certiorari (scrutatis registris)* whether Laurence de Manneby, presented to Ashby (Askeby) church by Henry III in the 54th year of his reign [28 Oct. 1269 – 27 Oct. 1270] was instituted and inducted in the same or not.
Teste me ipso, 6 June 1369.[1]

> 1   The only reference to Laurence de Manneby in Gravesend's register is as the deceased rector of Stiveton, Lincs., in 1270, *Rot. Gravesend*, pp. 45, 275.

91. [f. 19v] [Justice of Assize *inquiratis de bastardia*]. Simon Dod of Great Houghton brought in the king's court before Thomas de Ingelby and John Cavendish, justices of assize in the Northamptonshire, an assize of *novel disseissin* against Laurence Stratton of Northampton and Alice his wife and others, concerning tenements in Great Houghton, saying that he had been disseissed of two parts of two messuages, 9½ acres of land and one acre of meadow with appurtenances. To this Laurence and Alice came and said that they were the holders and that the case should not have been brought because one Richard de Halewyk, brother of John de Halewyk Alice's father, was seised of the property at his death; and after his death it passed to Alice, as next of kin, and Laurence her husband. Simon alleged that Alice could not inherit as she was a bastard, but Alice denied this. Mandate[1] to convene an enquiry, returnable before the justices at Northampton on the Monday before St. Margaret the Virgin [16 July].
Teste Thomas de Ingelby, 11 June 1369.

> 1   This writ is in intention, though not in form, an *inquiratis de bastardia*.

92. Hakthorn'
Exchequer *venire faciatis*, returnable on the octave of Michaelmas, against Thomas Peronell rector of Hackthorn to answer the king for 10s for certain tithes payable at the feast of St. Mark the Evangelist [25 April], by him to the priory of Willoughton, alien, for the time when it was in the king's hand because of the French war, as Richard de Ravenser clerk, has shown. Note of return of no lay fee by the sheriff of Lincolnshire on the quindene of Trinity [10 June] last.
Teste Thomas de Lodelowe, 25 June 1369.
RETURN. No goods of the said Thomas Peronell clerk could we find in our diocese at the time of the receipt of the writ, and therefore we could not execute it.

93. Lesyngham
Exchequer *levari faciatis de bonis et beneficiis ecclesiasticis*, returnable on the morrow of Michaelmas, against William rector of Leasingham (Lesingham), and Adam de Dunston chaplain and Roger Barbator his pledgers, for 20s being a debt to Philippa queen of England for a fine of £10 ('de auro suo de fine') being a licence to alienate in mortmain to the prior and convent of Nocton (Nokton) Park a certain tenement with appurtenances in the suburbs of Lincoln, payable to Richard de Ravenser, clerk, receiver of the said gold ('receptori auri predicti').[1]
Teste Thomas de Lodlowe, 26 June 1369.

RETURN. The present writ arrived too late for us to be able to execute it because of the shortness of the time.

¹ For Richard de Ravenser in the queen's household see Tout, *Chapters IV*, 170–1, 174–5.

94.   Concoreto

Exchequer *levari faciatis de bonis et beneficiis ecclesiasticis sicut pluries*, returnable on the morrow of Michaelmas, against Master John de Concoreto lately papal collector in England of the first fruits of John late supreme pontiff [John XXII] and of the quadrennial tenth imposed on the clergy of England by the said supreme pontiff of which half is due to us, for £600 of a certain debt of £1,127 0s 6¼d, identified by a certain view of account at the Exchequer as being the half due to us of that tenth, as appears by inspection of the rolls of our Exchequer.

Teste Thomas de Lodelowe, 6 June 1369.

RETURN. Itherius de Concoreto has been dead a long time and neither any of his goods nor his executors are left in the diocese and therefore we cannot raise the money, as we have certified many times before ('et sic vos quampluries certificavimus').

[See **19** and n.]

95.   [f. 20] Claro Rivulo

Exchequer *levari faciatis de bonis et beneficiis ecclesiasticis sicut pluries*, returnable on the morrow of Michaelmas, against:

the prioress of Clairruissel for £6 13s 4d for the administration of the fruits of Mapledurham church from 24 Edward III;

the prebendary of Sonning for the £10 from the first tenth of the biennial tenth granted 20 Edward III;

from the portion of Hendred church for 6s 8d for the second tenth of the same grant; Iffley church for 13s 8d for the same;

Henred church for 23s 4d for the first moiety of the tenth granted 20 Edward III; Harwell church for 26s 8d for the first moiety of the same.

Teste Thomas de Lodelowe, 20 June 1369.

RETURN. We caused the fruits of Mapledurham church to the value of 13s 4d and of Iffley, in sheaves, to the value named in the writ, 14s 8d, to be sequestrated and put up for sale, but because we could find no buyers we could not levy the money; Sonning Hendred and Harwell are not in our diocese therefore we could not in any way execute the writ.

[See **34**, **80**]

96.   Treven Prebend'

Exchequer *levari faciatis*, returnable on the morrow of Michaelmas, against the goods of the late Peter de Gildesborough rector of Biggleswade and prebendary of Tervin, who owes 10 marks for both parts of the biennial tenth granted 25 Edward III, 5 marks for the first part of the biennial tenth granted 20 Edward III, and 33s 4d for the second term of the same.

Teste Thomas de Lodelowe, 20 June 1369.

RETURN: No goods of the late Peter Gildesburgh could be found either in Biggleswade rectory or elsewhere and so we could not execute the writ.

[See **47**]

97. Blyburgh

Exchequer *venire faciatis sicut alias*, returnable on the octave of Michaelmas, against a group of rectors who owed money to the prior of Willoughton while the house was in the king's hands during the French war, viz. John Wythornwyk rector of Fillingham for 16s for tithes of Simon de Taillour payable at Michaelmas; John de Wynstowe rector of Blyborough for 40s for the tithes of two parts of all the sheaves of the whole lordship of Blyborough and two parts of the whole tithe on all sheaves of the whole lordship of Hugh Chaunce in the territory of Blyborough, and of a third part of all the tithes of all sheaves of the whole lordship of Robert Lennet in the same territory of Blyborough payable on the Purification of the Virgin; William Beauchamp rector of Harpswell for 20s for the tithes of the fee of Geoffrey de Neville payable at Michaelmas; Thomas de Helynge rector of Healing for 6s 8d for tithes of beans of the fee of Richard de Helynge payable at Michaelmas; and Thomas de Wilughby rector of Rippingale for 6s 8d for tithes arising from the fee of Robert Lennet payable at Michaelmas, as Richard de Ravenser clerk, who has investigated this on our behalf has shown that these sums are due to the crown. *Teste* Thomas de Lodelowe, 23 June 1369.
[See **88**]

98. [ff. 20–20v] Bekyngham

Exchequer *levari facaitis de bonis de beneficiis ecclesiasticis sicut pluries*, returnable on the morrow of Michaelmas, against Beckingham church, William de Tideswell, John de Hale, the prebendary of Nassington, the vicar of South Cadeby, St. Margaret's church Leicester, Adam de Beauchamp rector of Mablethorpe St. Peter, John Finchedon, the prebendary of Grantham Borialis. *Teste* Thomas de Lodelowe, 20 June 1369.
RETURN. Nassington and St. Margaret's Leicester were sequestrated to the value of the sums named but no buyers could be found; William de Tideswell is long since dead; the writ came so late that nothing could be done about the rest.
[See **31, 32**]

99. [20v] Sancti Aldati Oxon'

Common Pleas *fieri faciatis*, returnable on the quindene of Michaelmas, against William rector St. Aldate's church Oxford, of £4, to answer the abbot of Abingdon for a debt, being arrears of rent of 20s p.a. which the abbot recovered against him in the king's court at Westminster. *Teste* Robert de Thorp, 10 July 1369.
RETURN. The present writ arrived too late for us to be able to execute it.

100. Horpole

Common Pleas *fieri faciatis*, returnable on the octave of Michaelmas, against Nicholas Denc rector of Harpole (Horepole) church for 45s, to answer the abbot of St. Albans for arrears of rent of 30s p.a. which the abbot recovered in the king's court against John de Ithlyngburgh' lately rector of the said church and Nicholas' predecessor; and Nicholas should have paid the abbot 15s at the quindene of Easter 42 Edward III [23 April 1368], 15s at the following quindene of Michaelmas, 15s at the quindene of Easter 43 Edward III [15 April 1369] but he has not done so. Note of return of no lay fee by the sheriff of Northamptonshire. *Teste* Robert de Thorp', 12 July 1369.

RETURN. The profits of Harpole church to the said sum were sequestered by us but we could find no buyers so could not raise the money, and the profits were thus sequestered, and the rector swore to preserve the bishop unharmed ('et extit' fructus sicut sequestrata et iuravit rector de salvando dominum indempnem'.)
Simon Ward manu cepit salvare dominum indempnem.

101. [Unheaded] Exchequer *certiorari (scrutatis registris)*, returnable on the quindene of Michaelmas, against the holder of Corringham prebend in 8, 10, 11, 16, 18 Edward III.
Teste Thomas de Lodelowe, 12 July 1369.
RETURN. We could make no return because the writ arrived too late.
[See **31**, **32**]

102. Coryngham
Exchequer *certiorari (scrutatis registris)*, returnable on the morrow of All Souls [3 Nov.], concerning the holder of Corringham prebend in 8, 10, 11, 16, and 18 Edward III.
Teste Thomas de Lodlowe, 3 Oct. 1369.
RETURN. After looking in the registers and other memoranda we find that Anibaldus [Gaetani] once cardinal of Tusculum (St. Roman) [was prebendary of Corringham] in the years, 8, 10, 11, 16, and 18, as asked in the writ.
[f. 21] Certificatorium prebendarum de Coryngham, Nassyngton et Sancte Margarete Leycestr' per capitulum Linc.
Letter patent of the subdean and chapter of Lincoln saying that in answer to divers mandates of the bishop to scrutinise their records ('evidenciis nostris') about who held Corringham prebend in 8, 10, 11, 16, and 18 Edward III they certified that Anibaldus formerly cardinal was prebendary then; Lincoln 27 Oct. 1369.
'... item ... significamus quod fructus et proventus prebendarum de Coryngham, Nassyngton, et Sancte Margarete Leycestr' prout ad nos pertinuit ad valorem summarum in vestris litteris contentarum sequestravimus sicut alias scripsimus vestre paternitati reverendi, set levare pecuniam de eisdem non possumus nec audemus quia dicti fructus infra grangiam eorundem sunt inclusos quoad preben-dam de Norton, nunquam habuimus nec recepimus breve regium de levando lxvis viijd [66s 8d] ut dicitur debitos de eadem, et ideo nec sequestravimus nec pecuniam levare potuimus de eadem pro eo quod non habuimus potestatem sufficientem in hac parte'
29 Oct. 1369 Liddington 'prescripta littera fuit admissa'
Obligacio de Nassyngton
Memorandum that on 6 Nov. 1369 at Lidington there appeared one Richard rector of Stibbington (Stibyngton), in the archdeaconry of Huntingdon, and put himself under obligation to pay £10 sterling to the bishop of Lincoln at the next Christmas following, 'Et eodem die habuit diffesanciam se de 100s contra dictum dominum pro decima de Nassyngton petita indempnem preservet'.

103. [**Not a writ**] Atquietancia vicecomitis Lincoln' facta domino Episcopo Lincoln' pro quidusdam summis Regi a clero concessis
Let it be known to all by these presents that I, Thomas de Folnetby sheriff of Lincolnshire, have received from John bishop of Lincoln:
8d of the money imposed on him in payment in exoneration ('in exoneracione') of

the rector of Saddington (Sadyngton) church for the first moiety of the annual tenth
granted to the king by the clergy in 30 [Edward III];
7s 4d for Swithland (Swethelond) for both terms of the same tenth;
10s 8d for Shangton (Shanketon) for both terms of the same;
10s for [Great] Limber (Lymbergh') for first tenth of the triennial tenth granted 11
Edward III;
2s 6d for Toft [by Newton] for the ninth on wool of 14 Edward III;
14s for Rothwell (Rothewell) church near Grimsby for the biennial tenth granted
12 Edward III; and
14s 7d for Uffington (Uffyngton) church for the same years, 'de quibus quidem
summis faceor michi plenarie fore satisfactum et dictum Episcopum erga dominum
nostrum Regem et me inde esse quietum per presentes. In cuius rei testimonium
sigillum meum presentibus apposui.'
Dat' apud Westmonasterium 12 Nov. 1369

104. Recuperacio Roberti Bevyll cuiusdam debitum usque Gilbertum personam
ecclesie de Cesterton'
Exchequer *fieri faciatis de bonis et beneficiis ecclesiasticis*, returnable on the
quindene of Hilary, against Gilbert rector of Chesterton[1] executor of the will of
Thomas de Stikeleye deceased, for 10 marks which Robert Bevyll', yeoman
('valettus') of Master William de Askeby chancellor of the Exchequer, recently in
our court before the Exchequer barons, recovered against Gilbert for holding back
some of Thomas's debts, as appears by inspection of the Exchequer Rolls.
Teste Thomas de Lodelowe, 18 Nov. 1369.
EXECUTION. On 7 Dec. 1369 at Liddington the sequestrator in Huntingdon was
ordered to sequestrate the goods of the rectory to the sum mentioned and to levy
the money, and to cite the said rector to appear at Lidington on the Vigil of St.
Thomas the Apostle [20 Dec.] to preserve the bishop unharmed on the occasion of
this writ, and to certify the bishop before Christmas [of his actions].
   [See **89**]

   [1]   There are no references to this benefice between Registers 1 and 11; the latter contains no
   mention of a Gilbert vacating the rectory.

105. Ad satisfaciendum Regi
Persona ecclesie de Blyburgh'. Persona ecclesie de Herpeswell.'
Persona ecclesie de Helyng'. Persona ecclesie de Repynghale
Exchequer *venire faciatis sicut pluries*, returnable on the morrow of Hilary, against
the rectors of the following churches to answer the king for sums owed to the alien
priory of Willoughton while it was in the king's hands during the French war, lately
subtracted and cancelled viz., John de Wynstowe rector of Blyborough, for 40s for
tithes of two parts of the whole tithe of all the sheaves of the lordship of Blyborough
and two parts of all the tithes of the whole lordship of Hugh Chaunce in the territory
of Blyborough and also for the third part of all the sheaves of the lordship of Robert
Lennet in the same territory payable at the feast of the Purification of the Virgin
Mary; William Beauchamp rector of the church of Harpswell for 20s for tithes of
the fee of Geoffrey de Nevyll payable at Michaelmas; Thomas de Helyng rector of
Healing church for 6s 8d for tithes of beans of the fee of Richard de Helyns payable
at Michaelmas; and Thomas de Wylughby rector of Rippingale for 6s 8d for tithes
arising from the fee of Robert Lenn and payable at Michaelmas as Richard de

Ravenser clerk who sues for us can reasonably show that the said sums of money ought to pertain to us.

Teste Thomas de Lodelowe, 10 Oct. 1369.

[See **88**]

106.   [f. 21v] Ad satisfaciendum Regi

Persona ecclesie de Hakthorn'

Exchequer *venire faciatis*, returnable on the morrow of Hilary, against Thomas Peronell rector of Hackthorn to answer the king for 10s for certain tithes payable at the feast of St. Mark the Evangelist [25 April], by him to the priory of Willoughton, alien, for the time when it was in the king's hand because of the French war, as Richard de Ravenser clerk has shown.

Teste Thomas de Lodelowe, 10 Oct. 1369.

Executio

The Official of the archdeacon of Lincoln was written to to warn the rector and to cite him to appear before the bishop's commissary at Stamford on the Saturday after the feast of St. Thomas [22 Dec. 1369].

[See **92**]

107.   Ad satisfaciendum Regi

Willelmus Tydeswell persona ecclesie de Clifton. De prebendar' de Nassyngton. De ecclesia de Wywell'. De vicaria de Cateby. De Persona ecclesie de Malberthorp. De persona ecclesie de Ryceby. De J. de Fynchedon'. De prebenda Borialis de Grantham.

Exchequer *levari faciatis de bonis et beneficiis ecclesiasticis sicut pluries*, returnable on the morrow of Hilary, for the terms and persons named:

William de Tiddeswell clerk for 19s 4½d for loans at the Receipt of the Exchequer for his journeys;

John Hale rector of Clifton for half a mark for having writs of oyer and terminer;

Henry de Walton prebendary of Nassington, for 100s from the first moiety of the tenth granted 35 Edward III;

Wyville church, for 19s 4d from the tenth granted 35 Edward III;

the vicar of South Cadeby church, for 16s for the tenth granted 34 Edward III;

Adam de Beauchamp rector of Mablethorpe St. Peter for £20 for his pledges because he has not yet presented his bill against Thomas de Carleton and John atte Kirke for a plea of trespass;

John de Stretton rector of Risby, for 10s for having writs;

John de Fynchedon clerk, half a mark for writs of oyer and terminer;

the prebendary of Grantham Borialis, for 106s 8d for each of the biennial tenths granted 35 Edward III.

Note of return of no lay fees by William Haulay sheriff of Lincolnshire in his account on the morrow of Michaelmas, 39 Edward III.

Teste Thomas de Lodelowe, 12 Nov. 1369.

[See **31**, **32**, **45**, **56**, **81**, **98**]

108.   Ad satisfac'Regi

Pro parsona ecclesie de Toft

Exchequer *venire faciatis*, returnable on the morrow of Hilary, against John Dayns rector of Toft [by Newton] to answer the king for 6s 8d for the dues, tenths and profits of the manor of Toft, payable at the middle of Lent by the priory of Willoughton (Wylughton) which is in the king's hand because of the French war, as Richard de Ravenser, clerk, has testified. Note of return of no lay fee by the sheriff of Lincolnshire on the last morrow of Michaelmas.

Teste Thomas de Lodlowe, 24 Oct. 1369.

EXECUTION. The official of the archdeacon of Lincoln was written to to warn and to cite him to appear before the bishop's commissary at Stamford on the Saturday after St. Thomas the Apostle [22 Dec. 1369].

109. Ad satisfac' Regi

Pro prebendar' de Treven

Exchequer *levari faciatis*, returnable on the morrow of Hilary, for 10 marks for the first and second years of the biennial tenth granted 25 Edward III, and 5 marks for the first year of the biennial tenth granted 20 Edward III, and 33s 4d for the second moiety of the said tenth. We understand that Peter de Gildesburgh who was prebendary of Tervin in those years, it is said, has been dead a long time; mandate to raise the sums both from his rectory and elsewhere in your diocese.

Teste Thomas de Lodelowe, 8 Nov. 1369. By inspection of the Rolls of the Exchequer.

[See **47, 79, 96**]

110. [ff. 21v–22] Ad satisfac'Regi. Pro persona ecclesie de Thymelby. Pro persona ecclesie de Tateshale

Exchequer *venire faciatis*, returnable on the morrow of Hilary, against Alan Hened rector of Thimbleby (Thymelby) and Thomas de Kirkeby rector of Tattershall (Tateshale), executors of the will of John de Kirketon knight, deceased, to render account for the said John for one messuage and four shops in the town of Boston and 2½ perches ('parcium')[1] of arable land with appurtenances in the same town and 3½ acres of meadow in the same which belonged to John Baker on 24 June 12 Edward III, and afterwards were occupied by John de Kirketon, viz. from 22 to [f. 22] 33 Edward III during which time the said John de Kirketon occupied the property and took its profits but for which he has not accounted. Note of return of no lay fee by the sheriff of Lincolnshire on the morrow of Michaelmas.

Teste Thomas de Lodelowe, 16 Nov. 1369.

[1]   A perch, otherwise called a rod or pole, was a measurement of land; in length the standard measure was 5½ yards; a square perch was ⅟₁₆₀ of an acre.

111. [f. 22] [Unheaded]

Common Pleas *fieri faciatis de bonis ecclesiasticis sicut pluries*, returnable on the octave of Hilary, against William rector of St. Aldate's church Oxford, to answer the abbot of Abingdon for a debt of £4, being arrears of rent of 20s p.a. which the abbot recovered against him in the king's court at Westminster.

Teste Robert de Thorp', 3 Nov. 1369.

RETURN. The writ came too late.

[See **99**]

112. Adam de Borham

Exchequer *venire faciatis*, returnable on the quindene of Hilary, against Adam de Borham chaplain, executor of James Trumpwyn to answer the king for the said

James for £100 which James took and held at Lockington (Lokyngton), Nottinghamshire[1] from a certain large sum of money which belonged to Roger Mortimer, late earl of March on the day on which he was arrested, and which, by reason of his forfeiture, belongs to the king ('de quadam magna pecunie summa qui fuit Rogeri de Mortuo Mari nuper comitis March' die quo arestatus fuit que quidem pecunie summa racione forisfacture prefati comitis ad nos pertinet'). Note of return of no lay fee by the sheriff of Shropshire on the morrow of Michaelmas.
Teste Thomas de Lodelowe, 14 Oct. 1369.

    [1]   Now in Leics.

113.   Lesyngham

Exchequer *levari faciatis de bonis et beneficiis ecclesiasticis sicut pluries*, returnable on the quindene of the Purification of the Virgin [16 Feb.], against the rector of Leasingham, and Adam de Dunston chaplain and Roger Barbator his pledgers, for 20s being a debt to Philippa queen of England for a fine of £10 for a licence to alienate in mortmain to the prior and convent of Nocton Park a certain tenement with appurtenences in the suburbs of Lincoln, and which by the queen's death has become a debt to the crown.
Teste Thomas de Lodelowe, 4 Dec. 1369.
[See **93**]

114.   Persona ecclesie de Sybusdon'

Common Pleas *venire faciatis sicut alias*, returnable on the octave of Hilary, against Nicholas Shirburn' rector of Sibson (Sibusdon'), to answer the abbot of Lyre for a debt of £12 being arrears of rent of £4 p.a. Note of return of no lay fee by the sheriff of Leicestershire. And know that unless you execute our mandates we will proceed against you.
Teste Robert de Thorp, 12 Oct. 1369.

115.   Persona ecclesie de Trenge

Common Pleas *venire faciatis*, returnable on the octave of Hilary, against Robert de Stratford rector of Tring (Trenge), to answer the prior of the Hospital of St. John of Jerusalem for £50 being arrears of rent of 4 marks p.a. Note of return of no lay fee by the sheriff of Hertfordshire on the octave of Martinmas [19 Nov.]
Teste Robert de Thorp', 20 Nov. 1369.
EXECUTION. On 12 January [1370] at the Old Temple [London] the mandate was sent to the official of the archdeacon of Buckingham and the rector of Eversholt (Heversholt) to warn the said Robert to comply with the writ.

116.   [ff. 22–22v] Breve regium alienigenas concernens[1]

Exchequer *certiorari*, returnable on the morrow of the close of Easter [22 April], concerning alien clergy, both secular and regular, beneficed in the diocese, their names, the names of their benefices, the values and in which county or archdeaconry [they are].
Teste Thomas de Brantyngham, 16 Jan. 1370.[2]
Return [ff. 23v–24]
MEMORANDUM. Certificatorium brevis regii pro alienigenis.
This is the schedule of aliens, both seculars and regulars, holding ecclesiastical benefices in our diocese of Lincoln.

Chapter of Lincoln

The cardinal brother[3] of our lord the Pope is prebendary of the prebend of Sutton-cum-Buckingham (Sutton) with the churches of Buckingham (Bokyngham) and Harlestone (Herle), assessed at 260 marks.

The cardinal of Naples is prebendary of Milton Eccesia, assessed at 60 marks.

The cardinal brother of the aforesaid is prebendary of Thame, assessed at 168 marks.

The cardinal with the title of SS Marcellinus and Petrus is prebendary of Nassington, assessed at £100.

The cardinal of St. Martial is prebendary of Stow Longa (Langestowe), assessed at 63½ marks.

We do not know who is prebendary of Corringham (Coryngham), assessed at 190 marks; in the register of the chapter of Lincoln cathedral [there are] no receipts.

Huntingdon (Huntyngdon)

Brother Peter de Becko prior of the monastery of St. Neots is alien and has in the county and archdeaconry of Huntingdon the parish church of St. Neots [appropriated] to his own use, worth 31 marks; he also has Everton church worth 17 marks; he has a portion of Eynesbury, worth 10 marks.

A certain alien, whose name we do now know, is prebend of Stowe cum capella[4] worth 64 marks.

Northampton

John, rector of two parts of Boddington (Botyngdon) church, worth 20 marks.

Ralph prior of Weedon Lois (Wedon Pynkeneye) is rector of Weedon Lois worth 20 marks.

John prior of Ware is rector of Marston St. Lawrence (Merston) church worth 24 marks; the same John has a pension in Middleton Cheney (Midelton) church, 24s; John takes in Byfield (Byfeld) church a pension of 5s.

Thomas the prior and convent of St. Andrew Northampton have Sulgrave church to their own use worth 20 marks; the same prior and convent have the church of All Saints Northampton, worth £20; they have St. Sepulchre's church, Northampton, worth £10; they have St. Giles' church, Northampton, worth 10 marks; they have Exton church, worth £20; Ryhall (Ryale) church, worth £22[5]; they have Hardingstone (Hardyngesthorn iuxta Northampton) church, worth 20 marks; they have Moulton (Multon) church appropriated to their own use, worth £20.

Henry monk of the house of Cluny (Cluniacen') is rector of Mears Ashby (Assheby Mares) church, worth £10.

Walter prior of Ogbourne (Okeburn) priory has the parish church of Weedon Bec (Weden iuxta Flore), worth £10.

Brother Peter de Beko prior and the convent of St. Neots have Hemington (Hemmyngton) church appropriated to their own use, worth 20 marks.

Leicester (Leycestre)

The prior of Lewes (Lewys) has Melton Mowbray (Melton Moubray) parish church [appropriated] to his own use, worth £40 p.a.

The prior of Hinckley (Hynkle) has Hinckley (Hynkele) parish church worth 63 marks.

The prior of Ware has Peatling Magna (Petlyng Magna) church worth 18 marks.

Nicholas rector of Thurcaston (Thorkeston') church, worth 50 marks p.a.

Bedford (Bedeford)

The prior and convent of St. Neots have a moiety of Turvey (Torvay) church assessed at 13 marks.

Stow (Stowe)
Peter Ryther prior of the village ('ville') of Cammeringham (Cammeryngham) has
Cammeringham church [appropriated] to his own use, worth £10 p.a.
The prior and convent of Anjou (Andegavie) have a moiety of Willingham by Stow
[?] (Wylyngton) worth 11 marks p.a.
Lincoln
The prior of Long Bennington (Longebenyngton) has Long Bennington church
[appropriated] to his own use, assessed at 100 marks.
The prior of Hough (on the Hill) (How), of the order of St. Augustine, has Hough
church [appropriated] to his own use, assessed at £20.
The prior of (Great) Limber (Lymbergh) has Limber church [appropriated] to his
own use, worth £40 p.a.
The prior of Ravendale, Praemonstratensian order, has Ravendale church [appro-
priated] to his own use, worth 100s p.a.
The prior of Burwell, order of St. Augustine, has Burwell church [appropriated] to
his own use, worth 20 marks p.a.
The prior of Minting (Myntyng) has Minting church [appropriated] to his own use,
worth £20.
The abbot of St. Fromond (Frem') has Bonby (Bondby) church which is assessed
at [illeg.]
Buckingham Bukyngham)
William Dathy prior of Tickford (Tykford) has Newport Pagnell (Neuport Paynell)[6]
'cum villis evicinis', worth 80 marks p.a.
Brother John Felyng prior of [St. Nicholas] Ang[ers] has Wing (Wyngge) church
[appropriated] to his own use, assessed at 30 marks and worth 40 marks p.a.
James de Florencia is rector of Fingest (Fyngho), assessed at 55 marks and worth
£40 p.a.
Oxford (Oxon)
The prior of Cogges has Cogges church [appropriated] to his own use, assessed at
12 marks.
The prior of Minster Lovell (Minstre) has Minster [Lovell] church and Asthall
church, assessed at 17 marks.

1   The original of both the writ and return are in PRO, E179 (Subsidies, Clerical Series)/35/4.
2   Added from the original: Hauleye. Dorse [under ultra-violet light]: Breve infrascriptum
execucioni demandamus prout in cedula presenti annexa plenius continetur. William de Hauleye
was king's remembrancer of the Exchequer.
3   Anglicus Grimaud (Anglico Grimoard) cardinal bishop of Albano, occ. 1367–68; deprived
1381, *Fasti*, I.113; his brother Guillaume was Urban V, Sept. 1362 – Dec. 1370, J.N.D. Kelly,
The Oxford Dictionary of Popes (Oxford, 1986), pp. 223–5.
4   Perhaps Stow St. Mary or Stow-in-Lindsey. The *Fasti* list has no certain dates between
1368–69 and 1378–7.
5   Both Exton and Ryhall are in Rutland; the deanery of Rutland was usually treated as part of
the archdeaconry of Northampton.
6   'Paynell' interlined.

117. [f. 22v] Persona ecclesie Sancti Aldati Oxon'
Common Pleas *fieri faciatis de bonis ecclesiasticis sicut alias*, returnable on the
quindene of Easter [28 April], against William rector of St. Aldate's church Oxford,
to answer the abbot of Abingdon for a debt of £4, being arrears of rent of 20s p.a.
which the abbot recovered against him in the king's court at Westminster.
Teste Robert de Thorp, 23 Jan. 1370.

EXECUTION. On 28 Feb. the official of the archdeacon of Oxford was written to to sequestrate the goods of the said rector to the value mentioned and to certify before Easter, but he returned that he could find no goods to be sequestrated.

On 4 Dec. we sent another mandate to the same official ordering him to sequestrate the fruits.

[See **99**, **111**]

118A. Persona ecclesie de Sopmanford'

Exchequer *venire faciatis sicut alias*, returnable on the morrow of the close of Easter [21 April], against John Russell rector of 'Sopmanford' executor of John de Sautre yeoman and attorney of John Darcy knight lord of Knaith (Cnayt) to answer the king for the said John de Sautre for 30 ecus ('scuti') of gold which the said John owed to Walter de Chiryton and Gilbert de Wendlyngborgh' merchants of London 'et de quibus quidem xxx scutt' satisfieri volumus in partem satisfaccionis debitorum in quibus dict' mercatores bonis tenentur'.

Teste Thomas de Lodelowe, 18 Jan. 1370. By the pipe roll of 38 Edward III in London and a certain writ in the Treasurer's custody and a writ returned on the morrow of Hilary 41 [Edward III], and a writ returned on the morrow of Michaelmas by the sheriff of Cambridgeshire and Huntingdonshire. Edinesovere.

RETURN. Return was made that we made diligent enquiry for John Russell in our diocese but could not find him, therefore we could not execute the writ.

118B. Idem Breve est pro persona ecclesie de Sopmanford

Identical writ.

119. Persona ecclesie de Thymelby. Persona ecclesie de Tateshale

Exchequer *venire faciatis*, returnable on the morrow of the close of Easter [12 April], against Alan Hened rector of Thimbleby (Thymelby) and Thomas de Kirkeby rector of Tattershall (Tateshale), executors of the will of John de Kirketon knight, deceased, to render account for the said John for one messuage and four shops in the town of Boston and 2½ perches of arable land with appurtenances in the same town and 3½ acres of meadow in the same which belonged to John Baker on 24 June 12 Edward III, and afterwards were occupied by the said John de Kirketon, viz. from 22 to 33 Edward III during which time the said John de Kirketon occupied the property and took its profits but for which he has not accounted.

Teste Thomas de Lodewlowe, 16 Jan. 1370.

RETURN. Return was made in this way: we caused Alan and Thomas to be warned according to the form of the writ.

EXECUTION. On 30 Sept. 1370 at Stow Park a mandate was issued to the dean of Horncastle and the rector of Haltham on Bain (Holtham) to cite the said rectors to appear before the bishop or his commissary on the Thursday after the Translation of St. Hugh [10 Oct.], in the prebendal church of Stow; mandate also to sequestrate all the fruits of the said churches, and to certify. On that day and place, viz. 11 Oct. 1370,[1] the said Alan and Thomas appeared before Henry de Brok' and swore that they would make satisfaction and would preserve the bishop unharmed on account of the said writ and the sequestration arising therefrom. Present: Masters John de Banbury (Bannebury) and John Swafham and Simon de Messyngham proctors.

[Margin:] Afterwards the rectors paid by the hand of John Henry 60s by reason of the issues contained in the present writ.

[See **110**]

¹ 11 Oct. fell on a Friday that year. The Translation was observed on 6 or 7 Oct.

120. [f. 23] Parsona ecclesie de Blyburgh, Parsona ecclesie de Herpeswell, Parsona ecclesie de Helynga, Parsona ecclesie de Repynghale

Exchequer *venire faciatis*, returnable on the morrow of the close of Easter [22 April], against the rectors of churches named below to answer the king separately for sums owed to the alien priory of Willoughton while it was in the king's hands during the French war, viz. John Wythornwyk rector of Fillingham for 16s for tithes of Simon de Taillour payable at Michaelmas; John de Wynstowe rector of Blyborough for 40s for the tithes of two parts of all the sheaves of the whole lordship of Blyborough and two parts of the whole tithe on all sheaves of the whole lordship of Hugh Chaunce in the territory of Blyborough, and of a third part of all the tithes of all sheaves of the whole lordship of Robert Bennett in same same territory of Blybrough payable at the Purification of the Virgin; William Beauchamp rector of Harpswell for 20s for the tithes of the fee of Geoffrey de Neville payable at Michaelmas; Thomas de Helynge rector of Healing for 6s 8d for tithes of beans of the fee of Richard de Helynge payable at Michaelmas; and Thomas de Wilughby rector of Rippingale for 6s 8d for tithes arising from the fee of Robert Lennet and payable at Michaelmas, as the aforesaid Richard de Ravenser clerk has testified that these sums are due to us.

Teste Thomas de Ludlowe, 18 Jan. 1370.

EXECUTION. John de Wynstowe was warned, Thomas de Helyng was not in the diocese so could not be warned, William Beauchamp and Thomas de Wylughby are dead.

[See **88, 97**]

121. Parsona ecclesie de Hakthorn'

Exchequer *venire faciatis sicut pluries*, returnable on the morrow of the close of Easter, against Thomas Peronell', rector of Hackthorn to answer us about a debt of 10s being tithes payable at St. Mark's day [25 April] to the priory of Willoughton (Wylughton) for the time that it was in our hands because of the French war, on the information of Richard de Ravenser.

Teste Thomas de Lodelowe, 18 Jan. 1370.

RETURN. We have made diligent enquiry for Thomas Peronell in our diocese but cannot find him and because he remains in London diocese we cannot warn him. Thomas came to Stow Park 25 Nov. 1370 and swore that he would pay the said 10s before the Conception of the Virgin then following [8 Dec]. [In another hand:] He paid the same.

122. Prebend' de Treven

Exchequer *levari faciatis*, returnable on the morrow of the close of Easter [22 April], for 10 marks for the first and second tenths granted by the clergy in 25 Edward III, and 5 marks for the first tenth granted 20 Edward III and 23s 4d for the second moiety of the said tenth from the prebend of Tervin. We understand that Peter de Gildesburgh who held the said prebend in those years is dead and that on the day he died he had divers properties at Biggleswade (Brikeleswade) rectory.

Teste Thomas de Ludelowe, 17 Feb. 1370.

RETURN. We could find no goods of the said Peter de Gildesburgh at Biggleswade rectory or anywhere else in the diocese, therefore we could not execute the writ. [See **47, 109**]

123. Ecclesia de Mappelderham, prebend' de Sounnynges, porcio ecclesie de Henreth', ecclesia de Harwell'

Exchequer *levari faciatis de bonis et beneficiis ecclesiasticis sicut pluries*, returnable on the morrow of the close of Easter [22 April], against:

the prioress of Clairuissel for £6 of a debt of £6 13s 4d of arrears of the administration of the fruits of Mapledurham church from 34 Edward III;

the prebendary of Sonning £10 for the first year of the biennial tenth granted 19 Edward III;

a portion of Hendred church for the second year of the said tenth 6s 8d; from the same church for the first moiety of an annual tenth granted 20 Edward III 3s 4d; Harwell church for the first moiety of a tenth of 20 Edward III, 26s 8d.

Teste Thomas de Lodlowe, 17 Jan. 1370.

RETURN. Return was made in this form: no goods of the prioress of Clairruissel could be found to be sequestered, and also it is said that Mapledurham is in the king's hand because of the French war and one Master Edmund Bardolf[1] came and showed us a writ by which he is quit; the prebend of Sonning, Harwell church, Hendred church and any portion of it are not in our diocese and we have certified this many times.

[See **27, 28, 34**]

[1]   Prebendary of Banbury 1369–83, *Fasti* I.32.

124. [f. 23v] Parsona ecclesie de Lesyngham

Exchequer *levari faciatis de bonis et beneficiis ecclesiasticis sicut pluries*, returnable on the morrow of the close of Easter [22 April], against William rector of Leasinghm (Lesyngham), Adam de Dunston chaplain, and Roger Barbator pledger of the said William for 20s which they owed to the late Queen Philippa as part of a fine of £10 being a licence for the prior and convent of Nocton Park to acquire in mortmain certain property in the suburbs of Lincoln, and which on the queen's death has become a debt to the king.

Teste Thomas de Lodelowe, 18 Feb. 1370.

RETURN. No ecclesiastical goods of those persons could be found in our diocese though we made diligent search, and therefore we could sequestrate no goods.

125. Persona ecclesie de Clyfton, ecclesia de Wiwell, vicar' de Cateby, parsona ecclesie de Malberthorp, parsona ecclesie de Riseby, prebenda de Grantham, J. de Fyncheden

Exchequer *levari faciatis de bonis et beneficiis ecclesiasticis sicut pluries*, returnable on the morrow of the close of Easter [22 April], against:

William de Tideswell clerk, 19s 4½d owed to the king for William's journeys;

John Hale rector of Clifton ½ mark for his divers debts for hearing and treating ('de debitis plur' suis ad audiend' et tractand');

Wyville (Wywell) church for 19s 4d owed for the same tenth;

Cadeby (Cateby) vicarage 16s for the same;

Adam de Beauchamp rector of Mablethorpe (Malberthorp) £15 from a debt of £20 for his pleas as he has not yet executed his bill against Thomas de Carleton and John atte Kirke about a plea of trespass;

John de Stretton rector of Risby (Ryceby) 11s for having a writ; from John de Fyncheden ½ mark for having writs;

the prebend of Grantham Borialis 106s 8d from the said tenth. Returnable on the morrow of the close of Easter.

Teste Thomas de Lodelowe, 16 Feb. 1370.

RETURN. William de Tideswell and Adam de Beauchchamp are dead nor had they any ecclesiastical goods in the diocese as is known and we have often certified; John de Hale, John atte Kirke, John de Stretton are not in the diocese that we can find; and we can find no ecclesiastical goods for Wyville and Cateby.

[See **31, 34, 45, 56, 81, 107**]

126.   Adam de Borham

Exchequer *venire faciatis sicut alias* returnable on the quindene of Easter against Adam de Borham chaplain, executor of James Trumpwyn to answer the king for the said James for £100 which James took and held at Lockington (Lokyngton), Nottinghamshire, from a certain large sum of money which belonged to Roger Mortimer, late earl of March, on the day on which he was arrested, and which, by reason of his forfeiture, belongs to the king.

Teste Thomas de Lodelowe, 1 Feb. 1370.

RETURN. We made diligent enquiry but could find no ecclesiastical goods of the said Adam in our diocese.

[see **112**]

127.   [f. 24] Stanton Ecclesia

Prohibition against sequestering the goods of Stanton church, which owes a pension of 20 marks p.a. to Reading abbey, because cognition of annual pensions belongs to the crown.

Teste me ipso, 12 June 1370.

[See also **134, 283**, and, for execution, **318**]

128.   [f. 24v] Glatton Ecclesia

Exchequer *certiorari (scrutatis registris)*, returnable on the quindene of Michaelmas, concerning the holder of Glatton rectory in 25 Edward III.

Teste Thomas de Lodelowe, 12 June 1370.

RETURN. The registers and other memoranda were searched and it was found that Henry de Rusteshale of Campeden' was rector then.

129.   Herleston

Exchequer *venire faciatis sicut pluries*, returnable on the octave of Michaelmas, against the rector of Harlestone (Herleston) to answer the king and the prior of Lenton farmer of Lenton priory for a debt of £4, being arrears of a pension of 40s p.a. due from his church.

Teste Thomas de Lodelowe, 1 July 1370.

EXECUTION. 12 Sept. 1370 at Stow Park the dean of Haddon in the archdeaconry of Northampton was written to, in accordance with the force of this writ, to make the rector appear before the the bishop in his chapel at Stow Park on the first day after the feast of St. Matthew the apostle [Monday, 22 Sept.].

RETURN. This writ arrived too late to be executed.

130. Cortenhale ecclesia
Exchequer *venire faciatis sicut pluries*, returnable on the octave of Michaelmas, against Nicholas Rede rector of Courteenhall (Cortenhale) to answer the king and the prior of Lenton farmer of the alien priory for £4 of arrears of a pension of 6s 8d p.a. from his church, as the farmer cannot answer for his farm while the money is held back. We ordered you by another writ to make return to the Exchequer by last morrow of St. John Baptist but you said the writ came too late for you to execute it. We order you to execute this one diligently.
Teste Thomas de Lodelowe, 1 July 1370.
EXECUTION. The dean of Preston in the archdeaconry of Northampton was written to on 12 Sept. 1370 from Stow Park, to order and cite and certify in the [matter of the] preceding writ.
RETURN. The said rector of Courteenhall was warned according to the form of the said writ.

131. [f. 25] Cortenhale
Exchequer *supersedeatis et sequestrum relarxi faciatis* concerning the demand made to cause Nicholas Rede rector of Courteenhall to appear at the Exchequer.
Teste Thomas de Lodelowe, 14 Oct. 1370.
Relaxacio sequestri dicte ecclesie de Cortenhale.
On 17 Oct. 1370 at Stow Park the bishop wrote to the dean of Preston to relax the sequestration according to the writ.

132. [ff. 25–25v] Lincoln Stowe et Leyc' breve regium decime triennal' solucionem concernentes
[f. 25] We see by inspection of the Rolls of the Exchequer that the prior of St. Katherine's outside Lincoln, collector in the archdeaconries of Lincoln, Stow and Leicester of the triennial tenth, has still not accounted for these sums viz.:
2s 6d for Thorngate prebend;
3s 4d for the provosts' prebend;
33s 4d for Scamblesby with Melton church;
13s 4d for Louth vicarage;
33s 4d for Welton Ryval (Welton Rivail) [prebend] church;
£6 6s 8d for Corringham church;
13s 4d for Corringham vicarage;
23s 4d for Houghton (Houton) church;
½d for the pension of the nuns of St. Mary Magdalene in 'Kirkeby' church;
20s for Horkstow (Horkestowe) church;
5s 4d for Bonby (Bondeby) vicarage;
14s 8d for North Coates (Northcotes) church;
6s 8d for Tetney (Tetteneye) vicarage;
4s for West Ravendale (Westravendale) church;
8s for South Cadeby vicarage;
2½d for the portion of the prior of Covenham in St. Mary's church Covenham;
12d for the pension of the abbot of [Bury] St. Edmund in Wainfleet St. Mary (St. Mary's church Waynflete);
4s 2¼d for Tothill (Totyll) church;

26s 8d for West Halton (Halton) church;

13s 4d for Minting church;

7s 4d for Goulceby (Gouceby) church;

19d for the pension of the prior of Minting in the same;

21s 4d for Tattershall church;

8s 8d for Thornton le Moor church;[1]

13¼d for the portion of the abbot of Angers (Andeg') in Nocton (Noketon) church;

26s 4d for Ingoldsby (Ingoldesby) church;

4d for the pension of the abbot of Crowland (Croland) in the same;

11s 4d for Roxby (Rouceby) church;

8s 8d for the prior of Shelford's (Schefford) portion in Leasingham (Levesyngham) church;

6s for the same prior's portion in Dorrington (Diryngton) church;

8s for Folkingham (Folkynhgam) viz. for the rector's portion;

5s 4d for 'Kirkby' (Kirkeby) church for the rector's portion;[2]

12s for the moiety of South Witham (Southwyme), the rector's portion;

8s 8d for Wyville (Wiwell) church;

2s pension for the prior of Farley (Farle) in the same;

23s 4d for Wilsford (Willesford) church;

6s 8d for the prior of Wilsford's pension in the same;

8d for the prior of St. Fromond in the church of St. Mary in Cornstall, Stamford;

9s ¾d for the abbot of Angers' (Andeg') portion in Fillingham church;

6s 8d for his portion in Willoughton (Willughton);

2s 4½d for his portion in Hackthorn (Hakethorn) church;

[Leicestershire starts here]

9s 4d for Dunton Bassett (Dunton) church;

10s 8d for Ashby Magna (Magna Esseby) church;

12s 10d for Skeffington (Skeftyngton);

6d for the rector's portion in Rothley (Rotele);

37s 4d for Great Bowden (Boudon) church;

4s for the prior of Wolston (Wolfricheston)'s portion in Houghton on the Hill (Houton) church;

4s 4d for Packington (Pakyngton) vicarage;

10s for Breedon on the Hill (Bredon) vicarage;

42s for Hinckley (Hynkele) church;

4s 8d for the vicarage of St. Martin Leicester;

11s 10d for Broughton (Brocton) church;[3]

18d for the prior of Lenton's pension in the same;

8d for the abbot of Vaudey's pension in Saltby church;

16d for the prior of 'Cotesbyry's' pension in Coston church;

18d for his portion in Stapleford (Stapelford) church;

3s 4d for the prior of Monks Kirby (Kirkby Monachorum)'s pension in Melton Mowbray (Melton) church;

2s for the prior of St. Leonard's [hospital] York's pension in the same;

[Lincolnshire starts here]

5s 4d for Hundelby church;

4s 8d for Stixwould (Stikeswold) church;

21s 4d for Lavington (Lavyngton) church;

13s 4d for Thorpe on the Hill (Thorp) church;[4]

13s 4d for Honington (Honyngton) church;
12d for the prioress of Stixwould's portion in Alford church with Rigsby (Ryggesby) chapel;
commune capituli Lincoln pro decima trienn' £13 6s 8d for the commons of Lincoln Chapter;
26s 8d for [f. 25v] the pension of the said chapter in Gosberton (Gosberkirke) church;
40s for Bottesford (Botenesford) church;
6d for the chapter's pension in Scothern (Scothorne) vicarage;
3s 4d for the chapter's pension in Brattleby (Brotelby) [church];
18s for Mumby (Munby) church;
2s for the prior of Markby's pension in the same;
£6 for Holbeach church;
fieri faciatis de bonis et catallis and cause the money to be delivered to the said collector; unless the debtors can show you that they paid first, arrange that the acquittance shall be at the Exchequer on the morrow of the Purification of the Virgin [3 Feb.] and *supersedeatis* of the previous order.
Teste Thomas de Lodelowe, 21 Oct. 1370.

1 The only one of the three benefices called Thornton in Lincolnshire which was a rectory.
2 There are five places called Kirkby in Lincolnshire.
3 Either Broughton Astley or Nether Broughton, both rectories in Leicestershire.
4 Of the three 'Thorpe' benefices in Lincolnshire this is the only rectory.

133. [f. 25v] Breve pro decimis
Mandate to appoint collectors of the triennial tenth granted in the convocation held in St. Paul's cathedral London, and certify the names of collectors at the Exchequer before the octave of Trinity [23 June]
Teste me ipso, 20 April 1370.[1]

1 See *CFR 1369–77*, p. 72, where the date for the return of collectors' names is Ascension Day, which in 1370 fell on 23 May.

134. Breve pro ecclesias de Stanton
Prohibition against sequestering the goods of Stanton Harcourt (Stanton) church which owes a pension of 2 marks p.a. to Reading abbey because cognition of annual pensions belongs to the crown.
Teste me ipso, 12 June 1370.
EXECUTION. We wrote to stop the sequestration.
[See **127**]

135. Breve concernens Philipum de Weston' Rectorem de Goseberkirk'
Exchequer *inquiri faciatis* and *sequestrari faciatis*, returnable on the quindene of Hilary, concerning the goods of the late Philip de Weston, rector of Gosberton.
'Quia Philipus de Weston' clericus qui die suum clausit extremum ut accepimus tenebatur nobis die quo obiit in £66 4s [0d] per ipsum recept' de Thoma de Melchebourne et sociis suis firmariis omnium custumar' in diversis partibus Anglie in precio £33 2 gros' pro expeditione quorundam arduorum negociurum nostrorun in partibus Flandr', vobis mandamus quod per sacramentum virorum ecclesiasti-corum de dioc' vestra diligenter inquiri faciatis que bone et catalla ecclesiastica et cuius precii idem Philipus habuit tam apud Goseberkirk quam alibi in dicta dioc' vestra, et ad cuius vel quorum manus post mortem ipsius Philipi devenerunt et in

cuius vel in quorum manibus nunc existant, et de bonis et de catallis illis infra feodum ecclesiasticum in dicta dioc' vestra existentibus, sequestrari faciatis in manum nostram ad valenciam debiti predicti et ea sub sequestro salvo custodiri faciatis donec aliud inde a nobis habuitis in mandatis. Et constare faciatis Thes' et Baron' de Scaccario nostro apud Westm' a die sancti Hillar' in quindecim dies et sequestrari feceritis in manum nostram occasione premissa et ubi. Et remittatis ibi tunc hoc breve.

Teste Thomas de Lodelowe, 8 Oct. 1370.

RETURN. We could find no ecclesiastical goods of the said Philip at Goseberton or elsewhere in the diocese in ecclesiastical fee, therefore we could not sequestrate them. However, we made diligent enquiry and found that all the goods of the said Philip at the time of his death and even after his death, it is said, came to the hands of Ralph Bole of Swineshead and Ralph Bayle of Quadring (Quadryng) and they occupy them at present because they are the executors of Philip's will, but we do not know the value of the goods at present because this writ came too late so that we could not execute it.[1]

> 1 For Thomas (de) Melchbourn (Melcheborun) [of Lynn], see T.H. Lloyd, *The Medieval English Wool Trade* (Cambridge, 1977), pp. 194, 198–9, and E.B. Fryde, *Studies in Medieval Trade and Finance* (London, 1983), VII.1212–3, X.3–5, 8–11. I owe thanks to Prof. Mark Ormrod for these references. For the many references to Philip Weston's varied career in royal service see Tout, *Chapters*, VI.447–8.

136. [f. 26] <u>Eynesbury, Glatton, Leghton, Brouneswold, Stepilmordon'</u>

Exchequer *levari faciatis de bonis et beneficiis ecclesiasticis*, returnable on the morrow of the close of Easter [14 April], against:

the rector of Eynesbury for 10s for the second year of the biennial tenth granted by the clergy in 25 Edward III;

the rector of Glatton for 42s 4d from the same year of the same tax;

the prebendary of Leighton Buzzard (Leighton Brounneswold) for 35s 4d for the second moiety of the tenth granted 30 Edward III;

the rector of Steeple Morden (Stepilmordon) for £6 13s 4d for the second term of the tenth granted 30 Edward III.

Teste Thomas de Lodelowe, 18 Feb. 1371. By the great roll of 44 Edward III in Cambridgeshire and Huntingdonshire and in a certain schedule sent to the Exchequer by Nicholas de Styuecle sheriff in Cambs. and Hunts. which is among the sheriffs' returns for 44 Edward III and the memoranda roll 45 Edward III Hilary term *brevia retornabilia* roll one.

137. <u>Parsona ecclesie de Nethirkedyngton'</u>

Since by inquisition taken before Roger Elmerugg and others, our justices, and sent to the Exchequer it appears *inter alia* that Thomas de Williamscote chivaler and Hugh rector of Kiddington (Nethirkedyngton)[1] on Thursday on the vigil of All Saints 38 Edward III [31 Oct. 1364] by force and arms, in breach of the king's peace, took and imprisoned one John Patrik and held him at Broughton in detention until John Patrik made fine with the said Thomas and Hugh for 48 sheep worth 100s; Exchequer *venire faciatis*, returnable on the quindene of Michaelmas, against Hugh the rector, to answer along with Thomas who has also been summoned for that day. Note of no lay fee by the sheriff of Oxfordshire and Berkshire on the quindene of Trinity [22 June 1371].

Teste Thomas de Lodelowe, 3 July 1371. By the said inquisition held at the

Exchequer by David de Wollor lately clerk of the Rolls of Chancery 43 Edward III in the roll of the king's remembrancer and by return from the sheriff of Oxfordshire. RETURN. This writ arrived too late therefore we could not execute this because of the shortness of the time. Return was made that the rector of this church is not called Hugh but Richard and we could not find Hugh.

¹ Kiddington, Oxon. Possibly the 'nether' or 'inferior' arose from the fact that there was another settlement and benefice, Asterleigh, within the vill; see the LAO list of benefices.

138.   Ricardus de Hull' capellanus
Exchequer *venire faciatis*, returnable on the morrow of Michaelmas, against Richard de Hull' chaplain, executor of the will of William atte Hull deceased, to show why he should not answer for £154 18s 11½d being the price of 13 sacks 6 stones and 7 pounds of wool which in 11 Edward III were exported by the said William and on which customs have not been paid.
Teste Thomas de Lodelowe, 22 May 1371. By the memoranda roll of 36 Edward III Hilary term *Recorda*, and by the return on the morrow of Easter by the sheriff of Shropshire.
RETURN. We have made diligent enquiry in our diocese but can find no Richard de Hull' chaplain at the time of the receipt of the writ because the writ came so late that we could not execute it.
[See **36, 46**]

139.   Johannes Long' capellanus
Exchequer *venire faciatis sicut pluries*, returnable on the morrow of Michaelmas, against John Long' chaplain, executor of the will of William de Bergham of Bridgnorth' to answer the king for the said William for £35 2s 7½d the price of 2½ sack, 11 stones 4 pounds of wool removed in 11 Edward III by the said William and on which customs duties have not been paid.
Teste Thomas de Lodelowe, 12 July 1371.
RETURN. We made diligent enquiry but could not find John Long chaplain in our diocese at the time of the receipt of the writ, therefore we could not execute it.
[See **25**]

140.   [f. 26v] Eynesbury, Glatton, Leyghton Brouneswold'
Exchequer *levari faciatis de bonis et beneficiis ecclesiasticis sicut alias*, returnable on the morrow of Michaelmas, against:
the rector of Eynesbury for 10s for the second year of the biennial tenth granted by the clergy in 25 Edward III;
the rector of Glatton for 42s 4d from the same year of the same tax;
the prebendary of Leighton Buzzard (Leighton Brounneswold) for 35s 4d for the second moiety of the tenth granted 30 Edward III;
the rector of Steeple Morden (Stepilmordon) for £6 13s 4d for the second term of the tenth granted 30 Edward III.
Teste Thomas de Lodelowe, 8 July 1371.
RETURN. This writ arrived so late that we could do nothing because of the shortness of the time.
[See **136**]

141. [Unheaded]

[Incomplete] writ *[levari faciatis]* de bonis *[et beneficiis ecclesiasticis]* sicut *pluries* [no date of return], against William rector of Leasingham, Adam de Dunston chaplain, and Roger Barbator pledger of the said William for 20s which they owed to the late Queen Philippa as part of a fine of £10 being a licence for the prior and convent of Nocton Park to acquire in mortmain certain property in the suburbs of Lincoln, and which, on the queen's death has become a debt to the king.

[No attestor], 12 Nov. 1370.

Received at Stow Park 17 Aug. 1371.

[See **93, 113, 124**]

142. Robertus Austhorp'

Common plea *venire faciatis*, returnable on the octave of Hilary, against Robert de Austhorp clerk to answer the abbot of Peterborough for £11 5s 0d being arrears of 100s p.a. rent. Note of return of no lay fee by the sheriff of Northamptonshire on the octave of Michaelmas.[1]

Teste William de Fyncheden', 6 Oct. 1371.

> 1   For Robert Austhorp see *BRUO*, I.79, also Reg. 12, ff. 74, 74v–75; for his will dated London 17 Feb. 1373 see *ibid.*, f. 119, also Gonville and Caius MS 588/737, f. 47; examiner general of the court of Canterbury, I.J. Churchill, *Canterbury Administration* (London, 1933) II.241.

143. Thomas de Williamscote Hugo parsona ecclesie de Netherkydyngton

Exchequer *venire faciatis*, returnable on the quindene of Hilary, against Hugh rector of (Nether) Kiddington in the following case: since by inquisition taken before Roger Elmerugg and others, our justices, and sent to the Exchequer it appears *inter alia* that Thomas de Williamscote chivaler and Hugh rector of Kiddington, on Thursday on the vigil of All Saints 38 Edward III [31 Oct. 1364] by force and arms took and imprisoned one John Patrik and held him at Broughton in detention until John Patrik made fine with the said Thomas and Hugh for 48 sheep worth 100s; Hugh is to answer along with Thomas who has also been summoned for that day.

Teste Thomas de Lodelowe, 6 Dec. 1371

Memorandum that Richard is rector of Nether Kiddington now and Hugh, who used to be rector, is now vicar of North Aston (Northaston) in the archdeaconry of Oxford in Woodstock deanery.

[See **137**]

144. Midelton et Colyntre

Chancery *certiorari (scrutato registro)* to discover whether the towns of Middleton (Middelton) and Collingtree (Colyntre), Northamptonshire are one or two parishes and have one or two rectors, and whether any inhabitants of Collingtree are parishioners of Middleton church.

Teste me ipso, 1 Dec. 1371.

145. [Reg. 9C, p. 21][1] Wylden Ecclesia

Chancery *certiorari (scrutato registro et registris predecessorum vestrorum)*, returnable without delay, concerning the holders of Wilden (Wylden) church from 12 Edward I to 18 Edward III, who they were, how many, who were instituted, and at whose presentation, how, and in what manner.

Teste me ipso 5 Dec. 1372.   Stanb',

[1]   See the introduction, section i, for discussion and explanation of the text at this point.

[There follow two returns, one relating to **165** below, the other, which is incomplete, refers to debts and explains that, although the profits of the benefices in question have been sequestered, no buyers could be found, so that the bishop was unable to levy the sums named.]

146. [Reg. 9C, p. 21; a new hand begins here.] Bluntesham ecclesia
Chancery *ne admittatis* concerning Bluntisham (Bluntesham) church whose presentation we recently recovered, in our court before our justices, against John [Barnet] bishop of Ely and Nicholas Basset or Russel, clerk, with mandate to revoke, without delay, any action the bishop may already have taken.
Teste me ipso 4 Feb. 1373.   [John] Tam[worth][1]
    [1]   See Wilkinson, *Chancery*, pp. 66n., 76 and n.,77, 84, 85 and n., 86; Tout, *Chapters*, III.209, 212–13.

147. [Reg. 9C, p. 21] Hugo quondam[1] Rector ecclesie de Netherkedington
Since by inquisition taken before Roger Elmerugg and others, our justices, and sent to the Exchequer it appears *inter alia* that Thomas de Williamscote knight and Hugh rector of Kiddington on Thursday on the vigil of All Saints 38 Edward III [31 Oct. 1364] by force and arms, in breach of the king's peace, took and imprisoned one John Patrik and held him at Broughton in detention until John Patrik made fine with the said Thomas and Hugh for 48 sheep worth 100s; Exchequer *venire faciatis*, returnable on the morrow of the close of Easter [25 April 1373] against Hugh the rector, to answer, along with Thomas who has also been summoned for that day. Note of no lay fee by the sheriff of Oxfordshire and Berkshire on the quindene of Trinity [22 June 1371].
Teste Thomas de Lodelowe, 18 Feb. 1373.
[See **137**]
    [1]   'quondam' interlined.

148. [Reg. 9C, p. 22] Crudewell, Clifton, Wiwell, Cateby, Milberthorp' ecclesiae, Rykeby ecclesia, J. Fyncheden'
Exchequer, *levari faciatis de bonis et beneficiis ecclesiasticis sicut pluries*, returnable on the morrow of the close of Easter [10 April 1374], against:
William de Tydeswell, clerk, for 20s 4½d owed to us for loans of money received from the receipt of the Exchequer for his journeys;
John Hale rector of Clifton church, for ½ mark for divers debts for having writs of oyer and terminer;
Wyville church for 19s 4d owed for the first moiety of the annual tenth granted to us by the clergy 30 Edward III;
the vicar of [South] Cadeby for 16s for the same tenth;
Adam de Beauchamp rector of Mablethorp St. Peter for £15 of a certain debt of £20 owed for his pledges because he has not yet presented his bill against Thomas de Carleton and John atte Kirke for a plea of trespass;
John Stretton rector of Risby for 10s for having a writ;
John Fyncheden, clerk, for ½ mark which he owes for his writs of oyer and terminer.
Teste Thomas de Lodelow, 9 Nov. 1373.
[See **21**, **23**, **107**, **125**]

149. [Reg. 9C, p. 22] <u>Borham</u>
Exchequer *venire faciatis*, returnable on the morrow of the close of Easter [25 April 1373], against Adam de Borham chaplain, executor of James Trumpwyn to answer the king for the said James for £100 which James took and held at Lockington (Lokyngton), Nottinghamshire from a certain large sum of money which belonged to Roger Mortimer, late earl of March on the day on which he was arrested, and which, by reason of his forfeiture, belongs to the king. Note of return of no lay fee by the sheriff of Shropshire on the morrow of Michaelmas.
Teste Thomas de Lodelowe, 24 Jan. 1373.
[See **112, 126**]

150. [Reg. 9C, p. 22] <u>Theynton Wylwes Berkhamsted'</u>
Exchequer *levari faciatis*, returnable on the quindene of Easter [1 May], against the following clerks of the diocese:
'Theynton'[1] church for 8s 8d owed for the first moiety of the annual tenth granted 30 Edward III;
Welwyn (Welwes) church for 16s 8d owed for the same tenth;
Great Berkhamstead (Berkhamsted' Sancti Petri) church for 10s owed for the same tenth.
Teste Thomas de Lodelowe, 14 Feb.
RETURN was made in this form:[2] John Crysp rector of Welwyn was [illeg.] because no goods of the said rector or his church for the levying of the debt could be found; the rectors of the churches of 'Theynton' and Great Berkhamstead were [the subjects of] diligent enquiry but because of the shortness of the time from the reception of the writ we could find no goods of them by which the debts could be levied this time.
[Reg. 9C, p. 21] <u>Ecclesie de Wilberton et Stepilmordon</u>
The below mentioned Master John de Shropham[3] and Thomas de Edyngton are not beneficed in our diocese though we have made diligent enquiry for them and their benefices, therefore we are not able to levy the sums. Item, the churches of Wilburton (Wilberton) and Steeple Morden (Stepilmordon) are not within our diocese, therefore we are not able to levy the sums.[4]
[Reg. 9c, p. 23] <u>+Theynton</u>
'Infrascriptam summam octo solidorum et octo denar' de ecclesia de Theynton infracripta domino nostro Regi debit' non levavimus ista vice <u>cum</u> <u>sunt</u> due ville nuncupate Theynton videlicet super et inferior, quarum utraque habet ecclesiam paroch' ideo declaretis in eventu qu<u>oad</u> [illeg. word] summa<u>m</u> antedicta<u>m</u> sic levari poterit in eventu.'

    1   Possibly Theydon, of which there are three (Bois, Garnon and Mount), all in Essex.
    2   This is written in very small characters; it has obviously been squeezed in after the next writ was entered. All the return must be regarded as no more than a 'probable reading'.
    3   See *BRUC*, p. 526.
    4   Both benefices are in Cambridgeshire. For Steeple Morden see **136**.

151. [Reg. 9C, p. 22] <u>Prebenda de Stowe</u>
Exchequer *certiorari (scrutato registro et aliis memorandis)*, returnable three weeks from Easter [9 May 1373], conerning the holders of the prebend of Stow *cum Capella* in 30 Edward III.
Teste Thomas de Lodelowe, 4 May 1373 [*sic*].

152. [Reg. 9C, p. 22] <u>Breve super bastardia Philipi Pons</u>
Justice Itinerant (Assize) *inquiratis de bastardia*, returnable at Stamford on the Thursday next after the feast of St. James the Apostle [28 July 1373], because this matter lies within the cognisance of the Church, in the following case: William Pons of Pickworth (Pykeworth) and Margaret his wife, in a royal court, before John Cavendissh and Thomas Ingelby, justices of assize in Lincolnshire, brought an assize of *novel disseisin* against Philip son of Elizabeth de Limbyri and others, concerning two messuages, three tofts and two carucates of land and twenty acres of meadow, with appurtenances, in Silk Willoughby [next Quarrington] (Walling-bury iuxta Quryngton). In answer to this case Philip came into court before those justices and asserted that he was the son and heir of Roger de Thrikyngham. To this, Philip Pons and Margaret said that Philip could not be the son and heir of Roger because he was a bastard, but Philip replied that he was not.
Teste John Cavendissh, Lincoln, 3 March, 1373.
[EXECUTION]: the writ is contained in a mandate of the bishop to Masters John de Belvoir (de Belvero) official of Lincoln, Geoffrey le Scrope (Scroop) and Richard de Wynewyk canons of Lincoln [p. 23], to all or any two of them, to enquire into the case and to certify the bishop of their findings by letters patent and close.[1]
Old Temple, London, 8 May 1373.

    [1]   For Belvoir and Scrope see *BRUO*, I.164 and III.1658–9.

153. [Reg. 9C, p. 23] <u>Gilbertus de Arches</u>
Exchequer *fieri faciatis de bonis et beneficiis ecclesiasticis sicut pluries*, returnable on the morrow of Trinity [13 June], for 100 marks which John abbot of St. Nicholas, Angers (Andeg') recovered against Gilbert de Arches, as appears by an inspection of the rolls of the Exchequer, in part satisfaction of the arrears owed to the proctor of the abbot for the farm of lands and tenements and possessions of the abbot in England.
Teste Thomas de Lodelowe, 2 May 1373. By the *Memoranda* roll of 46 [Edward III], Easter *Recorda*.   [William de] Hauleye

154. [Reg. 9C, p. 23] <u>Agmundesham Ecclesia</u>
Chancery *certiorari (scrutatis registris)*, returnable without delay, to know who was rector of Amersham (Agmundesham) church from 34 Edward III to 36 Edward III.
Teste me ipso, 30 April 1373.   [Thomas] Midelton[1]

    [1]   See Wilkinson, *Chancery*, pp. 67n., 83n.

155. [Reg. 9C, p. 23] <u>Robertus Legat Rector ecclesiae de Navenby</u>
Exchequer *venire faciatis*, returnable on the octave of Michaelmas, against Robert rector of Navenby, to answer us for the farmer of the abbot of Séez (Sagio) of all the lands and possessions of the abbot in England, for £8, being arrears of a pension of 40s p.a., owed to the keeper of the lands in England, which are in our hand because of the French war, and which Robert unjustly detains. Note of return of no lay fee by the sheriff of Lincolnshire on the quindene of Trinity [3 July 1373].
Teste Thomas de Lodelowe, 6 July 1373.

156. [Reg. 9C, p. 23] <u>Willelmus Rector ecclesie de Pikewell'</u>
Common Pleas *venire faciatis*, returnable on the octave of Michaelmas, against William, rector of Pickwell (Pykwell), clerk, to answer Helena (Elena) who was the

wife of William de Curzon (Curson) knight, for a plea that he return to her two written obligations ('de placito quod reddat ei duo scripta obligatoria que sibi iniuste detinet, ut dicit'). Note of return of no lay fee by the sheriff of Leicestershire on the octave of Trinity [19 June 1373].
Teste William de Finch, 10 July 1373.

157. [Reg. 9C, p. 24] <u>Breve pro parliamento</u>
Mandate to attend parliament to discuss certain difficult and urgent business and for the king's war expedition overseas, at Westminster on the morrow of the feast of St. Edmund [17 Nov.], with *praemunientes* clause.
Teste me ipso Westminster, 4 Oct. 1373.[1]
[EXECUTION]: the writ is contained in a mandate of the bishop to the official of the archdeacon of Lincoln ordering him to order the clergy of his archdeaconry to be present in the church of St. Mary by the Bridge (*ad Pontem*), Stamford, on the Monday after the feast of St. Leonard the Confessor [7 Nov.] to elect two sufficient proctors to represent the clergy in parliament, and to certify to the bishop by letter patent what he has done.
Liddington, [blank in ms.] Oct. 1373.
<u>Commissio ad interessendum pro domino et ad videndum procurat' eligi et nominari pro parliamento</u>
Commission to Master John Barnet, official of Lincoln,[2] to represent the bishop in the church of St. Mary by the Bridge, Stamford on Monday after the feast of St. Leonard the Confessor [7 Nov.] and to receive the names of the proctors elected by the clergy for parliament.
Liddington, 4 Nov. 1373.

    1   Printed *RDP*, IV.659, and see *CCR 1369–74*, p. 586.
    2   For John Barnet junior see *BRUO*, I.113–14.

158. [Reg. 9C, p. 24] <u>Rector Ecclesie de Navenby</u>
Exchequer *venire faciatis sicut alias*, returnable on the octave of Hilary, against Robert Legat, rector of Navenby church to answer us for the farmer of the abbot of Séez (Sagio) of all the lands and possessions of the abbot in England, for £8, being arrears of a pension of 40s p.a., owed to the keeper of the lands in England which are in our hand because of the French war, and which Robert unjustly detains.
Teste Thomas de Lodelowe, 20 Oct. 1373.
<u>Breve Regium</u>
This writ was received at Liddington on 9 Dec. 1373. Return was made in this way: we caused diligent enquiry to be made for Robert Legat at Navenby and elsewhere in our diocese but we were not able to find him, therefore we were not able to order him to come, this time, 'et tradita fuit littera Talbot de mandato domini baronibus domini regi liberanda'.[1]
[See **155**]

    1   Professor Storey suggests that Talbot was the bishop's messenger.

159. [Reg. 9C, p. 25. A new gathering begins here.] <u>Thomas Vaux vicarius ecclesie de Bondeby</u>
Chancery *certiorari (scrutato registro)*, returnable without delay, concerning Thomas Vaux junior, vicar of Bonby (Bondeby) church, on what day he was instituted, and at whose presentation, how and in what way.

Teste me ipso, 5 Nov. 1371.

160. [Reg. 9C, p. 25] Middelton and Colyntre
Chancery *certiorari (scrutato registro)*, returnable without delay, to know whether
the vills ('ville') of Middleton (Middelton) and Collingtree (Colyntre) in the county
of Northampton are one parish or two parishes, and if they have one rector or two
rectors and if any inhabitants of the vill of Middleton are parishioners of the church
of Collingtree, or if any inhabitants of the vill of Collingtree are parishioners of the
church of Middleton.
Teste me ipso, 1 Dec. 1371.
[RETURN]. Because the writ came so late we were not able to execute it because of
the shortness of time.
[See **144**]

161. [Reg. 9C, p. 25] J. Chaworth persona ecclesie de Cusyngton
Exchequer *venire faciatis*, returnable before the Exchequer barons on the quindene
of Easter [11 April 1372], against John de Chaworth rector of Cossington
(Cusyngton), to anwer John de Denton, clerk of the Pleas of the Exchequer,
administrator of the goods and chattels which belonged to William de Denton
deceased, for 4 marks which he unjustly detains, to the great damage of the said
John [Denton], as he has been able to show, and for which John [Chaworth] should
answer. Note of return of no lay fee by Richard de Herthull sheriff in Leicestershire
on the quindene of Hilary.
Teste Thomas de Lodelowe, 20 Feb. 1372.
RETURN. The present writ came too late therefore we could not return it because of
the shortness of time.

162. [Reg. 9C, p. 25] Contra Arch[chidiaconatum] North[ampton]
Chancery prohibition[1] against doing anything in contempt of the king in the case
of the archdeaconry of Northampton whose patronage is in dispute in the royal
court between the king and the bishop.[2]
Teste me ipso, 3 March 1372.
[EXECUTION]. The present writ arrived too late so that, because of the shortness of
time, we were not able to execute it.

  [1] In intention a writ of *ne admittatis*, though these words do not occur in this writ.
  [2] See *Fasti*, I.11 and XII.14 for the holders in this period.

163. [Reg. 9C, p. 25] Johannes Tubeye persona ecclesie de Hardmed'
Common Pleas *venire faciatis*, returnable on the quindene of Michaelmas, against
John Tubeye rector of Hardmead (Hardmed'), clerk, to answer the prior of Merton
for a plea that he restore to him 50s, being arrears of rent of 20s p.a. Note of return
of no lay fee by the sheriff of Buckinghamshire at Westminster on the quindene of
Trinity [6 June].
Teste William de Fyncheden, 12 July 1372.

164. [Reg. 9C, p. 25] Rogerus de Sutton persona ecclesie de Glatton
Common Pleas *venire faciatis*, returnable on the octave of Michaelmas, against
Roger de Sutton rector of Glatton, clerk, to answer the abbot of Missenden

(Missynden) for a plea of £12, being arrears of rent of £4 p.a. [p. 26]. Note of return of no lay fee by the sheriff of Huntingdonshire on the quindene of Trinity [6 June]. *Teste* William de Fyncheden, 11 June 1372.

165. [Reg. 9C, p. 26] Johannes de Shropham custos aule scolar' Cantebrig'
Exchequer *levari faciatis de bonis et beneficiis ecclesiasticis*, returnable on the morrow of Michaelmas, against:
Master John de Shropham warden of the King's Hall, Cambridge for money received from the abbot of Waltham for his sustenance and journeys, £15 16s;[1]
the rector of Wilburton (Wilberton) church, £4 2s 8d for the first year of the biennial tenth granted 25 Edward III;
the rector of Steeple Morden (Stepilmordon), viz. Thomas de Etyngdon, 10 marks for the second year of the annual [*sic*] tenth granted 30 Edward III.
Note of return of no lay fees by Nicholas de Styuecle late sheriff of Cambridgeshire and Huntingdonshire on the morrow of Martinmas 45 Edward III [11 Nov. 1371].
Teste Thomas de Lodelowe, 21 June 1372. By the great roll of 45 [Edward III] in Cambridgshire and Huntingdonshire and a certain schedule presented to the court by the said former sheriff, among the responses of the sheriffs of that year and the [Pipe] Roll.
Retornatum eiusdem Return was made in this form: the present writ arrived too late and therefore because of the shortness of the time we were not able to execute it.

  [1]   Shropham was warden Oct. 1361 to 1363, see *BRUC*, p. 526. For the financial links between King's Hall and Waltham Abbey (Essex), see Alan B. Cobban, *The King's Hall within the University of Cambridge in the Later Middle Ages* (Cambridge, 1969), pp. 93–4, 163, 196, 203–4.

166. [Reg. 9C, p. 26] Commissio ad inquirendum super bastardia Willielmi Pirly
Common Pleas *inquiratis de bastardia* [no date for return] concerning William Pirly in the following case: William Pirley sued in our court at Westminster John Barkere of Parva Okele for 2s 6d rent with appurtenances owed to him in Parva Okele as his right and inheritance, and from which ('de quibus') John disseised Peter Pirly, William's father, whose heir William is. John came into our court and objected to William saying that he had no right in that rent with appurtenances as the heir of Peter, as he claimed, because William is a bastard. William denies this. Mandate to enquire into the truth of the matter because cognition of this belongs to the ecclesiastical jurisdiction.
Teste William de Fynchedon, 15 Oct. 1372.
EXECUTION. The writ is contained in a mandate to Master John de Bannebury and Ralph Crophill rectors of Ashby St. Ledger (Askebury) and Corringham churches, to enquire into this and to certify by letters close and patent to the bishop in suitable time ('tempore oportuno') their findings with the names of the witnesses and their full depositions.[1]
Buckden 20 Oct. 1372.

  [1]   For John Banbury (Bannebury) *alias* Fabian see *BRUO*, I.102–3. Crophill was not the prebendary of Corringham so could not have been the rector, so was probably the vicar.

167. [Reg. 9C, p. 27] Lillyngston' Ecclesia
Exchequer *certiorari (scrutato registro et aliis memorandis vestris)*, returnable on the octave of Martinmas, to know if Lillingstone Lovell (Lillingston) church,

Oxfordshire,[1] whose advowson we have given and granted to Notley (Notteley) abbey to hold in pure and perpetual alms, is appropriated to the said abbot and convent or not, and if it is, the day and year when it was appropriated.
Teste Thomas de Lodelowe, 8 Nov. 1372.
RETURN. Inspection of the registers in our possession shows that the parish church of Lillingstone Lovell has been appropriated to the said abbot and convent; however, the evidence for this appropriation is in the possession of the abbot and convent, and on 12 November Brother William de Dorcestre canon of Notley (Nottley) was instituted and inducted as rector [*sic*].

  [1] Now in Bucks.

168. [Reg. 9C, p. 27] Prebenda maior Bedeford et prebenda minor
Chancery *certiorari (scrutatis registris et aliis memorandis)* whether the prebendary of the prebend of Bedford Major in Lincoln cathedral has any portions in the vill of Kirkby Underwood (Kirkeby iuxta Repynghale) in the archdeaconry of Lincoln and Kilsby (Kildesby) in the archdeaconry of Northampton annexed to the prebend, and if the prebendary of the prebend of Bedford Minor in Lincoln cathedral has any portion in the vill of Boddington (Botyndon) in the archdeaconry of Northampton annexed to it and if the prebendaries have any portions outside the town of Bedford annexed to them in those vills or elsewhere; if so, which are these portions and in which towns they are, and whether they have been assessed *per se vel in grosso* and for what sums they have been assessed.
Teste me ipso, 24 November 1372.

169. [Reg. 9C, p. 27] Robertus Brembery Rector Ecclesie de Staunton Harecourt' de qua ecclesia infrascripte xx[ti] marce exiguntur
Common Pleas *venire faciatis sicut pluries*, returnable on the quindene of Hilary, against Robert Bremberc [rector of Stanton Harcourt] your clerk to answer the abbot of Reading (Redynges) for a plea that he return 20 marks, being arrears of rent of 20 marks p.a. owed to the abbot it is said. Note of return of no lay fee by the sheriff of Berkshire at Westminster on the octave of St. John the Baptist [1 July].
Teste William de Fyncheden, 16 Nov. 1372.

170. [Reg. 9C, p. 27] Ouston Ecclesia
Chancery *certiorari (scrutatis registris vestris et predecessorum vestrorum)* who was last admitted, instituted and inducted into the church of Owston (Ouston),[1] both the person and by which bishop your predecessor, and at whose presentation, and by what right the prior and convent of Newburgh (Neubourgh) obtained that church to their own use, and how and in what way.
Teste me ipso, 30 Oct. 1372.

  [1] There are two Owstons, one in Leics., the other in Lincs., but only the former was a parish.

171. [Reg. 9C, p. 27] Northburgh Ecclesia
Chancery *certiorari (scrutatis tam registris predecessorum vestrorum quam registro vestro)* who and how many persons have been admitted, instituted and inducted to the church of Narborough (Northburgh iuxta Leicester) from 1 January 5 Edward III by you and your predecessors.
Teste me ipso, 10 Nov. 1372.

172. [Reg. 9C, p. 28] [Unheaded]
Exchequer *certiorari (scrutatis registris)*, returnable on the quindene of Hillary, who was or were the rector or rectors of Iffley (Ziftele) church in 10, 11, 16, 18, 20 and 30 Edward III and if the church was at that time annexed to the archdeaconry of Oxford.
Teste Thomas de Lodelowe, 3 November 1372.
EXECUTION: Certificate of the same. After scrutiny of the registers and our other memoranda we found that Cardinal Albanen' et de Gordonia et de Aquen' archdeacon of Oxford [was the rector] and the parish church of Iffley (Zeftele) is annexed to that archdeaconry, and the church was so annexed during the years in question.[1]

> [1]   During these years, 1336 to 1356, the archdeacon of Oxford was Gaillard de la Motte, cardinal deacon of Santa Lucia in Orthea, who had held the archdeaconry since 1313, and who died 20 Dec. 1356, *Fasti*, I.14.

173. [Reg. 9C, p. 28] Edensore
Exchequer *levari faciatis de bonis et beneficiis ecclesiasticis*, returnable on the morrow of Hilary, against the following clerks of your diocese:
from the church of 'Theynton', 8s 8d owing from the first moiety of the tenth granted 30 Edward III;
from Welwyn (Welwes) church, 16s 8d owing from the same tenth;
from Great Berkhamstead (Berchampsted Sancti Petri), 10s owing from the same tenth.
Note of return of no lay fees by Thomas de Bassyngburn lately sheriff of Essex and Hertfordshire on the octave of Martinmas 45 Edward III.
Teste Thomas de Lodelowe, 23 Nov. 1372. By the great *Memoranda* Roll of the year 45 in Essex and Hertford and by a certain schedule lodged in the Exchequer by the said sheriff which is among the returns of the sheriffs, and by a writ returned on the morrow of Michaelmas last by the bishop of London.
RETURN was made that because the writ came too late we could not execute it because of the shortness of the time, at Liddington 10 Jan. 1373.

174. [Reg. 9C, p. 28] Austhorp
To the sheriff of Northamptonshire. Common Pleas *distringas episcopum*, returnable on the octave of Hilary, to have Robert de Austhorp, clerk, to answer the abbot of Peterborough (Burgo Sancti Petri), in a plea of £20 5s which are in arrears of a rent of 100s p.a., and to hear a judgment concerning other defaults ('Et audiendum iudicium tam de plur' defaltis').
Teste William de Fyncheden, 14 Nov. 1372.
[See **142**]

175. [Reg. 9C, p. 28] Wylden Ecclesia
Chancery *certiorari (scrutatis registris)*, who and how many persons have been presented, instituted and inducted to Wilden (Wylden) church from 18 [Edward I] until 44 Edward III.
Teste me ipso, 24 [?] Jan. 1373.   Stanl'
[For the original of this writ, and the return, see **Appendix A, no. 6**; see also **Appendix B, nos. 20, 21**]

176. [Reg. 9C, p. 29] <u>Breve ad certificandum nomina beneficiorum occupat' per alienigen'</u>
Chancery *certiorari*, returnable before the quindene of Easter [16 April 1374], which and how many benefices, as well archdeaconries and other dignities as parish churches, prebends and chapels are in the hands of aliens within your diocese, and of what kind they are and what their value p.a. by estimate or extent in your registers according to their true value, and the names of each and every alien who holds a benefice, their name, status, and condition, whether the benefices are held at farm and the names of the proctors or ministers and whether the aliens are resident or not.
Teste me ipso, 6 March 1374.

177. [Reg. 9C, p. 29] <u>Breve contra Rectorem de Horpole</u>
Common Pleas *fieri faciatis de bonis ecclesiasticis*, returnable in the quindene of Easter [16 April], against Nicholas Dene, clerk, rector of Harpole (Horpole), clerk in your diocese, to the answer the abbot of St. Albans for 60s, being arrears of a payment of 30s p.a. which the abbot recovered in the king's court before the justices at Westminster by consideration of the same court against a certain John de Irtlingburgh lately rector of that church; the rent is payable every year at the quindene of Easter and the quindene of Michaelmas by equal portions, and it therefore should have been paid, at the rate of 15s at Easter and Michaelmas in 46 and 47 Edward III.
Teste William de Fincheden, 22 Jan. 1374.
[See **100**]

178. [Reg. 9C, p. 29] <u>Breve pro Xª bien' solven'</u>
Exchequer *levari faciatis de bonis et beneficiis ecclesiasticis*, returnable on the morrow of the close of Easter [10 April], against:
Master John de Shropham warden of King's Hall, Cambridge (the hall of our scholars, Cantebr') for tenths received from the abbot of Waltham for the sustenance and journeys of the said warden, for £15 16s;
the rector of Wilburton (Wilberton) church for the first year of the biennial tenth granted by the clergy in 25 Edward III, for £4 2s 8½d;
the rector of Steeple Morden (Stepelmorden), viz. from Thomas de Edyngton for the second tenth of the biennial tenth granted 30 Edward III, for 10 marks.
Note of return of no lay fees by Nicholas de Stiucle late sheriff of Cambridgeshire and Huntingdonshire at the Exchequer on the morrow of Martinmas 45 Edward III.
Teste William Tauk', 9 Feb. 1374. By the great roll of year 45 in the counties of Cambridge and Huntingdon, and by a certain schedule of the court delivered by the said former sheriff which is among the sheriffs' returns of that year, and the Memoranda Roll of year 48, Michaelmas *brevia returnabilia*. Roll 11.
[See **165**]

179. [Reg. 9C, p. 29). <u>Consimilis Breve</u>
Exchequer *levari faciatis de bonis et beneficiis sicut pluries*, returnable on the morrow of the close of Easter [10 April], against 'Theynton' church for 8s 8d owed from the first moiety of the tenth granted 30 Edward III.
Teste William Tauk, 14 Feb. 1374. By the great roll of year 45, and by a certain schedule delivered to the Exchequer by Thomas de Bassynbourn' late sheriff of the

aforesaid counties [not named] and [p. 30] among the sheriffs' returns of year 45 and by a writ returned on the morrow of Michaelmas year 47 by the bishop of London and by the last writ returned on the morrow of Michaelmas.
[See **173**]

180.   [Reg. 9C, p. 30] <u>Horpole Ecclesia</u>
Common Pleas *fieri faciatis de bonis ecclesiasticis*, returnable on the octave of Michaelmas, against Nicholas Dene, clerk, rector of Harpole (Horpole), clerk in your diocese, for 60s and 15s to render to the abbot of St. Albans, being arrears of a payment of 30s p.a. which the abbot recovered in the king's court before the justices at Westminster by consideration of the same court against a certain John de Irtlingburgh lately rector of that church; the rent is payable every year at the quindene of Easter and the quindene of Michaelmas by equal portions, and it therefore should have been paid, at the rate of 15s at Easter and Michaelmas in 46 and 47 Edward III, and 15s at Easter 48 Edward III. Note of return of no lay fee by the sheriff of Northamptonshire.
Teste William de Wych', 18 June 1374.
Pas' 34   Ro 214   Petus
[See **177**]

181.   [Reg. 9C, p. 30] <u>Herleston Ecclesia</u>
Exchequer *venire faciatis*, returnable on the octave of Michaelmas, against Robert rector of Harlestone (Herleston) to answer the crown and the prior of Lenton, farmer of the priory, for £4, being arrears of a pension of 40s p.a., without which the prior cannot pay the farm of the priory, and which Robert unjustly detains so that the prior cannot satisfy the crown, to the prior's great damage. Note of return of no lay fee by the sheriff of Northamptonshire on the octave of Trinity.
Teste William Tauk, 13 June 1374.
[See **116, 129**]

182.   [Reg. 9C, p. 30] [Unheaded on this page but flagged on p. 31:] <u>Citacio concernens bastardiam Margerie uxoris Edmundi Waldeyene et Alice uxoris Gerardi Waldeyene</u>[1]
Common Pleas *inquiratis de bastardia*, returnable within a month of Michaelmas, in the following case: Edmund Waldeyne and Margery his wife and Gerard Waldeyne and Alice his wife brought a case in our court at Westminster against Thomas atte Cros concerning 10 acres of land with appurtanences in Mollington (Mollynton), Warwickshire,[2] and asserted the right of Margery and Alice to this land as daughters and heirs of Robert fitz Robert fitz Robert [*sic*] fitz Ralph de Bereford by writ of form of gift (*forma donacionis*). Thomas objected to Edmund, Margery, Gerard and Alice that those same four had no right of Margery and Alice as heirs of Robert fitz Robert fitz Robert fitz Ralph to claim those lands because, he alleged, Margery and Alice were bastards. This Edmund, Margery, Gerard and Alice denied. [p. 31] Marriage pertains to the spiritual power.
Teste William de Fyncheden, 17 May 1374.
EXECUTION. Mandate to the official of the archdeacon of Oxford, reciting the writ, and order, on pain of greater excommunication, to execute this in person; to cite, or cause to be cited, the said Edmund, Margery, Gerard, Alice, and Thomas and[3] to make proclamation in the church of St. Mary, Oxford and in other churches and places in the archdeaconry as seems most expedient, that all of these persons should

appear before us or the abbot of Ramsey OSB, the prior of Huntingdon priory OSA and Masters William de Tudenham and Thomas de Langeton bachelors in canon law, or two or three of them, in St. Mary's church, Huntingdon on the morrow of the feast of St. Matthew the Apostle [21 Sept.]; and to signify your actions in this matter.

Stow Park 26 August 1374.

Note that a similar letter was sent to the official of the archdeacon of Huntingdon [*sic*] to cite them, in the terms of the above letter, and, *especially in Kenilworth church**[4] to appear on the same day in the same place.

Note that a similar letter was issued to the official of the court of Coventry and Lichfield .

Commissio in negocio bastardie supradict'

Mandate to the abbot of Ramsey (Rameseye,) the prior of the canons of Huntingdon, and Masters William de Tudenham and Thomas de Langeton[5] to hold an enquiry and certify by letter close and patent, before the feast of St. Luke the Apostle [18 Oct.], including the names of the witnesses and their testimonies.

Stow Park 3 Sept. 1374.

[1]   The heading is written in a different ink and hand.
[2]   Now in Oxon.
[3]   A new hand and different ink start here; see note above.
[4]   The text between the asterisks is interlined.
[5]   For William Rede *alias* Tudenham, see *BRUC*, pp. 475–6, and for Langton (Langeton) *BRUO*, II.1101.

183.   [Reg. 9C, p. 32] [Unheaded]
Exchequer *levari faciatis de bonis et beneficiis ecclesiasticis sicut pluries* [no date given for return], against:

Master John de Shropham warden of the King's Hall, Cambridge, for money received from the abbot of Waltham for his sustenance and journeys, £15 16s;

the rector of Wilburton church, £4 2s 8d for the first year of the biennial tenth granted 25 Edward III;

the rector of Steeple Morden, viz. Thomas de Etyngdon, 10 marks for the second year of the annual [*sic*] tenth granted 30 Edward III.

Note of return of no lay fees by Nicholas de Stuecle lately sheriff of Cambridgeshire and Huntingdonshire on the morrow of Martinmas.

[No attestor given] 7 June 1374. By the great roll of year 45 in Huntingdonshire and by a schedule lodged at the Exchequer by the sheriff which is among the returns of the sheriffs in the same year 45 and a writ returned on the close of Easter. [John] Edenesovere

[See **165, 178**]

184.   [Reg. 9C, p. 32] Ecclesia de Braybroke
Common Pleas *fieri faciatis de bonis ecclesiasticis*, returnable on the quindene of Easter [27 April], against John rector of Braybrooke (Braybroke), clerk of your diocese, to answer the prior of Daventry for £4 19s, being arrears of rent of 44s p.a. which the prior recovered in our court, the rent payable at Michaelmas, Christmas, Easter and the Nativity of St. John the Baptist by equal portions, and *fieri faciatis de bonis ecclesiasticis*, returnable at the same time, for 11s, being arrears of rent which ought to have been paid at Christmas last.

Teste Robert Bealknapp, 7 January 1376. Ro 75

185.   [Reg. 9C, p. 32] [Unheaded]
Justice Itinerant (Assize) *inquiratis de bastardia*, returnable on the Friday after the feast of St. James the Apostle [28 July] because this matter lies within the cognisance of the church, in the following case: William Pons of Pykeworth and Margaret his wife, in a royal court, before John Cavendissh and Thomas Ingelby, justices of assize in Lincolnshire, brought an assize of *novel disseisin* against Philip son of Elizabeth de Limbyri and others, concerning two messuages, three tofts and two carucates of land and twenty acres of meadow, with appurtenances, in Silk Willoughby [next Quarrington] (Wallingbury iuxta Quryngton). In answer to this case Philip came into court before those justices and asserted that he was the son and heir of Roger de Trikyngham. To this, Philip Pons and Margaret said that Philip could not be the son and heir of Roger because he was a bastard, but Philip replied that he was not.
Teste me John Cavendissh, 18 June 1374.
[See **152**]

186.   [Reg. 12B, f. 27] Littera pro parliamento
[EXECUTION]. Letter of the bishop, dated Sleaford 10 Jan. 1376, ordering the election of suitable proctors for the parliament to be held on the Thursday after the Purification of the Virgin [6 Feb. 1376] in All Saints' church, Northampton. This mandate contains a writ of summons to a parliament at Westminster on 12 Feb., with *premunientes* clause.
Teste me ipso apud Langele, 28 Dec. 1375.[1]

   [1]   King's Langley, Herts., was a royal manor house. Printed *RDP*, V.662; see also *CCR 1374–77*, p. 282.

187.   Breve pro Rectore medietatis ecclesie de Segebrok' et Rectore ecclesie de Berughby
Exchequer *venire faciatis*, returnable three weeks from Easter [4 May], against John rector of a moiety of Sedgbrook (Segebrok') to answer the king and the prior of Eye, farmer of that priory, about a debt of £4, being arrears of a pension, and against Ralph Langele, rector of the other moiety, and Matthew Arsel, rector of Barrowby (Berughby), both for the same reason.[1]
Teste Henry Asty, 12 Feb. 1376.

   [1]   The prior and convent of Eye (Suffolk) were the patrons of Sedgebrook and took a pension of 20s p.a. for each moiety, Sutton, I.14.

188.   Willelmus Milner vicarius ecclesie de Baston'
Common Pleas *venire faciatis*, returnable on the quindene of Easter [27 April], against William Milner vicar of Baston, to answer the abbot of Crowland (Croyland) for a debt of 40s. Note of return of no lay fee by the sheriff of Lincolnshire on the octave of Hilary.
Teste Robert Bealknapp, 26 Jan. 1376.

189.   [ff. 27–27v] Breve pro rectore medietatis ecclesie de Segebrok' et Rectore alterius medietatis eiusdem ecclesie et Rectore de Berughby sicut pluries
Exchequer *venire faciatis sicut pluries*, returnable on the octave of Michaelmas, against John rector of a moiety of Sedgbrook (Segebrok') to answer the king and the prior of Eye, farmer of that priory, about a debt of £4 being arrears of a pension,

and against Ralph Langele, rector of the other moiety, and Matthew Arsel, rector of Barrowby (Berughby), both for the same reason.
Teste Henry de Asty, 20 June 1376.
[See **187**]

190. [f. 27v] Thomas Rector ecclesie de Dykeswell'
Common Pleas *venire faciatis*, returnable on the octave of Michaelmas, against Thomas rector of Digswell (Dykeswell) to answer the abbot of Walden for a debt of 40s.
Teste Robert Beaulknap, 18 June 1376.

191. Johannes Loned Rector ecclesie de Parva Kynbelle'
Common Pleas *venire faciatis*, returnable on the octave of Michaelmas, against the rector of Little Kimble (Parva Kynebell') to answer the abbot of St. Albans for a debt of 5s.
Teste Robert Bealkanpp, 20 June 1376.

192. Breve ecclesie de Toucestr'
Exchequer *levari faciatis de bonis et beneficiis ecclesiasticis*, returnable on the morrow of Michaelmas, against Laurence rector of Towcester (Toucester), for a debt of 113s 4d to the king from the issues of the forest.
Teste Henry Asty, 12 July 1376.
[f. 28] RETURN. Laurencius Rector Ecclesie de Toucestr'
Memorandum. This writ was received at Lincoln on 17 May 1377 and return was made that the writ arrived too late. We made diligent enquiry but could not find Laurence in our diocese.

193. [f. 27v] Certificatorium brevis regii super scrutinium registrorum pro capella de Cokthorp
Chancery *certiorari (scrutato registro)*, returnable without delay, to know if the chapel of Cokethorpe (Cokthorp) is annexed to Ducklington (Dokelyngton) church.
Teste me ipso, 20 Nov. 1376.
[EXECUTION]. The writ is contained in the bishop's reply saying that the chapel is annexed to the church.
Lidington, 15 Jan. 1377.

194. Rector ecclesie de Berughby
Exchequer *relaxari faciatis* since [Matthew Arsel] the rector of Barrowby (Berughby) has now satisfied the king and the prior of Eye.
Teste Henry de Asty, 6 Feb. 1377.
[EXECUTION]. On 14 Feb. 1377 at the Old Temple [London] the sequestration was relaxed and the dean of Grantham (Graham) was written to.
[See **187, 189**]

195. [ff. 27v–28] <u>Commissio in negocio bastardie [damaged] Ellesworth</u>
Common Pleas *inquiretis de bastardia*,[1] returnable on the octave of Trinity [14 June], concerning Alianora Ellesworth. She has brought an action in our court against William Clerk for one toft and three acres of land in Great Paxton, which she claims as the heir of Thomas Ellesworth; but William has alleged that Alianora is a bastard and so cannot inherit.
Teste Robert Bealknapp, 6 Feb. 1377.
EXECUTION. Mandate to the official of the archdeacon of Huntingdon and Master William Overton[2] ordering them to held an inquisition and to report back to the bishop in writing.
[f. 28] Stow Park, 13 May 1377.

> [1] The writ is contained in the bishop's mandate of execution.
> [2] See *BRUC*, p. 438.

196. [f. 28] <u>Robert Marrays</u>
Common Pleas *venire faciatis*, returnable on the octave of Trinity [14 June], against Robert Marrays to answer his brother John for a debt of 40s. Note of return of no lay fee by the sheriff of Lincolnshire.
Teste Robert Bealknapp, 1 May 1377.
RETURN. The writ arrived too late to be executed.

197.   <u>Breve pro decimis</u>[1]
Mandate to appoint collectors for the two tenths granted in the convocation on 5 December and payable [no date given]. The names of collectors are to be certified to the Exchequer by the octave of Hilary.
Teste me ipso, 8 Dec. 1377.[2]
[EXECUTION]. <u>Mandatum directum collectoribus pro dicto subsidio levando.</u> [ff. 28–28v]
Commission to the abbot of Peterborough to act as collector in the archdeaconry of Northampton.
Sleaford 22 Dec. 1377.
Note that the following were also committed as collectors:
the abbot and convent of Bardney in the parts of Lindsey and the archdeaconry of Stow;
the prior and convent of Sempringham in the parts of Kesteven and the deanery of Holland (Holand);
the abbot and convent of Croxton in the archdeaconry of Leicester;
the abbot and convent of Osney (Oseney) in the archdeaconry of Oxford;
the abbot and convent of Nutley (Nottley) in the archdeaconry of Buckingham;
the abbot and convent of Ramsey in the archdeaconry of Huntingdon;
the prior and convent of Newnham (Newenham) in the archdeaconry of Bedford.

> [1] This is the first writ in the register issued by the government of Richard II.
> [2] For the royal mandate to collect this tax see *CFR 1377–83*, pp. 42–3.

198.   <u>Breve pro alienigenis</u>
Exchequer mandate to know about secular aliens, both cardinals and others, beneficed in the diocese, what benefices they hold and their annual value, returnable on the morrow of Hilary.

Teste venerabili patre Thome [Brantingham] Exon' Episcopo Thesaurario nostro, 12 Dec. 1377.

EXECUTION. The writ is contained in a mandate to the archdeacon of Lincoln, or his official, ordering the names of all such aliens in the archdeaconry to be sent to the bishop before Epiphany [6 Jan.].

Sleaford 10 Jan. 1378.[1]

> [1] The original and return are in PRO, E179/35/6B.

199. Cortenhale

Exchequer *levari faciatis de bonis et beneficiis ecclesiasticis,* returnable on the octave of Michaelmas, against John de Bampton rector of Courteenhall (Cortenhale) for 6s 8d which he owes to the prior of Lenton.

Teste Henry de Asty, 7 July 1378.

[EXECUTION]. The dean of Preston was written to to sequestrate the property.

200. Breve pro ecclesia de Morbourne

Common Pleas *venire faciatis,* returnable on the octave of St. John Baptist [1 July], against William Cudy rector of Morborne (Morbourne) to answer the abbot of Crowland (Croyland) for a debt of 6 marks, being arrears of a pension of 26s 8d p.a. Note of return of no lay fee by the sheriff of Huntingdon.

Teste Robert Bealknap, 14 May 1379.

201. Prohibicio pro ecclesia de Grendon

Chancery *ne admittatis* concerning Grendon church whose advowson is disputed between the king and Simon Neylond master of the King's Hall Cambridge.[1]

Teste me ipso, 17 June 1379.

> [1] Grendon was appropriated to King's Hall by (or in) 1365–66, and brought an income of 25 marks p.a. (£16 13s 4d) to the college, Alan B. Cobban, *The King's Hall within the University of Cambridge in the Later Middle Ages* (Cambridge, 1969), p. 205. For Neylond see *BRUC*, p. 425.

202. Breve pro ecclesia de Grendon certiorari

[Chancery] *certiorari* to discover how many rectors of Grendon church there have been since 1250. [Incomplete writ.]

[See above, **201**]

203. [f. 29] Breve regium pro Willelmo de Blakebourne clerico

Chancery signification that the king has granted the bishop of Lincoln power to receive the attorneys of William Blakeburn who, by royal licence, is going to parts across the seas; they will take William's part in all pleas involving him in all the courts of England for one year. Mandate to receive the attorneys and to signify their names to the king under episcopal seal.

Teste me ipso, 4 June 1379.[1]

EXECUTION. [This is the next entry but one] The bishop committed John Haseber, John Seynnode and William Faxflete, Humphrey Daudes and John de Sadyngton as the attorneys of William Blakeburn according to the writ.

> [1] This letter is not recorded in the close rolls. Attorneys were normally received by the king's chancery clerks; see *CCR, passim.*

204. [Not a royal writ.] [Unheaded]
To John bishop of Lincoln from Cosmo Gentilis papal nuncio and collector:
[Prohibition against proceeding against Henry Mulshow and Thomas Elstow, agents
of John Mulsowe rector of Southoe who is in debt to the papal *camera* for the first
fruits of his benefice.]
Reverendo in Christo patri ac domino domino Johanni dei gracia Lincoln' Episcopo, Cosmatus Gentilis de Sulmona, licenciatus in decretis, prepositus Valuen'
sedis aposotice et camere Nuncius in Anglia et collector seipsum cum reverencia
et honore debit' tanto patri. Cum taxa sive primus fructus ecclesie parochialis de
Southo, vestre dioc', certis et legitimis de causis camere apostolice debeantur et de
eisdem nobis nomine eiusdem camere satisfactur', quidem Henricus Mulshow et
Thomas Elstow pro parte domini Johannis Mulsowe rectoris eiusdem debito modo
extiterunt obligati vobis, auctoritate apostolica qua fungimur in hac parte et virtute
sancte obediencie ac sub pena iuramenti prestiti quibus dicte sedi tenemini cum ea
qua decus reverencia firmiter iniungendo, mandamus et eciam tenore presencium
inhibemus, ne in huiusmodi fructibus nec contra prefatos Henricum et Johannem
quicquam attemptetis seu faciatis aliqualiter attemptari quousque nobis vel alteri
collectori, vel subcollectori, qui pro tempore fuerit in eisdem taxa sive primis
fructibus nomine eiusdem camere plenar' fuerit satisfactum, alioquin de interesse
vestro si quod habeatis in hac parte infra quatuordecim dies post prenunciam
prenotacionem vobis factam, nos certificare curetis per litteras vestras patentes
habentes hunc tenorem.
Dat' London sub sigillo nostro quo utimur in officio, 1 Nov. 1379.[1]

   1   Both John and Henry Mulsho (Mulshow, Mulso, Moulsoe) were evidently related to the
   prominent king's clerk [M.] William Moulsoe whose distinguished career (chamberlain of the
   Exchequer, clerk of the king's works, keeper of the wardrobe) may be followed from the
   references given in Tout, *Chapters*, VI.339. In 1379 both William and John were prebendaries
   of the college of St. Martin le Grand, London, A.K. McHardy, *The Church in London 1375–92*,
   London Record Society 13 (1977), no. 16. John became rector of St. Nicholas Cole Abbey,
   London, on 15 Dec. 1384, but vacated this by exchange in April 1387, G. Hennessy, *Novum
   Repertorium Ecclesiasticum Parochiale Londinense* (London 1898), p. 345. He was instituted
   to Southoe (Hunts.), 14 March 1376, Reg. 10, f. 317.

205.   Breve regium contra Rectorem de Farmyngho
Common Pleas *venire faciatis*, returnable on the quindene of Martinmas [25 Nov.],
against Thomas de Loweryngton rector of Farthinghoe (Farnyngho) to answer the
abbot of Leicester for a debt of 16 marks, being arrears of a rent of 4 marks p.a.
Note of return of no lay fee by the sheriff of Leicestershire[1] on the morrow of All
Souls [3 Nov.].
Teste Robert Bealknapp, 7 Nov. 1379.

   1   Farthinghoe is in Northants.

206.   [f. 29v] Breve Regium contra Rectorem de Estwell
Common Pleas *venire faciatis*, returnable on the quindene of Martinmas [25 Nov.],
against John atte Brigg of Grimsby rector of Eastwell (Estwell) to answer the abbot
of Leicester for a debt of 4 marks, being arrears of a rent of 13s p.a. Note of return
of no lay fee by the sheriff of Leicestershire on the morrow of All Souls [3 Nov.].
Teste Robert de Bealknapp, 7 Nov. 1379.

207. [Unheaded. **To the sheriff of Lincolnshire**]
Exchequer *venire facias* addressed to the sheriff of Lincolnshire, returnable on the morrow of Hilary, against John Karleton clerk to answer the king for £100 received and occupied by him of the fruits of Stickney (Stykeney) church, Lincolnshire, and other goods and chattels of Thomas Luffewyk outlaw, at the suit of John bishop of Lincoln, pertaining to the crown by reason of the outlawry promulgated against the said Thomas, as John Holt our sergeant 'qui pro nobis sequitur racionabiliter monstrare poterit quod inde respondere debet'.
Teste Henry Asty, 13 Nov. 1379. By the memoranda roll of Michaelmas term 3 Richard II, among the *Recorda*.

208. Breve regium pro subsidio levando
Mandate to levy the clerical subsidy granted in the convocation in St. Paul's cathedral [London] on the last day of February [29 Feb.]. Payment is to be at the rate of 16d in the mark on all assessed benefices of the province of Canterbury, including the exempt, privileged, royal and other free chapels and alien priories; the unassessed are to pay 16d in the mark on two parts [two thirds] of the value of their benefices; advocates, proctors, registrars and notaries public are to pay 2s each. The subsidy is payable by equal portions at the Ascension [3 May] and the Nativity of St. John Baptist [24 June]. Mandate also to signify the collectors' names to the Exchequer before the feast of St. George [23 April].[1]
Teste me ipso, 6 March 1380.
[EXECUTION AND RETURN, Reg. 12, f. 196v]
Certificat' Thes' et Baronibus de Scaccario domini Regis de nominibus collector' Lincoln' dioc'
Notification that in execution of the royal mandate of 6 March [recited] the bishop has appointed the following as collectors of the tax:
in the archdeaconries of Lincoln and Stow (Stowe): the abbot of Crowland
in the archdeaconry of Leicester: the abbot of Garendon (Gerendon)
in the archdeaconry of Northampton: the abbot of St. James, Northampton
in the archdeaconry of Oxford: the abbot of Osney (Oseney)
in the archdeaconry of Buckingham: the abbot of Nutley (Nottele)
in the archdeaconries of Bedford and Huntingdon: the abbot of Woburn (Woubourne)
Liddington (Lydyngton) 28 March 1380.
Commissio pro subsidio levando et colligendo in archidiaconatibus Lincoln' et Stowe.
Appointment of John [de Kirketon] abbot of Crowland as collector in the archdeaonries of Lincoln and Stow.
Liddington 27 March 1380.

    1   For the convocation see Reg. 12, ff. 189–189v and Lambeth Palace Library, Reg. Sudbury (Cant.), ff. 59v–60. For collection see *CFR 1377–83*, pp. 190 and 202; also PRO, E179 /35/19.

209. [Reg.12B, f. 29v] Breve Regium contra Rectorem ecclesie Sancti Benedicti Hunt'
Common Pleas *venire faciatis*, returnable on the quindene of Trinity [3 June], against William rector of St. Benedict's church, Huntingdon, to answer the prior of St. Mary, Huntingdon, in a plea of debt of 40 marks, being arrears of rent of 1 mark

p.a. Note of return of no lay fee by the sheriff of Huntingdonshire three weeks from Easter [15 April].
Teste Robert Bealknapp, 8 May 1380.
EXECUTION AND RETURN. It was returned that he had been warned.

210.   [f. 30] Breve regium pro recuperacione presentacionis ecclesie Omnium Sanctorum de Tetilthorp
Common Pleas *admittatis non obstante reclamatione* concerning the church of Theddlethorpe All Saints (Omnium Sanctorum Tetilthorp) whose presentation the abbot of Revesby recovered in the king's court before William de Skypwyth and Roger de Kirketon, justices of the Common Bench, at Wragby on the Wednesday before the middle of Lent last [28 Feb.] against Laurence Moigne of Theddlethorpe and Katherine his wife, William Anngevyn of Boston (St. Botolph), goldsmith, and Elizabeth his wife, and Robert Ardern clerk; notwithstanding this the bishop has not cared to admit anyone at the abbot's presentation.
Teste Robert Bealknapp, 14 April 1380.[1]

> [1]   Printed by A.R. Maddison, 'Original Document from a Volume of "Brevia Regia" Issued during the Episcopate of John Bokingham, Bishop of Lincoln', *Archaeological Journal* 44 (1887), pp. 403–4, with a note on the subsequent history of the Moigne family.

211.   Breve de nisi prius pro vicaria de Barton
Chancery *admittatis nisi prius* concerning the vicarage of Barton on Humber whose advowson the king has recently recovered in court against William de Blakeburn, chaplain.
Teste me ipso, 30 May 1380.

212.   Prohibicio contra presentacionem ecclesie de Sybertoft
Chancery *ne admittatis* concerning Sibbertoft (Sybertoft) church whose advowson is in dispute between the king and the abbot of Sulby.
Teste me ipso, 10 July 1380.

213.   [ff. 30–30v] Breve regium de veniendo ad parliamentum
Summons to attend parliament at Northampton on the Monday after All Saints [5 Nov.], with *premunientes* clause in the usual form for the warning of the dean of Lincoln, the archdeacons, and proctors.
Teste me ipso, 26 Aug. 1380.[1]
Commissio Offic'.
EXECUTION. The writ arrived on 25 Sept. [and in the register is contained in the] commission to the official of the archdeacon of Lincoln to appear in person [at the meeting to elect proctors] and to warn the clergy in his jurisdiction that the meeting to elect proctors of the clergy of the diocese would take place in the church of St. Mary *ad Pontem*, Stamford, on the Monday after the feast of St. Luke [22 Oct.]. Sleaford 20 Sept. 1380.
Capitulo Lincoln'.
Mandate, to execute the writ, to the chapter of Lincoln and to certify their actions in this matter to the bishop at Sleaford before the feast of St. Luke.

> [1]   Printed, *RDP*, IV.686; see also *CCR 1377–81*, p. 477.

214. [ff. 30v–31] <u>Littera ad exorandum pro Comite Buckyngham</u>
Request for the prayers of the clergy for Thomas earl of Buckingham constable of England[1] who is leading an expedition to France as the king cannot go in person.
Teste me ipso, 24 June 1380.[2]

  [1] Thomas of Woodstock, later (6 Aug. 1385) duke of Gloucester, youngest son of Edward III.
  [2] Printed, *Foedera*, VII.260; see also *CCR 1377–81*, p. 469. For comment see McHardy, SCH 18, pp. 217–18.

215. [f. 31] <u>Ne admittatis parsonam ad ecclesiam de Leek</u>
Chancery *ne admittatis* concerning Leake (Leek) church whose advoswon is being disputed in the royal court between Henry de Gedyngton warden of the college of the chantry of Nicholas de Cantilupe in Lincoln cathedral, and Andrew de Leek *chivaler* and Robert de Leek, *chivaler*.
Teste me ipso, 20 Oct. 1380.

216. [ff. 31–31v] <u>Breve regium pro subsidio levando</u>
Mandate to appoint collectors of the clerical subsidy granted in the convocation held in All Saints church Northampton, payable by equal amount at the feasts of St. Peter's Chair [22 Feb.] and the Nativity of St. John Baptist [24 June]. It is to be paid by all, both exempt and non-exempt, at two rates: 20 groats [6s 8d] by all regulars and seculars of whatever age, sex or order, advocates, proctors, examinators, registrars and notaries; 3 groats [1s] by deacons, sub-deacons, acolytes and all in clerical habit aged 16 or over. The names of collectors are to be certified to the exchequer before the Purification of the Virgin [2 Feb.].
Teste me ipso, 20 Dec. 1380.
EXECUTION. <u>Verba episcopi directa subditits [inten]dencia ad breve regium.</u>
Mandate [to an archdeacon, without greeting clause] to collect the names of all those who must pay, before the Tuesday after the Purification of the Virgin [5 Feb.], and to signify them in writing either to the bishop or to Masters John de Belvoir or Peter de Dalton his assessors and commissaries in this matter in All Saints church, Northampton, on that day. Either the archdeacon or his official is to be at the meeting of the clergy of the archdeaconry in person and is to cite one suitable rector from each deanery of the the archdeaconry to attend the diocesan meeting at Northampton.
Liddington, 10 Jan. 1381.

[ff. 31v–32] <u>Verba Episcopi directa capitulo Lincoln</u>
Similar mandate to the chapter of Lincoln cathedral concerning the clergy in the cathedral and close.
Lidington, 10 Jan. 1381.

[f. 32] <u>Littera archiepiscopi Cant'</u>
[Mandate [to the bishop] to order each archdeacon or his official to certify, by a given day [not specified], the name of every ecclesiastic, both regular and secular, of whatever condition – even the privileged and exempt – and the unbeneficed and nuns also. The information is to be gathered by two canons of the cathedral, if secular, otherwise by two sufficient clerics of the diocese, and by one rector from each deanery. The names of all those, both beneficed and unbeneficed, are to be calculated and inspected and reduced to one gross sum, and then, when everyone has been assessed, all the unbeneficed and all regulars and nuns below the rank of

prelate ought [to contribute] ten groats [40d = 3s 4d]. The remaining sum should be faithfully divided between all the beneficed so that, after a deduction of one third has been made from the amount payable by those with unassessed benefices, all should pay equally; with the proviso that prelates having temporalities and spiritualities should pay one sum in their own dioceses and not elsewhere.]

Simon archbishop of Canterbury to John bishop of Lincoln '. . . vobis tenore presencium intimamus videlicet quod quilibet episcopus in sua dioc' dirigat mandata sua singulis archidiaconis suis vel eorum officialibus ac etiam ecclesie sue cathedralis et iurisdictionibus exemptis infra sua dioc' constitutis quod ipsi ad certum diem limitand' certificent de nominibus omnium et singulorum prelatorum tam regularium quam secularium cuiuscumque status, gradus, ordinis vel condicionis fuerint ac clericorum quorumcumque promotorum eciam si exempti vel privilegiati extiterint, ac omnium presbiterorum non beneficiatorum eciam regularium et monialium infra dioc' suam existencium et quod quilibet episcopus ad dictum terminum assidentibus sibi suis archidiaconis vel eorum officiis ac eciam duobus canonicis ecclesie cathedralis si fuerit secularis vel officialibus duobus sufficientioribus [*sic*] clericis totius dioc' et uno rectore de singulis decanatibus qui invenerint et nomina dictorum tam beneficiatorum quam non beneficiatorum calculent et inspiciant et summam omnes et singulos contingentem in summam unam grossam redigant et tunc assessis singulis non beneficiatis inter quos omnes et singuli regulares et moniales citra statum prelatie includi debent ad decem grossos. Residuum integre summe inter omnes et singulos beneficiatos fideliter dividatur ita quod obtinentes beneficia taxata secundum taxam habentes vero beneficia non taxata secundum estimacionem valoris earundem deducta tercia parte equaliter solvere teneantur, proviso quod prelati habentes temporalia et spiritualia sub una summa taxata in dioc' suis solvant et non alibi. Quocirca vobis committimus et mandamus, firmiter iniungentes quatinus dictum subsidium quatenus vos et dioc' vestram concernet per collectores ydoneos et sufficientes per vos deputandos ad terminos in brevi regio contentes colligi et levari.
Lambeth 22 Dec. 1380.

RETURN. [Reg. 12, f. 221] Certicat' Thesaur' et Baronibus de Scaccario
[Certificate to the treasurer and barons of the Exchequer that the bishop has commissioned the following as collectors of the tax:]

'Nomine igitur iuxta et secundum modum et formam levandi dictum subsidium nobis et ceteris coepiscopis provincie antedicte ut prefertur reservat' et per eosdem et clerum predictum ordinat' omnes et singulos prelatos et alios quoscumque promotos ac presbiteros non beneficiatos et religiosos eciam moniales in nostra dioc' constitutos de quorum nominibus, vigore mandati nostri ad inquirendum de eisdem singulis officialibus archidiaconorum nostrorum directi, certificati fuimus ad solucionem dicti subsidii fideliter fecimus assideri. Et ad colligendum et levandum subsidium predictum a prelatis, clericis promotis, religiosis et monialibus, ac eciam presbiteris non beneficiatis sic assessis prout ipsos et eorum quemlibet concernit omnibus et singulis advocatis, procuratoribus, examinatoribus, registratoribus et notariis publicis singulis, videlicet viginti grossos. Necnon a quibuscumque clericis non beneficiatis, diaconis, subdiaconis, accolitis, et aliis in minoribus constitutis tres grossos de eorum quolibet terminis in brevi predicto

contentis persolvendis iuxta tenorem et exigenciam brevis predicti istos deputavimus et assignavimus collectores videlicet':

archdeaconries of Lincoln and Stow: the abbot of Barlings (Barlines)
archdeaconries of Leicester and Northampton: the prior of Daventry
archdeaconries of Buckingham and Oxford: the abbot of Notley (Nottele)
archdeaconries of Huntingdon and Bedford: the prior of Newnham (Newenham)

[And, because of the size of our diocese, we are not able to certify the names of all
those who ought to pay, we therefore certify the names of the collectors first. Under
the discretion which you have to excuse payment, the master and priors of the order
of Sempringham wish to have the nuns of the order excused, and the chancellor
wishes the same for the masters and scholars of the university of Oxford.]

'Et quia a tempore receptionis brevis predicti non potuimus propter amplitudinem
nostre dioc' de nominibus eorum quos ad dictum subsidium fecimus assideri prius
certificari cicius vobis non certificamus de nominibus collectorum predictorum,
super quo nos habere velit vestra discrecio excusatos Magistr<u>um</u> vero et Priores
ordinis de Sempingham nostre dioc' nomina monialium eiusdem ordinis ac cancel-
larius magistr<u>os</u> et scolares universitatis Oxon' licet debite requisiti nomina sua
tradere noluerunt, ideo quo ad eos et alios de quorum nominibus hucusque certificati non sumus citra primum terminum solucionis supradicte premissa exequi non
pot<u>erunt</u> nec valebunt. Et sic cum omni diligencia qua potuimus breve predictum
sumus executi que omnia et singula vobis reverenter intimamus'.
Northampton 8 Feb. 1381.
EXECUTION. [*Ibid.*, ff. 221–221v]. Commission to the collectors.
Northampton 8 Feb. 1381.[1]

[1] The granting and administration of this tax is discussed, with references, in LRS 81, pp.
xxii–xxiv and xvi–xviii.

217.   Breve regium contra Rectorem de Barnak'
Common Pleas *venire faciatis*, returnable on the quindene of Easter [28 April],
against William Kirkstede rector of Barnack (Barnak) to answer the abbot of
Peterborough about a plea of debt of 41s, being arrears of a rent of 10s p.a. Note
of return of no lay fee by the sheriff of Northamptonshire on the octave of the
Purification of the Virgin.
Teste Robert Bealknapp, 13 Feb. 1381   Roll 109 Baunford.

218.   [f. 32v] Breve regium utrum Willelmus Asselyn etc.
King's Bench *certiorari*, returnable without delay wherever we are in England, to
discover whether William Asselyn of Sutton married Juliana who was the wife of
Robert del Isle in the parish church of Brampton by Dingley (Brampton by
Dyngele), Northamptonshire, or not.
Teste John Cavendish at Northampton, 27 Nov. 1380. Shard.[1]

[1] Thomas Shardlow or Shardelow (younger son of John Shardlow, justice of the King's Bench),
king's attorney in King's Bench, appointed 9 Nov. 1366, until his death, which was before 21
Sept. 1385 when his successor was appointed. There are many forms of abbreviation of his name:
Sch., Schs., Schard., Shard., B.H. Putnam, *The Place in Legal History of Sir William Shareshull*
(Cambridge, 1950), p. 93.

219. Breve regium pro parte Abbatis de Croyland pro non sufficibus ad subsidium nuper domino Regi concessum

Exchequer *certiorari*, returnable on the morrow of St. John Baptist [25 June], concerning the clerical subsidy granted in February 1380 in St. Paul's cathedral [London] of 16d in the mark on assessed benefices, and 16d in the mark on unassessed benefices assessed at two-thirds of their value and 2s from all advocates, proctors, and notaries public,[1] as the abbot of Crowland, collector in the archdeaconries of Lincoln and Stow, has shown the king that many benefices in the said archdeaconries are destroyed, wasted and impoverished so that they cannot pay this tax, to discover which benefices within the archdeaconries of Lincoln and Stow are so wasted and destroyed.

Teste Robert de Plesyngton, 24 May 1380. By writ of privy seal among the Exchequer *communia* of Easter term 4 Richard II. Hauleye.

   [1] See **208** for the terms of this grant.

220. Breve regium de veniendo ad parliamentum

Summons to attend parliament at Westminster on the Monday after the Exaltation of Holy Cross [16 Sept.], with *premunientes* clause for the representation of the clergy of Lincoln diocese in person and by proctors.

Teste me ipso in the town of St. Albans, 16 July 1381.[1]

   [1] Printed, *RDP*, IV.688; see also *CCR 1381–5*, p. 79.

221. [f. 33] Breve de veniendo ad parliamentum apud Westmonasterium

Summons to attend a parliament at Westminster on the Monday after the Exaltation of Holy Cross which is now being prorogued to the morrow of All Souls [3 Nov.], with *premunientes* clause in the usual form concerning the representation of the clergy of Lincoln diocese in person and by proctors.

Teste me ipso Eltham, 22 Aug. 1381.[1]

   [1] Printed *RDP*, IV.691; see also *CCR 1381–5*, p. 81.

222. Breve regium pro Rectore de Burton Overay'

Exchequer *venire faciatis sicut pluries*, returnable on the quindene of Martinmas [25 Nov.], against John Neuport rector of Burton Overy, to answer the prior of the alien priory of Ware, farmer of that priory, about a debt of 18 marks, being arrears of a pension of 4 marks p.a. which is owed by his church. The rector is holding the money back so that the farmer cannot pay his annual farm to the king, in whose hand the priory is because of the war with France.

Teste Robert de Plesyngton, 23 Oct. 1381.

223. Breve regium pro Rectore de Hathern'

Common Pleas *venire faciatis*, returnable on the octave of Hilary, against Master James de Staunton[1] rector of Hathern church, to answer the abbot of Leicester about a plea of debt of £20 and 10 stones of wax, being arrears of a payment of 40s and 1 stone of wax p.a. Note of return of no lay fee by the sheriff of Leicestershire on the morrow of Martinmas [12 Nov.].

Teste Robert Bealknapp, 21 Nov. 1381.

   [1] See *BRUO*, III.1768–9.

224. Breve regium pro Willelmo Willy de bastardia
Chancery *certiorari* whether William de Willy of Kyngesclyve is a bastard or was born in lawful wedlock.
Teste me ipso Leeds (Ledes), 30 Aug. 1381.
[f. 33v] Certicator' Brevis et Processus Willelmi Willy
After making diligent enquiry we find that William Willy is not a bastard but the legitimate son of John Willy of Kyngesclyve and of Matilda Bate wife of the said John Willy.
Lidington 4 March 1382.

225. Breve Regium pro Simone de Sutton et Alicia Kynge causa divorcionis
Chancery *certiorari* whether there has at any time been a divorce between Simon de Sutton and Alice Kynge of Higham [Cold Higham or Higham Ferrers] (Hucham) before the bishop or any of his ministers in the courts Christian. Simon is said to have married Alice without celebration.
Teste me ipso, 6 Oct. 1381.
Commissio dicti brevis.
Mandate to Masters Thomas Boyvill rector of Seaton (Seyton) and Robert Palmere rector of Towcester (Toucester) ordering enquiry to be made and the findings signified to the bishop in writing.
[Undated.]
[f. 33v] Certificatorium brevis et processus Alicie Kynge
Certificate that Simon Sutton married Alice Kynge in church and has not divorced her.
Liddington 4 March 1382.

226. Breve contra Johannem parsonam de Ailleston et Johannem parsonam ecclesie de Killesworth'
Common Pleas *fieri faciatis de bonis ecclesiasticis*, returnable on the quindene of Easter [20 April], for 20s against John rector of Aylestone (Ayleston) church to answer Richard de Tretton and John de Bretton, clerks of the Common Bench, assigns of Roger Flamvill clerk, for 40s awarded to Roger in the king's court at Westminster as damages on the occasion of the detention of debts of 10 marks and chattels to the value of 100s; and *fieri faciatis de bonis ecclesiasticis*, returnable in the present term, against John Chamberlein rector of Kilworth [either North or South, both Leics.] (Killeworth) for 26s 8d, to answer the said clerks and assigns of the abbot of Leicester for £10 awarded to the abbot in the same court as damages on the occasion of the detention of the rent of 4 marks p.a., against him. Note of return of no lay fees by the sheriff of Leicestershire.
Teste Robert Bealknapp, 10 Feb. 1382.

227. Breve contra Magistrum Johannem Wyclif
Exchequer *levari faciatis de bonis et beneficiis ecclesiasticis*, returnable on the morrow of the close of Easter [14 April], against Master John Wyclif doctor (professor) of theology, for £7 17s 9d owed to the king from the remains of his account, recently returned to the Exchequer, for a certain journey made by him to the parts of Flanders in 48 Edward III.
Teste Robert Plesyngton, 16 Jan. 1382.[1]

¹   Printed in full, with comment and references, in A.K. McHardy, 'John Wycliffe's Mission to Bruges: a Financial Footnote', *Journal of Theological Studies* 26 (1973), pp. 521–2.

228.   Breve contra occupatorem Archidiaconatus Northampton'

Exchequer *venire faciatis*, returnable on the morrow of the close of Easter [14 April], against the occupier of the archdeaconry of Northampton, to answer the king for the subsidy of 16d in the mark granted to him by the clergy in 3 Richard II, and mandate to certify the name of the said occupier.¹

Teste Robert de Plesyngton, 16 Jan. 1382.

¹   Master Walter Skirlaw occ. 6 May 1381, *Fasti*, I.11. The archdeaconry was described as vacant on 19 June 1384, Reg. 11, f. 127v. Master Henry Bowet was installed 23 Feb. 1386, *Fasti*, I.11.

229.   Breve contra Rectorem de Bifeld

Exchequer *levari faciatis de bonis et beneficiis ecclesiasticis*, returnable on the morrow of the close of Easter [14 April], against William Griseley rector of Byfield (Bifeld) church for 22s 7½d owed to the crown for a loan at the receipt of the Exchequer on 22 March 45 Edward III and remaining in his hands for the tenth of his church.

Teste Robert de Plesyngton, 15 Jan. 1382.

230.   [ff. 33v–34] Breve regium de veniendo ad parliamentum

Summons to a parliament at Westminster on the morrow of St. John before the Latin Gate [7 May], with *premunientes* clause in the usual form.

Teste me ipso, 24 March 1382.¹

¹   Printed *RDP*, IV.694; see also *CCR 1381–5*, p. 121.

231.   Breve contra Ricardum de Ravenser

Common Pleas *fieri faciatis de bonis ecclesiasticis*, returnable on the quindene of Trinity [15 June], against Richard de Ravenser clerk of your diocese,¹ for 40 marks, to answer William Marmyon chivaler and Andrew Bround and William David for damages incurred because he unjustly impeded the presentation of a suitable person to the church of Brant Broughton (Brendbroghton) in their gift. Note of return of insufficient lay fee by the sheriff of Lincolnshire on the quindene of Easter [20 April] because it was in the king's hands for certain sums owed to the king by the said Richard, but certificate that he had sufficient ecclesiastical goods.

Teste Robert Bealknap, 8 May 1382.

[f. 36] Retornum pro Ricardo Ravenser'

We have made diligent enquiry in our diocese about the ecclesiastical goods of Richard de Ravenser, but we can find none by which the 40 marks can be distrained.

¹   Archdeacon of Lincoln occ. 1369–86, prebendary of Empingham 1363–84, *Fasti* I.6, 63; for other dignities at Lincoln held by Ravenser at other times see *ibid.*, pp. 4, 49, 123. See Tout, *Chapters*, VI.376 for references to his official career and relatives; III.215 and nn. deals especially with Ravenser as archdeacon of Lincoln. See also J.L. Grassi, 'Royal Clerks from the Archdiocese of York in the Fourteenth Century', *Northern History* V (1970), pp. 12–33; Colin Morris, 'The Ravenser Composition', *Lincolnshire Architectural and Archaeological Society Reports and Papers* 10, pt. 1 (1963), pp. 24–39.

232. [f. 34] <u>Breve contra Rectorem de Parva Byllyng'</u>
Common Pleas *venire faciatis*, returnable on the quindene of Trinity [15 June], against John Baukewell rector of Little Billing (Parva Byllyng) to answer the prior of St. Andrew Northampton about a plea of debt of 100s, being arrears of rent of 20s p.a. Note of return of no lay fee by the sheriff of Northamptonshire on the quindene of Easter [20 April].
Teste Robert Bealknap, 28 April 1382.
RETURN. Return was made that John was warned to be before the justices on the day and place mentioned.

233. [f. 34v] <u>Breve pro ecclesia de Erdeburgh'</u>
Chancery *certiorari (scrutato registro)* to know who and how many people have been presented to Yarborough (Erdebrugh) church.
Teste me ipso, 10 June 1382.
[ff. 35v–36] <u>Certificator' Brevis regii ecclesie de Erdburgh' pro Abbate de Oselveston'</u>
To the king from John [Buckingham] bishop of Lincoln in execution of the writ recently received. We have looked at our registers and those of our predecessors and find that the abbot and convent of Owston (Oselveston) presented Geoffrey de Burgh clerk to Burgh church in the time of Hugh of Wells; John de Nevile priest to Yarborough (Erdeburgh) church in the time of Richard Gravesend; William de Burgh chaplain to Burgh church in the time of Robert Grosseteste (Grostet), and John de Petling priest to the same church also in the time of Grosseteste;[1] Henry de Langton acolyte to Yarborough (Erdesburgh) in the time of Henry Burghersh; and the same abbot and convent presented John de Erdeburgh to the said church on an exchange with Thomas Beek rector of Fordham church London diocese; and William son of John Knossington priest to the same church in the time of John Gynewell. They were admitted, instituted and inducted by our said predecessors and no one else was admitted, instituted or inducted in any other way.
[f. 36] Sleaford, 23 Aug. 1382.

[1] Professor Smith points out that there seemed to be some chronological confusion in Buckingham's chancery about the order of his thirteenth-century predecessors.

234. [f. 34v] <u>Breve contra Ricardum de Ravenser clericum</u>
Common Pleas *fieri faciatis de bonis ecclesiasticis sicut alias*, returnable on the octave of Michaelmas, against Richard de Ravenser, clerk, for 40 marks, to answer William Marmyon chivaler and Andrew Bround and William David for damages incurred because he unjustly impeded the presentation of a suitable person to the church of Brant Broughton (Brendbroghton) in their gift. Note of return of insufficient lay fee by the sheriff of Lincolnshire on the quindene of Easter [20 April] because it was in the king's hands for certain sums owed to the king by the said Richard, but certificate that he had sufficient ecclesiastical goods.
Teste Robert Bealknap, 8 July 1382.
[See **231**]

235. <u>Breve pro excilitatibus beneficiorum certificand' in scaccario</u>
Exchequer mandate in respect of the clerical subsidy granted on the last day of February 3 Richard II [1380]of 16d in the mark on assessed benefices, 16d in the mark on two-thirds of the value of unassessed benefices, and 2s for all proctors,

notaries, etc. The abbot of Crowland (Croyland) has complained that many benefices in the archdeaconries of Lincoln and Stow where he is collector are destroyed,
wasted and impoverished. Mandate to send a list of these to the Exchequer as soon
as possible and at least by the morrow of Hilary.
Teste Robert de Plesyngton, 21 Nov. 1381. By writ of the great seal among the
communia, Easter Term, 4 Richard II.[1]
[ff. 34v–35] EXECUTION. Mandate of John [Buckingham], bishop of Lincoln to the
archdeacon of Lincoln and his commissary and Master Stephen [de Houghton]
rector of Potter Hanworth (Hanneworth)[2] to find out the values of the benefices on
the annexed schedule, which the abbot asserts are too poor to pay, and all the
circumstances of these benefices and their sufficiency and insufficiency, and to
signify their findings to the bishop by letters patent before Michaelmas.
Stow Park 28 August 1382.
[See **219**]

> [1]   See LRS 81, pp. xxi–xxii, for a discussion of this hybrid tax.
> [2]   *Ibid.*, no. 517 and n.

236.   [f. 35] Breve regium de veniendo ad parliamentum
Summons to a parliament at Westminster on Monday, the octave of Michaelmas,
with *premunientes* clause.
Teste me ipso, Woodstock 9 Aug. 1382.[1]
EXECUTION. Conclusio pro clero.
Mandate to the archdeacon of Lincoln, reciting the writ which was received on 26
August, ordering him to call the clergy before the bishop or his commissaries in the
parish church of All Saints Northampton on the Monday after the feast of St.
Matthew the Apostle [22 Sept.] to elect two proctors, and to certify what he did in
this matter on the same day and place.
Stow Park 30 Aug. 1382.
Conclusio pro capitulo.
Mandate to appoint a proctor and to signify to the bishop by Monday after St.
Matthew the Apostle, at Sleaford.
Stow Park 30 Aug. 1382.

> [1]   Printed *RDP*, IV.698; see also *CCR 1381–5*, p. 210.

237.   Breve contra Rectorem de Byfeld
Exchequer *levari faciatis de bonis et beneficiis ecclesiasticis sicut alias*, returnable
on the morrow of Michaelmas, against William Gryseley rector of Byfield (Byfeld)
church for 22s 7½d owed to the crown for a loan at the receipt of the Exchequer on
22 March 45 Edward III and remaining in his hand for the tenth of his church.
Teste Robert de Plesyngton, 19 May 1382.
[f. 35v] Conclusio brevis de Bifeld superius memorate
Mandate [to the sequestrator] to sequester the fruits of Chalfont (Chalfunte) church
which the said William holds at present, to the value named in the writ, and to cite
him to be before us or Masters Thomas de Brandon or Richard de Croxton to show
why, to indemnify us and our church, we should not sequester all the fruits and
income of his church of Chalfont for canonical reasons.
[f. 36] Returnum pro Rectore quondam de Byfeld
The said William, before the receipt of your writ and for a long time before, was

not and is not the rector of Byfield church, nor does he have any ecclesiastical goods in our diocese by which we can cause the writ to be executed.
[See **229**]

238. [f. 35] Breve contra Magistrum Johannem Moubray pro archidiaconatu North'
[f. 35v] Conclusio Brevis Antedect'
Exchequer *venire faciatis sicut alias*, returnable on the morrow of Michaelmas, against Master John Mowbray occupier of the archdeaconry of Northampton to answer for the subsidy of 16d in the mark granted by the clergy in 3 Richard II.
Teste Robert de Plesyngton, 14 July 1382.
[f. 36] Returnum pro Johanne Moubray.
The said John Moubray occupier of the archdeaconry of Northampton who has no goods pertaining to the archdeaconry by which he can be sufficiently distrained, was warned at Northampton to be at the Exchequer on the place and day named in the writ.[1]
[See **228**]

[1]   It is by no means clear who, if anyone, was archdeacon of Northampton at this time. Walter Skirlaw occ. 6 May 1381, and Henry Bowet was installed 23 Feb. 1386, *Fasti*, I.11, but the archdeaconry was described as vacant on 19 June 1384, Reg. 11, f. 127v. For Mr. John Mowbray see *BRUO* II.1326. For the administration of the archdeaconry after his death see Reg. 12, ff. 295–295v.

239. [f. 35v] Breve regium contra Rectorem ecclesie de Russhedon'
Common Pleas *venire faciatis sicut alias*, returnable on the quindene of Michaelmas, against Richard Wright rector of Rushton (Rushden) church to answer the prior of Lenton about a plea of debt of 40s, being arrears of a rent of 4s p.a. Note of return of no lay fee by the sheriff of Northamptonshire.
Teste Robert Bealknapp, 16 June 1382.

240. Prohibicio contra Rectorem de Whethamstede etc.
Chancery *ne teneatis*, addressed to the official of the bishop of Lincoln and his commissary, concerning a plea of trespass brought by Richard Claymound rector of Wheathampstead (Whethamstede) against Thomas Plumpton' of Whethamstead before you in the court Christian.
Teste me ipso, 27 June 1382.

241. Consultacio pro Rector de Whethamstede
Chancery *consultacio*, addressed to the bishop and his offical and their commissaries, in favour of Richard Claymound rector of Wheathampstead (Whethamstede) parish church who impleaded Thomas Plumpton of Whethamstead in the court Christian on a charge that Thomas had laid violent hands on him. Thomas, knowing that violence to the clergy pertains to the court Christian, and wishing to impede the plea by suggesting to our Chancery that the cause did not pertain to the church court, obtained a prohibition to stop proceedings in the church court.
Teste me ipso, 16 Aug. 1382.
[See **240**]

242.   [f. 36] Breve contra Rectorem de Billyng'
Common Pleas *venire faciatis* returnable on the octave of Michaelmas, against John Baukewell rector of Little Billing (Parva Byllyng) to answer the prior of St. Andrew Northampton about a plea of debt of 100s, being arrears of rent of 20s p.a. Note of return of no lay fee by the sheriff of Northamptonshire on the quindene of Easter [20 April].
Teste Robert Bealknapp, 10 July 1382.
Retornacio Sta' cur' pro eodem
The said John Baukewell was warned to be at the place on the day named in the writ.
[See **232**]

243.   Breve contra Rectorem de Aylyngton
Common Pleas *venire faciatis sicut alias*, returnable on the octave of Michaelmas, against Richard Carleton rector of Aylton (Aylyngton) to answer the abbot of Ramsey for a plea of debt of 100s being arrears of a rent of 5 marks p.a. Note of return of no lay fee by the sheriff of Huntingdonshire.[1]
Teste Robert Bealknap, 9 July 1382.
Tarde venit.

>   1   Aylton is in Herts.

244.   Breve Rotheley
Chancery *certiorari (scrutatis registris)* concerning the time of the appropriation of Rothley (Rotheley) church, Leicester, by whom it was appropriated and all the articles and circumstances.
Teste me ipso, 24 Sept. 1382.   [John] Burton[1]
Littera testimonialis super eodem.
26 Oct. 1382 at the Old Temple a letter testimonial was granted to the prior of the Hospital of St. John of Jerusalem in England concerning the time of the appropriation of Rothley (Roleya) church by the lord Richard [Gravesend], bishop of Lincoln, and to Master Thomas Rippleye,[2] whose tenor began as follows: Know all, that we, John, bishop of Lincoln have looked in the register of Richard of good memory, our predecessor, and we have found the following: a letter patent of Robert bp. of Lincoln, [the greeting and dating clauses only are given.]
Sleaford 10 Oct. 1382.

>   1   The career of this distinguished Chancery clerk may be followed in Wilkinson, *Chancery*, pp. 67n., 76, 76n; Tout, *Chapters*, III.43 n. 1, 442 n. 1, 450, VI.60, 173.
>   2   For Rippeley, a Cambridge graduate and canon lawyer, see *BRUC*, p. 482; he was official of the archdeaconry of Leicester compiling a formulary of canon law documents drawn largely from Leicester examples; Cambridge, Gonville and Caius College MS 288.

245.   Breve pro Rectore de Byfeld de supersedendo etc.
Exchequer *supersedeatis* of the writ *levari faciatis de bonis et beneficiis ecclesias-ticis*, until the quindene of Easter [20 April], concerning William Gryseley rector of Byfield (Byfeld) church for 22s 7½d owed to the crown for a loan at the receipt of the Exchequer on 22 March 45 Edward III and remaining in his hand for the tenth of his church *et sequestrum relaxetis*.
Teste Robert de Plesyngton, 21 Oct. 1382.
[See **229, 237**]

246. [f. 36v] Breve de certiorando Gnousale
Chancery *certiorari (scrutato registro)* concerning a resignation of a certain pre-
bend in Gnosall[1] collegiate church made into your hands, it is said, by Thomas de
Stathum in 1378.
Teste me ipso, 22 Oct. 1382.

   [1]   Gnosall, Staffs., and so in the diocese of Coventry and Lichfield, was a royal free chapel,
   see J.H. Denton, *English Royal Free Chapels 1100–1300* (Manchester, 1970). For its unusual
   constitution see *VCH Staffordshire* vol. 4 (1958), pp. 113, 128.

247. Breve contra Rectorem de Aylyngton'
Common Pleas *venire faciatis*, returnable on the octave of Martinmas, against
Richard Carleton rector of Aylton (Aylyngton) to answer the abbot of Ramsey for
a plea of debt of 100s being arrears of a rent of 5 marks p.a. Note of return of no
lay fee by the sheriff of Huntingdonshire.
Teste Robert Bealknap', 20 Oct. 1382.
[See **243**]

248. Prohibicio contra Juster
Chancery *ne teneatis*, addressed to the bishop and his official and their commissaries, concerning a plea of chattels and debt brought by John Juster of Bucknell
(Buckenhull) against Nicholas Bakere of Bicester in the court Christian, as pleas
of chattels and debt only pertain to church courts in cases of probate and matrimony,
and this case is neither of these.
Teste me ipso, 6 June 1381 [*sic*]

249. Consultacio eiusdem prohibicionis
Chancery *consultacio*, addressed to the bishop and his commissary in the case of
John Juster of Bucknell (Buckenhul) *versus* Nicholas Bakere of Bicester.
Nicholas's adultery with Matilda the wife of John was well known, and though
Nicholas swore on the gospels that he would not repeat this he did, and he pretended
that the plea was one of debt and chattels. The correction of his soul pertains to you.
Teste me ipso, 17 Nov. 1382.

250. Breve de certiorando de morte Johannis de Lincoln
Chancery *certiorari (scrutatis registris)* to know the day of the death of John de
Lincoln last warden of the chapel of Wykes near Bicker (Byker).[1]
Teste me ipso, 8 Dec. 1382.
Retornum. By inquisition we find that John de Lincoln last warden of Wykes chapel
near Bicker died on 3 Nov. The inquisition was made at Leadenham (Ledenham)
rectory by the official of the archdeacon of Lincoln and the witnesses were William
Foxworth, doms. John Brounflet and William de Hundelby chaplains, Brian Pynker,
William Mabot and John Bret etc. [Given] under the official's seal, Leadenham 15
Dec. 1382 'quod quidem certificatorium Thomas Wygtoft prosecutor dicti brevis
penes se habuit ad ipsius instantem peticionem'.

   [1]   Within the parish of Donington in Holland, D.M. Owen, 'Medieval Chapels in Lincolnshire',
   Lincolnshire History and Archaeology 10 (1975), p. 17.

251. Breve contra vicarium de Pyriton'
Common Pleas *venire faciatis*, returnable on the octave of Hilary, against Robert
Pateshull' vicar of Pirton (Pyriton) church to answer the prior of Hertford about a
plea of debt of 40s, being arrears of a rent of 22s p.a. Note of return of no lay fee
by the sheriff of Hertfordshire on the octave of Martinmas [18 Nov.].
Teste Robert Bealknap, 28 Nov. 1382.

252. [f. 37] Breve contra Rectorem de Folkesworth'
Common Pleas *venire faciatis*, returnable on the octave of Hilary, against Richard
de Sproxton rector of Folksworth (Folkesworth) to answer the abbot of Crowland
(Crowland) about a plea of debt of 40s being arrears of a rent of 6s 8d p.a. Note of
return of no lay fee by the sheriff of Huntingdonshire on the morrow of All Souls
[3 Nov.].
Teste Robert Bealknap, 7 Nov. 1382.

253. Breve de veniendo ad parliamentum
Summons to a parliament to be held at Westminster on Monday in the third week
of Lent [23 Feb.], with *premunientes* clause.
Teste me ipso, 7 Jan. 1383.[1]
Ad citandum et premuniendum clerum etc.
Unheaded mandate to summon the clergy to a meeting in the parish church of All
Saints, Northampton on Thursday after St. Juliana the Virgin [19 Feb.].
Buckden 4 Feb. 1383.
>   [1]   Printed *RDP*, IV.700; see also *CCR 1383–5*, p. 246.

254. [ff. 37–37v] Breve pro subsidio decime solvendo etc.
Mandate to appoint collectors for the moiety of the tenth granted in convocation at
St. Frideswide's, Oxford on 26 Nov. last, on benefices accustomed to pay, and due
on the Annunciation of the Virgin [25 March]; and in the same convocation at the
house of Friars Preachers, 21 Jan. another moiety [was granted] payable on the feast
of St. John the Baptist [24 June], on condition that the king goes in person to fight,
to collect both moieties. Collectors' names are to be at the Exchequer by the feast
of St. Mathew the Apostle [21 Sept.].
Teste me ipso, 26 Jan. 1383.
[f. 37v] Commissio pro collectoribus ad levandum decimam
Commission to the abbot of St. Mary de Pratis, Leicester, to collect these subsidies
in the archdeaconries of Lincoln, Stow, Leicester and the deanery of Rutland.
Buckden 6 Feb. 1383.
Note that a similar commission was sent to the prior of Newnham (Newenham) for
the archdeaconries of Northampton, Oxford, Buckingham, Bedford, and Huntingdon.
Certificatorium Thesaurario et Baronibus de scaccario de nominibus collect'
On the same day a certificate was sent to the Exchequer, saying that the writ had
been received on 2 Feb., and giving the collectors' names.

255. [f. 37v] Breve contra vicarium de Pyryton'
Common Pleas *venire faciatis sicut alias*, returnable on the quindene of Easter [5
April], against Robert Pateshull' vicar of Pirton (Pyriton) church to answer the prior
of Hertford about a plea of debt of 40s, being arrears of a rent of 22s p.a. Note of

return of no lay fee by the sheriff of Hertfordshire on the octave of Martinmas [18 Nov.].
Teste Robert Bealknap, 31 Jan. 1383.
Retornum.
On 17 March return was made that the said Robert was warned to be before the justices in the place and on the day required in the writ.
[See **251**]

256. [f. 38] Breve contra Rectorem de Aylyngton
Common Pleas *venire faciatis sicut pluries*, returnable on the octave of Trinity [24 May], against Richard Carleton rector of Aylton (Aylyngton) to answer the abbot of Ramsey for a plea of debt of 100s being arrears of a rent of 5 marks p.a. Note of return of no lay fee by the sheriff of Huntingdonshire.
RETURN. Return was made at the same term and sent by Robert Waryn.
[See **243**, **247**]

257. Breve regium pro parliamento
Summons to a parliament to be held at Westminster on the Monday before All Saints [26 Oct.], with *premunientes* clause.
Teste me ipso, 20 Aug. 1383.[1]
Conclusio pro clero.
[The writ is contained in a] mandate to the official of the archdeacon of Lincoln or his commissary ordering the clergy to elect two proctors in the parish church of All Saints, Northampton on the judgement day after the feast of 11,000 Virgins and to signify to the bishop's commissaries what he had done.
Nettleham 7 Sept. 1383.
[ff. 38–38v] Conclusio pro Decano et capitulo ecclesie Lincoln'
The writ was received on 7 Sept. Mandate to the dean to execute it and to certify his actions in this matter to the bishop at Sleaford before Michaelmas.
Nettleham 7 Sept. 1383.

    [1]   Printed *RDP*, IV.703; see also *CCR 1381–5*, p. 390.

258. [f. 38v] Breve contra Rectorem de Muresle
Common plea *venire faciatis*, returnable on the octave of Martinmas [18 Nov.], against Master John Wardeyn rector of Mursley (Muresley) to answer the prioress of Nuneaton (Newenton)[1] about a plea of debt of £10, being arrears of a rent of 40s p.a. Note of return of no lay fee by the sheriff of Buckinghamshire on the octave of Michaelmas.
Teste Robert Bealknap, 13 Oct. 1383.

    [1]   Nuneaton was the patron of Mursley, see *Rot. Gravesend*, p. 254. Thanks are due to Professor Smith for this identification.

259. Breve contra Rectorem de Gerthorp'
Exchequer *venire faciatis sicut pluries*, returnable on the quindene of Hilary, against John Rome rector of Garthorpe (Gerthorp)[1] to answer the king for the goods and chattels of John Scote lately parson of Garthorpe who feloniously killed himself by hanging in his room at Garthorpe on the Friday after St. Denys 2 Richard II [15 Oc. 1378] and whose goods and chattels to the value of £10 16s 3d are apportioned to the king and not yet sent.

Teste Robert de Plesyngton, 11 Dec. 1383. From the escheator's roll of Thomas Hore lately escheator in Warwickshire and Leicestershire in his accounts viz. from 12 Dec. 3 Richard II to the following 12 Dec. and by a writ returned on the morrow of the close of Easter 6 Richard II [30 March 1383]. Note of return of no lay fee by the the sheriff of Warwickshire and Leicestershire and the memoranda roll of 7 Richard II, Michaelmas among *brevia retornabilia*, roll 28.

    1   Garthorpe, Leics., since the Lincs. Garthorpe was not a benefice.

260.   Breve contra Rectorem ecclesie de Wychecok'

Exchequer *venire faciatis sicut pluries*, returnable on the quindene of Hilary, against Richard de Overton rector of Withcote (Wychecok') holder of the land and property belonging to William Hacellut, lately steward and keeper of the forest of Rutland to answer us for the said William, along with the heirs and executors of William's will, for £15 received of Simon Ward both for the repairing of the building and walls of Oakham Castle and for the lodge in the park there, which has not been sent to us or accounted for.

Teste Robert de Plesyngton, 12 Dec. 1383. From the account roll of Simon Ward, and of the castle and manor of Oakham from 16 Jan. 46 Edward III to the following 16 Jan. by return made on the morrow of Michaelmas 49 Edward III by the sheriff of Rutland, and the sheriff of Rutland made return of no lay fee on the morrow of Michaelmas 6 Richard II.

261.   [f. 39] Breve de levando decimam de subsidio etc. contra diversas personas ut infra

Exchequer *levari faciatis de bonis et beneficiis ecclesiasticis sicut pluries*, returnable on the morrow of Hilary, against the following [all in Lincolnshire], each of whom owe 6s 8d:

John [Snoring] rector of Southorpe, in the archdeaconry of Stow and the deanery of Corringham (Coryngham);[1]

Thomas Cardinal chaplain in West Halton (Halton), archdeaconry of Stow, deanery of Manlake (Manlak);

Thomas Pampylon' chaplain in Skillington (Skylington);

William Tykynton[2] rector of Stoke (Stokes), Beltisloe (Belteslowe) deanery;

John Forthyngton chaplain of Spilsby (Spillesby) in Bolingbroke deanery;[3]

Richard Wenton chaplain 'ad pollem for';

John Blakenham chaplain in St. Paul [in the Bail, Lincoln] church;[4]

John lately chaplain with James Bekeryng in the deanery of the Christianity of Lincoln;[5]

John Palgrave, chaplain of Beckingham chantry in Loveden (Lovedon) deanery;[6]

William chaplain with Simon Simeon;

John Robcot chaplain at the same;[7]

Richard chaplain in Lavington,[8] Belistloe (Belteslow) deanery;

Thomas chaplain in Kyme;

John Bunch chaplain in the same;

Thomas Evedon chaplain in Scredington (Screkyngton), Lafford deanery;

John Schefford, chaplain in Navenby;

William de Stepulton chaplain in Harmston (Hermeston);

John Reynes chaplain in Dogdyke (Dokdyk) chantry, Longoboby (Longouboby) [deanery];[9]

John de Leverington chaplain in 'Sutton';[10]
Bartholomew de Neuton chaplain of Tydd [St. Mary];[11]
Roger Rakedall chaplain in Frieston (Freston) [priory], Holland deanery;
Thomas chaplain with domina de Claythorpe (Clathorp) in Calcewaith [deanery];
Henry Besewyk chaplain in Grimsby;
Richard chaplain in Mareham Le Fen (Marum), Horncastle deanery;
John rector of Wyham (Wyhum) [Louthesk deanery];
William Conston chaplain in Barton upon Humber (Barton);
John chaplain in Barrow upon Humber (Barow);
William de Welton chaplain in 'Somerby';[12]
William chaplain in Searby (Seuerby);
John chaplain in Hundon;
William Cateryk rector of Wroot (Wrote);
Thomas de Topclyf chaplain of Walter de Topclyf of Somerby in Corringham (Coryngham) deanery;
Richard Beverlay chaplain in Broughton [by Brigg] (Berghton) in Manlake (Manlak) deanery;
which [the said] John rector of Southorpe, Thomas Cardinall etc. owe us for the subsidy granted 4 Richard II in the archdeaconries of Lincoln and Stow.
Teste Robert de Plesyngton, 13 Dec. 1383. From the Memoranda roll of 5 Richard II, Michaelmas, account roll 15.

1   See LRS 81, no. 835.
2   Or 'de Tykton', *ibid.*, no. 723.
3   See *ibid.*, no. 487.
4   *Ibid.*, no. 1781.
5   *Ibid.*, no. 1778.
6   For the chantry of the Blessed Mary of Beckingham see C.W. Foster and A. Hamilton Thompson, eds., 'The Chantry Certificates of Lincoln and Lincolnshire', *Associated Architectural and Archaeological Societies Reports and Papers* 36 (1921–22), 37 (1923–25), no. 107.
7   For these last two see LRS 81, no. 2058.
8   Otherwise known as Lavington, Lincs.
9   For Dogdyke chantry in the parish of Billinghay see 'Lincolnshire Chantries', no. 112.
10   Probably Sutton St. James which contained more chaplains than Sutton Le Marsh in this period.
11   See LRS 81, no. 755.
12   Unidentified; there are three places of that name in Lincs.

262.   [ff. 39–39v] Breve contra dominum Thomam Hervy
Exchequer *levari faciatis de bonis et beneficiis ecclesiasticis sicut pluries*, returnable on the morrow of Hilary, against Thomas Hervy for 16 marks owed to the king, being arrears for the custody of certain tenements in Billingsgate ward, London, which Mary de St. Pol (St. Paul) late countess of Pembroke held as dower after the death of Aymer de Valence (Adomar de Volencia) late earl of Pembroke of the inheritance of John son and heir of John Hastings late earl of Pembroke, who died under age and in the custody of Edward III, from 7 March 51 Edward III until the coming of age of the said heir.
[f. 39v] *Teste* Robert de Plesyngton, 24 Nov. 1383. From the great roll of 4 Richard II now in London and the memoranda roll of 7 Richard II *brevia retornabilia*.
Retornatum. This writ came too late for us to be able to execute it.

263. Breve ad deputandum collectores pro medietate decime persolvenda
Mandate to appoint collectors for the moiety of a tenth granted 2 December in the last convocation and payable on assessed benefices by 1 March [1384], and to send the names of the collectors to the Exchequer before Hilary.
Teste me ipso, 20 Dec. 1383.
Commissio pro eadem collecta colligend' etc.
Mandate addressed to the abbot of Garendon to act as collector in the archdeaconries of Lincoln, Stow, Leicester and the deanery of Rutland.
Sleaford [undated].
Note of a similar commission to the prior of Dunstable for the archdeaconries of Buckingham, Oxford, Bedford, Huntingdon and Northampton.
Memorand'.[1]

    [1] [f. 40] Infrascript' in prox fol' precedente The same writ is transcribed again.

264. [f. 39v] Breve contra Rectorem ecclesie de Muresle
Common Pleas *venire faciatis sicut alias*, returnable on the quindene of Hilary, against Master John Wardeyn rector of Mursley (Muresley) to answer the prioress of Nuneaton about a plea of debt of £10, being arrears of a rent of 40s p.a. Note of return of no lay fee by the sheriff of Buckinghamshire on the octave of Michaelmas.
Teste Robert Bealknap, 26 Nov. 1383.
[See **217**]

265. [ff. 39v–40] Breve contra Rectorem de Uppingham
Common Pleas *venire faciatis*, returnable on the octave of Hilary, against John Fransh rector of Uppingham to answer the abbot of Westminster about a plea of debt of 40s, being arrears of a rent of 40s p.a. Note of return of no lay fee by the sheriff of Rutland on the morrow of All Souls [3 Nov.].[1]
Teste Robert Bealknap, 8 Nov. 1383.

    [1] See *Westminster Abbey Charters 1066–c.1214*, ed. Emma Mason, London Record Society 25 (1988), nos. 46, 338.

266. Breve contra Rectorem de Carthorp'
Exchequer *supersedeatis et sequestrum relaxetis* until further notice, concerning John Rome rector of Garthorpe.
Teste Robert de Plesyngton, 27 Jan. 1384. By writ of the great seal sent to the Exchequer and enrolled among *Brevia directa baronibus* in Hilary term 7 Richard II.
[See **218**]

267. Breve pro parliamento
Summons to attend parliament at Salisbury on Friday after the feast of St. Mark the Evangelist [29 April], with *premunientes* clause.
Teste me ipso, 3 March 1384.[1]
[f. 40v] Commissio ad citandum et premuniendum clerum
Mandate to the official of the archdeacon of Lincoln in pursuance of the writ of summons to parliament, which the bishop received on 22 March, to cite the clergy of the archdeaconry to be at All Saints church, Northampton, on Thursday after the Sunday on which is sung *Quasimodo geniti* and to certify what you have done, to our commissaries on that day.

Stow Park 31 March 1384.
Commissio ad recipiendum certificator'
Mandate to the abbot of St. James' abbey Northampton and Master Thomas Boyvill[2] rector of Seaton (Seyton) church to be in All Saints church, Northampton, on the judgment day after the feast of 11,000 Virgins to inform us who are chosen proctors for the clergy, and to give them their powers and arrange for their expenses. [Undated.]

1   Printed *RDP*, IV.707; see also *CCR 1381–5*, p. 437.
2   See *BRUO*, I.239.

268.   [f. 41] Breve pro medietate decime solvende etc.
Mandate to appoint collectors of the moiety of a tenth granted in the convocation held at Salisbury on 1 May, being the moiety granted on conditions in the previous convocation held in London, payable at the feast of All Saints [1 Nov.], and to certify the collectors' names to the Exchequer before the next feast [not specified.]
Teste me ipso, 1 July 1384.
[f. 42v] Commissio ad colligendum medietatem decime
Mandate to the abbot of Revesby in execution of the writ on the previous folio, to collect the tax in the archdeaconries of Lincoln, Stow, Leicester, and the deanery of Rutland.
Liddington [day and month unspecified] 1384.
Note that the abbot of Ramsey was written to in similar form to collect in the archdeaconries of Huntingdon, Bedford, Oxford, Buckingham and Northampton.

269.   [f. 41] Breve contra non solventes subsidium vis viiid
Exchequer *levari faciatis de bonis et beneficiis ecclesiasticis sicut pluries*, returnable on the morrow of Michaelmas, against the following who have not paid the subsidy of 6s 8d:
John [Snoring] rector of Southorpe, in the archdeaconry of Stow and the deanery of Corringham;
Thomas Cardinal chaplain in West Halton, archdeaconry of Stow, deanery of Manlake;
Thomas Pampylon' chaplain in Skillington;
William Tykynton rector of Stoke, Beltisloe deanery;
John Forthyngton chaplain of Spilsby in Bolingbroke deanery;
Richard Wenton chaplain 'ad pollem for';
John Blakenham chaplain in St. Paul [in the Bail, Lincoln] church;
John lately chaplain with James Bekeryng in the deanery of the Christianity of Lincoln;
John Palgrave, chaplain of Beckingham chantry in Loveden deanery;
William chaplain with Simon Simeon;
John Robcot chaplain at the same;
Richard chaplain in Lavington, Belistloe deanery;
Thomas chaplain in Kyme;
John Bunch chaplain in the same;
Thomas Evedon chaplain in Scredington, Lafford deanery;
John Schefford, chaplain in Navenby;
William de Stepulton chaplain in Harmston;
John Reynes chaplain in Dogdyke chantry, Longoboby [deanery];

John de Leverington chaplain in 'Sutton';
Bartholomew de Neuton chaplain of Tydd [St. Mary];
Roger Rakedall chaplain in Frieston [priory], Holland deanery;
Thomas chaplain with domina de Claythorpe in Calcewaith [deanery];
Henry Besewyk chaplain in Grimsby;
Richard chaplain in Mareham Le Fen (Marum), Horncastle deanery;
John rector of Wyham (Wyhum) [Louthesk deanery];
William Conston chaplain in Barton upon Humber;
John chaplain in Barrow upon Humber;
William de Welton chaplain in 'Somerby';
William chaplain in Searby (Seuerby);
John chaplain in Hundon;
William Cateryk rector of Wroot;
Thomas de Topclyf chaplain of Walter de Topclyf of Somerby in Corringham deanery;
Richard Beverlay chaplain in Broughton [by Brigg] in Manlake deanery;
which John rector of Southorpe, Thomas Cardinall etc. owe us for the subsidy granted 4 Richard II in the archdeaconries of Lincoln and Stow.
Teste Robert de Plesyngton, 13 July 1384.
[See **261**]

270. [ff. 41–41v] Breve contra dominum Thomam Hervy pro 1 warda
Exchequer *levari faciatis de bonis et beneficiis ecclesiasticis sicut pluries*, returnable on the morrow of Michaelmas, against Thomas Hervy for 16 marks owed to the king, being arrears for the custody of certain tenements in Billingsgate ward, London, which Mary de St. Pol (St. Paul), late countess of Pembroke held as dower after the death of Aymer de Valence (Adomar de Volencia) late earl of Pembroke of the inheritance of John son and heir of John Hastings late earl of Pembroke, who died under age and in the custody of Edward III, from 7 March 51 Edward III until the coming of age of the said heir.
Teste Robert de Plesyngton, 16 July 1384.
[See **262**]

271. [f. 41v] Breve contra Rectorem de Billing Parva
Common Pleas *fieri faciatis de bonis ecclesiasticis*, returnable on the octave of Michaelmas, against John Baukewell rector of Little Billing (Billing Parva) to answer the prior of St. Andrew's Northampton for £8, being arrears of a rent of 20s p.a. recovered against him before John Holt justice of the common bench on the Thursday of Pentecost week at Rothwell (Rothewell), and *fieri faciatis de bonis ecclesiasticis* for £10 which the prior had as damages because of the detention of the rent.
Teste Robert Bealknapp, 12 July 1384.
[See **232, 242**]

272. Breve contra Rectorem ecclesie de Kyngham
Common Pleas *venire faciatis*, returnable on the quindene of Michaelmas, against William Aubyn rector of Kingham (Kyngham) to answer the abbot of Walden for a plea of debt of £6 being arrears of a rent of 20s p.a. Note of return of no lay fee by the sheriff of Oxfordshire.

Teste Robert Bealknapp, 25 June 1384.

Retornum.

Return was made that William the rector was warned to be at Westminster on the day named, as the writ required.

273. Breve de certiorando de alienigenis in dioc'

Chancery *certiorari* concerning the benefices in the diocese which are held by aliens, their annual value, and the names, state and condition of the holders.[1]

Teste me ipso, 20 Sept. 1384.

> [1] See *CCR 1381–5*, p. 481.

274. [ff. 41v–42] Breve pro parliamento

Summons to attend a parliament at Westminster on the morrow of Martinmas [12 Nov.], with *premunientes* clause.

Teste me ipso, 28 Sept. 1384.[1]

[f. 42] Commissio domini super eodem

Mandate to the official of the archdeacon of Lincoln to cause representatives of the clergy of his archdeaconry to attend the election of proctors for the clergy of the diocese in All Saints church Northampton on the Friday after All Saints [4 Nov.], and mandate to the abbot of St. James's Northampton and Master John de Banbury rector of one third of Waddesdon (Wodesdon) church to receive the certificates and to ordain the proctors' expenses and to report back to the bishop by the Thursday after St. Leonard the Abbot [10 Nov.].

Lidington 18 Oct. 1384. And in the same way the officials of all the archdeaconries of Lincoln diocese were written to in the usual form.[2]

> [1] Printed *RDP*, IV.711; see also *CCR 1381–5*, p. 586.
> [2] After this writ there is an unheaded fragment: Know all by these presents that I, John Bettelowe, bailiff of the liberty of Anne queen of England in Northamptonshire have received by the hand of John Ashby my clerk, from Alexander Vincent of Kilsby (Kyldesby) [the document ends here].

275. [ff. 42–42v] Breve ad orandum

Request for prayers for the safety of the king and his lieges and of the whole realm.

Teste me ipso, 20 Oct. 1384.[1]

> [1] Printed in Thomas Rymer, *Foedera, Conventiones, Litterae* vol. VII (London, 1709), pp. 444–5; calendared in *CCR 1381–5*, p. 590.

276. Prohibicio Seyton

Chancery *ne admittatis* concerning the rectory of Seaton (Seyton) vacant, if is said, whose advowson is being disputed in court between John Danneys knight, and John Tyndale, Master Robert Palmer' clerk and Nicholas Grenham clerk, until it is known whether the advowson belongs to John Danneys or to the said John, Robert and Nicholas.

Teste me ipso, 29 Oct. 1384.

277. Alia pro eadem

Chancery *ne admittatis* concerning Seaton church.

Teste me ipso, 28 Oct. 1384.

278.   Breve contra Rectorem de Billing Parva

Common Pleas *fieri faciatis de bonis ecclesiasticis*, returnable on the octave of Hilary, against John Baukewell rector of Little Billing (Billing Parva) to answer the prior of St. Andrew's Northampton for £8, being arrears of a rent of 20s p.a. recovered against him before John Holt justice of the common bench on the Thursday of Pentecost week at Rothwell (Rothewell), and *fieri faciatis de bonis ecclesiasticis* for £10 which the prior had as damages because of the detention of the rent.

Teste Robert Bealknap', 28 Oct. 1384.[1]

[See **232, 242, 271**]

> [1]   8 July 1383, 'Order to the justices of Common Pleas, on the prior's petition, to proceed to judgment in the case of the prior of St. Andrew's, Northampton *v.* John Baukewelle rector of Little Billyng for 100s being arrears of rent of 20s p.a. The defendant says that the rent was fully paid up when he was presented to the rectory and that he cannot pay without the consent of the king (because of the French war, since the priory is alien and in the king's hand for that reason), of the prior (patron of the living), and the bishop of Lincoln (the ordinary).' A similar order was made on 6 July 1384; *CCR 1381–5*, pp. 323, 462.

279.   Assheby la Zouche prohibicio

Chancery *ne admittatis* concerning the vicarage of Ashby de la Zouche (Ashby la Couche) whose advowson is being disputed in our courts between Hugh la Zouche chivaler, and the abbot and convent of Lilleshall (Lilleshull).

Teste me ipso, 1 Dec. 1384.

280.   Certificatorium Baronibus super primeva fundacione

Chancery *certiorari (scrutatis registris)*, returnable before the feast of St. Peter's Chair [22 Feb], concerning the foundation of the vicarage of Ashby de la Zouche and the holders of it, and by what title they held it.

Teste me ipso, 12 Jan. 1385.

RETURN: the writ is contained in the return to the treasurer and barons of the Exchequer *(sic)*. We have looked in our registers and find the following:

John de Ashby, deacon, was presented to the vicarage of Ashby la Zouche at the vacancy caused by the death of Roger the last vicar, by the abbot and convent of Lilleshall, and was admitted 14 Kal. Jan., in the 5th year [19 Dec. 1305] at Hinckley, after inquisition had been made by the official of the archdeacon of Leicester. The vicar took an oath that he would keep canonical residence. William Bromyerd chaplain was presented by the abbot and convent of Lilleshall on the resignation of John, and was admitted 7 Ides Dec. 15th year of the same pontificate [7 Dec. 1314]; William Lucas of 'Overton'[1] deacon was presented by the same abbot and convent on the resignation of William and admitted 17 Kal. April, 16th year of the pontificate [16 March 1315] of John bishop etc. In the time of John Gynewell our immediate predecessor, William de Dounton, priest was presented by the same abbot and convent on the death of Richard Page the last vicar, and admitted 1 Nov. 1349 at Stow Park, and the vicar took the oath on the gospels that he would reside. Liddington 12 Feb. 1385.[2]

> [1]   Probaby either Cold Overton (Leics.) or Market Overton (Rutland)
> [2]   The first three institutions took place in the bishopric of John Dalderby, 1300–20, and are recorded in LAO Reg. 2, ff. 200v, 208v, 210. The institution which took place during the bishopric of John Gynewell, Buckingham's immediate predecessor, 1347–62, is recorded in LAO Reg. 9, f. 346v.

281. [ff. 43–43v] Breve contra Alienigenas
Chancery *certiorari* which benefices are held by aliens, the annual value of those benefices and the names and status of the holders.
Teste me ipso, 16 Jan. 1385.
EXECUTION. The writ is contained in a mandate of the bishop to the official of the archdeacon of Lincoln ordering an inquisition to be made and a report sent to the bishop before the feast of St. Gregory the Pope [12 March].
Liddington 18 Feb. 1385.
Note that similar letters were written to the officials of all the other archdeacons in the diocese.

282. [f. 43v] Commissio ad colligendum medietatem unius decime
Mandate to appoint collectors of the tax of a moiety of a tenth granted in the convocation held at St. Paul's cathedral London on 19 Dec. last, and payable on the quindene of Easter [16 April]. Names of the collectors are to be certified to the Exchequer by the octave of the Purification of the Virgin [2 Feb.].
Teste me ipso, 11 Jan. 1385.
EXECUTION. The writ is contained in a commission to the prior of Markby to collect in the archdeaconries of Lincoln and Stow.
Liddington 3 Feb. 1385.
In a similar form these were written to and ordered to collect:
the abbot of Croxton in the archdeaconries of Leicester and Northampton, the archdeaconry of Northampton being vacant; the Prior of St. Frideswide's Oxford in the archdeaconries of Oxford and Buckingham; the abbot of Woburn in the archdeaconries of Bedford and Huntingdon; and a certificate to this effect was returned to the Exchequer.[1]

   [1] For the convocation and Archbishop Courtenay's certificate to the king dated 5 Jan. see Lambeth Palace Library, Reg. Courtenay (Cant.) I, ff. 79v–80.

283. Breve contra Rectorem ecclesie de Castre
Common Pleas *venire faciatis*, returnable on the quindene of Easter [16 April], against John Hervy rector of Castor (Craste *sic*) to answer the abbot of Leicester about a plea of debt of £16 and 8 stones of wax, arrears of 40s and 1 stone of wax p.a.
Teste Robert Bealknapp, 16 Feb. 1385.

284. [f. 44] Breve de excusando clericos de scaccario a non comparicione coram ord'
To the bishop or his commissary. Exchequer *ne teneatis* concerning a summons which was served on John Dautre rector of Leckhampstead (Leckhamstede) clerk of John de Hermesthorp' one of the chamberlains of the Exchequer to appear at Liddington on the morrow of Hilary before the bishop or his commissary. On that day he will be busy at the Exchequer, and the king's business ought to take precedence over any other sort, so he is not to be punished for non-appearance.
Teste Robert de Plesyngton, 17 Feb. 1385. By the Red Book of the Exchequer.

285.   Breve contra Rectorem de Berughby

Exchequer *venire faciatis*, returnable on the quindene of Easter [16 April], against John rector of Barrowby (Berughby), Lincolnshire, to answer the prior of Eye for 20 marks being arrears of a pension of 5 marks p.a. due from his church; and *venire faciatis*, returnable on the same day, against William rector of Welbourn (Welbourne), Lincolnshire to answer the said prior for 16 marks, being arrears of 4 marks p.a. pension due from his church.

Teste Robert de Plesyngton, 16 Feb. 1385. By the Barons because of note of no lay fee by the sheriff of Lincolnshire.

[See **187**, **189**, **194**]

286.   [ff. 44–44v] Breve contra Rectores de Hynham et Drayton

Exchequer *venire faciatis*, returnable on the morrow of St. John Baptist [25 June], against Master David Bradewell rector of Heyham on the Hill (Hynham) and Roger Walden rector of Fenny Drayton (Drayton) to answer John Clanvowe knight and Brother Ralph Maylok a foreigner, proctors of the abbot of Lyre (Lire) and our farmers about £14, being arrears of the pension of 40s p.a. due from Heyham church and [f. 44v] 70s, being arrears of a pension of 8s p.a. due from Fenny Drayton church, as the farmers cannot pay their farm until they get the money. Note of return of no lay fees by the sheriff of Leicestershire on the morrow of Ascension [12 May].

Teste Robert de Plesyngton, 14 May 1385.[1]

> 1   Bradewell is almost certainly to be identified with the Master David Bradwell listed in *BRUO*, I.246. Roger Walden was later archbishop of Canterbury 1397–99, and bishop of London 1404–6, *HBC* pp. 233, 258. For Sir John Clanvowe, a Chamber knight with lollard leanings, see Chris Given-Wilson, *The Royal Household and the King's Affinity* (Yale, 1986), pp 162f, 196, 217, 219; K.B. McFarlane, *Lancastrian Kings and Lollard Knights* (Oxford, 1972), pp. 139–232 *passim*, esp. 230–32.

287.   [f. 44v] Breve ad Inquirendum super bastardia pro Bernardo Brocas[1]

Common Pleas *inquiretis de bastardia*, returnable on the morrow of St. John Baptist [25 June], in the following matter: [Sir] Henry Langfield (Langefeld)[2] impleaded in our court at Westminster Bernard Brocas, junior, on the charge that with arms and force he broke the close and houses at Weekley (Wytle), Northamptonshire belonging to the said Henry and the he cut down and carried away trees to the value of 100s. The said Bernard came into court and said that one Agnes Vavasour his mother had died seised of Weekley (Witle) manor, and he had entered the manor as her son and heir, so that the supposed crime had taken place on his own property, and that it was Henry who was at fault if he had cut down any trees.[3] To which Henry replied that Bernard could not inherit the manor as he was a bastard and not legitimate, but Bernard denied this saying that he was not a bastard.

Teste Robert Bealknap', 15 May 1385.

Note: Look for the whole process of this writ in the memoranda book where it was written by order of the bishop's chancellor viz. from fol. 304.[4]

[Reg. 12, f. 306] Certificatorium processus pro Bernardo Brocas Junior viz. quod non est bastardus set legitimus.[5]

(i) Commission of the bishop to Masters Thomas Stowe archdeacon of Bedford and John Shillingford doctors of laws to hold an enquiry to investigate the matter named in the writ (recited in full), and to signify their findings under notarial instrument. Sleaford 30 May 1385.

(ii) Certificate that we, the commissaries, cited Bernard Brocas junior and Henry Langfield (Langeford) to appear before me, Thomas de Stowe, the said archdeacon, on a named day and place, namely Saturday 17 June 1385 in the church or chapel of Totteridge (Taterigg), Lincoln diocese, sitting as a tribunal in the presence of John called Sire de Katerington notary and Henry Northlode notary and John Westyerd clerks.

(iii) Mandate of Thomas Stowe archdeacon of Bedford and John Shillingford commissaries of the bishop of Lincoln [f. 306v] to Robert Ottele priest, John Grene and John Cotyler, layman, of Lincoln and York dioceses, to serve the citation on both parties to appear before the bishop's commissaries in the chapel of Totteridge (Taterigg) on the Saturday after the feast of St. Barnabas the Apostle.
London 2 June 1385.

(iv) Certificate of John Grene clerk of Lincoln diocese in respect of the commissaries' mandate which was received on 3 June. By authority of this he served the summons in person on Bernard Brocas and Henry Langeford [*sic*] on Saturday the 10 June 1385, in the presence of dominus John Sayvyle knight, John Woderove, Patrick de Martyn, John Faucus, William Faucus and Robert [f. 307v] Otolay specially recruited as witnesses. Bernard asserted his wish to appear in person before the commissaries, on the day and place named in the citation, and Henry wished, as he said, that you or others would proceed to expedite this matter, on the day and place named or on other days in other places, notwithstanding his absence. We have thus executed your mandate in every particular. In testimony of which we have caused the seal of the dean of the church of St. Mary Arches, commissary general in his deanery, to be applied to these presents, at the special request of John Grene.
London 16 June 1385.

(v) [Commissaries' certificate – continued]
When these letters had been read aloud in the presence of me, Thomas the commissary in the absence of my colleague Master John Schyllingeford, I caused the Henry Langfield (Langeford) named in the writ to be repeatedly called for ('preconizatum') in a loud and clear voice. Henry having failed to appear was pronounced contumacious, and we decided to proceed with the business named in the writ on the Monday following. With his consent Bernard was ordered to appear before me and my aforesaid colleague in the parish church of St. Olave Silver Street (Mugewell) London, for this business of the inquisition, by licence granted by Robert [Braybrooke] bishop of London for seeing and hearing whatever was necessary as the writ and commission required.

And when that Monday had come, namely 19 June [1385], in the presence of us, Thomas and John the commissaries, sitting as a tribunal in the Church of St. Olave [Silver Street] in the presence of Master John called Sire de Katrinton attesting notary, and Master Robert Northlode notary of Wells diocese and Roger Masoun' priest of Exeter diocese, Bernard appeared in person and there was read aloud a certain letter of the bishop of London sealed with his great seal in green wax ('sigillo magno in cera viridi impendenti sigillate') whose tenor is as follows:
Licencia Episcopi London' ad procedendum in civitate London'.
Robert [Braybrooke] bishop of London to Masters Thomas Stowe archdeacon of Bedford and John Schillingeford doctors of laws. With reference to a commission of John bishop of Lincoln to find out whether Bernard Brocas is a bastard or not,

dated Sleaford castle 30 May 1385, grant of special licence and free facility when
and as often as seems expedient to bring a final conclusion to this business.
Stepney (Stebenheth) manor, 16 June 1385.

When we had read this letter we, Thomas and John, ordered the said Henry to appear
before us in the said church of St. Olave [Silver Street.]

Petitio summar'

[Statement by Bernard Brocas]: In die nomine amen . . . Ego Bernardus Brocas
Junior clericus [*sic in ms.*] in negocio inquisicionis de et super [f. 307v] legitima-
cione et bastardia pretens' mei Bernardi predicti de mandato excellentissimi
principis domini nostri Ricardi dei gracia Regis Anglie et Francie et auctoritate dicti
patris faciend' pariter et capiende iuxta iuris exigenciam vim formam et effectum
brevis regii ad quod me refero et pro hic insertis haberi volo in hac parte impetrati
et dicto reverendo patri directi transmissi et liberati dico, allego pariter, et propono
quod ego Bernardus predictus de quo in prefato brevi regio fit mencio toto et omni
tempore meo vel in repplicacione de qua eciam in eodem brevi sit mencio est
deductum fui et sum legitimus et non bastardus et de legitimo matrimonio adductus
et procreatus . . .[6]

When this petition had been read to us and admitted, the same Bernard produced
four witnesses, viz: Master Arnaldus Brocas canon of Wells, dominus William
Hertmite priest, Walter Tanghurst of Windsor (de Wyndesor), Salisbury diocese,
and William Talour of Clewer, same diocese. Each of these was admitted and swore
on the gospels to tell the full and undiluted truth about the contents of this petition
('quilibet eorum sit admissus iuravit ad sancta die evangelia per ipsum corporaliter
tacta de dicendo plenam et meram veritatem super contentis in dicta peticione')

And afterwards in the parish church of St. Olave Silver Street in the presence of
Masters John and Robert notaries public the said four witnesses were secretly and
individually ('singillatim') examined and their depositions faithfully set down in
writing. Their tenor follows in these words. The witnesses were examined in the
parish church of St. Olave Silver Street (Mugewell) London on 19 June 1385 by
Masters John Shillingford and Thomas Stowe doctors of laws, commissaries of John
bishop of Lincoln.

[f. 307v] Examinacio primi testis

Arnold Brocas, canon of Wells cathedral, aged 40 years and more,[7] declared on oath
that Bernard Brocas was the natural and legitimate son of Bernard Brocas, now
knight,[8] and of Agnes Vavasour formerly the wife of Bernard Brocas knight, that
they were joined in lawful matrimony and cohabited for many years, and that
Bernard junior was and is publicly considered and reputed to be the natural and
legitimate son of Bernard and Agnes. The witness declared further that everything
he deposed was common knowledge in the county of Berkshire, Salisbury diocese,
and in other neighbouring places.

Examinacio secundi testis

Dominus William Ermyte priest, 60 years and more, parochial chaplain of Clewar
[Berks.] where the wedding took place.[9]

Dominus Willelmus Ermiyte presbyter lx annorum etatis et amplius ut dicit Iuratus
requisitus et diligenter examinatus super omnibus et singulis in dicta summaria
peticione content' ad que dicit iste iuratus quod omnia et singula in dicta summaria
petitione contenta sunt vera et hoc se dicit scire iste iuratus per hoc quod prefatum
Bernardum Brocas militem patrem dicti Bernardi per xlij annos et Agnetem

Vavasour per xlj annos ulterius preterit' et amplius ut dicit bene novit iste iuratus de visu sciencia et noticia suis ut dicit. Et dicit iste iuratus quod presens fuit iste iuratus in ecclesia paroch' de Cleware, Sar' dioc', cuius quidem ecclesie iste idem iuratus huic ad xl unum annos fuit capellanus parochialis ubi et quando iste idem iuratus banna matrimonialia tribus diebus dominicis a se distantibus intra missarum solempnia inter prefatos Bernardum patrem dicti Bernardi et Agnetem publice ut iuris [f. 308] est edidit et nullus apparuit contradictere, ut dicit. Et dicit iste iuratus quod prefati Bernardus pater dicti Bernardi et Agnes Vavasour in porticu dicte ecclesie parochialis de Clewar' coram domino Johanne Sengelton tunc ibidem presente matrimonium per verba de presenti contraxerunt sic dicendo videlicet: prefatus Bernardus nunc miles cepit dictam Agnetam per manum suam dexteram et dixit eidem Agneti, "Ego Bernardus accipio te Agnetem ab hac hora in antea in uxorem meam et ad hoc do tibi fidem meam", et tunc prefata Agnes dictum Bernardum per manum suam dexteram cepit et eidem Bernardo dixit, "Ego Agnes accipio vos Bernardum in virum meum ab hoc hora in antea et hoc do vobis fidem meam", et retractis manibus suis abinvicem extiterunt osculati, et tunc prefatus dominus Johannes Sengleton ipsos Bernardum et Agnetem in dictam ecclesiam adduxit ac missam de Sancta Trinitate coram eisdem Bernardo et Agnete et aliis in multitudine copiosa tunc ibidem in prefata ecclesia congregata celebravit ac ipsos Bernardum et Agnetem coram summo altari dicte ecclesie genuflectentes ut moris est benedixit ac nunc huiusmodi matrimonium ibidem inter eosdem solempnizavit isto iurato in premissis omnibus una cum domino Johanne Brocas patre dicti Bernardi contrahentis milite, Johanne Foxle, Hugone de Normanvile, Johanne Enfeld, Rogero Syfirwaste domino dicte ville de Clywar', Maugero Vavasour patre dicte Agnetis Vavasour, Thoma atte Ryde et Ricardo Normanvile domicell', ac Waltero Sanghurst et Willelmo Tailour contestibus suis presentibus et ea sic et fieri et dici, vidente, et audiente ut dicit. Dicit etiam iste iuratus quod circiter per duos vel tres annos postquam matrimonium huiusmodi inter prefatos Bernardum et Agnetem fuit solempnizatum et post solempnizacionem huiusmodi prefata Agnes fuit impregnata et peperit prefatum Bernardum in dicto brevi regio nominatum et deinde successive peperit duas proles Margaretam et Johannam. Et prefati Bernardus pater dicti Bernardi et Agnes ut vir et uxor per decem annos tunc prox' sequentes et ultra insimul steterunt de visu, auditu, sciencia et noticia istius iurati ut dicit. Dicit insuper iste iuratus quod prefati Bernardus et Agnes ipsum Bernardum ut filium suum a dicto tempore nativitatis sue et citra agnoverunt aluerunt et nominarunt ac pro filio eorum naturali et legitimo fuit et est dictus tentus, habitus, et reputatus de auditu, sciencia, and noticia istius curati ut dicit. Et dicit iste iuratus quod super premissis omnibus et singulis per istum iuratum superius depositis laboravit et laborant publica vox et fama in comitatu Bark' [sic] predictam et aliis locis convicinis de auditu, sciencia, et noticia istius iurati, ut dicit.

[f. 308] Examinacio tercii testis
Walter Sanghurst of the parish of Windsor, Salisbury diocese, illiterate, of free condition, aged 60 years and more, gave the same evidence.

[f. 308v] Examinacio quarti testis
William Taillour of the parish of Clewer (Cleware), Salisbury diocese, illiterate, of free condition, aged 50 years and more, gave the same evidence.

[f. 309] Pronunciacio et decretum

Pronouncement and decree that Bernard Brocas is legitimate and not a bastard. Commissaries' certificate to this effect sealed with the seal of Thomas Stow archdeacon of Bedford and Master John Sire de Katerington clerk of Winchester diocese, notary public.
London 19 June 1385.
Subscripcio.
Certificate of John Sire de Katerinton.
Certicatorium Thes' et baronibus.
We have caused diligent enquiry to be made and we find that Bernard Brocas is not a bastard but legitimate.
Sleaford 23 June 1385.

1 This case is discussed in the introduction, section iii pp. xviii–xix.
2 Sir Henry Langfield was the stepfather of Bernard Brocas junior, having been the second husband of Agnes Vavasour.
3 Agnes was dead by 26 Jan. 1385 when the writ was issued ordering an inquisition *post mortem* on her lands in Northants. Enquiry revealed that she held no lands in the county at the time of her death, presumably because this had been settled on her son at some earlier date, *Calendar of Inquisitions Post Mortem XVI (7–15 Richard II)*, no. 155.
4 LAO, Reg. 12, f. 304 is the contemporary foliation, the modern folio number is 306.
5 The following document is somewhat confusing to the modern reader, resembling as it does a Russian doll; the commissaries included in their certificate both the bishop's commission to them (which in its turn recited the writ), and the commission and return which they themselves had issued, and which also recited in its entirety the bishop's commission to them. In the interests of both clarity and brevity the form which the proceedings took are noted here in chronological order.
6 The statement continues for some time in the same vein, never departing from generalities.
7 Prebendary of St. Decumans, Wells, from 1366 until his death on 14 Aug. 1395; prebendary of Gretton, Lincoln, 1364–65, *Fasti*, I.67, VIII.61, XII.27, 80; occ. as clerk of the king's works 6 Nov. 1383, *CCR 1381–5*, p. 230; chamberlain of the receipt of the Exchequer, appointed 6 Jan. 1388, Tout, *Chapters*, III.430 n. 3. He was a bachelor in both civil and canon law, and occ. as rector of Compton (Berks.) in April 1391, T.C.B. Timmins, ed., *The Register of John Waltham, Bishop of Salisbury 1388–1395*, C&Y 80 (1994), p. 123.
8 For the career of the elder Bernard Brocas, c.1330–95, see *The Commons 1386–1421*, I.359–62; Agnes, his first wife, was the daughter and heiress of Mauger Vavasour whose principal property was at Denton, Yorks. See the introduction, pp. xviii–xix, for references and comment.
9 The following account of the wedding is exceptionally detailed and interesting. For comment on the value of such material see Christopher Brooke, *The Medieval Idea of Marriage* (Oxford, 1989), chap. 10, 'The Church Porch: Marriage and Architecture'.

288. [Reg. 12B f. 45] Breve ad habendum servicium Linc' Episcopi cum Rege
Order to have all services due from the bishop of Lincoln at Newcastle on Tyne on 14 July next to fight the Scots.
Teste me ipso Reading (Redyng), 4 June 1385.[1]

1 Printed *RDP*, IV.715; see also *CCR 1381–5*, p. 637. For comment see N.B. Lewis, 'The Last Medieval Summons of the English Feudal Levy, 13 June 1385', *English Historical Review* lxxiii (1958), pp. 1–26, and J.J.N. Palmer, 'The Last Summons of the Feudal Army in England (1985)', *ibid.* lxxxiii (1968), pp. 771–5.

289. Breve pro medietate decime levand'
Mandate to appoint collectors for the second moiety granted in the convocation at St. Paul's cathedral [London] on 19 Dec. last on condition that we go to war in person, and payable on the quindene of St. John Baptist [8 July]. The money is needed by the feast of St. Mary Magdalen [22 July] since we are about to fulfill the

condition by proceeding in person to Scotland. Collectors' names are to be at the Exchequer before the octave of St. John Baptist [1 July].
Teste me ipso, 12 June 1385.[1]
Collectors.
Sleaford, 2 July, the following commissions were issued:
to the prior of St. Katherine outside Lincoln for the archdeaconries of Lincoln and Stow;
to the prior of Bicester for the archdeaconry of Oxford;
to the abbot of St. James, Northampton for the archdeaconry of Northampton;
to the abbot of Owston for the archdeaconry of Leicester;
to the prior of Caldwell for the archdeaconry of Bedford;
to the rector of [the house of] Ashridge for the archdeaconry of Buckingham;
to the prior of Huntingdon for the archdeaconry of Huntingdon.

> [1] For the mandate to collect see *CFR 1383–91*, p. 97.

290. [ff. 45–45v] Breve contra non solventes subsidii vis and viijd
Exchequer *levari faciatis de bonis et beneficiis ecclesiasticis sicut pluries*, returnable on the morrow of Michaelmas, against the following persons in the archdeaconries of Lincoln and Stow who have not paid the subsidy of 6s 8d:
John [Snoring] rector of Southorpe, in the archdeaconry of Stow and the deanery of Corringham;
Thomas Cardinal chaplain in West Halton, archdeaconry of Stow, deanery of Manlake;
Thomas Pampylon' chaplain in Skillington;
William Tykynton rector of Stoke, Beltisloe deanery;
John Forthyngton chaplain of Spilsby in Bolingbroke deanery;
Richard Wenton chaplain 'ad pollem for';
John Blakenham chaplain in St. Paul [in the Bail, Lincoln] church;
John lately chaplain with James Bekeryng in the deanery of the Christianity of Lincoln;
John Palgrave, chaplain of Beckingham chantry in Loveden deanery;
William chaplain with Simon Simeon;
John Robcot chaplain at the same;
Richard chaplain in Lavington, Belistloe deanery;
Thomas chaplain in Kyme;
John Bunch chaplain in the same;
Thomas Evedon chaplain in Scredington, Lafford deanery;
John Schefford, chaplain in Navenby;
William de Stepulton chaplain in Harmston;
John Reynes chaplain in Dogdyke chantry, Longoboby [deanery];
John de Leverington chaplain in 'Sutton';
Bartholomew de Neuton chaplain of Tydd [St. Mary];
Roger Rakedall chaplain in Frieston [priory], Holland deanery;
Thomas chaplain with domina de Claythorpe in Calcewaith [deanery];
Henry Besewyk chaplain in Grimsby;
Richard chaplain in Mareham Le Fen (Marum), Horncastle deanery;
John rector of Wyham (Wyhum) [Louthesk deanery];
William Conston chaplain in Barton upon Humber;
John chaplain in Barrow upon Humber;

William de Welton chaplain in 'Somerby';
William chaplain in Searby;
John chaplain in Hundon;
William Cateryk rector of Wroot;
Thomas de Topclyf chaplain of Walter de Topclyf of Somerby in Corringham deanery;
Richard Beverlay chaplain in Broughton [by Brigg] in Manlake deanery;
which John rector of Southorpe, Thomas Cardinall etc. owe us for the subsidy granted 4 Richard II in the archdeaconries of Lincoln and Stow.
Teste Robert de Plesyngton, 16 May 1385. From the memoranda roll of Michaelmas 5 Richard II *visus compoti*, roll 15 and the memoranda roll of Michaelmas 8 Richard II, *brevia attorn' (sic)* roll 20.   Staverton.
[See **261**, **269**]

291. [f. 45v] Breve contra dominum Thomam Hervy
Exchequer *levari faciatis de bonis et beneficiis ecclesiasticis sicut pluries*, returnable on the morrow of Michaelmas, against Thomas Hervy for 36s 8½d owed to the king, being arrears for the custody of certain tenements in Billingsgate ward, London, which Mary de St. Pol, late countess of Pembroke held as dower after the death of Aymer de Valence, late earl of Pembroke of the inheritance of John, son and heir of John Hastings, late earl of Pembroke who died under age and in the custody of Edward III, from 7 March 51 Edward III until the coming of age of the said heir.
Teste Robert de Plesyngton, 24 April 1385.
[See **262**, **270**]

292. Breve contra Magistrum Thomam Brembre
Exchequer *levari faciatis de bonis et beneficiis ecclesiasticis*, returnable on the octave of Michaelmas, against Master Robert Brembre[1] for 106s 8d, being debts owed to the king by Thomas Brembre rector of Tusmore (Thoresmere)[2] viz. 24s for the two tenths granted by the clergy in 1 Richard II; 12s for the second tenth of the triennial tenth granted 43 Edward III; and against the warden of East Hendred (Esthenreth) chapel 3s 4d for a moiety of the clerical tenth granted 7 Richard II in the archdeaconry of Winchester (Wynton).[3]
Teste Robert de Plesyngton, 19 June 1385.

> [1] See *BRUO*, I.259.
> [2] The fullest discussion of the career and interests of Thomas Brembre is to be found in Patricia H. Coulstock, *The Collegiate Church of Wimborne Minster*, Studies in the History of Medieval Religion 5 (Woodbridge, 1993), chap. IX, 'The Chantry of Dean Thomas Brembre', pp. 147–160.
> [3] East Hendred, now in Oxon., was formerly in Berks. For some of the administrative complications of this place see *The Lay Subsidy of 1334*, ed. R.E. Glasscock (British Academy: London, 1975), pp. 8 and n. 4, 11.

293. Breve pro parliamento
Summons to attend parliament at Westminster on the Friday after the feast of St. Luke the Evangelist [20 Oct.], with *premunientes* clause.[1]
Teste me ipso, 3 Sept. 1385.
[f. 46] Ad premuniendum
EXECUTION. At Sleaford on 24 Sept. 1385 all the archdeacons' officials were written to to warn the clergy to be at All Saints church Northampton on Monday the feast

of St. Denys [9 Oct.], to elect proctors, and to the abbot of St. James, Northampton and John Boudon official of the archdeacon of Northampton, the archdeaconry being vacant, to receive the certificates and arrange the proctors' expenses, and to certify to the bishop the names of the proctors. However, they did not certify.

> 1   Printed *RDP*, IV.717; see also *CCR 1385–9*, p. 83.

294.   Breve de recipiendo iuramentum custumar' de Boston
Mandate to receive the oath of John de Holmton of Sleaford one of the collectors of customs of the port of Boston, and at once to inform Chancery when this had been done.
Teste me ipso, 11 Oct. 1385.[1]
RETURN. Certificate (in which the writ is contained) that the bishop has received the oath of John de Holmeton.
Sleaford 26 Oct. 1385.[2]
Forma iuramenti.

Vous jurrez que vous ferez continuele demeure en le port de Saint Botulp' et serverrez le charge de leyne, quirs, et peulz launuz, et toutz autres merchandises et choses custumables et le noumbr' des saks el dite porte et quantque en vous est ne soeffrez que nostre seigneur le Roy eit damage ne perde illoques et que loial acompt ont rendrez et des issues des dits custumes loialment respondrez sanx fauyime ou fraude faire en nul pointe. Si vous eide dieu et les seintz.

> 1   Holmton or Holmeton, a leading merchant of Boston (*CCR 1377–81*, pp. 168–9), was only briefly a customs collector in the town during the financial year 1385–6 (PRO E 356/14), though in 1388 he was a collector of tunnage and poundage in the same port (E356/5, 13). These references are derived from S.H. Rigby, 'Boston and Grimsby in the Middle Ages' (Ph.D. thesis, London, 1982), p. 402, who also provides a biography of Holmeton on pp. 424–5.
> 2   See Mabel H. Mills, 'The Collectors of Customs', in William A. Morris and Joseph R. Strayer, eds., *The English Government at Work, 1327–1336, Vol. II: Fiscal Administration* (Cambridge, Mass., 1947), pp. 170–6; also Anthony Steel, 'The Collectors of the Customs at Newcastle upon Tyne in the Reign of Richard II', in J. Conway Davies, ed., *Studies Presented to Sir Hilary Jenkinson* (Oxford, 1957), pp. 390–413.

295.   [ff. 46–46v. A new hand begins at this point.] Breve contra Rectores de Hyngham et Drayton'
Exchequer *venire faciatis sicut pluries*, returnable on the morrow of the Purification of the Virgin [3 Feb.], against Master David Bradwell rector of Heyham on the Hill and Roger Walden rector of Fenny Drayton to answer John Clanvowe knight and Brother Ralph Maylock a foreigner, proctors of the abbot of Lyre and farmers of his property in England, about £14 being arrears of the pension of 40s p.a. due from Heyham church, and 70s being arrears of a pension of 8s p.a. due from Fenny Drayton church, as the farmers cannot pay their farm until they recover the money. *Teste* Robert de Plesyngton, 10 Nov. 1385. Note of return of no lay fee by the sheriff of Leicestershire on the morrow of the Ascension [12 May].
Retornum.

On 24 Jan. 1386, at Sleaford, return was made in this form: the said David was warned to comply with the writ. We could not compel the said Roger Walden rector of Drayton because he is not a clerk in our diocese nor was he at the time of the receipt of the writ.
[See **286**]

296. [f. 46v] <u>Commissio ad colligendum et levandum decimam domino regi concessam</u>

Mandate to appoint collectors of the grant, made on 10 December last, of a tenth payable on the Annunciation of the Virgin [25 March] and the octave of Trinity [24 June 1386], and to signify the collectors' names to the Exchequer by the octave of Hilary.

Teste me ipso, 20 Dec. 1385.[1]

<u>Execution.</u> The writ is contained in a commission to the abbot of Missenden and Master John Evot archdeacon of Buckingham as collectors in the archdeaconry of Buckingham.

Sleaford 2 Jan. 1386.

<u>Certificatorium scaccario.</u>

Sleaford 10 Jan. 1386 a certificate was sent to the Exchequer of the collectors' names, viz.:

in the archdeaconries of Lincoln and Stow: the abbot of Thornton

in the archdeaconry of Leicester: the abbot of St. Mary [in the Meadows], Leicester

in the archdeaconry of Northampton: the abbot of Pipewell (Pipwell)

in the archdeaconry of Oxford: the abbot of Osney

in the archdeaconry of Buckingham: the abbot of Missenden and Master John Evot, archdeacon of Buckingham

in the archdeaconry of Bedford: the prior of Newnham

in the archdeaconry of Huntingdon: the abbot of Sawtry and the prior of St. Neots.

   [1]   See *CFR 1383–91*, pp. 124, 134.

297. [ff. 46v–47] [Unheaded]

Exchequer *levari faciatis de bonis et beneficiis ecclesiasticis sicut alias*, returnable on the quindene of Hilary, against Master Robert Brembre for 106s 8d, being debts owed to the king by Thomas Brembre rector of Tusmore (Thoresmere) viz. 24s for the two tenths granted by the clergy in 1 Richard II; 12s for the second tenth of the triennial tenth granted 43 Edward III, and against the warden of East Hendred chapel 3s 4d for the a moiety of the clerical tenth granted 7 Richard II in the archdeaconry of Winchester (Wynton).

Teste Robert de Plesyngton, 8 Dec. 1385. By the great roll of 7 Richard II in the counties of Oxfordshire and Berkshire and a certain schedule given to the court by John Holcote lately sheriff in Oxfordshire and Berkshire which is among the bills of Easter term 8 Richard II and the Memoranda roll of 9 Richard II, Michaelmas term, *brevia retornabilia* roll 9.

[See **292**]

298. [f. 47] <u>Breve contra Rectorem de Denham</u>

Common Pleas *venire faciatis sicut alias*, returnable on the quindene of Easter [6 May], against John Wyke rector of Denham to answer the abbot of Westminster for a plea of debt of £30, being arrears of a rent of 30s p.a. Note of return of no lay fee by the sheriff of Buckinghamshire.

Teste Robert Bealknapp, 8 Feb. 1386.

299. <u>Breve contra Rectorem de Passenham</u>

Common Pleas *venire faciatis*, returnable on the quindene of Easter [16 May], against Thomas Ravenser rector of Passenham to answer the abbot of Cirencester

for a plea of debt of 48 marks, being arrears of rent of 4 marks p.a. Note of return of no lay fee by the sheriff of Northamptonshire on the octave of Hilary.
Teste Robert Bealknap', 28 Jan. 1386.

300. Breve contra Rectorem de Peighelton'
Common Pleas *venire faciatis*, returnable on the quindene of Easter [16 May] against Simon rector of Peckleton (Peighelton) to answer the prior of Ware for a plea of debt of £6, being arrears of rent of 20s p.a. Note of return of no lay fee by the sheriff of Leicestershire on the Octave of the Purification of the Virgin [9 Feb.].
Teste Robert Bealknap', 16 Feb. 1386.

301. Breve contra Rectorem de Passenham sicut alias
Common Pleas *venire faciatis sicut alias*, returnable on the quindene of Trinity [1 July], against Thomas Ravenser rector of Passenham to answer the abbot of Cirencester for a plea of debt of 48 marks, being arrears of rent of 4 marks p.a. Note of return of no lay fee by the sheriff of Northamptonshire on the octave of Hilary.
Teste Robert Bealknap, 26 May 1386.
[See **299**]

302. [f. 47v. A new hand begins here.] Breve contra non solventes subsidium etc.
Exchequer *levari faciatis de bonis et beneficiis ecclesiasticis sicut pluries*, returnable on the morrow of Michaelmas, against the following who have not paid the subsidy of 6s 8d:
John [Snoring] rector of Southorpe, in the archdeaconry of Stow and the deanery of Corringham;
Thomas Cardinal chaplain in West Halton, archdeaconry of Stow, deanery of Manlake;
Thomas Pampylon' chaplain in Skillington;
William Tykynton rector of Stoke, Beltisloe deanery;
John Forthyngton chaplain of Spilsby in Bolingbroke deanery;
Richard Wenton chaplain 'ad pollen for';
John Blakenham chaplain in St. Paul [in the Bail, Lincoln] church;
John lately chaplain with James Bekeryng in the deanery of Christianity of Lincoln;
John Palgrave, chaplain of Beckingham chantry in Loveden deanery;
William chaplain with Simon Simeon;
John Robcot chaplain at the same;
Richard chaplain in Lavington, Beltisloe deanery;
Thomas chaplain in Kyme;
John Bunch chaplain in the same;
Thomas Evedon chaplain in Scredington, Lafford deanery;
John Schefford chaplain in Navenby;
William de Stepulton chaplain in Harmston;
John Reynes chaplain in Dogdyke chantry, Longoboby [deanery];
John de Leverington chaplain in 'Sutton';
Bartholomew de Neuton chaplain of Tydd [St. Mary];
Roger Rakedall chaplain in Frieston [priory], Holland deanery;
Thomas chaplain with domina de Claythorpe in Calcewaith [deanery];
Henry Besewyk chaplain in Grimsby;
Richard chaplain in Mareham le Fen, Horncastle deanery;

John rector of Wyham, [Louthesk deanery];
William Conston chaplain in Barton upon Humber;
John chaplain in Barrow upon Humber;
William de Welton chaplain in 'Somerby';
William chaplain in Searby;
John chaplain in Hundon;
William Cateryk rector of Wroot;
Thomas de Topclyf chaplain of Walter de Topclyf of Somerby in Corringham deanery;
Richard Beverlay chaplain in Broughton [by Brigg] in Manlake deanery;
which John rector of Southorp, Thomas Cardinall etc. owe us for the subsidy granted 4 Richard II in the archdeaconries of Lincoln and Stow.
Teste Robert de Plesyngton, 14 July 1386. From the memoranda roll of 5 Richard II, Michaelmas term, *visus compoti* roll 15 and the memoranda roll of 9 Richard II Michaelmas term *brevia retornabilia* roll 3.
[See **261**, **269**, **290**]

303.   Breve contra Robert Brembre
Exchequer *levari faciatis de bonis et beneficiis ecclesiasticis sicut pluries*, returnable on the quindene of Michaelmas, against Robert Brembre for 106s 8d, being debts owed to the king by Thomas Brembre rector of Tusmore (Thoresmere) viz. 24s for the two tenths granted by the clergy in 1 Richard II; 12s for the second tenth of the triennial tenth granted 43 Edward III, and against the warden of East Hendred chapel 3s 4d for a moiety of the clerical tenth granted 7 Richard II in the archdeaconry of Winchester.
Teste Robert de Plesyngton, 20 July 1386.
[See **292**, **267**]

304.   Breve contra dominum Thomas Hervy
Exchequer *levari faciatis de bonis et beneficiis ecclesiasticis*, returnable on the morrow of Michaelmas, against Thomas Hervy for 36s 8½d owed to the king, being arrears for the custody of certain tenements in Billingsgate ward, London, which Mary de St. Pol, late countess of Pembroke held as dower after the death of Aymer de Valence, late earl of Pembroke of the inheritance of John, son and heir of John Hastings, late earl of Pembroke who died under age and in the custody of Edward III, from 7 March 51 Edward III until the coming of age of the said heir.
Teste Robert de Plesyngton, 17 July 1386. By the memoranda roll of 9 Richard II Michaelmas term, *brevia retornabilia*.
[See **262**, **270**, **291**]

305.   Breve pro parliamento
Summons to attend a parliament at Westminster on 1 October, with *premunientes* clause.
Teste me ipso, Osney 8 Aug. 1386.[1]

   [1]   Printed *RDP*, IV.721; see also *CCR 1385–8*, p. 259.

306. [f. 48] <u>Breve contra Rectorem ecclesie de Blankenay</u>
Common Pleas *venire faciatis*, returnable on the octave of Michaelmas, against John rector of Blankney (Blaunkenay) to answer the prior of Thurgarton for a plea of debt of 13 marks, being arrears of rent of 1 mark p.a. Note of return of no lay fee by the sheriff of Lincolnshire on the octave of Trinity [24 June].
Teste Robert Bealknap', 8 July 1386.

307. <u>Breve contra Rectorem de Blaunkenay</u>
Common Pleas *venire faciatis sicut alias*, returnable on the quindene of Martinmas [25 Nov.], against the rector of Blankney, to answer the prior of Thurgarton [see **306** above].
Teste Robert Bealknap, 18 Oct. 1386.
<u>Iuramentum Rectoris predicti.</u>
On 21 Nov. 1386 at Sleaford, before Master John de Banbury, John rector of Blankney (Blankenay) swore that he would pay the money in accordance with the writ at the instance of the prior of Thurgarton, and pledged himself under pain of £20 in the presence of Master Thomas Dent vicar of Kirkby Green (Kyrkeby),[1] Richard Dalby, Robert Scarle, John Lidington, John Haversham and others.

   1   Kirkby Green is the adjacent parish to Blankney.

308. <u>Breve de inquirendo an Hugo Bray sit bastardus necne</u>
Itinerant Justices *inquiratis de bastardia*, returnable to the king's justices at Northampton on the Monday before St. Margaret the Virgin [16 July], in the following case. Know that since Hugh Bray of Broughton brought in our court before Roger de Fulthorp etc. justices of assize in Northamptonshire an assize of *novel disseisin* against John Latroner and Helena his wife and others and complained that they had disseised him of two messuages, one carucate and one virgate of land and two acres of meadow with appurtenances in Charwelton (Charlton) and West Farndon (Farendon) near Woodford Halse (Woodeford); to this John and Helena responded that they held the property in common with Thomas Bray of Wooton (Wotton) by which they held a moiety of the property, and the assize should never have been brought because one Henry Bray was formerly seised of a moiety of the property 'et de alia medietate in domino suo ut de feodo'; this Henry had two daughters, viz., Isabella and Alice, and Elena was the daughter of Isabella and was now the wife of the said John Latoner, and Thomas Bray was the son of Alice, and when Henry died Helena and Thomas entered his property as heirs and next of kin. To which Hugh asserted that he was the heir of Henry being the son of William son of Henry, but John and Helena said he was a bastard and could not inherit. He denied this. Mandate to convoke an enquiry as to whether Hugh Bray is a bastard.
Teste Robert de Fulthorp', Northampton, 7 Dec. 1386.
<u>Littera pro eodem.</u>
Sleaford 19 Dec. 1386 a commission was issued to the official of the archdeacon of Leicester, the abbot of Owston and Robert Oudeby rector of Stonton Wyville (Staunton Wyville) to hold an inquisition and to certify its findings before 12 July under authentic seal or the subscription of any notary.
EXECUTION. [Reg. 12, f. 340v] <u>Processus in causa bastardie pro Hugone Bray de Broghton'.</u>
To the bishop from the official of archdeacon of Leicester, the abbot of Owston and Master Robert rector of Stonton Wyville church: in virtue of these letters [the royal

writ and the episcopal commission, both recited] we convened an enquiry and found that Hugh Bray is legitimate and not a bastard. The names of the witnesses and their depositions are on the annexed schedule.

Gumley (Gummendele) 6 June 1387.

Admissio testium.

The witnesses were examined in the parish church of Bilstone (Billesdon), on 19 April 1387, in the presence of the three commissaries.

Examinacio testium in eadem causa.

Hugh Malozours aged 49 years, and of free condition and good fame [f. 341], deposed that William Bray was married in church to Joanna, and that Hugh Bray was born in wedlock. The marriage took place in Laughton (Laghton') church two years before the first plague, between the feasts of Easter and Pentecost.

Geoffrey Laronuz aged 60 years and more, of free condition and good fame, was present in Laughton church two years before the first plague between Easter and Pentecost when the marriage took place. William Bray and Joanna held hands and pledged themselves with the usual words saying, "I William Bray accept you Joanna as my wife for better for worse" ('Ego Willelmus Bray accipio te Johannam in uxorem mean pro meliori, pro peiori etc.'), and then Joanna likewise said, "I Joanna accept you William as my lawful husband for better for worse" ('Ego Johanna accipio te Willelmum in maritum meum legitimum pro meliori, pro peiori etc.'), and then the marriage was solemnized in the face of the congregation ('in facie ecclesie de Laughton'). There were present at this contract and solemnization both John Neuton and many other whose names he does not recall, and he said that afterwards William and Joanna lived at Lubbenham where Joanna gave birth to Hugh Bray, and he knew that Hugh was the natural and legitimate child of William and Joanna. He concurred in all respects with the evidence given by Hugh Malazours, and deposed that this was the public voice and opinion in the village of Lubbenham and surrounding places, and and his testimony was not influenced by entreaty or bribes ('non est corruptus prece nec precis').

John Sivert of Laughton aged 50 years and more, of free condition and good fame, was present when the contract was made between William Bray and Joanna for marriage.

John Mariot aged 60 and more, of free condition and good fame, concurred in all that Geoffrey Laronuz had testified.

John Neuton' aged 60 years and more gave evidence about the wedding of William and Joanna, between Easter and Pentecost two years before the first pestilence, and said that William and Joanna lived in the town of Lubbenham [Lubenham] (Lobenham) for three years and that in the middle of that time Joanna gave birth to Hugh [f. 341v] and that everyone knew that he was her legitimate son.

Geoffrey Sivert aged 60 years and more, of free condition and good fame, concurred in everything that Geoffrey Laronuz had said.

Thomas Wygeyn aged 60 years and more, of free condition and good fame, concurred in everything that Geoffrey Laronuz had said.

Walter Wygeyn aged 60 years and more, of free condition and good fame, said that William and Joanna lived in the town of Lubbenham [Lubenham] (Lobenham) for three years and that in the middle of that time Joanna gave birth to Hugh and that everyone knew that he was her legitimate son.

John Dawe aged 30 years and more, of free condition and good fame, concurred with Walter Wygeyn.

Certificatorium Justiciariis that Hugh Bray was legitimate.
London 28 June 1387.

309. [Reg. 12B, f. 48v] Breve contra non solventes subsidium sicut pluries.
Exchequer *levari faciatis de bonis et beneficiis ecclesiasticis sicut pluries*, return-able on the morrow of Hilary, against the following who have not paid the subsidy of 6s 8d:
John [Snoring] rector of Southorpe, in the archdeaconry of Stow and the deanery of Corringham;
Thomas Cardinal chaplain in West Halton, archdeaconry of Stow, deanery of Manlake;
Thomas Pampilon' chaplain in Skillington;
William Tykynton rector of Stoke, Beltisloe deanery;
John Forthyngton chaplain of Spilsby in Bolingbroke deanery;
Richard Wenton chaplain 'ad pollen for';
John Blakenham chaplain in St. Paul [in the Bail, Lincoln] church;
John lately chaplain with James Bekeryng in the deanery of Christianity of Lincoln;
John Palgrave, chaplain of Beckingham chantry in Loveden deanery;
William chaplain with Simon Simeon;
John Robcot chaplain at the same;
Richard chaplain in Lavington, Beltisloe deanery;
Thomas chaplain in Kyme;
John Bunch chaplain in the same;
Thomas Evedon chaplain in Scredington, Lafford deanery;
John Schefford chaplain in Navenby;
William de Stepulton chaplain in Harmston;
John Reynes chaplain in Dogdyke chantry, Longoboby [deanery];
John de Leverington chaplain in 'Sutton';
Bartholomew de Neuton chaplain of Tydd [St. Mary];
Roger Rakedall chaplain in Frieston [priory], Holland deanery;
Thomas chaplain with 'domina' de Claythorpe in Calcewaith [deanery];
Henry Besewyk chaplain in Grimsby;
Richard chaplain in Mareham Le Fen, Horncastle deanery;
John rector of Wyham, [Louthesk deanery];
William Conston chaplain in Barton upon Humber;
John chaplain in Barrow upon Humber;
William de Welton chaplain in 'Somerby';
William chaplain in Searby;
John chaplain in Hundon;
William Cateryk rector of Wroot;
Thomas de Topclyf chaplain of Walter de Topclyf of Somerby in Corringham deanery;
Richard Beverlay chaplain in Broughton [by Brigg] in Manlake deanery;
which John rector of Southorp, Thomas Cardinall etc. owe us for the subsidy granted 4 Richard II in the archdeaconries of Lincoln and Stow.
Teste Robert de Plesyngton, 14 Nov. 1386. By a note from the memoranda roll of 5 Richard II Michaelmas term, view of accounts roll 15, and the memoranda roll of 10 Richard II, Michaelmas term among *brevia retornabilia*.
[See **216**, **269**, **290**, **302**]

310.   Breve sicut pluries contra etc. Brembre

Exchequer *levari faciatis de bonis ecclesiasticis sicut pluries*, returnable on the quindene of Hilary, against Master Robert Brembre for 106s 8d, being debts owed to the king by Thomas Brembre rector of Tusmore (Thoresmere) viz. 24s for the two tenths granted by the clergy in 1 Richard II; 12s for the second tenth of the triennial tenth granted 43 Edward III, and against the warden of East Hendred chapel 3s 4d for a moiety of the clerical tenth granted 7 Richard II in the archdeaconry of Winchester.

Teste Robert de Plesyngton, 23 Nov. 1386. By the Great Roll of 7 Richard II in Oxfordshire [and] Berkshire, and by a certain schedule delivered to the court by John Holcote lately [sheriff] of Oxfordshire and Berkshire which is among the bills of Easter term 8 Richard II and the memoranda roll of 10 Richard II, Michaelmas term among *brevia retornabilia* roll 13.

[See **292, 297, 303**]

311.   Breve de certiorando Temesford

Chancery *certiorari* concerning the last person admitted and instituted to Tempsford (Temesford) church by the bishop or his commissary.

Teste me ipso, 30 Oct. 1386.

312.   Breve sicut pluries Blaunkenay

Common Pleas *venire faciatis sicut pluries*, returnable on the quindene of Hilary, against John rector of Blankney (Blaunkenay) to answer the prior of Thurgarton for a plea of debt of 13 marks, being arrears of rent of 1 mark p.a. Note of return of no lay fee by the sheriff of Lincolnshire on the octave of Trinity [24 June].

Teste Robert de Bealknap, 28 Oct. 1386.

RETURN. On 14 Jan. 1387 at Sleaford return was made in this manner: John, rector of Blankney was warned to comply with the writ and to appear at the day and place given.

[See **306, 307**]

313.   [f. 49] Breve de certiorando Stokton'

Chancery *certiorari (scrutatis registris)* concerning the tenor of the letters of institution and induction of James Walsh to the church of Great Staughton (Stokton) made at the presentation by Edward III, and the inquisition made by the then archdeacon of Huntingdon or his official or commissary.

Teste me ipso, 24 1385 [*sic*, 9 Richard II].

314.   Breve de certiorando Midelton and Colyntre

Chancery *certiorari (scrutatis registris)* concerning those presented to a moiety of the church of Middleton and Collingtree from the first year of Henry father of John king of England ('ab anno regni domini H. patris domini Johannis quondam Regis Anglie progenitoris nostri primo'),[1] and by whom they were presented, and on what title.

Teste me ipso, 26 Nov. 1386.

[See **144**]

---

[1]   1 Henry II, 19 Dec. 1154 – 18 Dec. 1155; this is earlier than the limit of legal memory which was set by Edward I at 3 Sept. 1189.

315.   [f. 49] <u>Breve sicut pluries contra Rectorem de Passenham</u>
Common Pleas *venire faciatis sicut pluries*, returnable on the octave of Hilary, against Thomas Ravenser rector of Passenham your clerk to answer the abbot of Cirencester for a plea of debt of 48 marks, being arrears of rent of 4 marks p.a. Note of return of no lay fee by the sheriff of Northamptonshire on the octave of Hilary.
Teste Robert Bealknapp', 22 Oct. 1386.
[See **299, 301**]

316.   <u>Breve contra Rectorem de Kyngham</u>
Common Pleas *venire faciatis*, returnable on the quindene of Hilary, against William Aubyn rector of Kingham, to answer the abbot of Walden for a plea of debt of £6 being arrears of a rent of 20s p.a. Note of return of no lay fee by the sheriff of Oxfordshire.
Teste Robert Bealknap', 24 Nov. 1386.
[See **272**]

317.   <u>Breve pro subsidio levando</u>
Mandate to appoint collectors of the moiety of a tenth granted in the convocation of 5 November last in St. Paul's cathedral [London] and payable on the quindene of Easter [21 April], and to notify the Exchequer of the collectors' names by the quindene of the Purification [16 Feb.]
Teste me ipso, 17 Jan. 1387.[1]
EXECUTION. These collectors were deputed:
in the archdeaconries of Lincoln and Stow: the abbot of Crowland
in the archdeaconry of Oxford: the prior of Bicester
in the archdeaconry of Leicester: the prior of Launde
in the archdeaconry of Northampton: the prior of Chacombe
in the archdeaconry of Bedford: the abbot of Woburn
in the archdeaconry of Huntingdon: the abbot of Ramsey
in the archdeaconry of Buckingham: the abbot of Biddlesden (Biddledon)

[1]   For the summoning of this convocation see Reg. 12, ff. 333v–334. The request for a tax grant was greeted with great suspicion and the grant was made only grudgingly; the first moiety, the subject of this writ, was absolute, but the second was granted only on conditions, and was not to be raised if the king concluded a truce or peace, Lambeth Palace Library, Reg. William Courtenay (Cant.) I, f. 84v. The gathering of this tax provoked considerable opposition in Lincoln diocese, see *CPR 1385–9*, p. 282.

318.   <u>Breve contra Rectorem de Alesby</u>
Common Pleas *venire faciatis*, returnable on the quindene of Easter [21 April], against Henry rector of Aylesby (Alesby) to answer the dean and chapter of Lincoln about a plea of debt of £10, being arrears of rent of £10 p.a. Note of return of no lay fee by the sheriff of Lincolnshire on the octave of the Purification [9 Feb.].
Teste Robert Bealknap, 12 Feb. 1387.

319.   <u>Breve contra Rectorem de Muresleye</u>
Common Pleas *venire faciatis*, returnable on the quindene of Easter [21 April], against John Wardeyen rector of Mursley (Muresleye) to answer the prioress of Nuneaton (Newenton) about a plea of debt of £10 being arrears of a rent of 40s p.a.

Teste Robert Bealknap, 8 Feb. 1387.
[See **258**, **264**]

320. [f. 49v] Breve contra Rectorem de Passenham
Common Pleas *venire faciatis sicut pluries*, returnable on the quindene of Easter
[21 April], against Thomas Ravenser rector of Passenham to answer the abbot of
Cirencester for a plea of debt of 48 marks, being arrears of rent of 4 marks p.a.
Teste Robert Bealknap, 28 Jan. 1387.
[See **309**, **315**]

321. Breve contra certas personas pro subsidio levando
Exchequer *levari faciatis de bonis et beneficiis ecclesiasticis sicut pluries*, return-
able on the morrow of the close of Easter [15 April] against the following who have
not paid the clerical subsidy levied at the rate of 6s 8d:
John [Snoring] rector of Southorp, in the archdeaconry of Stow and the deanery of
Corringham;
Thomas Cardinal chaplain in West Halton, archdeaconry of Stow, deanery of
Manlake;
Thomas Pampilion chaplain in Skillington;
William Tykynton rector of Stoke, Beltisloe deanery;
John Forthyngton chaplain of Spilsby in Bolingbroke deanery;
Richard Wenton chaplain 'ad pollen for';
John Blakenham chaplain in St. Paul [in the Bail, Lincoln] church;
John lately chaplain with James Bekeryng in the deanery of Christianity of Lincoln;
John Palgrave, chaplain of Beckingham chantry in Loveden deanery;
William chaplain with Simon Simeon;
John Robcot chaplain at the same;
Richard chaplain in Lavington, Beltisloe deanery;
Thomas chaplain in Kyme;
John Bunch chaplain in the same;
Thomas Evedon chaplain in Scredington, Lafford deanery;
John Schefford chaplain in Navenby;
William de Stepulton chaplain in Harmston;
John Reynes chaplain in Dogdyke chantry, Longoboby [deanery];
John de Leverington chaplain in 'Sutton';
Bartholomew de Neuton chaplain of Tydd [St. Mary];
Roger Rakedall chaplain in Frieston [priory], Holland deanery;
Thomas chaplain with domina de Claythorpe in Calcewaith [deanery];
Henry Besewyk chaplain in Grimsby;
Richard chaplain in Mareham Le Fen, Horncastle deanery;
John rector of Wyham, [Louthesk deanery];
William Conston chaplain in Barton upon Humber;
John chaplain in Barrow upon Humber;
William de Welton chaplain in 'Somerby';
William chaplain in Searby;
John chaplain in Hundon;
William Cateryk rector of Wroot;
Thomas de Topclyf chaplain of Walter de Topclyf of Somerby in Corringham
deanery;

Richard Beverlay chaplain in Broughton [by Brigg] in Manlake deanery;
which John rector of Southorp, Thomas Cardinall etc. owe us for the subsidy
granted 4 Richard II in the archdeaconries of Lincoln and Stow.
Teste John Cary, 14 Feb. 1387. By the memoranda roll of 5 Richard II Michaelmas
term, among view of accounts roll 15, and the memoranda roll of 10 Richard II
Michaelmas term, *brevia retornabilia* roll 5.
[See **261, 269, 290, 302, 309**]

322. Breve ut supra
Exchequer *levari faciatis de bonis et beneficiis ecclesiasticis sicut pluries*, return-
able on the morrow of the close of Easter [15 April], against Master Robert Brembre
for 106s 8d, being debts owed to the king by Thomas Brembre rector of Tusmore
(Thoresmere) viz. 24s for the two tenths granted by the clergy in 1 Richard II; 12s
for the second tenth of the triennial tenth granted 43 Edward III, and against the
warden of East Hendred chapel 3s 4d for a moiety of the clerical tenth granted 7
Richard II in the archdeaconry of Winchester.
Teste John Cary, 20 Feb. 1387.
[See **292, 297, 303, 310**]

323. [f. 50] Breve ad orandum pro comite darundell'
Request for prayers for the campaign of Richard earl of Arundel whom the king has
appointed to sail on his service at sea, the lords and others of his company.
Teste me ipso, 20 March 1387.[1]
EXECUTION. Conclusio pro eodem.
Contained in a mandate from the bishop to the archdeacon of Lincoln or his official,
ordering execution of the writ by all religious and seculars; solemn processions are
to be made on the fourth and sixth ferias (working days) and masses celebrated and
special prayers said, for the king and for the church and people of England and
especially the expedition of the noble earl and for John [of Gaunt] king of Castile
and Leon, duke of Lancaster, with an indulgence of 40 days for those who comply.
Sleaford 2 April 1387.

   [1] Printed, Rymer, *Foedera* VII.554–5; calendared *CCR 1385–9*, p. 309. See also SCH 18, pp.
215–28.

324. Breve contra rectorem de Staunton Harecourt
Common Pleas *venire faciatis*, returnable three weeks from Easter [28 April],
against John Harewell rector of Stanton Harcourt, your clerks to answer the abbot
of Reading (Redyng) for a plea of 90 marks being arrears of rent of 20 marks p.a.
Note of return of no lay fee by the sheriff of Oxfordshire before the justices at
Westminster on the octave of the Purification of the Virgin.
Teste Robert Bealknapp', 10 Feb. 1387.
[See **127, 134**]

325. Breve contra Rectorem de Kyngham
Common Pleas *venire faciatis sicut alias*, returnable on the quindene of Easter [21
April] against William Aubyn rector of Kingham, to answer the abbot of Walden
for a plea of debt of £6 being arrears of a rent of 20s p.a. Note of return of no lay
fee by the sheriff of Oxfordshire.
Teste Robert Bealknap, 12 Feb. 1387.

EXECUTION. The bishop caused the said William to be warned to appear at the place and day mentioned in execution of the writ.
[See **272**, **316**]

326.   [f. 50v] Breve contra Rectorem ecclesie de Drayton
Exchequer *venire faciatis*, returnable on the morrow of Ascension [17 May], against Master David Bradwell rector of Heyham on the Hill and Roger Walden rector of Fenny Drayton to answer John Clanvowe knight and Brother Ralph Maylock a foreigner, proctors of the abbot of Lyre and farmers of his property in England, about £14 being arrears of the pension of 40s p.a. due from Heyham church, and 70s being arrears of a pension of 8s p.a. due from Fenny Drayton church, as the farmers cannot pay their farm until they recover the money. Note of return of no lay fees by the sheriff of Leicestershire on the quindene of the Purification [3 Feb.].
Teste John Cary, 20 Feb. 1387.
[See **286**, **295**]

327.   Breve contra Rectorem de Alesby
Common Pleas *venire faciatis sicut alias*, returnable on the quindene of Trinity [17 June], against Henry rector of Aylesby (Alesby) to answer the dean and chapter of Lincoln about a plea of debt of £10, being arrears of rent of £10 p.a. Note of return of no lay fee by the sheriff of Lincolnshire.
Teste Robert Bealknap, 12 May 1387.
[See **318**]

328.   Breve contra Rectorem de Passenham sicut pluries
Common Pleas *venire faciatis sicut pluries*, returnable on the octave of Michaelmas, against Thomas Ravenser rector of Passenham to answer the abbot of Cirencester for a plea of debt of 48 marks, being arrears of rent of 4 marks p.a.
Teste Robert Bealknap, 10 July 1387.
[See **299**, **301**, **315**]

329.   [f. 51] Breve pro Hugone Bray etc.
Itinerant Justices *inquiratis de bastardia*, returnable before the king's justices at Northampton on the Monday in the first week of Lent [25 Feb.], whether Hugh Bray is a bastard and mandate to conduct an enquiry to discover his status.
Teste Roger de Fulthorp, Northampton, 16 July 1387.
[See **308**]

330.   Breve de certiorando Boseworth'
Chancery *certiorari (scrutatis registris)* concerning who and how many people have been presented to Husbands Bosworth church from 1314 to 1371 and at whose presentation.
Teste me ipso, 20 June 1387.

331.   Consultacio pro parte prioris de Bello Loco
To the bishop and his official and their commissaries: Chancery *consultacio* on behalf of the prior of Beaulieu to whom the church of Clophill (Clophull) is annexed, who lately sued Walter Alnthorp of 'Caynho'[1] for cutting down the tithe

of wood and brushwood belonging to the prior and the rector [*sic*] of the church; Walter, when sued in the church court, maliciously signified in Chancery that he was being sued for debt, so a prohibition was issued, but the prior has now told the king the facts. Mandate to proceed with the case provided that you do not hold a plea of great tithes on trees.

Teste me ipso, 2 Sept. 1387.[2]

1   Unidentified, but perhaps Haynes, immediately to the north of Clophill.
2   See Norma Adams, 'The Judicial Conflict over Tithes', *English Historical Review* 52 (1937), 1–22.

332.   [ff. 51–51v] <u>Breve sicut pluries contra diversas personas</u>
Exchequer *levari faciatis de bonis et beneficiis ecclesiasticis sicut pluries*, returnable on the morrow of Michalmas, against the following who each owe 6s 8d:
John [Snoring] rector of Southorpe, in the archdeaconry of Stow and the deanery of Corringham;
Thomas Cardinal chaplain in West Halton, archdeaconry of Stow, deanery of Manlake;
Thomas Pampylon' chaplain in Skillington;
William Tykynton rector of Stoke, Beltisloe deanery;
John Forthyngton chaplain of Spilsby in Bolingbroke deanery;
Richard Wenton chaplain 'ad pollen for';
John Blakenham chaplain in St. Paul [in the Bail, Lincoln] church;
John lately chaplain with James Bekeryng in the deanery of Christianity of Lincoln;
John Palgrave, chaplain of Beckingham chantry in Loveden deanery;
William chaplain with Simon Simeon;
John Robcot chaplain at the same;
Richard chaplain in Lavington Beltisloe deanery;
Thomas chaplain in Kyme;
John Bunch chaplain in the same;
Thomas Evedon chaplain in Scredington, Lafford deanery;
John Schefford chaplain in Navenby;
William de Stepulton chaplain in Harmston;
John Reynes chaplain in Dogdyke chantry, Longoboby [deanery];
John de Leverington chaplain in 'Sutton';
Bartholomew de Neuton chaplain of Tydd [St. Mary];
Roger Rakedall chaplain in Frieston [priory], Holland deanery;
Thomas chaplain with 'domina' de Claythorpe in Calcewaith [deanery];
Henry Besewyk chaplain in Grimsby;
Richard chaplain in Mareham Le Fen, Horncastle deanery;
John rector of Wyham, [Louthesk deanery];
William Conston chaplain in Barton upon Humber;
John chaplain in Barrow upon Humber;
William de Welton chaplain in 'Somerby';
William chaplain in Searby;
John chaplain in Hundon;
William Cateryk rector of Wroot;
Thomas de Topclyf chaplain of Walter de Topclyf of Somerby in Corringham deanery;
Richard Beverlay chaplain in Broughton [by Brigg] in Manlake deanery;

which John rector of Southorpe, Thomas Cardinall etc. owe us for the subsidy granted 4 Richard II in the archdeaconries of Lincoln and Stow.
Teste John Cary, 20 May 1387.
[See **261, 269, 290, 302, 309, 321**]

333.   Breve sicut pluries Brembre

Exchequer *levari faciatis de bonis et beneficiis ecclesiasticis sicut pluries*, return-able on the morrow of Michaelmas, against Master Robert Brembre for 106s 8d, being debts owed to the king by Thomas Brembre rector of Tusmore (Thoresmere) viz. 24s for the two tenths granted by the clergy in 1 Richard II; 12s for the second tenth of the triennial tenth granted 43 Edward III, and against the warden of East Hendred chapel in the archdeaconry of Winchester 3s 4d for a moiety of the clerical tenth granted 7 Richard II in the archdeaconry of Winchester (Wynton).
Teste John Cary, 7 July 1387.
[See **292, 297, 303, 310, 322**]

334.   Breve sicut pluries contra Rectorem de Alesby

Commom Pleas *venire faciatis sicut pluries*, returnable on the octave of Michael-mas, against Henry rector of Aylesby (Alesby) to answer the dean and chapter of Lincoln about a plea of debt of £10, being arrears of rent of £10 p.a. [17 June]. Note of return of no lay fee by the sheriff of Lincolnshire.
Teste Robert Bealknap, 8 July 1387.
[See **318, 327**]

335.   Brevel contra Rectorem de Cerchesden'

Common Pleas *venire faciatis*, returnable on the octave of Michaelmas, against John Magnell rector of Chesterton (Cerchesden) to answer the prior of St. Frides-wide, Oxford, about a plea of debt of 7 marks, being arrears of rent of 1 mark p.a. Note of return of no lay fee by the sheriff of Oxfordshire on the quindene of Trinity [16 June].
Teste Robert Bealknap, 24 June 1387.

336.   Breve contra Rectorem de Muresle

Common Pleas *venire faciatis*, returnable on the quindene of Michaelmas, against John Warden rector of Mursley to anwer the prioress of Nuneaton (Newenton) about a plea of debt of £10 being arrears of a rent of 40s p.a.
Teste Robert Bealknap, 12 July 1387.
[See **258, 264, 319**]

337.   [f. 52] Breve contra Rectorem de Adyngton

Common Pleas *venire faciatis*, returnable on the morrow of Martinmas [12 Nov.], against John Adam rector of Addington (Adyngton) to answer the prior of the Hospital of St. John of Jerusalem in England for a debt of 6 marks, arrears of rent of 40s p.a. Note of return of no lay fee by the sheriff of Buckinghamshire on the octave of Michaelmas.
Teste Robert Bealknap, 10 Oct. 1387.

338. Breve de certiorando Birchemore
Chancery *certiorari (scrutatis registris)* concerning a composition made between
the abbot of Woburn, then rector of Birchmoor (Birchemore) church, and the vicar,
concerning profits and emoluments.
Teste me ipso, 24 Oct. 1387.

339. Prohibicio Haversegge
To the bishop and his official and their commissaries: Chancery *ne teneatis*
concerning Hathersage (Haversegge) church whose patronage is being disputed in
our court between the prior of Launde and the heirs of Roger Colman.
Cum prior de Lauda Lincoln' dioc' nuper certa terras et tenementa cum pertinenciis
in Haversegge, ad que advocacio ecclesie de Haversegge pertinet Rogero Colman,
iam defuncto, ad firmam ad certum terminum dimisisset, iamque intellexerimus
quod licet ecclesia predicta de laicali patronatu Ricardi Colman, fratris et heredis
ac executoris testamenti predicti Rogeri existat, Ricardusque de Brentyngby ecclesiam illam virtute presentacionis ipsius Rogeri sibi inde facte canonice sit adeptus,
et eam in eodem iure obtineat, quidam tamen machinantes ipsos Ricardum et
Ricardum super iure suo in hac parte, ac ipsum priorem occasione dimissionis
predicte coloribus quesitus et indebitis per processum coram vobis in Curia Christianitatis gravare et inquietare prefatum Ricardum Colman ad respondendum coram
vobis in Curia Christianitatis, super iure patronatus sui in hac parte ac ipsum
Ricardum de Brentyngby super iure possessionis sue eiusdem ecclesie, quam in
iure patronatus ipsius Ricardi Colman ut premittitur obtinet, necnon prefatum
priorem occasione dimissionis predicte citari et placitum inde ibi teneri facere
intendunt in nostrum et corone nostre prejudicium nostrumque et ipsius Ricardi
Colman exherredacionem manifestam, necnon ipsorum prioris et Ricardi de Brentyngby dampnum gravissimum, que nolumus nec debemus aliqualiter tollerare,
vobis prohibemus ne quicquam in hac parte quod in nostrum contemptum vel
prejudicium aut nostri seu corone nostre exherredacionem vel legum aut consuetudinum regni nostri Anglie subversionem vel derogacionem cedere valeant
quacumque auctoritate attemptetis, nec per alios facere aliqualiter attemptari. Et si
quid in contrarium per vos seu mandatum vestrum in premissis attemptatum fuerit,
id sine dilacione revocari faciatis.
Teste me ipso, 8 Nov. 1387.

340. Breve contra Rectorem de Adyngton'
Common Pleas *venire faciatis sicut alias*, returnable on the octave of Hilary, against
John Adam rector of Addington to answer the prior of the Hospital of St. John of
Jerusalem in England for a debt of 6 marks, arrears of rent of 40s p.a. Note of return
of no lay fee by the sheriff of Buckinghamshire on the octave of Michaelmas.
Teste Robert Bealknap, 16 Nov. 1387.
EXECUTION AND RETURN. We caused the said John Adam to be warned to comply
with the writ.
Sleaford 20 Dec. [1387]
[See **337**]

341. Breve pro parliamento
Summons to attend parliament at Westminster on the morrow of the Purification
of the Virgin [3 Feb.], with *premunientes* clause.
Teste me ipso apud Wyndsore' [*sic*] 17 Dec. 1387.[1]
Execucio eiusdem.
The writ is contained in a mandate of the bishop to the archdeacon of Lincoln or
his official indicating that it arrived on 26 Dec., and ordering him to cite the clergy
to appear in All Saints church, Northampton, on Tuesday after the feast of SS. Fabian
and Sebastian [27 Jan. 1388], to elect diocesan proctors.
[f. 52v] Sleaford 26 Dec. 1387.
Note that the other archdeacons were written to in the above form.
Conclusio capitulo.
Mandate to the dean [of Lincoln cathedral] to attend parliament in person and to
the chapter to elect a suitable proctor, and to certify their dealings to the bishop
before the Conversion of St. Paul [25 Jan.].
The abbot of St. James Northampton, Master James Brigg sequestrator in the
archdeaconry of Northampton, and Hugh Grenham were committed to receive the
certificates and to transmit them [to the bishop] before the Conversion of St. Paul.

[1]   See *RDP*, IV.724; see also *CCR 1385–9*, p. 456.

342. Breve contra vicarium de Coldassheby
Exchequer *venire faciatis sicut pluries*, returnable on the morrow of Hilary, against
Henry Russell vicar of Cold Ashby (Coldassheby) executor of Simon Ward late
sheriff of Northamptonshire, to render Simon's account along with William Wrygth
rector of Rothersthorpe (Rotheresthorp'), the other executor who has also been
summoned for that day. Elizabeth Ward, who was Simon's wife, holder of the lands
and tenements which were Simon's, Theobald Ward and Nicholas Ward sons and
heirs of Simon are also summoned, for the profits of the hundred of Fawsley
(Fallewesle) with appurtenances in Northamptonshire, which Philippa, lately queen
of England, had in dower for life, by grant of Edward III, viz. from Michaelmas 46
Edward III to Michaelmas 47 Edward III, and to answer for the concealment of the
profits of the place in his account. Note of no lay fee on the morrow of the close of
Easter [15 April] by the sheriff of Northamptonshire.
Teste John Cary, 30 Oct. 1387. By the Memoranda roll of 10 Richard II Michaelmas
term among the *Recorda* and by writ saying that Simon was dead, returned on the
morrow of Hilary, and by return of no lay fee on the morrow of the close of Easter
10 Richard II by the sheriff of Northamptonshire on the morrow of the close of
Hilary 'ulterius preter' quoad predictum Simonem Ward' primi return' mortuum et
breve return' in crastino clausi Pasche 10 Richard II nunc quoad prefatum Henr'
Russell et William Wryghth' primi return' exec' et quoad Elizabeth Ward primo
retorn' teneret' terre et ten' que fuerunt predicti Simonis Theobaldum et Nicholaum
filios et her' eiusdem Simonis, et Rotulum memor' de dicto anno Xmo Reg' nunc
Michaelis Recorda ubi cont' quod predicto Elizabeth, Theobaldus et Nicholaus hab'
diem in premissis'.

343.   Breve contra diversas personas pro subsidio
Exchequer *levari faciatis*, returnable on the morrow of Hilary, against:
the vicar of South Cadeby (Cateby), Louthesk deanery, for 32s for the two tenths granted 1 Richard II;
the rector of Wyville (Wywell), Grantham (Graham) deanery, for 17s 4d for the subsidy granted 4 Richard II;
the same rector for 17s 4d for both moieties of the tenth granted 7 Richard II;
Raymond Pelegrini (Pilgryni) prebendary of Milton Manor for 11s 4d, for the subsidy granted 4 Richard II;
Simon Parys vicar of Holbeach (Holbech), Holland deanery, for 6s 8d for the same subsidy;
Henry Snaith (Sneyth) prebendary of Gretton, for 11s 4d for the same subsidy;
Master John Mowbray (Moubray) prebendary of Cropredy (Croppud),[1] 11s 4d for the same subsidy;
William Islep prebendary of Bedford Major, 11s 4d for the same subsidy;
Thomas Thelwall' prebendary of Thorngate, 6s 8d for the same subsidy;
Master John de Waltham prebendary of Carlton Kyme (Carleton), 6s 8d for the same subsidy;
William Gunthorp' prebendary of Grantham Australis,[2] 6s 8d for the same subsidy;
Roger Braybrok prebendary of All Saints, Lincoln, 11s 4d for the same subsidy;
the rector of Wyville (Wywell), Grantham deanery, 17s 4d for the tenth granted 6 Richard II, and 10s 8d for the first moiety [of tenth] granted 9 Richard II, and 10s 8d for the second moiety [of tenth] granted 8 Richard II.
Teste John Cary, 27 Nov. 1387. By the great roll of 10 Richard II in Lincolnshire, and by a certain schedule sent to the Exchequer by Philip de Tilney lately sheriff of Lincolnshire, which is in the bag ('baga') of sheriffs' returns in the custody of the remembrancer.

  [1]   This is the only mention of Master John Mowbray as prebendary of Cropredy, though Simon Bate, who held the prebend from 1371 to 1386 appears to have been challenged, *Fasti*, I.58. For other references to Mowbray see *BRUO*, I.1326; *Fasti*, VI.67, 86.
  [2]   In Salisbury cathedral, see *Fasti*, III.54.

344.   Breve etc. Brembre
Exchequer *levari faciatis de bonis et beneficiis ecclesiasticis sicut pluries*, returnable on the morrow of Hilary, against Master Robert Brembre for 106s 8d, being debts owed to the king by Thomas Brembre rector of Tusmore, viz. 24s for the two tenths granted by the clergy in 1 Richard II; 12s for the second tenth of the triennial tenth granted 43 Edward III, and against the warden of East Hendred chapel for 3s 4d for the moiety of the clerical tenth granted 7 Richard II in the archdeaconry of Winchester.
Teste John Cary, 13 Nov. 1387.
[See **292, 297, 303, 310, 322, 333**]

345.   [f. 53] Breve contra Rectorem de Muresle
Common Pleas *venire faciatis sicut alias*, returnable on the quindene of Hilary, against John Warden rector of Mursley (Muresley) to answer the prioress of Nuneaton (Newenton) about a plea of debt of £10 being arrears of a rent of 40s p.a.
Teste Robert Bealknapp, 12 Nov. 1387.
[See **258, 264, 319, 336**]

346.   Breve contra Brembre

Exchequer *levari faciatis de bonis et beneficiis ecclesiasticis sicut pluries*, return-able on the morrow of the close of Easter [6 April], against Master Robert Brembre for 106s 8d, being debts owed to the king by Thomas Brembre rector of Tusmore, viz. 24s for the two tenths granted by the clergy in 1 Richard II; 12s for the second tenth of the triennial tenth granted 43 Edward III, and against the warden of East Hendred chapel for 3s 4d for the moiety of the clerical tenth granted 7 Richard II in the archdeaconry of Winchester.

Teste John Cary, 28 Jan. 1388.

[See **292, 297, 303, 310, 322, 333, 344**]

347.   Breve ad recipiendum iuramentum vic' Roteland

Mandate to receive the oath of John Wyttilbury the new sheriff of Rutland, according to the form given in the annexed schedule, and then to give the sheriff his letters patent of appointment, and to signify to Chancery that this has been done.

Teste me ipso 28 Feb. 1388.[1]

Forma iuramenti

Vous jurrez que bien et loialment servirez au Roy en loffice de viscont de Rotel' et le prou le Roy ferez en tantz choses que a vous appendent a faire solonc vostre seu et vostre poair et ses droitures et quantque a la corone appent loialment garderez ne nassenterez a destres ne au concelement des droites et des fraunchises le Roy et par la ou vous saverez les droites le Roy, ou de la corone soit en terres soit en rentes, ou en fraunchises, ou en surites concelez en sustrez vostre loial poair mettrez de ceo repeller, et si vous ne le poez faire, vous le dirrez au Roy ou a ceux de soun conseil des queu vous soiez certain quils le dirront au Roy, et les dettes le Roy pur doun ne pur favour ne respiterez par la ou vous les purrez saunz tresgrande grevance de dettours lever, et que loialment et a droitur' tretrez le poeple de vostre baille, et a checun ferez droit aux bien as povres come as Riches en ce que a vous appent a faire, et que pour doun ne pour promesse ne pour favour, ne pour haiour tort ne ferez a nully, ne autry droiture ne destourberez, et que loialment acquiterez al Escheqer les gentz des queux vous averez rien resceu des dettes le Roy, et que rien ne prendrez par qoi le Roy perde ou par q[u]oi droiture soit destourbe ou la dette le Roy perde ou par q[u]oi droiture soit destourbe ou la dette le Roy delaie, et que ferez retourner et loialment servir les brefs le Roy a vostre seu, et a vostre poair, et que vous remuerez le soutz viscount que fuist lan darrein passe et que vous ne prendrez nul baillif en vostre service mes pour qi vous vaillez respondre et vous ferez vos baillifs faire a tiel serement come a eux lappent et que nul bref resceiverez par vous, ne par les voz nient enseale ne soitz seal des Justices forsque en eir ou autres Justices assignez en mesme le countee en Justices de Neugate et que vous mettrez voz baillifs des plus loialx de pais. Si Deux vous eide et ses seintz.

Return was made under the same form by which the writ to receive the oath of John Holington customs-collector of the town of Boston, as in the preceding quaternion, was received.

[See **294**]

1   Commission to J. Wyttelbury issued 16 Feb. 1388, *CFR 1383–91*, p. 208.

348. Breve contra Rectorem de Passenham
Common Pleas *venire faciatis sicut pluries*, returnable on the quindene of Easter [12 April], against Thomas Ravenser rector of Passenham to answer the abbot of Cirencester for a plea of debt of 48 marks, being arrears of rent of 4 marks p.a. Note of return of no lay fee by the sheriff of Northamptonshire.
Teste Robert Bealknap, 28 Jan. 1388.
[See **299, 301, 315**]

349. Breve pro subsidio levando
Mandate to appoint collectors of the moiety of a tenth granted in the convocation held at St. Paul's [cathedral] London, on 26 February last, and payable on 1 May, and to certify the collectors' names to the Exchequer by the octave of Easter [5 April].
Teste me ipso 14 March 1388.[1]
Execution.
The following were committed to act as collectors in the usual form, as found elsewhere, viz.:
in the archdeaconries of Lincoln and Stow: the prior of Bullington
in the archdeaconry of Leicester: the abbot of St. Mary de Pratis, Leicester
in the archdeaconry of Northampton: the prior of Daventry
in the archdeaconry of Oxford: the abbot of Eynsham
in the archdeaconry of Buckingham: the rector of the House of Ashridge
in the archdeaconry of Bedford: the prior of Dunstable
in the archdeaconry of Huntingdon: the prior of Wymondley and the prior of Bushmead.
Return.
The treasurer and barons were certified.

> [1]   See *CFR 1383 91*, p. 223.

350. [f. 53v] Breve contra Rectorem de Stevenache
Common Pleas *venire faciatis*, returnable on the octave of Trinity [31 May], against John Dyne rector of Stevenage (Stevenache), to answer the abbot of Westminster for £7 10s, being arrears of rent of 50s p.a. Note of return of no lay fee by the sheriff of Hertfordshire on the quindene of Easter [12 April].
Teste Robert Cherlton, 6 May 1388.

351. Breve contra Passenham
Common Pleas *venire faciatis sicut pluries*, returnable on the octave of St. John Baptist [1 July], against Thomas Ravenser rector of Passenham to answer the abbot of Cirencester for a plea of debt of 48 marks, being arrears of rent of 4 marks p.a. Note of return of no lay fee by the sheriff of Northamptonshire.
Teste Robert de Cherlton, 6 May 1388.
[See **299, 309, 315, 328, 248**]

352. Breve de certiorando pro ecclesia de Cresselowe
Chancery *certiorari (scrutatis registris)* concerning the presentation to Creslow (Cresselawe) church of Master William Stuecle,[1] and who presented and instituted him.

Teste me ipso 26 April 1388.
    [1]   Probably William Styvecle for whom see *BRUO*, III.1812.

353.   Breve ad orandum pro comite Darundell admarall'
Request for prayers for the earl of Arundel, our admiral, who is about to set out on an expedition against the king's enemies.
Teste me ipso 12 June 1388.[1]
EXECUTION. At Louth Park 25 June 1388, the archdeacons and their officials were written to and ordered to execute the writ, and the form used was the same as for the other writ to pray enrolled in this register.
[See **323**]
    [1]   This writ is not printed in T. Rymer, *Foedera*, or calendared in the *CCR*.

354.   Breve de certiorando pro ecclesia Omnium Sanctorum Oxon'
Chancery *certiorari (scrutato registro)* concerning the presentation of Alexander Spurman to All Saints church Oxford, in 37 Edward III by the king, and the reason for that presentation.
Teste me ipso 2 July 1387 [*sic, rectius* 1388][1]
    [1]   The MS has the regnal year as 'undecimo', probably a mistake for 'duodecimo'.

355.   Breve retorn' contra Rectorem de Passenham
Common Pleas *venire faciatis sicut pluries*, returnable on the quindene of Michaelmas, against Thomas Ravenser rector of Passenham to answer the abbot of Cirencester for a plea of debt of 48 marks, being arrears of rent of 4 marks p.a. Note of return of no lay fee by the sheriff of Northamptonshire.
Teste Robert de Cherlton, 6 July 1388.
RETURNUM. At Sleaford 2 Oct. 1388 return was made that the rector was warned etc.
[See **299, 309, 315, 328, 348, 351**]

356.   [f. 54] Breve pro parliamento
Summons to a parliament at Cambridge on the morrow of the Nativity of the Virgin [9 Sept.], with *premunientes* clause.
Teste me ipso Oxon' 28 July 1388.[1]
    [1]   Printed *RDP*, IV.729; see also *CCR 1385–9*, p. 603.

357.   Breve pro subsidio levando etc.
Mandate to appoint collectors for the tenth granted on condition of the king going in person to war before next Michaelmas, granted in the convocation at St. Paul's [cathedral], London on the 12 Oct. last, whose terms are the quindene of Easter [2 May 1389] and the Translation of St. Thomas the Martyr [7 July], and to certify collectors' names to the Exchequer by the octave of Hilary.
Teste me ipso 28 Oct. 1388.[1]
EXECUTION: The following were committed as collectors in the usual form:
in the archdeaconries of Lincoln and Stow: the abbot of Bardney
in the archdeaconry of Leicester: the abbot of St. Mary de Pratis, Leicester
in the archdeaconry of Northampton: the abbot of Pipewell
in the archdeaconry of Oxford: the prior and convent of St. Frideswide, Oxford

in the archdeaconry of Buckingham: the abbot of Notley
in the archdeaconry of Bedford: the abbot of Chicksands
in the archdeaconry of Huntingdon: the abbot of Ramsey
Sleaford 10 Jan. 1389.
RETURN. On the same day a certificate was sent to the treasurer and barons of the
Exchequer.

> 1   See *CFR 1383–91*, p. 264, for details of the conditions under which this grant was made.

358.   Breve contra Rectorem de Sautre
Chancery *certiorari (scrutatis registris)* concerning the true annual value of St.
Andrew's church Sawtry (Sautry), and of two parts of its tithes, and whether the
said two parts constitute a fourth part of the goods of the church, as a case is pending
in the court Christian between the prior of St. Mary, Huntingdon, and Thomas de
Alyngton rector of St. Andrew's church, Sawtry about two parts of all tithes of the
church coming from Lord de Belmes in Sawtry (Saltreia), and Thomas has suggested in Chancery that the two parts of the tithes form a fourth part of the goods
of the church, and therefore we issued a prohibition concerning this case.
Teste me ipso 26 Jan. 1389.
RETURN. We have looked in our registers and those of our predecessors and find
that the annual value of the church is estimated at 12 marks and the worth of two
parts of the tithes is 20s, and it does not attain the value of fourth part of the goods.
Sleaford 4 Feb. 1389.

359.   Breve contra Rectorem de Staunton Harecourt'
Common Pleas *fieri faciatis de bonis ecclesiasticis*, returnable on the quindene of
Easter [2 May], against John Harewell rector of Stanton Harcourt (Staunton
Harecourt) for 70 marks, to answer the abbot of Reading for arrears of a rent of 20
marks p.a. which the abbot recovered against the said John before our justices at
Westminster, payable at the feasts of All Saints, the Purification, Easter and the
Nativity of St. John Baptist by equal portions, at Reading; similar mandate for 20s
returnable at the end of the present term for damages; similar mandate returnable
at the same time for 10 marks, the amount payable at the last Nativity of St. John
Baptist and the feast of All Saints following it.
Teste Robert de Cherlton, 6 Feb. 1389.
[f. 54v] Execucio Brevis.
On 10 March 1389 at Sleaford the bishop wrote to Master John Thomas, sequestrator,[1] as follows: we have received the following writ, Richard, etc.; we order you
to execute it and in person to sequester the fruits up to the sums mentioned, by sale
of goods, and inform us what you have done by Pentecost [6 June], if you wish to
avoid the king's wrath and to receive his benevolence in the future.
[See **127, 134, 324**]

> 1   Probably of the archdeaconry of Oxford, since this is where Stanton Harcourt lies. Thomas
> is one of John Buckingham's few identifiable relations, see *BRUO*, III.1861.

360.   Breve de certiorando Boseworth'
Chancery *certiorari (scrutatis registris)* concerning the holders and patron of
Husbands Bosworth (Bosworth) church from 1328 to 1380, and at whose presen-
tation.
Teste me ipso 12 Aug. 1389.

RETURN. Master Henry le Despenser in the time of bishop Gynewell and William Sleaford in the time of the present bishop, with prohibition and consultation. Sleaford 12 Sept. 1389.[1]
[See **330**]

   [1]   The benefice is identified from Reg. 9, f. 377v; Reg. 10, f. 249; Reg. 11, f. 231v.

361.   [ff. 54v–55] Breve contra Robertum Bolton' clericum[1]
Exchequer *venire faciatis*, returnable on the morrow of Michaelmas, against Robert Bolton clerk, lately receiver of Michael de la Pole late earl of Suffolk, to render account for the profits of the manor of Saxlingham Nethergate (Saxlyngham iuxta Hemnale) with the advowson of Saxlingham Thorpe (Saxlynghamthorp)[2] church with appurtenances, Norfolk, which the said former earl held on 1 October 10 Richard II, on which day he forfeited his lands and tenements for divers losses ('perdicionibus'),[3] viz. from 1 Oct. 10 Richard II until Michaelmas 11 Richard II [1 Oct. 1386 – 29 Sept. 1387];

venire faciatis against the same Robert de Bolton, returnable on the same day, to render account for the profits of the manors of Wingfield (Wyngefeld), Syleham (Sillyam), Stradbrook (Stradbrok), Fressingfield (Fresyngfeld) and Sternfield (Sternesfeld), with the advowsons of the churches of Stradbrook and Saxmundham (Saxmondham), with appurtenances, Suffolk, which the same earl held on 1 October 10 Richard II by the law of England after the death of Katherine his wife of the inheritance of Michael son and heir of Katherine, which manors were held of the crown in chief, from 1 October 10 1386 to 29 Sept. 1387;[4]

and against the same clerk to render account for the profits of the manor of Stratford St. Mary (Stratford) which is called 'Veyses cum Leta' there which the earl held in his lordship and fee on that 1 October, with the advowson of the church of that manor which Robert received to the use of the earl, from 1 Oct. 1386 to 29 Sept. 1387;[5]

and against the same clerk to render account for the profits of £20 p.a. rent from the town and castle of Orford, Suffolk which the earl held in his lordship and fee of our gift and which Robert had received to the earl's use, from 1 Oct. 1386 to 29 Sept. 1387;[6]

and against the same clerk to answer for the account of the profits of a certain tenement called 'Haukers' in Farnham with appurtenances, Suffolk, consisting of thirty-seven acres of [arable] land and three acres of meadow which the earl held in his lordship as of the aforesaid fee, from 1 Oct. 1386 to 29 Sept. 1387;

and against the same clerk to render account for the profits of a [f. 55] tenement called 'Bretones' which belongs in Baylham (Beilham), Suffolk which the earl held in his lordship and fee along with John Janne, and because it was held of Anne queen of England as of the hundred of Bosmere, and of her manor of Benhall (Benhale) by service of 4s 4d p.a., by Robert de Bolton to the use of the earl, from 1 Oct. 1386 to 29 Sept. 1387;[7]
and for which he has not yet accounted.
Teste John Cassy, 31 May 1389. Through scrutiny of the escheator's rolls of account viz. of John Cranewys escheator in Norfolk and Suffolk, from 30 Nov. 11 Richard II to 30 Nov. 12 Richard II.

   [1]   For the background to this, and the following writ, see J.S. Roskell, *The Impeachment of Michael de la Pole, Earl of Suffolk in 1386* (Manchester, 1984); the appendix, 'Michael de la

Pole's Own Estates', pp. 205–8, has proved especially useful for identifying place-names. See also *Complete Peerage*, vol. XII, pt. 1, pp. 437–40, s.n. 'Suffolk'.
2　The description 'near Hempnall' identifies this as Saxlingham Nethergate.
3　The 'Wonderful Parliament'.
4　Michael de la Pole married Katherine, daughter and heiress of Sir John Wingfield of Wingfield, Suffolk; she died before 1 Oct. 1386, *Complete Peerage* XII, pt. 1, p. 440.
5　Suffolk, see Roskell, *op. cit.*, p. 124.
6　*Ibid.*, p. 120. On uses see J.L. Barton, 'The Medieval Use', *Law Quarterly Review* 81 (1965), 562–77.
7　Roskell, *op. cit.*, pp. 120–1, 125, 149.

362.　Breve contra Robert Bolton' clericum
Exchequer *venire faciatis*, returnable on the morrow of Michaelmas, against Robert Bolton clerk, receiver of Michael de la Pole, late earl of Suffolk, on the occasion of the judgement against him in parliament on the morrow of the Purification, 11 Richard II [13 Feb. 1388],[1] to render account for the profits of two parts of one messuage and one carucate of [arable] land and four acres of meadow, with appurtenances in Normanton and Weston[2] which belonged to the earl at the time of that judgement against him and forfeit, from 1 Oct. 10 Richard II [1386] until 6 March 11 Richard II [1388], on which day they were seized into the king's hand; *venire faciatis* against the same Robert de Bolton clerk, returnable on the same day, to render account of the profits of a messuage with appurtenances in Suthwhetele, now ruinous, and anciently called 'Poleplace', and of another messuage with appurtenances there which formerly belonged to John Whetele, which Michael de la Pole occupied through Robert from 1 Oct. 1386 to 6 March 1388 and for which he has not yet accounted.
Teste John Cassy, 9 July 1389. By the escheator's roll of John de Briggeford lately escheator in Nottinghamshire and Derbyshire.[3]

1　The 'Merciless Parliament'.
2　Unidentified; both are common names.
3　Robert de Bolton, whose career would repay closer study, was still in the service of Edmund de la Pole, the earl's younger brother, in Feb. 1391, *CPR 1388–92*, p. 381.

363.　Breve directum episcopo sub forisfactura etc. pro novis imposicionibus et novitatibus subsidii summo pontifico solvendi
[Prohibition against collecting a papal tax.
The king is bound by oath to conserve the laws and customs of the kingdom, and by that law and custom no tax should be levied on his people without the common counsel and consent of the kingdom. The community of the realm petitioned the king in a recent parliament to provide a remedy against taxes demanded by the pope from the clergy, and suggested that anyone bringing any papal bulls ordering the levying of such taxes or for making novelties, or anyone who should cause such taxes or novelties to be levied without the consent of the king and realm should be adjudged a traitor and executed. This was granted by the king with the assent of parliament. The king has learned that a subsidy imposed by the pope is being collected by you without the common counsel and consent of the realm, contrary to the said custom and grant. Such a novelty has never been seen before and ought not to be seen at this time. Order, under pain of total forfeiture to desist from these new impositions and exactions, to revoke your mandates for the levy of the subsidy, to repay and restore to the payers any money already collected and not to contribute to the subsidy yourself.]

Licet vos non lateat qualiter ad conservacionem iurium et consuetudinum regni nostri Anglie ac indempnitatis et recte gubernacionis populi nostri eiusdem vinculo iuramenti simus astricti, ac de iure et consuetudine predictis imposicio aliqua eidem populo nostro absque communi consilio et assensu eiusdem regni fieri seu levari non debeat ab eodem quovismodo supplicante insuper nobis in parliamento nostro apud Westmonasterium nuper[1] tento communitate eiusdem regni contra huiusmodi imposiciones clero regni nostri predicti per summum pontificem eo tempore publicatas et exactas remedium apponere et quod qui extunc ligeorum nostrorum vel alius aliquas bullas papales pro huiusmodi imposicionibus levandis aut aliis novitatibus faciendis perantea minime usitatis que in nostri vel regni nostri dampnum cedere possent deferret vel si quis de huiusmodi imposicionis vel novitate publicationem seu huiusmodi imposicionem vel novitatem sine assensu nostri et regni nostri predicti colligi vel levari seu solvi facerit tanquam proditor nobis et regno predicto adiudicarem et execucionem haberet de assensu eiusdem parliamenti per nos concessum fuisset ibidem quod nichil foret levatum vel solutum quod in oneracionem vel dampnum regni nostri predicti vel ligeorum nostrorum eiusdem cedere posset: Nichilominus iam de novo, ut accepimus, quedam imposicio clero eiusdem regni nostri ad quoddam subsidium denar' eidem summo Pontifici ad imposicionem suam solvend' et auctoritate vestra sive ad mandatum vestrum levand' absque huiusmodi communi consilio et assensu regni nostri predicti facta existit contra consuetudinem et concessionem predictas, de quo miramur, maxime cum aliquo tempore transacto in regno nostro predicto, nova talia visa non fuerunt nec audita, et nos nova huiusmodi in regno nostro predicto fieri temporibus nostris pati non debeamus, sicuti nec possumus, salvo iuramento nostro predicto, Vobis in fide qua nobis tenemini et sub foresfactura omnium que nobis forisfacere poteritis iniungimus et mandamus quod ab huiusmodi novis imposicionibus et exaccionibus clero nostro predicto faciendis omnino desistentes, ea omnia et singula per vos seu ad mandatum vestrum pro levacione et exaccione huiusmodi subsidii sive imposicionis facta vel attemptata, sine dilacione et difficultate quacumque revocetis et revocari, ac summas denariorum quascumque si quis per vos seu ad mandatum vestrum in hac parte exacte et levate fuerint, integre et sine dilacione restitui et resolvi faciatis, Vobis insuper ex habundanti iniungentes et mandantes ne huiusmodi subsidio sive imposicioni contribuatis aut summam aliquam ex hac causa quomodolibet solvere presumatis sub fide et forisfactura antedictis.

Teste me ipso 10 Oct. 1389.[2]

[1] This must refer to the parliament which began on 3 Feb. 1388 at Westminster since the most recent parliament, which began on 9 Sept., was held at Cambridge.

[2] For the background to this writ see W.E. Lunt, *Financial Relations of the Papacy with England 1327 to 1534: Studies in Anglo-Papal Relations during the Middle Ages* II (The Medieval Academy of America: Cambridge, Mass., 1962), pp. 116–18.

364. Breve contra Rectorem de North' Withum

Common Pleas *venire faciatis*, returnable on the morrow of Martinmas [12 Nov.], against Richard rector of North Witham (Withum), to answer William abbot of Owston for 40s being arrears of 40s p.a. rent. Note of return of no lay fee by the sheriff of Lincolnshire on the octave of Michaelmas.

Teste Robert de Cherlton, 12 Oct. 1389.

EXECUTION. At Sleaford 28 Oct. 1389 the dean of Beltisloe (Belteslowe) was written to to execute this.

365. Breve contra Thomas Basset de Weldon'

Common Pleas *venire faciatis*, returnable on the octave of Hilary, against Thomas son of Ralph Basset of Weldon your clerk, to answer William la Zouche of Totnes (Totteneis) concerning a plea that he should be held to an agreement made between them concerning an enfeoffment made for William of all the lands and tenements with appurtenances which are of the inheritance of Thomas after the recovery of those lands and tenements at William's expense, and to be held by William and his heirs in perpetuity. Note of return of no lay fee by the sheriff of Northamptonshire on the morrow of Martinmas [12 Nov.].

Teste Robert de Cherlton, 30 Nov. 1389.[1]

> [1]   William la Zouche of Harringworth (Northants.) kt. held the castle and manor of Totnes (Devon) at his death, 23 April 1382, *Calendar of Inquisitions Post Mortem XV (1–7 Richard II)*, p. 259. Thomas Basset was evidently the son of that Ralph Basset who succeeded his father in 1341 and who became a canon of Launde priory, Leics., in 1368, and who was the father of only one son, another Ralph, *Complete Peerage*, II.11–12.

366. [ff. 55–55v] Breve contra Rectorem de Parva Billyng

Common Pleas *fieri faciatis de bonis ecclesiasticis*, returnable on the octave of Hilary, against John Baukewell rector of Little Billing (Parva Billyng) for 50s being arrears of rent of 20s p.a. payable to the priory of St. Andrews Northampton at Michaelmas and Easter. The prior of St. Andrews Northampton recovered the sum in court at Westminster in Trinity Term 8 Richard II before Robert Bealknap and other justices, and afterwards recovered the execution against John by his default. Note of return of no lay fee by the sheriff of Northamptonshire on the octave of Michaelmas.

Teste Robert de Cherlton, 28 Nov. 1389.

[See **232, 251, 271, 278**]

367. Breve contra Willclmum Haunay clericum

Exchequer *venire faciatis sicut pluries*, returnable on the morrow of Hilary, against William Haunay clerk to answer the king for 144 boards called rigolts [Riga deals] ('bord' vocat' Rygold')[1] received by indenture by William from William Sleaford clerk[2] late supervisor of the king's works in the time of Edward III at the Palace of Westminster and the Tower of London and not yet answered or accounted for.

Teste John Cassy, 7 Dec. 1389. By the account roll of William de Sleaford in the said work from 20 Sept. 48 Edward III until 21 June 51 Edward III, by a writ returned on the morrow of Michaelmas 13 Richard II certifying no lay fee by the sheriff of London. Staverton'

> [1]   For Riga deals, or righolts, and '. . . the differentiation of Eastland boards as wainscots and righolts' in the early fourteenth century, see L.F. Salzman, *Building in England down to 1540* (Oxford, 1952), pp. 21, 246. Riga (Latvia) was the great centre from which timber from the eastern Baltic was exported to western Europe. Riga deals, oak planks already roughly prepared and cut into standard lengths, were much prized by naval shipbuilders into the early nineteenth century. I am indebted to Miss P.K. Crimmin for this information.
>
> [2]   Sleaford was clerk of works at Westminster and the Tower from 14 Nov. 1361 to 21 June 1377. Haunay, his successor, held office from 21 June 1377 to 14 April 1378. R. Allen Brown, H.M. Colvin and A.J. Taylor, *The History of the King's Works* (London, 1963), II.1047. Clerks of works were paid 1s a day and received robes in addition. Sleaford's ecclesiastical promotions included a prebend in, and later the deanery of, St. Stephen's chapel, Westminster, *ibid.*, I.173.

368.   Breve contra vicarium de Colde Assheby

Exchequer *venire faciatis sicut pluries*, returnable on the morrow of the close of Easter [26 April], against Henry Russell vicar of Cold Ashby, executor of Simon Ward late sheriff of Northamptonshire, to render Simon's account to the Crown, along with William Wrygth rector of Rothersthorpe, the other executor who has also been summoned for that day. Elizabeth Ward, who was Simon's wife, holder of the lands and tenements which were Simon's, Theobald Ward and Nicholas Ward sons and heirs of Simon are also summoned, for the profits of the hundred of Fawsley with appurtenances in Northamptonshire, which Philippa, lately queen of England, had in dower for life, by grant of Edward III, viz. from Michaelmas 46 Edward III to Michaelmas 47 Edward III, and to answer for the concealment of the profits of the place in his account. Note of no lay fee on the morrow of the close of Easter [15 April] by the sheriff of Northamptonshire.

Teste John Cassy, 31 Jan. 1390.

[See **342**]

369.   Breve contra Rectorem de Wynceby

Exchequer *venire faciatis sicut pluries*, returnable on the morrow of the close of Easter [26 April], against Henry Herdeby rector of Winceby (Wynceby), to answer the king, along with John Hungate of Leake (Leke), for the account of the profits of one toft and one bovate of land with appurtenances in Winceby which belonged to Alice de Supholm' of Winceby, viz. from 7 Richard II to 20 Jan. 9 Richard II, and not yet accounted for.

Teste John Cassy, 7 Feb. 1390. By the escheator's roll of John de Feryby lately escheator in Lincolnshire, from 11 Nov. 8 Richard II to 4 Feb. 9 Richard II, and by return of no lay fee by the sheriff of Lincolnshire on the morrow of the close of Easter 12 Richard II, and the Memoranda roll of 13 Richard II Michaelmas term among the *brevia retornabilia*. Staverton.

370.   Breve contra Willelmum Haunay clericum

Exchequer *venire faciatis sicut alias*, returnable on the morrow of the close of Easter [26 April], against William Haunay, clerk, to answer the king for 144 boards called righolts received by indenture by William from William Sleaford clerk lately supervisor of the king's works in the time of Edward III at the Palace of Westminster and the Tower of London and not yet answered or accounted for.

Teste John Cassy, 20 Feb. 1390.   Staverton.

[See **367**]

371.   [ff. 55v–56] Breve de placito inter Robertum Stynt et Rectorem de Bolingbrok

Chancery *certiorari*, returnable without delay, concerning the annual value of Bolingbroke (Bolingbrok) church and of its tithes and whether the tithes form a fourth part of its value. Robert Stynt rector of West Keal (Westerkele) church has shown us that he ought to have the right to take and have the tithes of a certain place commonly called 'Lynghowe'[1] inside the limits of his parish, and they have been taken by his predecessor, and he has impleaded [f. 56] before your official, in the the court Christian, Master John Warde rector of Bolingbroke (Bolyngbrok) that John has gone out of the limits of his parish and taken tithes of the pasture of

Lynghowe for seven years and usurped them contrary to Robert's will. John appealed to the court of Canterbury and suggested in Chancery that the advowson of the church of Bolingbroke [sic] belonged to the prior of Spalding (Spaldyng) but that Robert had been presented by the abbot of Crowland, William Anngwyn and Elizabeth his wife and Laurence Moigne and Katherine his wife, and that the case should not be heard in a church court. We therefore addressed a writ of prohibition to the official of the court of Canterbury not to proceed until we knew to whom the advowson belonged and we do not wish to take cognition of what belongs to the church's sphere.[2]

Teste me ipso 4 May 1390.   [William de] Rondon'.[3]

   [1] Lynghowe was in Bolingbroke, and this appears as an early name of the area which was known in the sixteenth century as 'Hallhill or Lyngewoode' and from the seventeenth century as Hallhill. The present-day Hall Hill Farm may mark the site. I owe thanks to Professor Ken Cameron for this information.
   [2] For William Anngwyn and Elizabeth his wife, and Laurence Moigne and Katherine his wife, see also **210**.
   [3] See *CPR 1381–5*, pp. 117, 158.

372.   Breve contra Rectrem de Stangrond'

Exchequer *venire faciatis*, returnable on the morrow of Trinity [14 June], against Robert rector of Stanground (Stangrond), to answer the king along with Robert Huscher who has a writ to be there on the same day, about a horse worth 13s 4d which killed John the rector's servant. Note of no lay fee by the sheriff of Cambridgeshire and Huntingdonshire, Edmund atte Pole, on the morrow of the close of Easter.

Teste John Cassy, 4 May 1390. By the escheator's roll among the accounts of Thomas More of Balsham lately escheator of Cambridgeshire and Huntingdonshire from 2 Feb. 10 Richard II to 30 Nov. following, and by a writ returned on the morrow of the close of Easter last by the sheriff of Cambridgeshire and Huntingdonshire and its endorsement by which it was conceded that execution should be against Robert Huscher.[1]   Staverton.

   [1] Since it was the horse which had caused the death its value became a deodand: 'a personal chattel or thing which had been the cause of the death of a person, and as such was forfeit to the crown to be applied to pious uses'. The practice was not abolished until 1846; *The Oxford Dictionary of the Christian Church*, ed. F.L. Cross and E.A. Livingstone, 3rd ed. (Oxford, 1997), p. 470.

373.   Breve de certiorando Tykeford

Chancery *certiorari* concerning the last person to be admitted to Tickford (Tykford) priory, at whose presentation and when.

Teste me ipso 12 June 1390.   [Thomas] Brayton'[1]

   [1] See Tout, *Chapters*, III.153, VI.13–15.

374.   [f. 56v] Breve contra Rectorem de Stangrond'

Exchequer *venire faciatis sicut pluries*, returnable on the morrow of Michaelmas, against Robert rector of Stanground (Stangrond), to answer the king along with Robert Huscher who has a writ to be there on the same day, about a horse worth 13s 4d which killed John the rector's servant. Note of no lay fee by the sheriff of Cambridgshire and Huntingdonshire, Edmund atte Pole, on the morrow of the close of Easter.

Teste John Cassy, 12 July 1390. By the escheator's roll among the accounts of

Thomas More of Balsham lately escheator of Cambridgeshire and Huntingdonshire from 2 Feb. 10 Richard II to 30 Nov. following, and by a writ returned on the morrow of the close of Easter last by the sheriff of Cambridgeshire and Huntingdonshire and its endorsement by which it was conceded that execution should be against Robert Huscher.   Staverton.
[See **372**]

375.   Breve contra Willelmum Haunay clericum
Exchequer *venire faciatis sicut pluries*, returnable on the morrow of Michalmas, against William Haunay clerk to answer the king for 144 'bord' vocat' Rygold' received by indenture by William from William Sleaford clerk lately supervisor of the king's works in the time of Edward III at the Palace of Westminster and the Tower of London and not yet answered or accounted for.
Teste John Cassy, 18 May 1390.   Staverton.
[See **367**, **370**]

376.   Breve contra Rectorem de Wynceby
Exchequer *venire faciatis sicut pluries*, returnable on the morrow of Michaelmas, against Henry Herdeby rector of Winceby, to answer the king, along with John Hungate of Leake, for the account of the profits of one toft and one bovate of land with appurtenances in Winceby which belonged to Alice de Supholm' of Winceby, viz. from 7 Richard II to 20 Jan. 9 Richard II, and not yet accounted for.
Teste John Cassy 18 June 1390. By the escheator's roll of John de Feryby lately escheator in Lincolnshire, from 11 Nov. 8 Richard II to 4 Feb. 9 Richard II, and by return of no lay fee by the sheriff of Lincolnshire on the morrow of the close of Easter 12 Richard II, and the Memoranda roll of 13 Richard II Michaelmas term among the *brevia retornabilia*. Staverton'.
[See **369**]

377.   Breve contra vicarium de Colde Assheby
Exchequer *venire faciatis sicut pluries*, returnable on the morrow of Michaelmas, against Henry Russell vicar of Cold Ashby (Colde Assheby), executor of Simon Ward late sheriff of Northamptonshire, to render Simon's account to the Crown, along with William Wrygth rector of Rothersthorpe, the other executor who has also been summoned for that day. Elizabeth Ward, who was Simon's wife, holder of the lands and tenements which were Simon's, Theobald Ward and Nicholas Ward sons and heirs of Simon are also summoned, for the profits of the hundred of Fawsley with appurtenances in Northamptonshire, which Philippa, lately queen of England, had in dower for life, by grant of Edward III, viz. from Michaelmas 46 Edward III to Michaelmas 47 Edward III, and to answer for the concealment of the profits of the place in his account. Note of no lay fee on the morrow of the close of Easter [15 April] by the sheriff of Northamptonshire.
Teste John Cassy, 16 June 1390.
[See **342**, **368**]

378.   [ff. 56v–57] Breve pro parliamento
Summons to a parliament at Westminster on the morrow of Martinmas [12 Nov.], with *premunientes* clause.

Teste me ipso 12 Sept. 1390 *per ipsum regem et concilium.*¹   Lunde.

> ¹ Printed *RDP*, IV.735; see also *CCR 1389–92*, pp. 283–4.

379. [f. 57] <u>Breve contra Rectorem de Swafeld</u>
Common Pleas *venire faciatis*, returnable on the octave of Trinity [20 June], against John rector of Swayfield (Swafeld), your clerk, to answer the prior of Thurgarton for a debt of 40s being arrears of rent of 13s 4d p.a. Note of return of no lay fee by the sheriff of Lincolnshire on the quindene of Michaelmas.
Teste Robert de Cherlton, 18 Oct. 1390
Roll lxxxxv   Perb'

380. <u>Breve contra Rectorem de Benyfeld</u>
Common Pleas *venire faciatis*, returnable on the octave of Hilary, against John rector of Benefield (Benyfeld)¹ to answer John de Bretton for 8 quarters of corn worth £4 which he unjustly detains. Note of return of no lay fee by the sheriff of Northamptonshire on the morrow of Martinmas [12 Nov.].
Teste Robert de Cherlton, 16 Nov. 1390.
Roll   cccxxij   Wakefeld

> ¹ There are now two villages, Upper and Lower Benefield.

381. <u>Breve contra Willelmum de Pychelesthorn'</u>
Exchequer *levari faciatis de bonis et beneficiis ecclesiasticis*, returnable on the morrow of Hilary, against William de Pychelesthorn lately receiver of all rents and profits at the castle and honour of Berkhamstead (Berkhamsted)¹ for £18 5s 7¼d from his account from Michaelmas 5 Richard II to the Nativity of St. John Baptist 8 Richard II.
Teste John Cassy, 14 Oct. 1390. By the great roll of 12 Richard II in London and Middlesex.   Staverton.

> ¹ The honour of Berkhamstead was one of the 'foreign manors' of the earldom of Cornwall, Tout, *Chapters*, V.290.

382. <u>Breve ad recipiendum sacramentum Johannis Bozon' Escaetoris</u>
Mandate to receive the oath of John Bozon the new escheator in Lincolnshire, to give him his letters patent of appointment, and to certify Chancery when this has been done.
Teste me ipso 4 Feb. 1391.
<u>Forma iuramenti</u>
Vous jurrez que bien et loialment servirez le Roy en loffice del Eschetour en le countee de Nicole et le prou [*sic*] le Roy f[e]rez en toutes choses que a vous appendent a faire selonc vostre seu et vostre poair et ses droitures et quantque a la corone appent loialment garderez, ne nassenterez a destres ne a concelement des droitz ne des franchises le Roi et par la ou vous saverez les droitz le Roi ou de sa corone soit en terres, soit en rents, ou en franchises, ou en suites concelez ou sustretz vostre loial peine mettrez de ceo repeller; et si vous ne le poez faire vous le dirrez au Roi ou a ceux de soun conseill' des queux vous soiez certein qils le dirront au Roi, et que loialment et a droiture tretez le poeple de vostre baillie et a chescun f[e]rez droit auxibien as povres come as riches en ceo que a vous appent a faire, et pur doun ne promesse ne pour haiour [*sic*] tort ne ferez a nully ne aucu[n] droit ne

destourberez et que rien ne prendrez par quoi le Roi perde ou par quoi la droiture
soit destourbe. Et que loialment ferez retourner et loialment servir les briefs le Roi.
Et que en propre persone les estentz des terres selonc lour verroie value et enquestes
ferez et retournez a vostre seu et a vostre poair si tost qils soient pris et ce deinz un
mois, et que vous ne prendrez null' baillif en vostre service pur qi ne voillez
respondre, et que vous f[e]rez vos baillifs faire au tiel serement come a eux appent
et que loial acompt rendrez al Escheqer le Roi des issues de vostre dite baillie. Et
que vous prendres voz enquestes en lieux appiertz et nemie privez et ce par
endenture selonc le purport de lestatut ent fait. Si Dieux vous eide et ses seintz.[1]

> [1]   See E.R. Stephenson, 'The Escheator', in William A. Morris and Joseph R. Strayer, eds.,
> *The English Government at Work, 1327–1336* vol. II (Cambridge, Mass., 1947), esp. pp. 110–13.

383.   Breve ad recipiendum sacramentum constabularii stapule
Mandate to receive the oaths of Robert de Ledes mayor of the staple of Lincoln and
of William de Bliton and Robert de Messyngham, constables.[1]
Teste me ipso 4 Feb. 1391.
Forma iuramenti
Vous jurrez que bien et loialment servirez au Roi et au poeple en loffices de mair
et conestables de lestaple de Nicol a queles vous estes esluz et loialment tretiez les
merchauntz de mesme lestaple et owel droit ferez as toutz sibien as privees come
estranges selonc les ordinances ent faitz par nostre seigneur le Roy et soun conseil
et la leie marchande. Si dieu vous eide et ses seintz.
Sleaford 1 April 1391 the writs were returned in the form contained elsewhere in
the book.

> [1]   See Francis Hill, *Medieval Lincoln* (Cambridge, 1965), pp. 249 and nn. 1, 3; 250–1. The
> parliament which met from 12 Nov. to 3 Dec. 1390 'was concerned almost exclusively with
> matters of trade and its determination to secure the return of the staple [from Calais] was given
> statutory sanction. The staple was to return to England by 9 January 1391 at the latest and was
> to be held in those towns named in the statute of 1354 . . . The legislation of 1390 proved to be
> a total failure and was reversed in the parliament which sat during November 1391', T.H. Lloyd,
> *The English Wool Trade in the Middle Ages* (Cambridge, 1977), p. 232.

384.   [57v] Breve contra Rectorem de Wynceby
Exchequer *venire faciatis sicut pluries*, returnable on the morrow of the close of
Easter [3 April], against Henry Herdeby rector of Winceby, to answer the king, along
with John Hungate of Leake, for the account of the profits of one toft and one bovate
of land with appurtenances in Winceby which belonged to Alice de Supholm' of
Winceby, viz. from 7 Richard II to 20 Jan. 9 Richard II, and not yet accounted for.
Teste John Cassy, 28 Jan. 1391. By the escheator's roll of John de Feryby lately
escheator in Lincolnshire, from 11 Nov. 8 Richard II to 4 Feb. 9 Richard II, and by
return of no lay fee by the sheriff of Lincolnshire on the morrow of the close of
Easter 12 Richard II, and the Memoranda roll of 13 Richard II Michaelmas term
among the *brevia retornabilia.*
Return: was made that he is dead.
[See **369, 376**]

385.   Breve contra Rectorem ecclesie de Stangrond'
Exchequer *venire faciatis sicut pluries* returnable on the morrow of the close of
Easter [3 April], against Robert rector of Stanground to answer the king along with
Robert Huscher who has a writ to be there on the same day, about a horse worth 13s

4d which killed John the rector's servant. Note of no lay fee by the sheriff of Cambridgeshire and Huntingdonshire, Edmund atte Pole, on the morrow of the close of Easter.

Teste John Cassy, 30 Jan. 1391. By the escheator's roll among the accounts of Thomas More of Balsham lately escheator of Cambridgshire and Huntingdonshire from 2 Feb. 10 Richard II to 30 Nov. following, and by a writ returned on the morrow of the close of Easter last by the sheriff of Cambridgeshire and Huntingdonshire and its endorsement by which it was conceded that execution should be against Robert Huscher.

[See **372**, **374**]

386.   Breve retornum contra Rectorem ecclesie de Swafeld

Common Pleas *venire faciatis*, returnable on the quindene of Easter [9 April], against John rector of Swayfield, your clerk, to answer the prior of Thurgarton for a debt of 40s being arrears of rent of 13s 4d p.a. Note of return of no lay fee by the sheriff of Lincolnshire on the quindene of Michaelmas.

Teste Robert Cherlton, 14 Feb. 1391.

Returnum. The said John was warned to be before the justices at Westminster on the said day to do and answer for everything required by the writ.

[See **379**]

387.   Breve de certiorando Emberton

Chancery *certiorari (scrutatis registris et memorandis)* to discover who were presented to Emberton church from Edward III [no year given], who presented, and by what title, on those occasions.

Teste me ipso 12 Oct. 1390.

388.   Breve retornum pro archidiacono Buckyngham'

The bishop to Richard II: we recently received your writ with its order to scrutinize the registers, whose tenor is below. 'Reverendo . . . de resignacione vero prefati magistri Willelmi Gynwell' clerici qui nuper archidiaconatum Buk' per collacionem Johannis Gynwell' nuper episcopi Lincoln' predecessoris nostri obtinuit an prefactus Magister Willelmus Gynwell' predictum archidiaconatum in manus nostras resignaverit [*sic*] non constat nobis, nec quicquam de resignacione huiusmodi in Registris nostris reperimus'.

Sleaford etc. [undated].

Tenor eiusdem brevis:

Breve de certiorando Buckyngham

Chancery *certiorari* whether Master William Gynewell clerk who lately obtained the archdeaconry of Buckingham by collation of John Gynewell bishop of Lincoln, it is said, resigned the archdeaconry into your hands, and afterwards gained the archdeaconry by virtue of collation made by Edward III it is said, was by you admitted, instituted and inducted, or not, and if he was, then on what day, in which year, where, in what place, how and in what way, and whether 'archidiaconi loci illius pro tempore existentes, per vos et predecessores vestros episcopos Lincoln', ad archidiaconatum predictum primo in aliqua ecclesia infra eundem archidiaconatum totis temporibus retroactis, institui et induci, et super institucione et induccione ill' stallum in choro ecclesie beate Marie Lincoln' predictis archidia-

conis assignari an in stallo predicto installari et induci et postmodum ad archidiaconatum predictum mitti consueverunt, vobis mandamus quod . . .
Teste me ipso 8 Dec. 1390.[1]   [James] Billyngford.[2]

   [1]   The archdeaconry of Buckingham had a troubled history for most of the fourteenth century.
   William Gynewell was collated by his kinsman, John Gynewell, Bishop Buckingham's predecessor, in 1352 and managed to retain the dignity until 1380, despite papal hostility, *Fasti*, I.15.
   See also introduction, section iii, p. xxviii.
   [2]   See Wilkinson, *Chancery*, p. 85; Tout, *Chapters*, III.488 n. 3, 492 n. 2.

389.   [f. 58] <u>Breve contra vicarium de Rouceby</u>
Common Pleas *venire faciatis sicut pluries*, returnable on the octave of St. John
Baptist [1 July], against John vicar of Roxby (Rouceby), your clerk, to answer the
prior of Shelford (St. Mary Sheiford) concerning a plea of debt of £8, being arrears
of rent of 20s p.a. Note of return of no lay fee by the sheriff of Lincolnshire.
Teste Robert de Cherlton, 10 May 1391.

390.   <u>Breve de exhibendo registrum, Buckyngham</u>
[Mandate to the bishop to send his register to Chancery under the care of his agents
before the morrow of St. John Baptist.]
'Ricardus dei gracia Rex Anglie et Francie et dominus Hibernie venerabili in
Christo patri J. eadem gracia Episcopo Lincoln' salutem, Cum placitum pendeat
coram nobis inter nos et Magistrum Johannem Evot de Archidiaconatu Buckyng-
hamie, ac pro evidentiori declaracione et salvacione iuris nostri in hac parte,
inspeccionem Registri vestri desideremus, vobis mandamus quod integrum Registrum vestrum quod a tempore consecracionis vestre fieri fecistis, sub custodia
alicuius ministrorum vestrorum cui fidem credulam adhibetis, nobis in cancel-
lariam nostram sub sigillo vestro citra crastinam Sancti Johannis Baptiste [25 June]
proximo futur*am* mitti et deferri fac<u>iatis</u> hoc breve nobis remittentes. Et hac sicut
ius in hac parte preservare volueritis nullatenus omitatis.'
Teste me ipso 4 June 1391.[1]

   [1]   John Evot, who had been archdeacon of Buckingham since Nov. 1380, was challenged by
   royal grants of the dignity to John Stacy, in Feb. 1390, and William Ashton, in Sept. 1391. Both
   were ineffective and Evot remained in possession until 1 July 1392 when he exchanged the
   archdeaconry for the subdeanery of York, *Fasti*, I.15, XII.15.

391.   <u>Breve retornum pro archidiacono Buckyngham</u>
Mandate to send the bishop's entire register into Chancery, in the same words as
390, with the following addition:
'Et hac sicut ius nostrum illesum in hac parte preservare volueritis, nullatenus
omittatis vel causam nobis significetis quare mandatum nostrum al' vobis inde
directum exequi noluistis vel non potuistis.'
Teste me ipso 10 June 1391.
RETURN. Certificate was made to the crown concerning those two writs in this form:
We have scrutinised our register and send a full copy of the relevant matter, but we
are not able to send our whole register.
'Brevia excellentis vestre magestatis presentibus interclusa die veneris in vigilia
Sancti Johannis Baptiste apud Sleford hora vesperarum recepimus reverenter prout
decuit, quorum tenores eff<u>ec</u>tualiter attendentes Registrum nostrum prout alias
vestre regali celsitudini transmissimus fecimus diligenter perscrutari In quo quidem
Registro nostro, prout in forma et modo sequentibus, nul addendo vel minuendo,

comperimus contineri eo qui sequitur sub tenore: Reverendo etc. ut in Registro prout al' certificat' fuit. In qu<u>arum</u> quidem scrutacionis et compercionis testimonium vigore brevium vestrorum predictorum nobis transmissorum quia Registra nostra integra ex tam brevi premunicione vobis hac vice destinare non valemus. Sigillum nostrum fecimus hiis apponi.'
Sleaford, the vigil of St. John Baptist, viz. 23 June 1391.

392. [f. 58v] Breve contra Rectorem de Thurcaston
Common Pleas *venire faciatis*, returnable on the octave of Michaelmas, against Thomas Haule rector of Thurcaston, your clerk, to answer the prior of Ware about a debt of £10 being arrears of a payment of 40s p.a. Note of return of no lay fee by the sheriff of Leicestershire on the quindene of Trinity [4 June].
Teste Robert de Cherlton, 12 June 1391.

393. Breve contra Rectorem de Burton Novery
Common Pleas *venire faciatis*, returnable on the octave of Michaelmas, against John Barnabas, your clerk [rector of Burton Overy], to answer the prior of Ware about a debt of 20 marks being arrears of a payment of 4 marks p.a. Note of return of no lay fee by the sheriff of Leicestershire on the quindene of Trinity [4 June].
Teste Robert de Cherlton, 12 June 1391.

394. Breve pro parliamento
Summons to a parliament at Westminster on the morrow of All Souls next [3 Nov.], with *premunientes* clause.
Teste me ipso 7 Sept. 1391.[1]
[Execution:] Note that the archdeacons or their officials were written to.

> [1] Printed *RDP*, IV.738; see also *CCR 1389–92*, pp. 489–90.

395. Breve ad orandum pro pace
Request for the prayers of every one of the clergy, secular and regular, for the tranquillity of the kingdom and for peace.
Teste me ipso 28 Aug. 1391.[1]
Mandatum execucionis brevis predicti archidiaconis.
Mandate to the archdeacon of Lincoln or his official to order the prayers, with an indulgence of 40 days given by the bishop to all who comply.
[No date.]
Mandatum capitulo.
Similar order to the chapter of Lincoln.

> [1] Writ printed in T. Rymer, *Foedera* (original ed.), VI.704; calendared *CCR 1389–92*, p. 491. See also McHardy, SCH 18.

396. [f. 59] Prohibicio pro archidiaconatu de Buckyngham
Chancery *ne admittatis* concerning the archdeaconry of Buckingham.
Teste me ipso 18 Oct. 1391.
[See **388**, **390**, **391**]

397. Prohibicio Stokton
Chancery *ne admittatis* concerning the church of Great Staughton (Stokton) whose advowson is in dispute. The advowson was held by the London Charterhouse for many years, but John Excestr' clerk obtained the church by colour of a royal presentation, and when he resigned Walter Aumeney clerk was also appointed in this way. A writ was sent to the sheriff of Huntingdon to cause the said Walter to be in Chancery on a certain day to show why the presentation should not be revoked and the advowson restored to the prior. We now hear that Walter is making malicious machinations against the prior, by exchanging this benefice, and we do not wish the priors [cause] to be injured in this way: ('Walterus machinans ipsum priorem maliciose se prosecucione sue in hac parte impedire ecclesiam predictam permutare intendit in prosecucionis ipsius prioris huiusmodi adnullacionem manifestam, Nos nolentes eundem priorem taliter iniurari, Volentes quod in hac parte fieri quod est iustum vobis prohibemus ne aliquem personam ad ecclesiam predictam admittatis pendente placito predicto in Curia nostra discusso'.)
Teste me ipso 7 Nov. 1391.

398. Prohibicio Northmymmes
Chancery *ne admittatis* concerning North Mimms (Northmymmes) church whose advowson is being disputed between William Swanlond and Beatrice Mounviron, and John prior of the London Charterhouse.
Teste me ipso 20 Dec. 1391.

399. Breve contra Rectorem de Hadyngton
Exchequer *venire faciatis*, returnable on the quindene of Hilary, against Thomas rector of Haddington (Hadyngton) to answer the abbot of Bourne and John Hermesthorp clerk the farmers of Wilsford alien priory about a debt of £8 being arrears of a pension of 40s p.a. due from that church and which the said Thomas is unjustly withholding. Note of return of no lay fee by the sheriff of Lincolnshire at the Exchequer on the quindene of Martinmas last [25 Nov.].
Teste John Cassy, 28 Nov. 1391.

400. Breve de certiorando Olney
Chancery *certiorari (scrutato registro)* returnable with all speed, concerning the rectors of Olney from the time of the coronation of Richard lately ['nuper'] king of England, until 13 Richard II, who presented them and how.
Teste me ipso 10 June 1391.

401. Olney certiorari
Chancery *certiorari (scrutatis registris)*, returnable without delay, concerning the incumbents of Olney church from 1240 until now.
Teste me ipso 10 Jan. 1392.

402. [f. 59v] Northmymmes Prohibicio
Chancery *ne admittatis* concerning North Mimms church whose advowson is in dispute between Beatrice who was the wife of John Moveroun and the prior of the Charterhouse of London.
Teste me ipso 10 Feb. 1391.
[See **398**]

403.   Breve ad levandum medietatem decime Regi concesse

Mandate to appoint collectors of the moiety of a tenth granted in the convocation held in St. Paul's cathedral on the morrow of the Conception of the Virgin [9 Dec.] and payable on 1 April next, and to certify their names at the Exchequer by 16 Feb. next.

Teste me ipso 30 Jan. 1392.[1]

Collectores.

The following were written to in the usual form and ordered to collect the moiety viz.:

archdeaconries of Lincoln and Stow : the abbot and convent of Newhouse [Newsham]

archdeaconry of Leicester: the prior and convent of Kirby Bellars (Kirby on Wrethek)

archdeaconry of Northampton: the prior and convent of St. Andrew's Northampton

archdeaconry of Oxford: the abbot and convent of Eynsham

archdeaconry of Bedford: the abbot and convent of Warden

archdeaconry of Huntingdon: the abbot and convent of Sawtry

> [1]   See *CFR 1391–9*, p. 33. No record survives of the proceedings of that convocation, but the writ ordering its meeting was dated 7 Oct. 1391, D.B. Weske, *Convocation of the Clergy* (London, 1937), p. 267; *CCR 1389–92*, p. 495.

404.   Breve de certiorando sicut alias Olney

Chancery *certiorari (scrutatis registris)*, returnable without delay, concerning the incumbents of Olney church from 1240 until now.

Teste me ipso 1 Feb. 1392.

[See **400, 401**]

405.   Olney Prohibicio

Chancery *ne admittatis* concerning Olney church whose advowson is being disputed between the king and John Graunt clerk.

Teste me ipso 10 Feb. 1392.

406.   Breve contra Rectorem de Northwythum

Common Pleas *fieri faciatis de bonis ecclesiasticis*, returnable on the octave of Michaelmas, against Richard rector of North Witham (Northwythum), for £8 which William abbot of Owston recovered against him in the [court of] Common Pleas, being arrears of payment of 40s p.a., and mandate also to cause to be raised from the said Richard 18½ marks which the abbot recovered before the justices at Westminster for his damages ('pro dampnis suis') because he held back the annual payments, in accordance with a certain judgement given in the presence of William Thyrnyng justice of the Common Bench on the Thursday after the Feast of St. Peter in Chains [8 Aug.] at Grantham. Note of return of no property within his jurisdiction ('Ricardus nulla habet bona nec catalla, terras nec tenementa in balliva sua . . .')

Teste Robert Cherlton, 10 Feb. 1392.

Roll 493   Sproxton

Executio eiusdem.

Stow Park 19 April 1392. The dean of Beltisloe (Belteslowe) and John Kylpesham *domicellus* were written to to levy the said sum and hand it over to the bishop wherever he should be in the diocese on the [feast of] the Exaltation of Holy Cross next [14 Sept.], and to certify on that day what they had done.

407.   Breve contra Rectorem de Thurcaston
Common Pleas *venire faciatis sicut pluries*, returnable on the quindene of Easter [28 April], against Thomas Haule rector of Thurcaston, your clerk, to answer the prior of Ware about a debt of £10 being arrears of a payment of 40s p.a. Note of return of no lay fee by the sheriff of Leicestershire on the quindene of Trinity [4 June].
Teste Robert Cherlton, 23 Jan. 1392.
[See **392**]

408.   [f. 60] Breve contra vicarium de Coldeassheby
Exchequer *venire faciatis sicut pluries*, returnable on the morrow of the close of Easter [22 April], against Henry Russell vicar of Cold Ashby executor of Simon Ward late sheriff of Northamptonshire, to render the account of the said Simon to the crown, along with William Wrygth rector of Rothersthorpe the other executor who has also been summoned for that day. Elizabeth Ward, who was Simon's wife, holder of the lands and tenements which were Simon's, Theobald Ward and Nicholas Ward sons and heirs of Simon, are also summoned, for the profits of the hundred of Fawsley with appurtenances in Northamptonshire, which Philippa lately queen of England had in dower for life by grant of Edward III, viz. from Michaelmas 46 Edward III to Michaelmas 47 Edward III, and to answer for the concealment of the profits of the place in his account. Note of return of no lay fee by the sheriff of Northamptonshire.
Teste John Cassy, 20 Feb. 1392.
[See **351**, **368**, **377**]

409.   Breve contra Johannem Barnebe
Common Pleas *venire faciatis sicut pluries*, returnable on the quindene of Easter [28 April], against John Barnabas, your clerk, [rector of Burton Overy] to answer the prior of Ware about a debt of 20 marks being arrears of a payment of 4 marks p.a. Note of return of no lay fee by the sheriff of Leicestershire on the quindene of Trinity [4 June].
Teste Robert de Cherlton, 23 Jan. 1392.
[See **393**]

410.   Breve bastardie Ricardi Clerc' et Agnetis uxoris eius
Common Pleas *inquiretis de bastardia*, returnable on the octave of Trinity [16 June], in the following case: Richard Clerk and Agnes his wife are seeking in our court, against Robert Constable knight, Juliana Gatesham and Richard Assheby and Agnes his wife, a third part of the manor of Lubbesthorpe (Lubbesthorp) with appurtenances. The plaintiffs claim that this was the dower of Agnes now wife of Richard Clerk, by the endowment of William Zouche (Souche) formerly her husband, but Robert has alleged that this cannot be claimed as dower as Agnes and William were never joined in lawful wedlock. Since this lies within the cognisance of the church court we order you to hold an inquiry in your presence and certify the result by letters patent and close.

Teste Robert Cherlton, 16 May 1392.[1]

1   Despite the form of the writ this is not really a case of bastardy but of validity of marriage. Agnes' marriage to William Zouche, her uncle by marriage, surely within the prohibited degrees, would have made the union invalid on the grounds of affinity. For discussion see R.H. Helmholz, *Marriage Litigation in Medieval England* (Cambridge, 1974), esp. pp. 77–87.

411.   [f. 60v. A new hand begins here.] <u>Breve pro elemosinis quer' et ad suscipi-endum pro curatorem domus de Acon' London'</u>
Since by our letters patent[1] we granted to John Peyntneye chaplain, nuncio and proctor of the master and brothers of the house of St. Thomas the Martyr, Acon, London, leave to collect alms anywhere in our kingdom for the completing of the new works of their church in London and the supporting of other burdens and necessities, we order you and other prelates and ecclesiastical persons to allow him to enter churches, chapels and other ecclesiastical places and to receive him kindly and allow him to collect alms and take them away, as we now understand that some of our lieges have not allowed this. We order you to command all your subordinates to let John carry out his business on behalf of the house, and to publish our letters patent concerning this.
Teste me ipso Stamford 28 July 1392.[2]

1   Not in *CPR*. Grant to John Peyntney, chaplain, of the wardenship of St. James' Hospital, Dulwich, at Stamford, 28 July 1392, *CPR 1391–6*, p. 135.
2   This was a house of notorious poverty. See David K. Maxfield, 'A Fifteenth-Century Lawsuit: the case of St. Anthony's Hospital', *Journal of Ecclesiastical History* 44 (1993), 199–223, for references to the fortunes of the hospital during this period.

412.   <u>Breve ad inquirendum in causa etc. W. Souche versus Robertum Constable chivaler</u>
Common Pleas *inquiretis de bastardia*, returnable at York[1] three weeks from Michaelmas, in the following case: Richard Clerk and Agnes his wife are seeking in our court, against Robert Constable knight, Juliana Gatesham and Richard Assheby and Agnes his wife, a third part of the manor of Lubbesthorpe (Lubbes-thorp) with appurtenances. The plaintiffs claim that this was the dower of Agnes now wife of Richard Clerk, by the endowment of William Zouche (Souche) formerly her husband, but Robert has alleged that this cannot be claimed as dower as Agnes and William were never joined in lawful wedlock. Since this lies within the cognisance of the church court we order you to hold an inquiry in your presence and certify the result by letters patent and close.
Teste Robert de Cherlton, York 6 July 1392.
<u>Informacio pro causa eiusdem</u>
'Willelmus de Bredon desponsavit Agnetem sororem Willelmi la Zouche de Lobes-thorp' militis et habuerunt exitum inter se quendam Radulphum qui desponsavit Agnetem que modo est uxor Ricardi Clerk et predicti Radulphus et Agnes uxor eius fuerunt etatis novem annorum et amplius antequam predictus Radulphus morie-batur et post mortem predicti Radulphi predictus Willelmus la Zouche desponsavit predictam Agnetem que fuit uxor predicti Radulphi et modo predictus Ricardus Clerk et predicta Agnes uxor eius petunt dotem de hereditati predicti Willelmi la Zouche.'
[See **410**]

1   Richard II moved the courts to York in the summer of 1392 in the course of his quarrel with the city of London; see Caroline M. Barron, 'The Quarrel of Richard II with London 1392–7',

and John H. Harvey, 'Richard II and York', in F.R.H. Du Boulay and Caroline M. Barron, eds., *The Reign of Richard II: Essays in honour of May McKisack* (London, 1971), pp. 173–201, 202–217.

413. [ff. 60v–61]. Breve pro Parliamento apud Eboracum
Summons to parliament at York on the morrow of the Translation of St. Edward the King [30 April], with *premunientes* clause.
Teste me ipso Windsor 23 July 1392.[1]

   [1] Printed *RDP*, IV.741; see also *CCR 1392–6*, p. 83.

414. [f. 61] Breve de prorogando parliamentum et notificandum subditos etc.
Prorogation of the parliament which was to have been held at York on the morrow of the Translation of St. Edward the King [30 April].
Teste me ipso Windsor Castle 8 Sept. 1392.[1]

   [1] Printed *RDP*, IV.744; see also *CCR 1392–6*, p. 77.

415. Breve de veniendo ad parliamentum Wynchestre
Summons to a parliament to be held at Winchester on the octave of Hilary next with *premunientes* clause.
Teste me ipso York 23 Nov. 1392.[1]
Execucio eiusdem brevis.
The dean and chapter of Lincoln cathedral were written to ordering the dean to go to parliament in person and the chapter to appoint a proctor. They are to report to the bishop what they have done in this matter by the Nativity of the Virgin [8 Sept.]. [Undated.]
The archdeacons, or their officials, were written to, ordering them to attend in person and to cite the clergy to be at the parish church of All Saints Northampton on the Tuesday after Epiphany [7 Jan. 1393] to elect two proctors. The abbot of St. James, Northampton and Master John Hauberk were committed to receive the certificates of the archdeacons or their officials reporting what they had done.

   [1] Printed *RDP*, IV.746; see also *CCR 1392–6*, p. 105.

416. [f. 61v] Breve de certiorando an Matilda Huntercombe monialis de Burn-ham sit professa
Chancery *certiorari*, returnable without delay, to find out on what day and year Maud daughter of John Huntercombe (Undercombe) knight assumed the religious habit at Burnham [abbey] and whether or not she is professed in the order.
Teste me ipso 6 July 1391.[1]

   [1] See *CCR 1389–92*, p. 363, *CCR 1392–6*, pp. 70–1; PRO, C 269/8/18 is the final writ on this matter and the bishop's return following an inquisition, see **Appendix A, no. 17**; also PRO, C 145/254/2 and SC 8/97/4804. This case is discussed further in the introduction, section iii.

417. Aliud Breve de certiorando
Chancery *certiorari sicut alias*; [as above **416**].
Teste me ipso 18 Oct. 1391.
Commissio ad inquirandum virtute dicti brevis Regii.
Commission to Masters John Shillingford, Thomas Southam, Thomas Stowe, William Ryde and John Burbache doctors of laws, to investigate the matter asked

for in the writ, and to report back in writing by letters patent and close what they have done, the names of those giving evidence, and their depositions.
Sleaford 16 July 1392
22 Oct. 1391 at Stow Park the mandate was sent out to the said commissaries to certify all their proceedings.

418. Breve de supersedendo ab ulteriori processu
Chancery *supersedeatis* of the previous two writs.
Teste me ipso 6 Nov. 1391.

419. Breve pro causa Huntercombe et Bekering
Chancery *inquiratis*, returnable in Chancery wherever it is on the octave of Hilary, concerning the following: Giles French, one of our servants, by virtue of a writ directed to him to be before us in Chancery on a day now passed, wherever it then was, to answer Thomas Bekeryng knight, and Elizabeth his wife, Philip Skydemore and Agnes his wife, and Richard Lile and Margaret his wife, should have been present to answer the charge against him; this was, that he had unjustly disseised the said Thomas, Elizabeth, Philip, Agnes, Richard and Margaret of two parts of the manors of Huntercombe and Eton, Buckinghamshire. The plaintiffs held this property because Elizabeth, Agnes and Margaret were the heirs of Elizabeth who was the wife of Robert Cherlton justice of the Bench, and after his death they entered into possession. This is contained in a petition to the parliament held at Westminster on the morrow of All Souls 15 Richard II [3 Nov. 1391] presented by the plaintiffs, and endorsed and sent into Chancery. The said Giles, appearing in Chancery by virtue of a mandate, said that when Elizabeth the wife of Robert, who was seised of the property in question, died without heirs of her body, the land passed to Maud, her sister and heir. He, Giles, married Maud, and she ought to hold the property. The plaintiffs, appearing in Chancery, said that Maud was a nun in the Augustinian house of Burnham and was professed seven years before the death of Elizabeth, and was now aged 24. But Giles alleged that she was a secular and had been for a long time before Elizabeth's death. Mandate to find out the truth.
Teste me ipso York 13 Nov. 1392.

420. [ff. 61v–62] Breve sicut alias
Chancery *inquiratis*, returnable wherever the Chancery is on the octave of the Purification of the Virgin [9 Feb.] on the same matter as the previous writ.
Teste me ipso Winchester 18 Jan. 1393.[1]

> [1] For the final writ on this subject, and Buckingham's return, see **Appendix A, no. 17**.

421. Breve contra vicarium ecclesie de Watford
Common Pleas *venire faciatis*, returnable on the quindene of Easter [20 April], against William Blokle vicar of Watford, your clerk, to answer the abbot of St. James, Northampton for a plea of debt of 7 marks, being arrears of a rent of 26s 8d p.a. Note of return of no lay fee by the sheriff of Northampton on the octave of the Purification [9 Feb.].
Teste Robert de Cherlton, 12 Feb. 1393.

422.   Breve de levando medietatem decime domino Regi concesse
Mandate to levy the moiety of a tenth on assessed benefices granted in the convocation at St. Paul's cathedral on 24 February last, and payable on the feast of the Translation of St. Thomas the Martyr [7 July], and to certify collectors' names to the Exchequer before 1 May next.
Teste me ipso 3 April 1393.
Collectores deputati.
The following were written to in the usual form to levy and collect the moiety, viz.:
archdeaconries of Lincoln and Stow: the abbot and convent of Barlings
archdeaconries of Leicester and Northampton: the abbot and convent of St. Mary's Leicester
archdeaconries of Oxford and Buckingham: the prior and convent of Bicester
archdeaconries of Bedford and Huntingdon: the prior and convent of Newnham (Newenham)

423.   Breve de certiorando pro hospic' de Seint Dewes iuxta Kyngesthorp'
Chancery *certiorari (scrutatis registris)*, returnable without delay, to discover how many people have been admitted, presented or collated to the hospital of Holy Trinity called Saint Dewes,[1] Kingsthorpe (Kyngesthorp), from 1 Edward III to the present.
Teste me ipso 8 June 1393.
[Both this and two subsequent writs on this subject, **445**, **447**, seem to have arisen from a challenge to the mastership of the hospital of Richard Bollesore, since it can scarcely be coincidence that the bishop was ordering an enquiry into this matter at the same time as this first of the sequence of writs was issued. On 28 May 1393 Buckingham issued two commissions, one to the abbot of St. James, Northampton and Robert Palmer rector of Towcester (Toucestr') bachelor in laws, to enquire whether Richard Bollesore chaplain was the rightful warden of the hospital of Holy Trinity Kingsthorpe; the other to the dean of Brackley (Brackele) and Thomas rector of Stoke Bruern (Stoke Bruer') ordering them to cite Richard Bollesore to appear before the commission of enquiry in All Saints church Northampton on the Saturday after Corpus Christi [7 June] to show his title to the wardenship. On the appointed day Bollesore appeared and showed that he had been the warden for a long time, exhibiting evidence and producing several witnesses to this effect.][2]

   [1]   St. Dewi's, that is, St. David's.
   [2]   PRO, C 270 (Ecclesiastical Miscellanea)/30/6. This hospital attracted a lot of attention from the crown since the class contains a number of items relating to it, from 1304 to 1537, C 270/30/4–11.

424.   Breve de certiorando Welton
Chancery *certiorari (scrutatis registris)*, returnable without delay, to discover in what year the church of Welton was appropriated to the prior and convent of Daventry and in what way, who was the last rector before appropriation and who the first vicar after, at whose presentation the rector and vicar were admitted, instituted and inducted.
Teste me ipso 1 March 1393.

425. [ff. 62–62v] <u>Aliud breve sicut alias pro eadem</u>
Chancery *certiorari (scrutatis registris)*, returnable without delay, on the same matter as the previous writ.
Teste me ipso 6 March 1393.

426. <u>Breve sicut pluries de certiorando Welton. Returnum</u>
Chancery *certiorari sicut pluries*, on the same matter as the previous two writs, concluding with a complaint that the bishop has disregarded earlier writs on this matter and has spurned crown mandates; with order to the bishop to be in Chancery on the quindene of Easter [20 April], wherever it is, to explain his contempt for earlier mandates.
Teste me ipso 12 March 1393.
RETURN. We have searched in our registers and archives and we cannot find the year in which Welton church was appropriated, nor who was the last rector before appropriation, nor who presented. [Undated.]

427. <u>Breve ad levandum debita regia</u>
Exchequer *levari faciatis de bonis et beneficiis ecclesiasticis* from the following men, viz.:
the vicar of Catesby in the deanery of Louthesk,[1] for 22s owed to us for two clerical tenths; [unfinished in ms.]

> 1   Obviously an error; Catesby is in central Northants., Louthesk in east Lincs.

428. [f. 63] <u>Breve contra Rectorem ecclesie de Boseworth'</u>
Common Pleas *venire faciatis*, returnable on the morrow of All Souls [3 Nov.], against William de Sleaford rector of Husbands Bosworth (Boseworth) to answer John de Elvet archdeacon of Leicester about a plea of debt of 40s being arrears of an annual rent of 3s 6d. Note of return of no lay fee by the sheriff of Leicestershire before the justices at Westminster on the quindene of Michaelmas.
Teste Robert de Cherlton, 20 Oct. 1393.
EXECUTION. The said William, rector of Bosworth was warned to be before you at the place and day named, as the writ required.

429. <u>Breve de certiorando pro ecclesia de Northmymmes</u>
Chancery *certiorari (scrutatis registris)*, returnable without delay, to know who and how many people have been presented to North Mimms church from 1 Edward III until now, by whom they were presented, and in what way.
Teste me ipso 20 Oct. 1393.
[See **398**, **402**]

430. <u>Breve sicut alias pro eadem</u>
Chancery *certiorari sicut alias* about the same matter as the previous writ, adding that the bishop should give the reason why he will not, or cannot, execute the mandate.
Teste me ipso 30 Oct. 1393.

431. <u>Adhuc breve pro eadem ecclesia de Northmymmes</u>
Chancery *certiorari (scrutatis registris)* on the same subject as the previous two

writs, with strictures about the bishop's delay and contempt, with order to be in
Chancery on the octave of Hilary to explain his non-return of the earlier writs.
Teste me ipso 16 Nov. 1393.[1]

  [1]   Not, as we might expect, *certiorari sicut pluries*. See **Appendix 1, no. 18** for another writ
  on this matter, C 269/8/20.

432.   Breve pro parliamento
Summons to attend a parliament to be held at Westminster on the quindene of Hilary
next, with *premunientes* clause.
Teste me ipso 13 Nov. 1393.[1]
Execucio brevis.
The dean and the archdeacons were written to and ordered to be in parliament in
person, the chapter to be represented by one proctor, and clergy of the diocese by
two; and the archdeacons, or their officials, and the dean were ordered to cite the
clergy to be present in the church of St. Peter in Eastgate Lincoln on the Wednesday
after St. Hilary [14 Jan. 1394] to elect two proctors for the parliament.

  [1]   Printed *RDP*, IV.749; see also *CCR 1392–6*, p. 233.

433.   [ff. 63–63v] Breve contra Rectorem ecclesie de Paunton' Magna
Common Pleas *venire faciatis*, returnable on the octave of Hilary, against John de
Rothewell rector of Great Ponton (Magna Pounton) to answer John de Yerburgh'
prebendary of Grantham Australis[1] about a plea of debt of £20, being arrears of a
rent of 10 marks p.a. Note of return of no lay fee by the sheriff of Lincolnshire
before the justices at Westminster on the octave of Martinmas [18 Nov.].
Teste Robert Cherlton, 26 Nov. 1393.

  [1]   *Sic, rectius* Grantham Borealis, *Fasti*, III.56.

434.   [f. 63v] Breve contra Rectorem de Mynyngesby
Common Pleas *venire faciatis*, returnable on the octave of Hilary, against Thomas
de Ely rector of Miningsby (Mynyngesby), your clerk, to answer Robert de Mumby
about a plea of debt of 40s. Note of return of no lay fee by the sheriff of Lincolnshire
before the justices at Westminster on the morrow of All Souls [3 Nov.].
Teste Robert Cherlton, 12 Nov. 1393.

435.   Breve contra Rectorem ecclesie de Parva Boudon'
Common Pleas *venire faciatis*, returnable on the octave of Hilary, against Thomas
rector of Little Bowden (Parva Boudon) your clerk to answer Walter Baldok prior
of Launde (Lauda) about a plea of debt of 6 marks, being arrears of a rent of 1 mark
p.a. Note of return of no lay fee by the sheriff of Northamptonshire before the
justices at Westminster on the morrow of All Souls [3 Nov.].
Teste Robert de Cherlton, 8 Nov. 1393.

436.   Breve de certiorando Dodyngton
Chancery *certiorari (scrutato registro)*, returnable without delay, to know on what
day and year, in what way and by what title Thomas Sedeyn chaplain was presented
to Doddington Pigot (Dodyngton) church.[1]
Teste me ipso 4 Feb. 1394.

  [1]   Thomas Sedeyn priest was presented by the crown to Doddington Pigot church and admitted
  11 Sept. 1393, Reg. 11, f. 66.

437. Breve contra Rectorem de Craft

Common Pleas *venire faciatis*, returnable on the quindene of Easter [3 May], against John Holbek rector of Croft (Craft) to answer Philip [Repingdon] abbot of Leicester about a plea of debt of £20 and 10 stones of wax, being arrears of a rent of 40s and one stone of wax p.a. Note of return of no lay fee by the sheriff of Leicestershire on the quindene of Hilary.

Teste Robert de Cherlton, 6 Feb. 1394.

Retornum fuit.

438. Breve contra vicarium de Thirneby

Common Pleas *venire faciatis*, returnable on the quindene of Easter [3 May], against Robert Nelot to answer Philip [Repingdon] abbot of Leicester about a plea of debt of 100s being arrears of rent of 30s p.a. Note of return of no lay fee by the sheriff of Leicestershire at Westminster on the quindene of Hilary.

Teste Robert de Cherlton, 6 Feb. 1394.

Retornum fuit.

439. Breve contra vicarium de Thornton'

Common Pleas *venire faciatis*, returnable on the quindene of Easter [3 May], against John Bulker vicar of Thornton to answer Philip [Repingdon] abbot of Leicester about a plea of debt of 20 marks being arrears of rent of 4 marks p.a. Note of return of no lay fee by the sheriff of Leicestershire at Westminster on the quindene of Hilary.

Teste Robert de Cherlton, 6 Feb. 1394.

Returnum fuit.

440. Breve contra parsonam de Magna Paunton'

Common Pleas *venire faciatis*, returnable on the quindene of Easter [3 May] against John de Rothewell rector of Great Ponton (Magna Pounton) to answer John de Yerburgh' prebendary of Grantham (Australis) [*rectius* Borealis] about a plea of debt of £20, being arrears of a rent of 10 marks p.a. Note of return of no lay fee by the sheriff of Lincolnshire before the justices at Westminster on the octave of Martinmas [18 Nov.].

Teste Robert de Cherlton, 24 Jan. 1394.

Retornum fuit.

[See **433**]

441. [f. 63v] Breve contra parsonam de Myngyngesby

Common Pleas *venire faciatis*, returnable on the octave of Hilary, against Thomas de Ely rector of Miningsby, your clerk, to answer Robert de Munuby about a plea of debt of 40s. Note of return of no lay fee by the sheriff of Lincolnshire on the morrow of All Souls.

Teste Robert de Cherlton, 24 Jan. 1394.

Retornum fuit.

[See **434**]

442.   Breve contra parsonam de Denham
Common Pleas *venire faciatis*, returnable on the quindene of Easter [3 May], against John Mayfield rector of Denham to answer the abbot of Westminster about a plea of debt of £6, being arrears of rent of 30s p.a. Note of return of no lay fee by the sheriff of Buckinghamshire on the octave of Hilary.
Teste Robert de Cherlton, 24 Jan. 1394.

443.   [f. 64] Prohibicio Welton
Chancery *ne admittatis* concerning the vicarage of Welton whose advowson is being disputed between the king and the prior of Daventry.
Teste me ipso 16 Feb. 1394.
[See **424**, **426**]

444.   Breve de certiorando Dodyngton
Chancery *certiorari*, returnable without delay, to know on what day and in what year, in what way and by what title Thomas Sedeyn chaplain was presented to Doddington Pigot church.
Teste me ipso 4 Feb. 1394.
[See **436**]

445.   Breve de certiorando Seint Dewes iuxta Kingesthorp
Chancery *certiorari (scrutatis registris)* returnable without delay, to discover how many wardens have been admitted, presented or collated to the hospital of Holy Trinity called Saint Dewes, Kingsthorp, from 1 Edward III to the present.
Teste me ipso 11 Feb. 1394.[1]
[See **423**]

   [1]   See Reg. 12, ff. 405–405v for the case against Richard Bollesore chaplain, warden of the hospital, in the church court. The church court was held in All Saints church, Northampton.

446.   Chancery *venire faciatis*,[1] returnable on the quindene of Easter [3 May], before the king and council in Chancery against Amia Palmer[2] a prisoner detained in the bishop's prison at Banbury, it is said, along with the cause of her arrest and detention.
Teste me ipso 26 March 1394.[3]
Breve retornum Palmere.
John [Buckingham] bishop of Lincoln to Richard II. We have recently received your writ 'vigore cuius Annam [*sic*] Palmere in custodia nostra apud Bannebury deten-tam vestre Regie maiestate ac consilio vestro in cancellar*ia* vestra destinamus, causamque et capcionem ac detencionem eiusdem Amie in custodia nostra predicta seriose exponentes prout tenor brevis predicti exigit et requirit. Nam fama publica et referente ad nostram dudum pervenit noticiam quod nonnulli filii tenebrarum villam seu opidum de Northampton nostre dioc' tunc inhabitantes errores atque hereses alia que enormia catholice fidei ac determinacioni sancte matris ecclesie repugnancia publice tenuerunt et in stratis publicis ac domibus clam et palam docuerunt populum eiusdem ville quasi pro maiori parte a fide catholica dampnabiliter pervertendo; unde ne pestiferi veneni eorundem infusio amplius dilataretur et animas Christi fidelium inficeret eosque a tramite veritatis et fidei orthodoxe faceret fallaci sermone et simulata simplicitate deviare nostros commis-sarios primo et deinde venerabilem confratrem nostrum dominum Willelmum dei

gracia episcopum Pisenensem[4] suffraganeum nostrum secundo ad villam predictam pro reformacione premissorum et execucione mandatorum nostrorum contra certas personas in hac parte tunc fienda transmisimus olim per litteras nostras patentes, set hiisdem commissariis nostris in exequendo mandatorum huiusmodi in tantis periculis ibidem per lollardos tunc fautoresque eorundem constitutis quod ad vestiarium ecclesie Omnium Sanctorum[5] in villa predicta cum magna difficultate ob vite eorum tutelam fugerunt. Nos ob id ne sanguis ipsorum de manibus nostris in extremo iudicio requeretur, ad videndum utrum clamorem aperte complenerant ad villam de Northampton predictam personaliter descendebamus, et ibidem in ecclesia Omnium Sanctorum diebus Jovis, Veneris et Sabbati proximis ante festum Exaltacionis Sancte Crucis ultimo elapsum inquisicionem fecimus diligentem generalem per probiores et digniores ville predicte ac locorum vicinorum, per quam quidem inquisicionem comperimus quod prefata Amia Palmere tunc anchorita et in quadam domo ecclesie Sancti Petri in villa predicta contigua inclusa fuit principalis receptrix lollardorum in domo sua noctanter et presertim Thome Patteshull, Johannis Chory, Simonis Colyn, Johannis Wolf, Johannis Whelewryght' capellani et Thome Whelwright' capellani principalium lollardorum pro tunc manencium in villa predicta, in cuius eciam domo occulte fiebant conventicule et illicite congregaciones, ac quod ipsa Amia Palmere ac prefati Thomas Patteshull', Johannes, Simon, Johannes, Johannes, et Thomas articulos presentibus annexos palam et publice tenuerunt et docuerunt. Et propterea eandam Annam de incontinencia eciam inquisicione nostra predicta detectam iussimus et fecimus ad iudicium coram nobis ad articulum predictum ac ad articulos subsequentes presentibus annexos responsuram evocari, ipsa tamen Amia in iudicio coram nobis personaliter comparens palam et publice coram copiosa multitudine dixit nos esse Antichristum clericos que nostros esse discipulos Antechristi, et recitatis eidem Amie articulis subsequentibus seriatim per cancellarium nostrum in Wlgari, eadem Amia contumaciter et vultu protervo dixit se nolle respondere ad articulos eosdem preterquam ad articulum de incontinencia quam negavit. Quocirca premissorum intuitu nos habentes eandam Amiam de heresibus et erroribus ac lollardica pravitate vehementer suspectam ipsam occasione premissorum et propter suas manifestas contumacias coram nobis contractas ne ceteros inficeret Christi fideles, custodie deputavimus carcerali et ipsam in prisona nostra apud Bannebury fecimus detineri quousque ad gremium sancte matris ecclesie ipsa Amia decreverit se reversuram. Que omnia et singula vestre excellencie Regali nostras litteras clausas sigillo nostro consignatas transmittimus per presentes.
Lincoln 27 April 1393.

Articuli.

Articuli subscripti in inquisicione generali per nos Johannem Episcopum Lincoln' Episcopum in ecclesia Omnium Sanctorum Northampton' capta detecti contra Annam [*sic*] Palmere nuper anchoritam in Northampton', Thomam Patteshull', Johannem Cory', Simonem Colyn, Johannem Wolf, Johannem Whelewright capellanum et Thomam Whelewright capellanum ac tenti et publice docti per eosdem prout publica vox et fama in villa Northampton' et aliis locis vicinis contra eosdem et ipsorum quemlibet volat' et laborat':

In primis dicitur quod prefata Amia et ceteri supradicti dicunt palam et expresse quod Innocentes ad dominum migrantes nec in inferno nec in paradiso post decessum collocantur set in medio loco sunt examen extremi iudicii expectantes.

Item quod cuilibet christiano sufficiens est dei mandata servare in cubili vel in campo deum secrete adorare, nec in domo materiali publice precibus incumbere, ne phariseis se conformans ypocrita computetur, nec ecclesia materialiter constructa apud illos pro sacra ecclesia reputatur ymmo quedam domus materialis et apud quosdam constructa castellum 'caym' vocatur.

Item qui proximus est deo in hac vita sanctitate causante papa confirmatur, nec papa quem nos dicimus summum pontificem pontificem [*sic*] potestatem habet a pena et culpa veniam peccancium concedendi. Et quod tempore sancti Silvestri pape erat universalis ecclesia simoniace dotata. Et sic usque in hodierum diem residet toxicata et ideo de potestate pape et aliorum prelatorum eis omnino desperatur.

Item cum iniungatur alicui nomine penitencie propter peccata peregre proficisci affirmant illi lollardi magis meritorium quantitatem summe illius in peregrinacionis itinere expendend, fore pauperibus erogand, quam penitenciam sibi pro commissis iniunctam peragere iuxta [f. 64v] canonis instituta. Et dicunt quod post annum millenium a nativitate domini sathanas erat solutus a nexibus et omnes quos postmodum natos reputamus fore sanctos taliter credunt diabolice infectos quod cicius credendos est illos fore dampnatos quam salvatos et huiusmodi sanctos vocant sanctos millenos.

Item sanctum Thomam Cantuar' vel alium sanctum quem peregrini in partibus anglicanis adorant pro sancto affirmare omnino indubio suspendent nec credunt articulos fore licitos nec divine commendabilies voluntati pro quibus sanctus Thomas persolvit tributum condicionis humane.

Item affirmant quod capellanus non tenetur matutinas et horas canonicas dicere ante celebracionem divinorum neque postea nisi ex mera sua voluntate eiusdem capellani nec indiget confiteri nisi soli deo ante celebracionem.

Item si sacerdos sit in mortali peccato caret potestate sacramentum Eukaristie et baptismi consecrand' et idem capellanus diabolus est.

Item ita quod meritorium est ut eis videtur ostulare [*sic*] lapides in campo iacentes sicut pedes crucifixi in ecclesia vel aliquas ymagines in ecclesia cum luminibus adorare vel munera eis offerre.

Item quod oblaciones facte in sponsalibus et sepulturis mortuorum sunt subtrahend' eo quod in simoniam penitus redundant.

Item quod si aliquis commiserit aliquod peccatum mortale et illud oblitus fuerit et inde obierit non confessus licet misericordiam dei pecierit, dampnatus est pro illo peccato mortali oblito et quod non est in potestate dei ipsum salvare per misericordiam.

Item quod non est licitum sacerdotibus fore stipendarios pro celebracione divinorum.

Item quod est licitum cuilibet christiano informare fratrem suum in decem mandatis et sanctis evangeliis ut ea sciat et predicet et quod quilibet paterfamilias respondebit pro se et commissis familie sue.

Item dicunt, ut dicitur, quod est cassum dare alicui mendicanti elemosinam nisi solummodo claudis et curvis et cecis que fuerint debiles aut paralitice iacentes et quod omnes contribuentes huiusmodi elemosinam sunt fautores et sustentatores dictorum mendicancium in peccatis et qui ita dat elemosinam servit diabolo.

Item affirmant, ut dicitur, quod si aliquis in mortali peccato existens audieret missam quod illa missa erit sibi in dampnacionem.

Item dicunt, ut dicitur, quod omnes indulgencie concesse a domino papa in remissionem peccatorum vel ad relevacionem alicuius hospitalis seu alterius loci propter elemosinas dandas et querendas per questores sunt false casse et vane et in cupidinem redundant absque salute anime quia questores et receptores huiusmodi elemosinarum inde superbiose et delicate vivunt et nullum aliud bonum inde provenit.

Ad articulos predictos in vulgari expositos prefata Amia monita per nos Johannem Episcopum supradictum atque iussa, noluit ut palam dixit respondere ad eosdem.

¹ This writ is in common form. It is not, as might have been expected, a *corpus cum causa.*
² The scribe who copied this writ and return was far from conscientious about dotting his letter 'i'. However, on balance the lady's name was probably Amia, rather than Anna, as I once thought.
³ The return to this writ and the articles of belief have previously been printed and discussed in McHardy, 'Bishop Buckingham and the Lollards of Lincoln Diocese', in *Schism, Heresy and Religious Protest*, ed. Derek Baker, Studies in Church History 9 (1972), pp. 138–45. For the similarity of these beliefs to the tract known as the *Twenty-five Articles*, see *Knighton's Chronicle 1337–1396*, ed. and trans. Geoffrey Martin (Oxford, 1995), pp. 434–7, and 435 n. 2.
⁴ William Egmund, suffragan bishop, see David M. Smith, 'Suffragan Bishops in the Medieval Diocese of Lincoln', *Lincolnshire History and Archaeology* 17 (1982), 17–27, esp. p. 25.
⁵ All Saints church, Northampton, was the usual meeting place for diocesan gatherings, for example to elect proctors to represent the clergy in convocation and in parliament.

447. [f. 64v] Breve de certiorando Seint Dewes
Chancery *certiorari (scrutatis registris)* returnable without delay, to discover how many wardens have been admitted, presented or collated to the hospital of Holy Trinity called Saint Dewes, Kingsthorp, from 1 Edward III to the present.
Teste me ipso 11 Feb. 1394.
[See **423, 445**]

448. [f. 65] Breve contra Rectorem de Walton iuxta Ramsey
Exchequer *levari faciatis de bonis et beneficiis ecclesiasticis*, returnable on the morrow of Michaelmas, against William Pichelesthorn, chaplain, rector of Wood Walton church near Ramsey, Huntingdonshire, lately receiver of all rents and profits at the castle and honour of Berkhamsted for £18 5s 7¾d owed to the crown being debts incurred in that office, and seen in his accounts at the Exchequer, from Michaelmas 5 Richard II to the Nativity of St. John Baptist 8 Richard II [29 September 1381 – 24 June 1384].
Teste John Cassy, 20 July 1394.
Execution. The writ is contained in a mandate of the bishop to the archdeacon of Huntingdon or his official, and the dean of Yaxley (Jakesley) ordering sequestration of the amount and a report to be before the bishop by the feast of St. Matthew the Apostle [21 Sept.], along with the money, and threatening royal and episcopal indignation if this were not done.
Stow Park 10 Aug. 1394.
[See **381**]

449. [f. 65] Breve de certiorando Merston
Chancery *certiorari (scrutatis registris)* to know who, and how many, have been presented to Marston Moretaine (Merston) church near Bedford since the coronation of Henry [III] son of King John, by whom and by what title.
Teste me ipso 16 July 1394.

450. <u>Mandatum de colligendo medietatem decime domino Regi concesse</u>
Mandate to collect the grant made in the convocation held at St. Paul's cathedral,
London, on 21 May, of a moiety of a tenth on assessed benefices, payable on the
feast of St. Andrew [30 Nov.], on condition that the benefices of poor nuns are
exempt, and certification of the names of collectors to the Exchequer by 21 October.
Teste me ipso 10 Aug. 1394.
<u>Execution</u>: the writ is contained in a commission to the abbot and convent of Thame
to act as collectors in the archdeaconry of Oxford. The writ was received on 16 Oct.
in the bishop's palace at Lincoln.
Note that the following were also appointed:
in the archdeaconries of Lincoln and Stow: the abbot and convent of Kirkstead
in the archdeaconry of Leicester: the abbot and convent of Croxton
in the archdeaconry of Northampton: the abbot and convent of Biddlesdon
in the archdeaconry of Oxford: the abbot and convent of Thame
in the archdeaconry of Buckingham: the rector and convent of [the house of]
Ashridge
in the archdeaconry of Bedford: the prior and convent of Caldwell
in the archdeaconry of Huntingdon: the abbot and convent of Ramsey.
Stow Park 20 Oct. 1394.

451. [65v] <u>Breve pro testamento Cary</u>
Chancery *certiorari (scrutato registro)*, returnable without delay, concerning the
registration of the will of Richard Cary of Oxford made in your register, it is said.
The bishop is to look to see if he could find it.
Teste me ipso 1 Aug. 1394.[1]

> [1] This case is discussed in the introduction, section iii, p. xxi. Cary, a prominent Oxford citizen,
> died in the Black Death. For his career and bequests see *VCH Oxfordshire*, IV.19, 43, 59, 67,
> 371, 385.

452. <u>Breve sicut alias pro eodem</u>
Another writ on the same subject as the above.
Teste me ipso 16 Aug. 1394.
<u>Return. Breve sicut pluries retornum testamentum infrascript' in libro memorand'.</u>
We received your writ on 22 Sept. We found the will copied out word for word
among our memoranda, *In dei nomine amen etc.*[1]
Stow Park 22 Sept. 1394.[2]

> [1] The will of Richard Cary is in Reg. 12, ff. 367v, 371. The main provisions are printed by
> Alfred Gibbons, *Early Lincoln Wills* (Lincoln, 1888), p. 39.
> [2] See original letter patent 10 May 1391, Reg. 12, f. 370. Letter close of 26 Nov. 1394, original
> *ibid.*, f. 369, calendared in *CCR 1392–6*, p. 323; see also *CPR 1391–6*, p. 82, for background
> notes.

453. <u>Breve retornum pro testamento Cary de Oxon'</u>
Chancery mandate, returnable before the octave of the Purification of the Virgin [8
Feb.], concerning the will of Richard Cary of Oxford. At an inquisition taken by
William Dagvyll, John Hikkes, Edmund Kynyan and John Merston, our commissaries, and returned into Chancery, it was found that Richard Cary of Oxford had
left certain lands and tenements in Oxford, with appurtenances, to John his son,
also dead, and the legitimate heirs of his body, but that the will was a forgery, as

was shown by a jury before [the said] William [Dagvyll] on 9 March 15 Richard II. We understand that the will was copied into your register, and we asked for a copy of this to be sent into Chancery. Having made careful collation we find that the will copied into your register is also a forgery; we therefore order you to annul and abolish the copy in your register.

Teste Edmund duke of York guardian of England, 18 Jan. 1395.[1]

Return: We received the writ on 3 Feb. 1395 and we have caused the registrar of our Chancery to annul the will.[2]

Stow Park 3 Feb. 1395.

> [1]   The original of this writ is sewn into Reg. 12 at f. 368.
> [2]   The will in Reg. 12, ff. 367v, 371, is crossed through.

454.   Breve sicut alias pro ecclesia de Merston

Chancery *certiorari (scrutatis registris)* to know who, and how many, have been presented to Marston Moretaine (Merston) church near Bedford since the coronation of Henry [III] son of King John, by whom and by what title.

Teste Edmund duke of York guardian of England, 18 Oct. 1394.

[See **449**]

455.   [ff. 65v–66] Breve sicut pluries

Chancery *certiorari* concerning Marston Moretaine church with mandate ordering the bishop to be in Chancery on the octave of Hilary to explain why he had ignored earlier writs.

Teste Edmund duke of York guardian of England, 15 Nov. 1394.

[f. 66] Breve retornum pro ecclesia de Merston.

Return: addressed to the King, informing him that the bishop has caused the registers of his predecessors to be scrutinised from the time of Hugh II,[1] when Gilbert de W.[2] was instituted, and sends a full list.

Stow Park 8 Jan. 1395.

> [1]   Hugh of Wells, bishop of Lincoln 1209–35.
> [2]   For Gilbert de Wyville's institution see *Rot. Wells*, III.29.

456.   Breve retornum super sacramento Escaetoris Lincoln' capto

Chancery mandate to receive the oath of John Meres escheator in Lincolnshire according to the form contained in the annexed schedule, and afterwards to give him the letters patent by which the crown appoints him to this office.

Teste Edmund duke of York guardian of England, 14 Nov. 1394.

Return. To the king; the oath of John Meres was received according to the form contained in the annexed schedule and the letters patent were given to him.

Stow Park 6 Dec. 1394.[1]

> [1]   This writ was also entered in Reg. 12, f. 420.

457.   Breve pro exoneracione pauperum monialum

Exchequer mandate, returnable on the octave of Hilary, to send a list of the benefices of poor nuns which are exempt from payment of the moiety of a tenth granted in St. Paul's cathedral on last 21 May, and which is payable on the feast of St. Andrew [30 Nov.] on condition that the benefices of poor nuns would be excused.

Teste L[awrence]. de Allerthorp, 5 Dec. 1394.

458.   Breve pro parliamento in XV<u>a</u> sancti Hillar'

Summons to attend the parliament at Westminster on the quindene of Hilary, with *premunientes* clause.

Teste Edmund duke of York guardian of England, 20 Nov. 1394.[1]

> [1]   Printed *RDP*, IV.752; see also *CCR 1392–6*, pp. 386–7.

459.   [ff. 66–66v] Breve contra Rectorem de Botyngdon

Common Pleas *venire faciatis*, returnable on the quindene of Hilary, against William rector of a moiety of Boddington (Botyngdon) church to answer the prior of Chacombe about a plea of debt of 100s, being arrears of a rent of 13s 4d p.a. Note of return of no lay fee by the sheriff of Northamptonshire on the morrow of the Annunciation [26 March].

Teste Robert Cherlton, 13 Nov. 1394.

460.   Prohibicio regia pro placitis de advoc' ecclesiarum etc.

To the bishop and his commissary: Chancery *ne teneatis* concerning Dorney church whose advowson is in dispute between the abbess and convent of Burnham, long time patrons of the church which has been appropriated to their use by royal licence, and John Newenham who claims the right of presentation and who has presented one John Leyre clerk to the church; the case started in the church court should be stopped at once, and any action taken in connection with this should be revoked without delay.

Teste Edmund duke of York guardian of England, 5 Oct. 1394.

461.   Breve contra Rectorem de Boseworth

Common Pleas *venire faciatis*, returnable on the octave of Trinity [13 June], against William Sleaford rector of Husbands Bosworth who was indicted before the court of Common Pleas by John Elvet archdeacon of Leicester on a plea of debt of 40s being arrears of rent of 3s 6d p.a. at Westminster on the octave of Michaelmas, and the case was adjourned *sine die* because William de Ferrers (Ferrariis), Elizabeth who was the wife of Edward le Despenser, Thomas de Nevill *chivaler* and Joan his wife, and Walter Derose and Agnes his wife patrons of the church, and John [Buckingham] bishop of Lincoln the ordinary, who also sought William in the king's court, could do nothing because he was about to set out with the king to Ireland and had royal proctection from 26 Sept. 18 Richard II [1394] for six months. Note of return of no lay fee by the sheriff of Leicestershire at Westminster five weeks from Easter [16 May].[1]

Teste Robert de Cherlton, 23 May 1395.

[See also **428**]

> [1]   For William Sleaford and his family see Tout, *Chapters*, IV.384 and n. 2, 458 n. 3.

462.   Breve pro X<u>a</u> domino Regi concessa levando

Mandate to appoint collectors for the tenth granted in the convocation held at St. Paul's cathedral on 5 Feb. last, payable in equal portions at the Translation of St. Thomas the Martyr [7 July] and the following feast of St. Andrew the Apostle [30 Nov.], on assessed benefices, but excluding the benefices of nuns or religious women, and to notify the collectors' names to the Exchequer by Trinity [6 June].

Teste me ipso 15 May 1395.

[ff. 66v–67] Execution.
Mandate to the abbot and convent of Peterborough to act as collectors in the archdeaconry of Northampton, except from the prioress and convent of Sewardsley (Sewardesle).[1]
The other collectors were:
in the archdeaconries of Lincoln and Stow: the abbot and convent of Barlings
in the archdeaconry of Leicester: the abbot and convent of Leicester
in the archdeaconry of Northampton: the abbot and convent of Peterborough
in the archdeaconry of Oxford: the abbot and convent of Thame
in the archdeaconries of Buckingham and Bedford: the abbot and convent of Warden
in the archdeaconry of Huntingdon: the prior of St. Mary's Huntingdon.

[1] Northants., probably Cistercian. 'The convent was always small and poor', Knowles and Hadcock, *Medieval Religious Houses: England and Wales* 2nd ed. (London, 1971), p. 275.

463. Breve de certiorando Thornton'
Chancery *certiorari (scrutatis registris)* to know whether the vicarage of Thornton, Leicestershire, is pensionary or portionary and, if it is, to whom and for what sums and in what way, by searching the registers of the bishop and his predecessors from the time of Hugh II [Hugh of Wells] onwards.
Teste me ipso Northampton 1 Aug. 1395.
Return. This writ came too late for us to execute its mandate.

464. Breve sicut alias de certiorando Thornton'
Chancery *certiorari sicut alias* [as above writ] with clause expressing displeasure at the bishop's delay in executing mandates.
Teste me ipso Beverley 3 Sept. 1395.

465. [f. 67v] Breve de certiorando Thornton
Chancery *certiorari* [as in the two previous writs] with a longer clause expressing severe displeasure and order to be in Chancery on the Monday before Michaelmas to explain why the bishop has not executed the previous writs.
Teste me ipso Kingston on Hull 13 Sept. 1395.
Retornum. We have made diligent scrutiny of the rolls of Hugh II and we report as follows: Thornton (Thoryngton) church etc.[1]
Sleaford 16 Sept. 1395.
[See **463, 464**]

[1] Thornton was appropriated to Leicester abbey, see *Rot. Wells*, I.247.

466. Breve de levando etc. Walton iuxta Ramsey
Exchequer *levari faciatis de bonis et beneficiis ecclesiasticis sicut pluries*, returnable on the morrow of Michaelmas, against William Pichelesthorn chaplain rector of Wood Walton near Ramsey, Huntingdonshire, lately receiver of all rents and profits at the castle and honour of Berkhamsted for £18 5s 7¾d owed to the crown being debts incurred in that office, and seen in his accounts at the Exchequer, from Michaelmas 5 Richard II to the Nativity of St. John Baptist 8 Richard II [29 September 1381 – 24 June 1384].
Teste John Cassy, 15 June 1395.
[See **423, 445**]

467.   Breve de certiorando Hals in parochia de Brakley
Chancery *certiorari (scrutatis registris)* by looking in the registers from Hugh II onwards, to know who finds a chaplain to serve, by celebrating and performing the other duties, the chapel of Halse (Hals) in the parish of Brackley, Northamptonshire.
Teste me ipso Northampton 1 Aug. 1395.
[See **Appendix A, no. 19** for the original and return.]

468.   Breve pro eodem
Chancery *certiorari (scrutatis registris)* [on the same subject as the previous writ] with clause expressing displeasure that the first writ was not executed.
Teste me ipso Beverley 3 Sept. 1395.
[f. 68. Breve de certiorando Brakley. The same writ was copied again.]

469.   Breve pro eodem
Chancery *certiorari (scrutatis registris)* on the same subject as the previous two writs with complaint that the bishop has not replied to earlier writs and mandate to be in Chancery on the morrow of All Souls [3 Nov.] to explain himself.
Teste me ipso Windsor 2 Oct. 1395.

470.   [ff. 67v–68] Breve de certiorando Leycestr'
Chancery *certiorari (scrutatis registris)* to know in what sums of money the churches of St. Mary de Castro, St. Leonard and St. Martin, all in the town of Leicester, are bound to pay p.a. to the bishop of Lincoln and the archdeacon of Leicester, by searching the rolls and registers from the time of Hugh of Wells onwards, from what time and in what way.
Teste me ipso Northampton 1 Aug. 1395.

471.   Breve de certiorando Leycestr' pro certis ecclesiis
Chancery *certiorari (scrutatis registris)* on the same subject as the previous writ with clause that the bishop should explain why he could not execute the earlier one.
Teste me ipso Windsor 2 Oct. 1395.
Retornum eiusdem brevis: We have looked at our registers and we do not find in what annual sums the churches of St. Mary de Castro, St. Leonard and St. Martin in the town of Leicester are bound to us and the archdeacon of Leicester, but we do find among other things, 'The church of St. Mary etc.' which we make known by these presents.
Stow Park 26 Oct. 1395.

472.   Breve de certiorando Usflet
Chancery *certiorari* whether Robert de Ursflet clerk holds a benefice and if so what kind and how.
Teste me ipso 8 Nov. 1395.
Retornum eiusdem.
We have searched diligently in our registers and other deeds and we cannot find that Robert de Ursflet holds an ecclesiastical benefice.[1]
Stow Park 14 Nov. 1395.

----

[1]   Robert Ursflet had been rector of Reepham, Lincs., instituted Aug. 1366, Reg. 10, f. 128; he was still there in 1377, but not in 1381, LRS 81, nos. 799, 2149.

473. Breve de certiorando Cammeringham
Exchequer *certiorari*, returnable on the quindene of Hilary, to know who has occupied the church of Cammeringham[1] which is appropriated to the alien abbot and convent of Blanchelande (Blaunchelande)[2] from 10 Aug. last.
Teste John Cassy, 28 Nov. 1395.
Retornum eiusdem.
We have searched our registers and other acts and our answer is John de Sneed, priest, present etc.
Stow Park 18 Jan. 1396.

> [1] See Knowles and Hadcock, *Medieval Religious Houses*, pp. 184, 186. The alien priory of Cammeringham was sold to Hulton abbey, Staffs., in 1396.
> [2] Normandy.

474. [ff. 68–68v] Breve contra Rectorem de Walton iuxta Ramsey
Exchequer *levari faciatis de bonis et beneficiis ecclesiasticis sicut pluries*, returnable on the quindene of Easter [16 April], against William Pichelesthorne rector of Wood Walton lately receiver of all rents and profits at the castle and honour of Berkhamsted for £18 5s 7¾d owed to the crown being debts incurred in that office, and seen in his accounts at the Exchequer, from Michaelmas 5 Richard II to the Nativity of St. John Baptist 8 Richard II [29 September 1381 – 24 June 1384].
Teste John Cassy, 24 Jan. 1396. By the great roll of 16 Richard II now in London [and] Middlesex, and the Memoranda roll of 19 Richard II, among *brevia retornabilia*, roll 13.
[See **381**, **448**, **466**]

475. [f. 68v] Breve contra Johannem Rectorem de Scoter
Common Pleas *venire faciatis*, returnable on the quindene of Easter [16 April], against [Master] John Bannebury rector of Scotter (Scoter')[1] to answer the abbot of Peterborough about a plea of debt of £6, being arrears of rent of 40s p.a. Note of return of no lay fee by the sheriff of Lincolnshire on the octave of Hilary.
Teste William Thirnyng, 27 Jan. 1396.

> [1] Admitted 4 June 1394, see *BRUO*, I.102.

476. Breve de certiorando Armeston'
Chancery *certiorari (scrutatis registris)* who and how many wardens have been presented to St. John's Hospital, Armston from 50 Edward III to last Christmas and at whose collation or presentation, when and in what way, and what form is the foundation of the hospital and whether it is compatible with a benefice with cure.
Teste me ipso Woodstock (Wodestok) 15 Jan. 1396.
Retornum. We have made diligent search in our register and send you what is there, word for word, but whether or not the hospital is compatible with a benefice with cure of souls we cannot at present certify.
Stow Park 24 Feb. 1396.

477. Adhuc Armeston'
Chancery *certiorari (scrutatis registris) sicut alias* on the same matter as the previous writ.
Teste me ipso York 1 March 1396.
Retornum. In answer to your first writ we sent a reply to you by Benedict Nicol

chaplain, who has presented your writs to us on several occasions. As to whether the hospital is or is not compatible with a benefice with cure we cannot yet say, but we have set in motion an enquiry and will let you know quickly as soon as we can do so.
Stow Park 13 March 1396.
Armeston Inquisitio. [ff. 68v–69]
Report to the bishop from William de Burton rector of Easton on the Hill (Eston)[1] to investigate the status and history of Armston hospital, with recital of the bishop's letter of commission dated Stow Park 12 March 1396. The inquisition was held on the feast of St. Edward the Martyr last [18 Feb.] in the parish church of Polebroke. He quotes in full the foundation charter of Ralph and Alice de Trubleville in the time of Hugh of Wells,[2] complete with witness list.[3] Then follows a list of all the holders of the mastership and which other benefices they have held with it.
Lincoln 23 March 1396.

  [1]   See *BRUO*, I.322.
  [2]   1232, Knowles and Hadcock, *English Religious Houses*, pp. 313, 339.
  [3]   The original is in the PRO, Ancient Deeds C 3119. See also *Rot. Wells*, II.256–8.

478.   [f. 69v] Breve de certiorando Armeston'
Chancery *certiorari (scrutatis registris) sicut pluries* concerning presentations to Armston hospital, [as the previous two writs], with mandate to appear in Chancery on the quindene of Easter [16 April] to show why you cannot execute the mandates. *Teste me ipso* Pontefract (Pomfret) 9 March 1396.
Retornum: [ff. 69v–70] In answer to your writ we have caused diligent enquiry to be made and we find that the hospital is lacking cure of souls and everything else that would make it incompatible with a benefice with cure of souls and that from the foundation to the present time the warden is accustomed to be presented and instituted by the bishop of the place,[1] and at the present time it is held by a secular.
Stow Park 13 April 1396.

  [1]   For evidence of patronage see LAO Reg. 10, ff. 178, 223; Reg. 11, ff. 154v, 164.

479.   [f. 70] Breve de certiorando Armeston'
Chancery *certiorari (scrutatis registris)* concerning the form of the foundation and ordination of Armeston hospital made in the time of Robert Grosseteste it is said. *Teste me ipso* 3 May 1396.
Retornum.
In answer to your enquiry we made diligent search among the registers of Robert Grossetete but could not find anything about the foundation of the hospital in his time. However, we did find an *inspeximus* of two charters, one of Hugh of Wells[1] and the other of Lady Alice de Trublevile in these words etc.[2] as in the register; and we have looked in the register for the charters of these two and send you their wording etc.
Stow Park 28 May 1396.
[See **Appendix A, no. 23** for the original of the writ and return.]

  [1]   1232. The original, owned by the duke of Buccleuch, is at Boughton House, Kettering, Northants., doc. B.1.470; printed *Rot. Wells*, II.256–8.
  [2]   *Rotuli Roberti Grosseteste*, ed. F.N. Davis (C&Y 10, 1913), pp. 187–8.

480. [Unheaded]
Chancery *certiorari (scrutatis registris)* concerning the rectors of Market Deeping
(St. Guthlac Estdepyng) from 1 Edward III to Christmas 1395, and the patrons of
the living.
Teste me ipso 22 April 1396.
Retornum. We recently received your writ which we return, and we have made
diligent scrutiny of the registers of our predecessors from the first year of Henry
Burghersh[1] onwards, and we send you the results word for word.
Stow Park 28 May 1396.

   [1]   Bishop of Lincoln 1320–40.

481.   Breve de certiorando Bolewyk
Chancery *certiorari (scrutatis registris)* concerning the rectors of Bulwick
(Bolewyk) church from the time of Henry II [*sic*] to the feast of Hilary last, and the
patrons of the living.
Teste me ipso Nottingham 30 Jan. 1396.

482.   Item aliud Breve
Chancery *certiorari (scrutatis registris)* concerning the rectors of Bulwick from the
time of Henry III [*sic*].
Teste me ipso York 4 April 1396.

483.   [ff. 70–70v] Prohibicio Burford
[Mandate against admitting Walter Eymer to the vicarage of Burford, in the
patronage of the abbot of Keynsham (Somerset), because he has been prosecuted
in court of King's Bench for obtaining the presentation by papal provision, in
contravention of the Statue of Provisors of 1390.]
Chancery *prohibicio* to the bishop 'executori quarundam litterarum apostolicarum
vobis et quibusdam aliis ad prosecucionem cuiusdam Walteri Eymer'[1] capellani a
sede apostolica, ut dicitur, directarum ac commissariis vestris in hace parte salutem.[2] Cum in statuto [in parliamento] nostro apud Westmonasterium nuper tento
edito[3] inter cetera contineatur quod de quibuscumque beneficiis ecclesiasticis que
vicesimo nono die Januarii anno regni nostri Anglie terciodecimo [29 January
1390] seu postea de facto vacare inceperunt vel extunc infra idem regnum nostrum
vacaverint, quoddam statutum in parliamento domini Edwardi nuper Regis Anglie
avi nostri apud Westmonasterium anno regni sui Anglie vicesimo quinto tento
editum[4] in omnibus imperpetuum firmiter teneatur et debite execucioni deman-
detur de tempore in tempus, si quis aliquam acceptacionem de aliquo beneficio
ecclesiastico in contrarium dicti statuti in parliamento nostro predicto editi fecerit
et hoc debite probato habeat penam in dicto statuto in parliamento nostro predicto
edito contentam, et quod de aliqua dignitate vel beneficio ecclesiastico que vel
quod dicto vicesimo nono die Januarii plena vel plenum extitit aliquis occasione
alicuius doni, collacionis, reservacionis, provisionis aut alterius vel cuiuscumque
gracie sibi per dominum summum pontificem de huiusmodi beneficio ecclesiastico
facti et ante eundem vicesimum novum diem Januarii minime executi execucionem
inde sub eadem pena nullatenus prosequatur prout in eodem statuto in parliamento
nostro predicto edito plenius contineturi, Jamque intellexerimus quod cum Henricus Derlyng capellanus vicarius [f. 70v] ecclesie de Boreford [Burford][5] per

collacionem abbatis de Keynesham [Keynsham] eiusdem vicarie, ut dicitur, patro-
num legitime fuisset adeptus et in corporali possessione eiusdem eodem vicesimo
nono die Januarii et antea extitisset predictus Walterus, colore cuiusdam provisionis
sibi a sede apostolica ut dicebatur facte, et non ante predictum vicesimum nonum
diem Januarii nec eodem die execute contra formam statutorum predictorum
quandam acceptacionem de vicaria predicta fecisset, pro quod nos in Curia nostra,[6]
coram nobis varios processus versus ipsum Walterum iuxta formam statutorum
predictorum prosecuti fuerimus prout per recorda et processus inde habita plenius
poterit apparere; quidam machinantes processus predictos ac iudicia in Curia nostra
in hac parte reddita maliciose adnullare, quamplures processus coram vobis in
Curia christianitatis versus prefatum Henricum pro vicaria predicta ad opus predicti
Walteri recuperanda in adnullacionem processuum et iudiciorum predictorum ac
contra vim, formam et effectum statutorum predictorum prosecuti fuerunt et indies
prosequuntur minus iuste in nostrum contemptum et preiudicium nostrumque et
corone nostre exheredacionis periculum manifestum. Nos qui ad illesam obser-
vacionem iurum corone nostre vinculo iuramenti astringimur nolentes talia tollerare, vobis prohibemus ne quicquam in hac parte quod in nostrum contemptum vel
preiudicium seu corone nostre exheredacionem aut iudiciorum sive statutorum
predictorum adnullacionem vel derogacionem cedere valeat attemptetis seu attemptari faciatis sub periculo quod incumbit.
Teste me ipso 10 Oct. 1395.

[1]   Grant to Walter Eymer, priest, of the diocese of Limerick, of the office of notary, he having
been examined by Master Francis de Lanzanico, papal secretary, 6 Dec. 1389, *Calendar of Papal
Letters*, IV.320.
[2]   An almost identical writ citing this statute is printed in R.L. Storey, 'Clergy and Common
Law in the Reign of Henry IV', in R.F. Hunnisett and J.B. Post, eds., *Medieval Legal Records in
Memory of C.A.F. Meekings* (London, 1978), p. 392.
[3]   The third Statute of Provisors, 1390; there had been a second passed in 1365.
[4]   The Statute of Provisors, 1351.
[5]   There is no reference in the LAO Index to parishes to a presentation of Burford vicarage
during the episcopate of John Buckingham, though see Reg. 11, ff. 319, 322. 'Very few provisors
are recorded in bishops' registers as being instituted or collated to a benefice, even though many
graces can be proved to have been successful. This is because the induction of provisors was in
the hands of executors appointed by the pope or subexecutors named by them, and was carried
out without regard for the ordinary diocesan administration', A.D.M. Barrell, *The Papacy,
Scotland and Northern England, 1342–1378* (Cambridge, 1995), p. 82.
[6]   That is, King's Bench.

484.   Breve de certiorando Benyngton'
Chancery *certiorari (scrutatis registris)* concerning the rectors of Benington [in
Holland] (Benyngton)[1] church from I Edward III to Easter last, and the institutors,
inductors and patrons.
Teste me ipso 28 June 1396.
[See **Appendix A, no. 25** for the original.]

[1]   'Benyngton' may be identified confidently as Benington in Holland because Long
Benington, the only other possible benefice, was a vicarage. Both villages are in Lincolnshire.

485.   Breve pro Armeston
Chancery *certiorari (scrutatis registris)* who and how many wardens have been
presented to St. John's Hospital, Armston from 50 Edward III to last Christmas and
at whose collation or presentation, when and in what way, and what form is the
foundation of the hospital and whether it is compatible with a benefice with cure.

Teste me ipso 20 June 1396.
[See **Appendix A, no. 24** for the original.]

486. [f. 71] <u>Breve de certiorando Armeston'</u>
Chancery *certiorari (scrutatis registris) sicut alias* concerning the holders of Armston hospital.
Teste me ipso 3 July 1396.

487. <u>Armeston</u>
Chancery *certiorari (scrutatis registris) sicut alias* concerning the holders of Armston hospital with mandate to appear in Chancery on the octave of Michaelmas to explain why earlier writs have not been executed.
Teste me ipso 7 July 1396.
[See **476–9**]

488. <u>Breve de certiorando Benyngton</u>
Chancery *certiorari (scrutatis registris) sicut alias* concerning the rectors of Benington [in Holland] (Benyngton) church from I Edward III to Easter last, and the institutors, inductors and patrons.
Teste me ipso 6 July 1396.
[See **484**]

489. <u>Breve de recipiendo sacramentum vicecomiti Lincoln'</u>
Mandate to receive the oath of Roger Welby sheriff of Lincolnshire according to the form on the enclosed schedule, and to hand him his letter patent of office.
Teste me ipso 1 Dec. 1396.
Return was made from Stow Park 13 Dec. 1396 on which day the bishop received the oath of the said Roger according to the form on the schedule which begins Vouz iurrez etc. while touching the gospels, and after the oath was received handed over the royal commission to the office and other letters patent concerning it. Present: Masters Thomas Welborn, William Gretwell, John Haversham, John Lidington, clerks, and Adam Frydey, etc.

490. <u>Breve pro parliamento</u>
Summons to a parliament at Westminster on the feast of St. Vincent [22 Jan.], with *premunientes* clause.
Teste me ipso 13 Nov. 1396.[1]
<u>Execution.</u>
The dean, chapter, and archdeacons were written to, in the usual form, to execute the writ.

[1] Printed *RDP*, IV.755; see also *CCR 1396–9*, p. 74.

491. [f. 71v] <u>Breve de certiorando Dorney</u>
Chancery *certiorari (scrutatis registris) sicut alias* concerning the number of rectors presented to Dorney church, Buckinghamshire, from 1 Edward III until the present, and the patrons of the living.
Teste me ipso 13 Feb. 1397.[1]

[1] For the vicarage of Dorney, established at this time, see Reg. 11, ff. 165v, 394v–395, 402v, 407, 411v, 418.

492. Prohibicio Oundell'
To the bishop or his commissary: Chancery *ne admittatis* concerning Oundle church, Northamptonshire, against the form of the statute.[1]
Teste me ipso 16 Jan. 1397.

> [1] See above, **483** for references.

493. Breve contra Rectorem de Wytherley
Exchequer *venire faciatis sicut pluries*, returnable on the quindene of Easter [6 May], against William Bulcote rector of Witherley (Wytherley) to answer Brother Ralph Mayloc, proctor of the abbot of Lyre and lately farmer of all the abbot's lands in England, for £60 being arrears of a pension of 20s p.a. due from that church; also against Ralph Bromley rector of Sibstone [Sibson] (Sybbesdon), clerk, to answer the same proctor for £12 being arrears of £4 p.a. pension from his church, for which pensions the proctor is bound in his account to the king, and he cannot satisfy the king until the money is paid, which William and Ralph are witholding.
Teste John Cassy, 4 Feb. 1397.
Retornum. We caused Ralph Bromley to be warned to comply with the writ, but we could not find William Bulcote because a long time before he exchanged his church of Witherley for Barrowby (Berughby) church, Northamptonshire.

494. Breve de certiorando Omnium Sanctorum Hunt'
Chancery *certiorari (scrutatis registris)* concerning the holders and patrons of All Saints church Huntingdon from 1 Edward III until Easter last.
Teste me ipso 5 June 1397.

495. Prohibicio Toucestr'
Chancery *ne admittatis* concerning Towcester church, vacant, it is said, whose advowson is being disputed in the royal court between the king and the bishop of Lincoln, and William Broughton and Thomas Broughton clerk.
Teste me ipso 14 May 1397.

496. [f. 72] Breve pro parliamento
Summons to a parliament at Westminster on Monday after the Exaltation of Holy Cross, with mandate to execute the *premunientes* clause.
Teste me ipso 18 July 1397.[1]
Execution. The dean and chapter and the archdeacons were written to to cite the clergy to attend in All Saints church Northampton on the Monday after the Nativity of the BVM [10 Sept.] to elect two proctors, and to certify the outcome on the same day.
A commission was issued to Masters John Haversham and Thomas Tibberay sequestrator in the archdeaconry of Northampton to receive the certificates, see that the proctors were elected, arrange their expenses and inform the bishop before the Exaltation of Holy Cross [14 Sept.].

> [1] Printed *RDP*, IV.758; see also *CCR 1396–9*, p. 204.

497. [ff. 72–72v] Breve contra Rectorem de Walton iuxta Ramsey
Exchequer *levari faciatis de bonis et beneficiis ecclesiasticis sicut pluries*, returnable on the morrow of Michaelmas, against William Pychelesthorn chaplain, rector

of Wood Walton lately receiver of all rents and profits at the castle and honour of Berkhamsted for £18 5s 7¾d owed to the crown being debts incurred in that office, and seen in his accounts at the Exchequer, from Michaelmas 5 Richard II to the Nativity of St. John Baptist 8 Richard II [29 September 1381 – 24 June 1384]. *Teste* John Cassy, 10 May 1397.
[See **381, 448, 466, 474**]

498. [f. 72v] Breve de certiorando Stoke Goldyngton
Chancery *certiorari (scrutatis registris)* concerning the patrons and rector of Stoke Goldington (Stoke Goldyngton) from 1 Edward III until Easter last.
Teste me ipso 28 May 1397.

499. Prohibicio pro ecclesia de Parva Berkhamstede
Chancery *ne admittatis* concerning Little Berkhamsted (Parva Berkhamstede) church whose advowson is being disputed in the royal court between the prior of Lewes, and the bishop of Lincoln and Ralph Waterman chaplain, Nicholas Hemyngford clerk, Elizabeth who was the wife of William Botreux, Peter Rous chaplain and Thomas Bryce chaplain.
Teste me ipso 14 July 1397.

500. Breve de certiorando Benyngton
Chancery *certiorari (scrutatis registris)* concerning the rectors and patrons of Benington in Holland church from 1 Edward III to Easter last, and the institutors, inductors and patrons.
Teste me ipso 20 Sept. 1397.
[See **484, 488**]

501. Sicut alias pro eadem ecclesia
Chancery *certiorari (scrutatis registris) sicut alias* concerning Benington in Holland church, as in the previous writ.
Teste me ipso 2 Oct. 1397.

502. Sicut pluries pro eadem ecclesia
Chancery *certiorari (scrutatis registris) sicut pluries* concerning the rectors and patrons of Benington in Holland church from 50 Henry III to I Edward III, with mandate to appear in Chancery on the morrow of Martinmas [12 Nov.] to explain why earlier mandates were not executed.
[ff. 72v–73] Breve primum returnum pro Benyngton. [Damaged by water stain.]
We have searched our registers and the list of our findings is as follows: Master Richard Talebot etc. as contained in the Register.
Sleaford 1 Jan. 1398.
[See **484, 488, 500–2**]

503. [f. 73] Breve de certiorando in quodam divorcio Middilton'
Common Pleas mandate, returnable on the quindene of Hilary, to make an inquisition and report on whether there was a divorce between Richard de Middleton and Anne his wife. Anne who was the wife of Richard Middleton impleaded in the king's court at Westminster William Audby who by default of John Middleton was

admitted to the defence of her right to a third part of two[1] messuages, 30 acres of land and 10 acres of meadow with appurtenances in Bisbrooke (Bisbrok), as her dower by the endowment of the said Richard formerly her husband. William came into court and alleged that after the marriage of Richard and Anne they had been divorced during Richard's lifetime before the official of the archdeacon of Northampton. Anne said that there had never been a divorce. We wish to know the truth. *Teste* William Thirning, 28 Nov. 1397.

Execution. The writ is contained in the bishop's mandate to the archdeacon of Northampton or his official, ordering him to scrutinise his register of ecclesiastical causes held before him or his commissary, or in other ways to ascertain if there has been a divorce or to make diligent enquiry if there has been a divorce, and to submit a written report on the whole case, to the bishop or his commissaries Master John Burbache[2] or John Kyngton, at Sleaford prebendal church on the morrow of Hilary. Sleaford 31 Dec. 1397.

[1]   Probable reading; the manuscript is damaged at this point.
[2]   See *BRUO*, I.305–6.

504.   Prohibicio regia contra sequestrum interpositum
To the bishop of his commissary: Chancery *sequestrum relaxetis* concerning the fruits of St. Andrew's priory, Northampton while it is in the king's hand because of the war with France. The king by letters patent committed the keeping of the priory and all its property to Thomas More and John Everdon clerks, from Michaelmas 19 Richard II[1] during the war with France. We hear that you are citing the farmers, their servants and proctors to show the right and title of the churches which have been appropriated to the priory from time immemorial, and for that reason have caused the fruits to be sequestered, in contempt of the king and to the damage of the farmers whose farm is hindered.
Teste me ipso 14 Dec. 1397.

[1]   Grant made 7 Dec. 1395, *CFR 1391–9*, p. 171.

505.   [Damaged] Breve sicut pluries Middilton
Common Pleas *certiorari sicut pluries* concerning the alleged divorce between Richard Middleton and Anne his wife. Anne who was the wife of Richard Middleton impleaded in the king's court at Westminster William Audby who by default of John Middleton was admitted to the defence of her right to a third part of two messuages, 30 acres of land and 10 acres of meadow with appurtenances in Bisbrooke, as her dower by the endowment of the said Richard formerly her husband. William came into court and alleged that after the marriage of Richard and Anne they had been divorced during Richard's lifetime before the official of the archdeacon of Northampton. Anne said that there had never been a divorce. We wish to know the truth. *Teste* William Thyrnyng, 9 May 1398.
[See **503**]

506.   [f. 73v] Breve ad inquirendum de Bastardia vel non Bastardia domine Katerine Hebden'
Justices Itinerant, *inquiretis de bastardia*, returnable before the justices of assize at Lincoln on Friday after St. James the Apostle [28 July 1396], in the following case: John la Warr knight brought in our court before William Thirning and Richard Sydenham justices of assize in Lincoln, at Lincoln, an assize of *novel disseisin*

against Nicholas Hebeden knight and Katherine his wife and John Verdon of Gosberkirk junior, for his free tenure in Gosberton (Gosberkirk), Surfleet (Surflet'), Quadring (Quadryng), Donnington [near Spalding] (Donyngton), Pinchbeck (Pynchebek), and Swineshead (Swyneshede) and the plea was that he was disseized from the manor of Beaurepaire of 4 messuages, 100 acres of land, 80 acres of meadow, 50 acres of pasture and £10 of rent with appurtenances, and the said Nicholas and Katherine 'quo ad unam medietatem manerii terrarum ten' et redditus predictorum et tricesimam partem alterius medietatis manerii predicti cum pertinenciis excepta tricesima parte medietatis duorum mesuagiorum et decem libratarum reddit' predict' tricesimo partis cum pertinenciis placitaverunt in barram assise predict' prout in recordo predicto liquet manifeste'. They alleged in their plea that the whole residue of the manor, lands, and rents was the property of one William de Cressy chivaler who granted it to Nicholas son of Nicholas de Rye and Margaret his wife and to the heirs of their bodies; and Nicholas and Margaret were seized in fee tail, and when they died the property descended to Edmund their son and heir, and then to Nicholas son and heir of Edmund. But Nicholas had no heirs of his body, so the property passed to Beatrice, Joan and Elizabeth his sisters and heirs. Elizabeth's share passed to her son George. Joan died without heirs of her body, so her share passed to Beatrice her sister and to George her relative, Elizabeth's son; and one William de Wyham married Beatrice in the church of Holy Trinity, in the city of Lincoln after the banns had been proclaimed and the marriage took place with all due ceremony. And after the marriage William and Beatrice had issue Katherine. And afterwards William de Wyom and Beatrice died, and the said George died without heirs of his body. And after George, William and Beatrice died, Katherine, as their heir, entered into possession of the property. John la Warr' claimed that George and Beatrice died without heirs and that the property should be his by escheat, but Nicholas and Katherine said that this was not so, to which John la Warre replied that Katherine was altogether a bastard, but she and her husband denied this. Mandate to call witnesses and hold an enquiry into the truth of the matter.
Teste William Thirnyng, Lincoln, 3 March 1396.

507. [ff. 73v–74] <u>Aliud Breve pro eadem Materia</u>
Justices Itinerant *inquiretis de bastardia*, returnable before William Thirnyng and John Woderove justices of assize on the Monday before the feast of St. Emerentiana next [17 Jan. 1397] on the same matter as the previous writ.
Teste William Thirnyng, Lincoln 28 July 1396.

508. [ff. 74–74v] <u>Aliud Breve sicut alias pro eodem</u>
Justices itinerant *inquiretis de bastardia sicut alias*, returnable at Lincoln on Thursday after St. Peter in Chains [2 Aug.], concerning the alleged bastardy of Katherine Hebden, as in the previous two writs.
Teste William Thirnyng, Lincoln 6 March 1397

509. [ff. 74v–75] <u>Quartum et ultimum Breve super eadem materia bastard'</u>
Justices Itinerant *inquiretis de bastardia sicut pluries*, returnable before William Thirnyng and Robert Tirwhit justices of assize at Lincoln on Monday after St. James the Apostle [29 July], concerning Katherine Hebden's alleged bastardy, as in the previous three writs.

Teste William Thirnyng, Lincoln 4 March 1398.

[f. 74v] <u>Require sentenciam lat' in ista causa in libro memorandorum cccclx fol'</u> [Reg. 12 ff. 464–467v][1]

[f. 467–467v] <u>Tenor Commissionis</u>

The bishop's commission to Mr. John Burbache. On 5 June [f. 467v] we received the following writ, *Teste* William Thirnyng, 3 June 1396.

Stow Park 12 June 1396.

[f. 464] <u>Sentencia in causa bastard' lat' pro domina Katerina Hebden'</u>

Report of John Burbach, doctor of laws, the bishop's commissary. Humphrey de Patryngton clerk was the proctor of John la Warr knight. He certifies that Katherine wife of Nicholas Hebden knight is legitimate and not a bastard.

<u>Libellus oblatus pro parte domini la Warre.</u>

He alleged that Beatrice had been married to William de Gamilthorp in church but had committed adultery with William de Wyhom a clerk in holy orders and had lived with him in sin [f. 464v] and it was common knowledge that he was the father of Katherine.

[f. 464v] <u>Materia iustificat' proposita per partem domine Katerine</u>

Katherine's evidence in person. She said that Beatrice was for a long time separated from William [de Gamilthorp] and was freed from all conjugal chains and her marriage dissolved, and that she married William Whyom esquire who was certainly not in holy orders, and did so after the calling of the banns, in the face of the church, and that the wedding was openly and publicly contracted and solemnized and that they lived as man and wife until the death of Beatrice. Lord La Warr defamed Beatrice in speaking of her as an adulteress.

[f. 465] <u>Materia repplic' pro parte attric' minstrat'</u>

[f. 466] <u>Materia dupplic' proposit' pro parte rea</u>

The replication of the evidence was because the same business was also heard in the consistory court of York, *sede vacante*. [f. 467] The evidence is also found in the registers and archives of the consistory court of York.

<u>Prelacionis sentencie</u>

[Reg. 12B, f. 75] <u>Certificatorium Justic' domini Regis.</u> To William Thirnyng and Robert Tirwhit: we have made diligent enquiry and we find that Katherine wife of Nicholas Hebden knight was and is legitimate and not a bastard.

Sleaford 11 July 1398.[2]

---

1   The editor's reference is to the modern foliation of the Memoranda Register.

2   About this time the Hebdens' enemy died; the will of Lord John de la Warr was written on 8 January and proved on 1 Aug. 1398, *Complete Peerage*, IV.150. William Wyhom of Gosberton died shortly afterwards (1 Nov. 1390 x 28 Feb. 1391), but left no personal bequests, Reg. 12, f. 378. See Introduction, p. xviii.

APPENDIX A

SOME WRITS ADDRESSED TO JOHN BUCKINGHAM NOW IN THE PUBLIC RECORD OFFICE

The writs in this appendix are now in the PRO class C 269, *certiorari* ecclesiastical. The writs in this class were formerly in Chancery Miscellanea (C 47), Chancery Files (C 202 series C), and unsorted Miscellaneous Writs.

All the writs in this appendix were issued by Chancery at Westminster, and were returnable without delay, unless otherwise stated.

1. [C 269/4/29. Both writ and return are in very poor condition.] *Certiorari* if Alice (Alesia) daughter of John de Everyngham is a nun of Haverholme.
1 December 1367.   [John de] Brank[etre][1]
[Dorse] We made enquiry as the writ demanded and we find that the said Alesia is not a professed nun of the house of Haverholme.
[The original of the writ registered in 12B, ff. 11v–12; see **44**.]

> [1]   [M.] John de Branketre. For his distinguished career in Chancery, where he was a greater clerk 1355–75, and as a diplomat see the references in Wilkinson, *Chancery*, and in Tout, *Chapters*, VI s.n. Brancaster.

2. [C 269/4/30] [Face] *Certiorari (scrutato registro)* on which day and by whose death the church of Haverholme was last vacant, and who was presented to it and admitted, by whom and by what title, how and in what way, and also the name and surname of the last rector presented by William de la Plaunk patron, it is said, or his predecessors, and by what title.
4 May 1369.   [John de] Branketre
[Dorse] Per J. de Brank'
By looking at our registers and those of our predecessors we find that Haverholme church last became vacant on 7 October 1361 by the death of the last rector Robert, whose surname we cannot discover from the register. Thomas de Evere clerk was presented by William son of Fulk de Berningham after an inquisition had been made by the official of the archdeacon of Buckingham, and he was admitted and instituted by John Gynewell of good memory our immediate predecessor. We also discovered that Roger de Aston priest was presented by William de la Plank' knight to this church on the death of Richard de Donyngton and was admitted by our same predecessor on 17 June 1347 at the Old Temple, London. We are not able to establish from the registers the authenticity of the titles of these presentations.
Swafham[1] [this name is surrrounded by penwork which may indicate a simple notarial sign.]

> [1]   Probably John Swafham; see **119**.

3. [C 269/5/2] [Face] *Certiorari (scrutatis registris)* who was rector of Stanford on Avon (Staneford) church before John de Wynewyk,[1] lately rector, at whose patronage and by what title he was admitted.
20 May 1369.   [John] Freten'[2]
[Dorse] Richard de Baldock was rector of Stanford on Avon as the immediate predecessor of John de Wynewyk with the prebend of Weighton (Wighton) in the church of York, which prebend the said Richard held earlier . . .[3] [the rest of the return is damaged by a brown stain beyond the possibility of reading].

    1   Winwick (Wynewyk), had been Buckingham's predecessor as keeper of the privy seal, 1355–60. A king's clerk of the highest distinction, his career may be traced from the many references listed in Tout, *Chapters*, VI.451. See also *BRUO*, III.2063–4.
    2   For John Freten see the references in Wilkinson, *Chancery*, esp. p. 179.
    3   M. Richard de Baldock was prebendary of Weighton 1324–33, *Fasti*, VI.88. He became rector of Stanford 23 Oct. 1338 and had vacated it by April 1341, *BRUO*, I.96.

4. [C 269/5/10] [Face] *Certiorari (scrutato registro)* if anyone was admitted to the prebend of Stow Longa (Longestowe) in Lincoln cathedral at our presentation before 18 Edward III [1344–45], and if so, on what day, year, who and in what way.[1]
10 Dec. 1370.   [Robert de] Far[yngton][2]
[Dorse] Per H. de Burt[on]
We have scrutinised our registers and those of our predecessor and we find that on 17 September 1342 at the king's presentation Philip Weston formerly [a word is omitted here] of Thomas de Bek then bishop of Lincoln was admitted, and subsequently on 23 January 1346 there came royal writs to the same Thomas bishop of Lincoln saying that you had recovered by court action the presentation of Stow Longa against the said bishop and that he should admit Philip to that prebend at your presentation, notwithstanding your recovery, and so bishop Thomas committed his deputies Peter de Gildesburgh clerk of Lincoln and Augustine de Stokton to admit Philip to the prebend and stall in the choir and chapter assigned to it. We cannot find anything else relevant in the registers. It is said that a certain Reginald de Themunis [Theminis] is now the incumbent but for how long he has been the incumbent we do not know.[3]
[C 269/5/11] [Piece 1, face] To the dean and chapter of Lincoln Mandate to discover if Master Philip de Weston was admitted and installed in the prebend of Stow Longa at the king's presentation, by authorization of the ordinary, or not, and if so on what day, year, and how.
4 March 1371.   [Robert de] Faryngton
[Dorse] The reply appears on the schedule sewn to this writ.
[Piece 2] Return: We cannot find anything about the admission and installation of the said Philip despite looking diligently, nor can we find any mandate of yours to any of the bishop's predecessors from 1335 onwards to admit or install Philip to Stow Longa prebend.
Lincoln chapter House on the feast of St. Edward the King and Martyr [20 Nov.] 1370 [*sic, rectius 1371*][4]

    1   For Philip Weston's tenure of Stow Longa which lasted from 1342 until at least 1360 see *Fasti*, I.111.
    2   Identified from *CCR 1385–9*, p. 737.
    3   The former PRO reference was C 202/168/58. See *Fasti*, I.111. Raynald de Theminis was a papal provisor, see *Calendar of Papal Registers: Papal Letters*, IV.92.
    4   This was formerly C 47/16/5/15.

5. [C 269/5/36] [Piece 1. Both the writ and return are in very poor condition.] *Certiorari (scrutatis registris)* concerning the names of the holders of Churchill (Chirchull) church from the coronation of King Richard [I].[1]
30 December 1372.   [Nicholas] Spaigne[2]
[Piece 2][3] Illeg., but see *The Cartulary of the Monastery of St. Frideswide*, ed. S.R. Wigram vol. II (Oxford Historical Society, 31, 1896), pp. 289–91, and C.R. Cheney, *English Bishops' Chanceries 1100–1250* (Manchester, 1950), p. 102.[4]

    [1]   That is, from the limit of legal memory, 3 Sept. 1189.
    [2]   A Chancery clerk from 1343 until 1374 or 1375; see Tout, *Chapters*, VI.15; Wilkinson, *Chancery*, 6, 7 n., 148 n., 172, 173, 179, 180 and n., 202, 207.
    [3]   The former reference was C 47/16/1/16.
    [4]   See also, Reg. 12, ff. 104–104v.

6. [C 269/5/38] *Certiorari (scrutatis registris)* who and how many persons were presented to Wilden (Wylden) church from the eighteenth year of our grandfather's reign until the forty-fourth year of our reign [1289/90 – 1370/71], their institution and induction and at whose presentation.
24 January 1373.
[Piece 2] We have looked at our registers and here is the information asked for, in order.
First, in the register of Oliver [Sutton], 1298 Wilden was vacant by the death of the rector, Malcolm de Harle. John Ridel knight presented Simon de Pabenham clerk and Ralph Tyrel de Wylden presented Thomas Haliday of Bedeford clerk to the bishop. Inquisition was made by the official of the archdeacon of Bedford and then a second one about the age of Simon de Pabenham, and finally Simon was ordained subdeacon and deacon on 31 May [1298][1] at Brampton near Huntingdon.
In the register of Henry [Burghersh], 1321, when the church was vacant by the death of Simon Pabenham the last rector, John de Pabenham clerk was presented by John de Pabenham knight. Inquisition was made by the official of the archdeacon of Bedford by whom he was admitted 19 December 1321.
In the register of Thomas [Bek], 1343, Edmund de Pabenham clerk was presented by Joanna lady of Wilden on the vacancy caused by the death of John de Pabenham the last rector, and he was admitted on 27 January 1344 at Buckden.
In the register of John [Gynewell], Master Robert Braybrok clerk[2] was presented by William Borstall on the vacancy caused by the death of Edmund the last rector, and he was admitted 7 February 1362 at Biggleswade (Bygleswad').
In the same register Robert de Eston priest was presented by W[illiam] Borstall on the vacancy caused by the resignation of Master Robert Braybrook, and admitted 11 May 1362 at Liddington.

    [1]   The date, illegible in this return, has been supplied from Sutton, VIII.123.
    [2]   The future bishop of London; see *BRUO*, I.254–5.

7. [C 269/6/24] *Certiorari (scrutato registro)* whether the chapel of Cokethorpe (Cokthorp) is part and annexed to Ducklington (Dokelynton') church, and, if it is, then for how long it has been so annexed and whether it is a benefice with cure, who was last presented and when, how, and with what title.
20 November 1376.   [John] Burton
[Dorse] After consulting the registers and *memoranda* of ourselves and our predecessors we find that Cokethorpe chapel is a part and annexed to Ducklington church

and has been since time out of mind, but it is not a benefice with cure and no one has been presented, admitted or instituted to it by us or our predecessors.
Liddington 15 January 1382.[1]

1   The chapels of Cokethorpe and Hardwick are mentioned as part of Duckington church from the episcpate of Oliver Sutton, LAO Reg. 1, f. 344.

8.   [C 269/7/1, piece 1] *Certiorari (scrutato registro)* whether Thomas Priour lately rector of Holywell (Halywell) church, it is said, was presented to the church by Edward III or someone else, and by what right or title he was admitted by you or one of your predecessors.
28 August 1377.   [Geoffrey] Martyn[2]
[Piece 2] Return. We looked diligently at the register of John Gynewell our immediate predecessor of good memory and finally we found that in 1349 Thomas Priour clerk was presented by Edward then king of England to Holywell church, vacant by the death of William Drax the last rector, and that the king made the presentation because the temporalities of Ramsey abbey were then in his hands. We also found that on 14 July in that same year at Newark (Newerk) Thomas Priour was admitted to Holywell church and canonically instituted as rector, and was inducted by the official of the archdeacon of Huntingdon, all of which we notify to you by these presents.
Sleaford 15 September 1377.

1   For Geoffrey Martin or Martyn, see the references in Tout, *Chapters*, VI.331, and Wilkinson, *Chancery*, pp. 85 and n., 86.

9.   [C 269/7/6, piece 1] *Certiorari, inquiretis de bastardia*, concerning William Willy of Kyngesclyve of your diocese, using the best ways and means to acquire this information.
Leeds (Ledes) 30 August 1381.   [John] Lilleston[1]
[Piece 2] Return: We have made diligent enquiry and find that William is not a bastard but the legitimate son of John Willy of Kyngesclive and of Matilda Bate his wife, now deceased, and this we signify to you by these our letters close and patent.
Liddington 4 March 1382.

1   Identified from *CCR 1381–5*, p. 689.

10.   [C 269/7/10, piece 1] *Certiorari (scrutatis registris)* to discover on which day John de Lincoln, last warden of the chapel of Wykes next Bicker (Wykes iuxta Byker)[1] died.
8 December 1382.   [Richard de] Holm'[2]
[Dorse] per John de Walth[am][3]
By inquisition we discovered that John Lincoln last warden of the chapel of Wykes near Bicker died 11 November last in the rectory of Leadenham (Ledenham).

1   In the parish of Donington in Holland, Dorothy M. Owen, 'Medieval Chapels in Lincolnshire', *Lincolnshire History and Archaeology* 10 (1975), 17.
2   See *CPR 1381–5*, pp. 281, 385.
3   There was more than one man of that name in royal service, but this is probably the future keeper of the privy seal, treasurer, and bishop of Salisbury, for whom see Tout, *Chapters*, VI.425, Waltham, John (3).

11. [C 269/7/15, piece 1] *Certiorari (scrutatis registris)*, returnable before the Feast of St. Peter's Chair [22 February] concerning the foundation or ordination of the vicarage of Ashby de la Zouche (Assheby la Zouche), and who has or have been presented to it from its foundation, by what title and in what way.

12 January 1385.   [John] Scarle[1]

[Dorse] Per John de Waltham

[On the writ, in a nineteenth-century archival hand, is written: Inq. P.M. 8 Rich.2 no. 132].

[Piece 2] The following have been presented:

In the register of John [Dalderby] once bishop of Lincoln, John Esseby deacon was presented by the abbot and convent of Lilleshall to the church [*sic*] of Ashby de la Zouche vacant by the death of Roger the last vicar. Inquisition was made by the official of the archdeacon of Leicester by whom he was admitted 19 December in the 5th year of the episcopate [1304.]

Later in the time of the same bishop, William Bromyard chaplain was presented by the abbot and convent of Lilleshall to the said vicarage of Ashby de la Zouche (Esseby la Zouche) vacant by the resignation of John the last vicar, on the [illeg.] December in the 15th year of the episcopate [1314.]

Later in the time of the same bishop, William Lucas of Overton deacon was presented by the abbot and convent of Lilleshall, vacant on the resignation of William the last vicar, on 21 March in the 16th year [1315.][2]

In the register of John Gynewell our predecessor, William de Dounton priest was presented by the same patron on the vacancy caused by the death of Richard the last vicar. Inquisition was made by the official of the archdeacon of Leicester by whom he was admitted 1 November 1349 at Stow Park, and as a perpetual vicar was warned to reside in person and he swore an oath on the gospels in the form of the constitution of Ottobono,[3] and the official was ordered to induct him.

Liddington 12 February 1385.

[1] For the very distinguished career of John Scarle (junior), a native of Lincolnshire, see the references given in Tout, *Chapters*, VI, Wilkinson, *Chancery*, pp. 66 n., 80, and Charles W. Smith, 'A conflict of Interest? Chancery Clerks in Private Service', in Joel Rosenthal and Colin Richmond, eds., *People, Politics and Community in the Later Middle Ages* (Gloucester, 1987), pp. 176–91.

[2] See LAO, Reg. 2, ff. 200v, 208v, 210.

[3] See M. Powicke, *The Thirteenth Century*, 2nd. ed. (Oxford, 1962), pp. 472–4.

12. [C 269/7/21, piece 1] *Certiorari* concerning the names of those presented to a moiety of the churches of Middleton [Milton Malzor] and Collingtree (Midelton et Colyntre) from the first year of Edward [I] son of Henry king of England, by whom, by what title and in what way.

12 April 1386.   [William de] Roundon[1]

[Dorse] Per Johannen de Waltham.

[Piece 2] First, in the time of John Dalderby our predecessor, at the vacancy caused by the death of Thomas de Malleshovers, Edward king of England exercised the patronage because the lands of Simon de Patteshil deceased tenant-in-chief were in his hands. He presented John de Hemmyngburgh deacon. John son of Simon de Patteshill presented William de Rylesham, and William le Vineter de Creck presented Almaric de North[ampton] clerk successively, and an inquisition was made by the official of the archdeacon of Northampton. There was litigation in the king's court between John son of Simon, and William le Vincer about the right of patronage of the said moiety. Finally there was shown to the bishop a royal writ in this form: Common Pleas *admittatis* concerning the moiety of the church of Middleton and Collingtree because Simon de Pateshull has recovered the presentation against William le Vint' de Creek; *Teste* R[alph] de Hengham 18 November 1308.

The same John de Hemmyngburgh was admitted to the moiety on 23 November 1308 at Burnham, was canonically instituted and swore an oath of obedience to the bishop in the usual form, and the archdeacon's official was written to, etc.

In the time of John Gynewell our immediate predecessor, we find that William Baldewyn priest was presented by William de Pateshull to a moiety of the churches of Milton Malzors and Collingtree near Northampton on the vacancy caused by the death of John de Hemmyngburgh, and he was admitted 3 March 1353 at Stow Park. [This return is in poor condition. The history of this benefice may be followed in these references from the LAO Index: Reg. 1/259v (Sutton); 2/112v, 114v, 134v (Dalderby); 4/185, 188v, 239; 9/175v, 196, 198, 233. This the last reference until Reg. 16.]

   1   See *CPR 1381–5*, pp. 117, 158.

13. [C 269/7/25, piece 1] *Certiorari* whether the bishop has carried out the mandate to admit and install John Stacy to whom the king granted the prebend of Leighton Buzzard (Leghton Busard) in Lincoln cathedral, by letters patent in his own right; the bishop is to describe all the circumstances of the execution of the writ, along with the names of any who impede it.
13 December 1387.

[Piece 2] Mandate of the bishop to the prior of Dunstable, Order of St. Augustine, and Master Thomas Stowe, doctor of laws, archdeacon of Bedford, reciting the royal grant of the prebend to John Stacy because the temporalities of the bishopric of Lincoln were recently in the hands of the king's grandfather, dated 16 November 1387; to hold an inquiry into the vacancy, namely whether one exists, and if so when it began, who has the right of presentation, and also into the character, orders and benefices of John Stacy, and if the king has the right of patronage and John is a sufficient person to admit him to the prebend and canonry of Lincoln cathedral and assign him a competence, returning a report to the bishop.
Nettleham, 25 Nov. 1387.

Report of the commissaries of the inquiry held in the chapel of Tebworth (Tebbeworth) within the parish of Chalgrave, which found that the prebend of Leighton Buzzard was vacant and had recently begun to be so by the death of John Pipe who died on the feast of St. Lawrence in August 34 Edward III [10 Aug. 1360]; that the king did enjoy the right of presentation by inheritance from his grandfather, and that John Stacy was a man of good life and honest character, in priestly orders, rector of Blunham, Lincoln diocese and prebendary of Sucarshall (Seukesworth) in Gnosall collegiate church, Lichfield diocese.[1] There is no canonical objection to the said John Stacy. Wherefore John Stacy was admitted to the prebend of Leighton Buzzard. The names of the inquisitors are: John and Mr. Roger rectors of the parish churches of Battlesden (Badlesdon) and Steppingley (Stepyngle), and John, Thomas, William, John, Richard, Walter, Richard, William, Nicholas and John perpetual vicars of the churches of Sundon (Sonyngdon), Wymington (Wynton), Houghton Regis, Chalgrave, Tilsworth (Tillesworth), Westoning (Westonynge), Totternho (Tetorulio Segeuly), Ampthill and Studham (Stodham).

Dunstable 4 Dec. [1387] under the seal of the dean of Dunstable.
After receiving this report John Stacy was admitted and installed to his prebend in Lincoln cathedral. The bishop therefore signifies that he has executed the above writ.
Sleaford 16 Jan. 1388.[2]
[C 269/7/34 piece 1][3] *Certiorari (scrutatis registris)* addressed to the dean and chapter of Lincoln concerning the holders of the prebend of Leighton Buzzard from 1 Edward III.
29 Jan. 1389.   [Thomas] Middelton[4]
[Dorse] Per Johannem de Burton
[Piece 2] Diligent scrutiny of the registers of admissions of canons of the church of Lincoln and other books and memoranda deposited in our archives showed that on the death of John de Puy Barzac (Podio Bersaco) John Pype was presented by Edward [III] and installed on 13 Dec. 1343. After the death of John Pipe, William Gynewell was installed before the feast of the deposition of St. Hugh which is celebrated every year on 17 November.[5] Lincoln chapter house, 21 Feb. 1389.[6]

1   Not a truly collegiate church, see *VCH Staffordshire*, IV.113, 128; see also **246** and n.
2   The promotion of John Stacy is excessively well documented, see *Fasti*, I.80 n., XII.31.
3   Formerly C 47/16/3/9, part.
4   See Wilkinson, *Chancery*, pp. 67 n., 83 n.
5   To distinguish it from the other feast of St. Hugh, 6 or 7 Oct.
6   *Fasti*, I.79–80.

14. [C 269/7/33, piece 1][1] *Certiorari* concerning the true annual value of the church of St. Andrew, Sawtry (Sautre) and the value of two parts of the tithes, and whether the value of those two parts is worth a fourth part of the annual value of the goods of the church, since a plea is pending in court Christian between the prior of St. Mary, Huntingdon and Thomas de Alyngton rector of St. Andrew, Sawtry concerning two parts of all the tithes from the lord of Belmes in Salteris; Thomas claimed in Chancery that those two parts of tithes would be worth a fourth part of the goods of the church, so a prohibition was issued not to proceed in the case, but now we wish to be informed whether the two parts of those tithes are a fourth part of the value of St. Andrew's church.
22 Jan. 1389.   [John de] Burton
[Dorse] J. de Burton
[Piece 2] Notification that the value of St. Andrew's church is 12 marks p.a., and the value of two parts of the tithes is 20 shillings; and so those two parts do not attain the value of a fourth part of the church's goods.
Sleaford 4 Feb. 1389.

1   Formerly C 202/090/178.

15. [C 269/7/36, Piece 1; pencil note on the writ: 20/8][1] *Certiorari (scrutatis registris) sicut pluries*, returnable on the morrow of Ascension [28 May], concerning the holders of Leighton Buzzard prebend in Lincoln cathedral from 1 Edward III, who was admitted, at whose collation, and on what days and years.
8 May 1389.   [John] Lilleston
[Piece 2, pencil note: 21/8] Scrutiny of the registers of ourself and from the time of John Gynewell our immediate predecessor shows that on 8 October 1361 at Wooburn (Woubourn) the bishop conferred the prebend of Leighton Buzzard,

vacant by the death of Master John Pipe, on William Gynewell, priest, who was canonically instituted and installed.
Sleaford 19 May 1389.

    [1]   Formerly C 47/16/319 part.

16. [C 269/8/9, piece 1][1] *Certiorari (scrutatis tam registro vestro quam registris predecessorum vestrorum)* which benefices Master Henry Chaddesden, now deceased it is said,[2] held within the diocese of Lincoln, by whose presentation, how long he held them, and whether these were compatible benefices.[3]
12 Oct. 1391.
[Piece 2] We have made diligent scrutiny of the registers of our predecessors and in the register of Thomas Bek of good memory we find the following:
M. Henry de Chaddesden clerk was presented by Hugh de Courteney earl of Devon to the portion of Waddesdon (Wodesdon) church, commonly known as 'attegrene',[4] by way of exchange with Master Henry Motoun, with whom he also exchanged the archdeaconry of Stow for the prebend of St. Martin in Dernestall [in Lincoln cathedral].[5] He was admitted to that portion on 31 December 1346 at Nettleham in the person of Thomas de Derby clerk his proctor. Subsequently we find that the said venerable father lord Thomas Bek died at Nettleham on 15 February 1347.
During the vacancy before the episcopate of John Gynewell our immediate predecessor [began] on 14 June 1347, in the middle of the vacancy, in the register of the late Master William Bachiler official and keeper of the spiritualities,[6] we find the following: On 8 May 1347 in the chapter house of Lincoln cathedral Master William Bachiler official of Lincoln *sede vacante* declared that Master Henry Chaddesden archdeacon of Leicester and rector of the portion of attegrene in Waddesdon church had enjoyed both those benefices peacefully for a month and more, was contumacious by his absence, and had incurred the penalties laid down by the constitution *Execrabilis* issued by pope John XXII.[7] He therefore deprived Henry both of the archdeaconry and of the rectory, and pronounced the sentence in written form attested by Augustine Stokton, John Kelleseye, and Alan (Aleyn) the notary.[8]
Finally, afterwards, in the time of John Gynewell our immediate predecessor as we find in his register, Nicholas de Chaddesden clerk was presented by Hugh de Courtenaye earl of Devon to the portion of Waddesdon church called attegrene, vacant by the free resignation of Master Henry Chaddesden the last rector. No inquisition was taken and he was admitted on 27 April 1354 at the Old Temple, London.[9] The dean of Waddesdon was written to to induct him. How Henry Chaddesden was admitted to the archdeaconry of Leicester cannot be found in our registers because he was admitted at a time of vacancy by the chapter of Lincoln [cathedral] church, as appears clearly enough in the chapter register.[10] The portion of attegrene in Waddesdon rectory and the archdeaconry of Leicester which he held simultaneously are incompatible benefices with cure of souls, it is thought ('Rectoria . . . de Wodesdon et archidiaconatus Leycestr' . . . sunt beneficia incompatibilia et curata et pro talibus reputantur . . .')
Returned under letter close, Stow Park, 4 Nov. 1391.
[Dorse] Memorandum that on 15 November in the same year these certificates were exemplified in the required form at the request of John Botlesham clerk.[11]

    [1]   Formerly C 47/19/4/19, part.
    [2]   Dead by 12 May 1354, *Fasti*, I.12, 89. Chaddesden is not listed in Dr. Emden's volumes of graduates' biographies but he was the uncle of M. Nicholas Chaddesden for whom see *BRUO*,

I.380–1. The younger Chaddesden was an executor of his uncle's will, and he himself died at Rome in 1390.

3   Though he cannot be connected with certainty to either university Henry Chaddesden was clearly a highly skilled canon lawyer; he was appointed official of London diocese, *sede vacante*, on 20 April 1354, though evidently declined to act, Irene J. Churchill, *Canterbury Administration* (London, 1933), II.247 and n.

4   The church of Waddesdon, Bucks., was divided into three portions of which the third was called de la Grene, or atte Grene, LAO Index.

5   Archdeacon of Stow from 1339 until Dec. 1346 when he became prebendary of St. Martin's in Dernstall, by exchange, and held the dignity until his death in spring 1354, *Fasti*, I.18, 89.

6   Prebendary of Corringham 1328–49, *ibid.*, I.56. Not listed by Dr. Emden.

7   Issued 19 Nov. 1317, which forbade the holding of two or more benefices with cure of souls.

8   Chaddesden's tenure of the archdeaconry was recognized by the pope by 12 June 1348, and he held it until his death, *Fasti*, I.12.

9   The London residence of the bishops of Lincoln, on the east side of Chancery Lane.

10   LAO, Dean and Chapter, A.C. As/35, ff. 31v–32.

11   Bottlesham was granted the archdeaconry in 1390, but after litigation he withdrew in favour of Cardinal Poncellus de Orsini who had held the dignity since 1380, *Fasti* I.12.

17.   [C 269/8/18. piece 1][1] *Certiorari* whether Maud Huntercombe is a nun, arising out of a petition presentated to parliament 3 November 1391. Winchester 12 Feb. 1393.

[Piece 2] Having made diligent enquiry, at great trouble and expense ('cum magnis laboribus et expensis'), about the truth of the matter we find that Maud Huntercombe, sister of the late Elizabeth who was the wife of Robert de Cherlton formerly justice of the Bench entered into a religious house of nuns of the order of St. Augustine of Burnham at the age of discretion, and is legitimately a member of that order, and Maud is a professed nun and was for a long time before the death of Elizabeth wife of Robert Cherlton. Stow Park, 20 April 1391.

[Dorse] 'Excellentissimo in Christo principi et domino nostro domino Ricardo dei gracia Regi Angl' et Franc' et domino Hibern' illustrissimo'.
[See **416–20**][2]

1   Formerly C 47/18/5/7.
2   See also PRO C 145/254/2; SC 8/97/4804; *CCR 1392–6*, pp. 70–1.

18.   [C 269/8/20. The document is damaged along the left-hand side.][1]
[The writ has not survived; it was evidently a *certiorari* concerning the holders of the church of North Mimms, similar to, though not identifical with, those of **429–31**.]

We have inspected the registers and articles of institutions to churches from the times of John Dalderby, Henry Burghersh, Thomas Beck, and John Gynewell our predecessors. The institutions to North Mimms church are as follows, word for word from our predecessors' registers.

In the time of Dalderby. The vacancy was caused by the death of John de Kirkeby. Sara who was the wife of Walter de Castello presented Adam Bacun, and dominus Ralph Montchesney (de Monte Caviso) presented John de Sandale subdeacon. Inquisition was made by the official of the archdeacon of Huntingdon and there was litigation in the king's court by which Ralph Montchesney (de Monte Caniso) recovered the advowson against Sara widow of Walter de Castello. By virtue of a Common Pleas writ of *admittatis*, *Teste* R[alph] de Hengham 22 May 1 Edward II

[1308], the bishop admitted John de Sandale at Buckden, [illeg.] May 1308 in the person of Nicholas de Loughteburg' his proctor.

On the resignation of John Sandale, Gilbert de Wyggeton priest was presented by [illeg.], and after an inquisition by the archdeacon's official he was admitted at Sleaford (Lafford), 28 March 1312 and instituted in the person of Master Nicholas, vicar of Empingham [Rutland] (Empyngham), priest, his proctor.

In the time of Henry Burghersh. On the resignation of Gilbert de Wyggeton, Gilbert de Sandale priest was presented by King Edward,[2] and after inquisition he was admitted at [?] Louth, 7 July 1323 in the presence of Masters Thomas Louth (de Luda) treasurer, Walter de Maidenstane and Roger Louth (de Luda) clerk.

On the death of Gilbert de Sandale, John de Wynewyk acolyte[3] was presented by King Edward because the lands and rights of Giles de Badlesmere, deceased, were in his hands, and after inquisition by the dean of Berkhamstead (Berkhamstede) he was admitted at the Old Temple, London, 4 March 1340.

On the resignation of John Wynewyk, Henry de Wynewyk clerk, was presented by Elizabeth de Badlesmere, and admitted in the person of John de Wynewyk king's clerk his proctor, at Lincoln, 19 April 1341.

In the time of Thomas Beck. On the resignation of Henry Wynewyk, William de Kesteven priest, rector of Potterspury [Northants.] (Potterspirie), was presented by Hugh le Despenser kt., by way of exchange, and after inquisition by the archdeacon's official he was admitted at Thame, 27 May 1344.

In the time of J[ohn] Gynewell. On the death of William de Kesteven, Thomas de Horton clerk, was presented by Simon de Swanlond kt., and after inquisition by the dean of Berkhamstead was admitted at Nutley (Nottele), 17 September 1361.

In our time. On the resignation of Thomas de Horton, William Burgeys, priest, rector of Great Billing (Billyng Magna), was presented by John de Thorp, Nicholas de Thornton and Thomas de Bedewynde clerks, by way of exchange, and after inquisition by the archdeacon's official was admitted at Liddington, 4 May 1372. Stow Park, 31 Dec. 1393.

  1   Formerly C 47/16/4/4.
  2   No reason for the crown's exercise of patronage is given.
  3   For whom see **Appendix A, no. 3**.

19. [C 269/8/26][1] Return to a writ, now lost, which was enregistered at 12B, f. 68v. See **467** for both the writ and the copy of the original return explaining why the bishop has not been able to execute earlier writs.

  1   Formerly C 47/16/8/29.

20. [C 269/8/27][1] The original of the writ concerning the chapel of Halse in Brackley parish, Northamptonshire, registered in 12B, f. 76v [**467**].   [James] Billyngford

[Dorse] After receiving this writ we diligently scrutinised our registers and those of Hugh II our predecessor and of our other predecessors according to the requirements of the writ but we found nothing material to the said writ therein.

  1   Formerly C 47/91/4/25.

21. [C269/8/28, piece 1][1] *Certiorari (scrutatis registris)* to know what sums the Leicester churches of St. Mary *de Castro*, St. Leonard, and St. Martin owe annually to the bishop and to the archdeacon of Leicester.

Northampton, 1 Aug. 1395.   [James] Billyngford
[Piece 2] In obedience to the writ we have looked at the register and we cannot find in what sums the churches of St. Mary *de Castro*, St. Leonard and St. Martin, Leicester, are bound to us and to the archdeacon, but *inter alia* we find[2] that St. Mary *de Castro* is assessed according to an ancient assessment at 12 marks. Also, the church of St. Mary *de Castro* is of the patronage of the abbey of St. Mary *de Pratis* and has been appropriated to its use since the foundation of the canons,[3] except for the oblations and obventions of the altar which are due to seven deserving clerks who serve the church in person, and to two chaplains, except for a third of the tithes which the abbot of Saint-Evroul (St. Ebrulfus) has taken since ancient times. The abbot's portion is worth about 60s.[4] The church of St. Leonard is in the same patronage and has been appropriated to the same abbot for a long time; its value is 2 marks. The church of St. Martin is in the same patronage and is assessed at 11 marks.
We cannot find any more material relevant to this writ in the registers of Hugh II or of any other of our predecessors.
Stow Park, 26 Oct. 1395.

  [1]   Formerly C 47/16/8/10.
  [2]   The rest of the return is largely copied from *Rot. Wells*, I.238.
  [3]   The house was first founded in 1107 as a secular college with a dean and twelve canons; in 1143 the new house of Augustinian canons of St. Mary in the Meadows superseded the secular college to which all its endowments were transferred. The church of St. Mary *de castro* was part of the first foundation, A. Hamilton Thompson, *The Abbey of St. Mary of the Meadows, Leicester* (Leicester, 1949), pp. 1–2, 5.
  [4]   The relationship of the college of St. Mary *de castro* to the abbey of St. Mary *de Pratis*, Leicester, is described in *VCH Leicestershire* II (1954), p. 45, which reports that after about 1220 'The college existed in obscurity for the rest of the middle ages.'

22.   [C 269/8/32, piece 1, writ; piece 2, return]
The original of the writ and return concerning St. John's hospital Armston, which was registered in Reg. 12B, ff. 69v–70; see **478**.
Pontefract, 9 March 1396.   [James] Billyngford.

23.   [C 269/8/34, piece 1] *Certiorari* concerning Armston hospital.
Teste me ipso 3 May 1396.   [James] Billyngford
[The original of **479**]
[Piece 2. Return] We have searched the registers of Robert Grosseteste and cannot find the foundation charter of Armston hospital but we have found the confirmation of two charters dating from his episcopate whose tenor is as follows:
Recites the *inspeximus* now printed *Rotuli Roberti Grosseteste, episcopi Lincolniensis*, ed. F.N. Davis (C&Y x, 1913), pp. 187–8; and also the beginning of the foundation charter now printed *Sutton* II.149–51.
Stow Park, 28 May 1396.
[See also the return to **479**]

24.   [C 269/8/35] *Certiorari* concerning the foundation of Armston hospital and its holders.
Teste me ipso 20 June 1396.
[In the same form as C 269/8/34 above; see **479**]
[Piece 2, return] In the same form, word for word, as C269/8/34 above.]
Stow Park, 20 Sept. 1396.

25. [C 269/8/38, piece 1] *Certiorari (scrutatis registris)* concerning the rector of Benington [in Holland] church from I Edward III to Easter last, and the names of the institutors, inductors and patrons.
Teste me ipso 28 June 1396.
[The original of **484**]
[Piece 2. Return] Master John de Leke subdeacon was presented by Ada de Stykeney widow of John de Stykeney on the vacancy caused by the death of John de Bohun. Inquisition was first made by Master William de Makeseye, commissary-general of the official of Lincoln, by whom he was admitted on 24 April 1328 at Stamford. Robert de Driffeld acolyte was presented by Philippa queen of England at the vacancy caused by the resignation of John de Leek, and was admitted on 27 Oct. 1349 at Newark (Newerk) in the person of John Mallyng his proctor. On Robert's free resignation the same Robert de Driffeld was presented by Queen Philippa and admitted 30 March 1353 at Stow Park.
Richard de Rocheford clerk was presented by Robert de Derby of Boston (St. Botolph) at the vacancy caused by the death of Robert de Driffeld and was instituted on 27 October 1359 at Sleaford (Lafford). Saer de Rocheford clerk was presented by Robert de Derby of Benyngton to the parish church of Benington in Holland (Benyngton in Holand) at the vacancy caused by the death of Richard de Rocheford, and was admitted on 23 March 1375 at Nocton (Nokton). Henry de Brauncewell priest was present by Robert de Derby at the next vacancy and admitted in the bishop's church at Stow Park on 6 September 1381. Robert Hull clerk was presented by Thomas Gerard citizen of Norwich at the vacancy caused by Henry Brauncewell's death and was admitted in the chapel within the manor of Stow Park on 9 March 1396 by William rector of a moiety of Leverton church, John vicar of Butterwick (Butterwyk), William vicar of Frampton, Adam Eykwell de Boston, John Bull, John Suton and Robert Gyboun faithful laymen, lawfully sworn in this matter, who said on oath that there were two sisters to whom the advowson pertained alternately. One of them was Alice wife of the late Robert Derby who had in right of his wife presented Henry Brauncewell to the church; the other was called Ada wife of John de Feriby de Barton, and of this marriage there was a daughter Elizabeth now deceased whom Thomas Gerard who was now presenting had married, and of this marriage there were several children. And after her death he had under English custom the right of presentation for this turn ('et post cuius mortem de consuetudine regni Anglie habet ius presentandi ad eandem ista vice'). And when the suitability of his person had been established the same Robert was presented to the bishop and admitted and instituted as rector.
Stow Park 20 Sept. 1396.

26. [C 269/8/39; piece 1] *Certiorari* concerning those presented to Benington in Holland church from 50 Henry III until 1 Edward III.
20 Sept. 1397.   [Henry de] Shelford
[Piece 2] In answer to your writ we reply as follows: Master Richard Talebot treasurer of St. Paul's [cathedral] London was presented by Henry de Bathonia at the vacancy caused by the death of Master Henry le Aungevyn the last rector [no date].[1] Peter de Yatingdon subdeacon was presented by Nicholas de Yatingdon knight on the vacancy caused by Master Richard Talebot's death, inquisition was made by Master Alexander official of the archdeacon of Lincoln, and in the

presence of Master Roger archdeacon of Lincoln, at Buckden (Bugeden) he was admitted etc.[2] William Dous de Paris (Parys) deacon was presented by John de Bath (Bathonia) knight on the death of Peter de Jatingdon, and after inquisition by William archdeacon of Lincoln was admitted on 4 November in the sixth [episco-pal] year [of Oliver Sutton, 1285] at the Old Temple, London.[3] William de Parys deacon was re-presented to Benington in Holland church vacant because William had not been ordained priest within a year of [his previous] institution, and was instituted at the Old Temple, London, 18 October 1286.[4] Roger de St. John subdeacon was presented by lady Joanna de Boune daughter and heiress of dominus John de Bath at the vacancy caused by the death of William de Parys the last rector, and was admitted 5 April in the twelfth [episcopal] year [1292], at Fingest.[5] John de Bohun subdeacon was presented by William de Bohun and Edmund his brother at the vacancy caused by the death of Master Roger de St. John, and admitted 29 July in the seventh year [of bishop John Dalderby, 1306] at Biggleswade (Bik-leswade) and instituted in the person of the rector of Salmonby his proctor. Master John de Leke subdeacon was presented by Ada de Stykeney widow of John de Stykeney at the vacancy caused by the death of John de Bohoun the last rector. An inquisition was held by Master William Makeseye commissary-general of the official of Lincoln by whom he was admitted 24 April 1328 at Stamford.
Sleaford 1 Jan. 1398.

1 1260–61, supplied from *Rot. Gravesend*, p. 5.
2 1262–63, *ibid.*, p. 12.
3 *Sutton*, I.73.
4 *Ibid.*, p. 89.
5 *Ibid.*, p. 165.

27. [C 269/15/38; piece 1][1] *Certiorari*, returnable before the Ascenion [14 May], who and how many aliens hold benefices, both parish churches and dignities, in the diocese of Lincoln and for how long they have been so occupied.
16 April 1374.
[Piece 2[2]] By virtue of this writ [recited in full] we have made diligent enquiry and send the return on the annexed roll.
Liddington, 6 May 1374.
[The schedule has now become detached; it is possible that it survives in the PRO as E 135/25/7.]

1 Formerly C 202/072/10.
2 Formerly C 47/18/3/15.

APPENDIX B

SELECT WRITS ADDRESSED TO BISHOP BUCKINGHAM WHICH WERE COPIED INTO HIS OTHER REGISTERS

As is explained in section iv of the Introduction, a considerable number of writs came into Buckingham's chancery and were engrossed elsewhere than amongst the writ collection. Those listed here were all issued in connection with lawsuits about advowsons, the right of presentation to an ecclesiastical benefice, which could be heard only by the lay courts. Most are, in the main, of one of two types. Prohibitions – the margin flag says <u>Prohibicio</u> – were writs of *ne admittatis* issued by Chancery; they forbade the bishop to admit an incumbent to a particular benefice because its advowson was being disputed before a royal court. Writs called consultation (<u>Consultacio</u>) were Common Pleas writs of *admittatis* following the conclusion of a case; the writ informed the bishop which party to the suit had been victorious. Often there had been not two, but three or four competing interests, and this explains the number of prohibitions which might be issued in a single case. Chancery consultations ordered the bishop to do what pertained to his office in regard to the vacant benefice, since the crown no longer had an interest in the matter.

All the benefices concerned were rectories, unless otherwise stated.

ASHWELL (Herts., Archdeaconry Huntingdon)
Consultation, 9 May 1393.
Reg. 11, f. 267v.

AYNHO (Northants.)
Consultation, 10 Oct. 1386; consultation, 10 Oct. 1386; consultation, 7 Nov. 1386.
Reg. 11, f. 139.

BARNOLBY LE BECK (Lincs.)
Consultation, 4 Feb. 1371.
Reg. 10, f. 45v.

BERKHAMSTEAD, LITTLE (Herts., Archdeaconry Huntingdon)
Prohibition, 6 Feb. 1397; prohibition, 8 Dec. 1397.
Reg. 11, f. 285v.

BRAMPTON (Hunts.), prebend.
Consultation, 11 Oct. 1387; consultation, 13 Oct. 1387; consultation, 9 Oct. 1387.
Reg. 11, f. 254.

BRINGTON (Northants.)
Consultation, 12 May 1386; consultation, 12 May 1386.
Reg. 11, f. 136.

BROUGHTON (near Newport Pagnell, Bucks.)
Consultation, 12 Oct. 1386.
Reg. 11, f. 391v.

BROUGHTON, BRANT (Lincs.)
Prohibition, 20 Sept. 1381 (copied twice); consultation, 13 Feb. 1382.
Reg. 10, f. 117v.

BUCKINGHAM (Bucks.), archdeaconry.
Prohibition, 18 Oct. 1391.
Reg. 11, f. 428.

BULWICK (Northants.)
Prohibition, 29 Jan. 1396; consultation, 25 April 1396.
Reg. 11, f. 180–180v.

CAREBY (Lincs.)
Prohibition, 16 Oct. 1369; consultation, 28
Nov. 1369.
Reg. 10, f. 37v.

CRICK (Northants.)
Prohibition, 18 April 1368; prohibition, 18
April 1368; prohibition, 6 May 1368;
prohibition, 25 May 1368; Chancery
consultation, 3 Nov. 1368.
Reg. 12, f. 67v.

CROPREDY (Oxon.), vicarage.
Prohibition, 3 Jan. 1376; consultation, 24
May 1376.
Reg. 10, f. 364.

DESBOROUGH (Northants.)
Consultation, 6 Nov. 1382.
Reg. 10, f. 228v.

EATON SOCON (Beds.), vicarage.
Consultation, 24 Jan. 1386.
Reg. 11, f. 344.

FLIXBOROUGH (Lincs.).
Prohibition, 22 Oct. 1394.
Reg. 11, f. 115.

GRAVELEY (Herts., Archdeaconry.
Huntingdon)
Prohibition, 5 April 1385; prohibition, 10
April 1385; consultation, 14 June 1385.
Reg. 11, f. 249v.

HATFIELD (Herts., Archdeaconry.
Huntingdon)
Prohibition, 6 Feb. 1389; consultation, 26
May 1389.
Reg. 11, f. 259.

HORTON (near Windsor, Bucks.)
Prohibition, 28 July, 1395.
Reg. 11, f. 416v.

IRBY ON HUMBER (Lincs.)
Consultation, 4 April 1386.
Reg. 11, ff. 22v–23.

KETTLEBY, AB (Leics.)
Prohibition, 14 March 1378; consultation,
15 June 1378; consultation, 19 June 1378.
Reg. 10, f. 269v.

LEICESTER (Leics.), archdeaconry.
Prohibition, 18 July 1392; consultation, 25
July 1392; consultation *sicut alias* 26 July
1392; consultation *sicut pluries* 27 July
1392; [letter patent revoking presentation,

1 Aug. 1392]; Chancery consultation, 1
Aug. 1392.
Reg. 11, f. 436–436v.

LEIGHTON BUZZARD (Beds.), prebend.
Chancery *certiorari*, 13 Dec. 1387.
Reg. 11, f. 347.

MARSTON MORETAINE (Beds.)
Prohibition, 21 March 1373; prohibition,
26 March 1373; consultation, 22 June
1373; consultation, 22 June 1373;
consultation, 26 June 1373; consultation,
29 June 1373.
Reg. 10, f. 388v.

MIDDLETON and COLLINGTREE
(Northants.)
Prohibition, 30 March 1386; prohibition,
29 March 1386; consultation, 12 Feb.
1387.
Reg. 11, f. 142v.

OFFORD CLUNY (Hunts.)
Prohibition, 18 June 1394; [letter patent
revoking presentation, 20 June 1394];
Chancery consultation, 1 July 1394.
Reg. 11, f. 274v.

OUNDLE (Northants.)
Consultation, 18 Oct. 1371.
Reg. 10, ff. 185v–186.

OVERTON MARKET (Rutland)
Chancery *certiorari*, 24 Aug. 1390;
prohibition, 20 Nov. 1390; prohibition, 28
April 1391; [letter patent revoking
presentation, 6 May 1391]; Chancery
certiorari, 31 Aug. 1391; [letter patent
revoking presentation, 6 Nov. 1391];
consultation, 17 Nov. 1391; [letter patent
of presentation, 11 Oct. 1391].
Reg. 11, f. 160.

OXCOMBE (Lincs.)
Prohibition, 2 Aug. 1380; consultation, 31
Jan. 1383.
Reg. 10, f. 122v.

OXFORD, St. Michael at the South Gate
(Oxon.)
Consultation, 10 May 1386.
Reg. 11, f. 304v.

OXFORD, St. Peter in the Bail (Oxon.)
Consultation, 10 Feb. 1387.
Reg. 11, 306v.

SEATON (Rutland)
Prohibition, 28 Oct. 1383; prohibition, 29 Oct. 1384; consultation, 18 Dec. 1384.
Reg. 11, f. 131.

STANGROUND (Hunts.)
Consultation, 9 Feb. 1392.
Reg. 11, f. 266v.

THURCASTON (Leics.)
Consultation, 9 March 1387.
Reg. 11, f. 205v.

UPPINGHAM (Rutland)
Prohibition, 8 Dec. 1390; prohibition, 8 Dec. 1390; [letter patent of renunciation, 14 Dec. 1390].
Reg. 11, f. 157.

WASHINGLEY (Hunts.)
Prohibition, 5 Nov. 1372; consultation, 1 April 1373.
Reg. 10, f. 304.

WESTON TURVILLE (Bucks.)
Consultation, 7 Feb. 1376.
Reg. 10, f. 439v.

WILDEN (Beds.)
Prohibition, 20 Oct. 1373; consultation, 3 Nov. 1373.
Reg. 10, f. 389.

YELVERTOFT (Northants.)
Consultation, 20 July 1397; prohibition, 8 Feb. 1397; prohibition, 24 Feb. 1397; prohibition, 12 Feb. 1397.
Reg. 11, f. 186–186v.

APPENDIX C

ATTESTING JUDGES

The references are to writ numbers in the text[1]

Note. While Richard II was in Ireland (2 Oct. 1394 – 7/11 May 1395) Chancery writs were attested by **Edmund, duke of York, guardian of England**.
Attested six writs, the earliest 5 Oct. 1394, the latest 3 Feb. 1395.
Numbers: 453, 454, 455, 456, 458, 460.

COMMON PLEAS

Belknap (Bealknapp), Robert, chief justice, appointed 10 Oct. 1374; vacated 30 Jan. 1388.
Attested fifty-five writs, the earliest 7 Jan. 1376, the latest 28 Jan. 1388.
Numbers: 184, 188, 190, 191, 195, 196, 200, 205, 206, 209, 210, 217, 223, 226, 231, 232, 234, 239, 242, 243, 247, 251, 252, 255, 256, 258, 264, 265, 271, 272, 278, 283, 287, 298, 299, 300, 301, 306, 307, 312, 316, 318, 319, 320, 324, 325, 327, 328, 334, 335, 336, 337, 340, 345, 348.

Charlton (Cherlton), Robert, chief justice, appointed 30 Jan. 1388; his last term was Michaelmas 1395.
Attested thirty writs, the earliest 6 May 1388, the latest 23 May 1395.
Numbers: 350, 351, 355, 359, 364, 365, 366, 379, 380, 386, 389, 392, 393, 406, 407, 409, 410, 421, 428, 433, 434, 435, 437, 438, 439, 440, 441, 442, 459, 461.

Finchdean (Fyncheden), William de, second justice, appointed 29 Oct. 1365; chief justice appointed 14 April 1371; his last term was Trinity, 1374.
Attested eight writs, the earliest 6 Oct. 1371, the latest 17 May 1374.
Numbers: 142, 156, 163, 164, 166, 169, 177, 182.

Thirning (Thirnyng), William, second justice, appointed 11 April 1388; chief justice appointed 15 Jan. 1396; he served to the end of the reign and was appointed chief justice by Henry IV, 30 Sept. 1399; Henry V reappointed him, 2 May 1413, but he was dead by 26 June 1413.
Attested seven writs, the earliest 27 Jan. 1396, the latest 5 May 1398.
Numbers: 475, 503, 505, 506, 507, 508, 509.

---

[1]   The biographical information in this appendix is derived from *Officers of the Exchequer*, compiled by J.C. Sainty, List and Index Society Special Series 18 (1983), Sir John Sainty, *The Judges of England 1272–1990*, Selden Society Supplementary Series 10 (1993), and *HBC*, unless otherwise stated.

Thorpe, Robert de, chief justice, appointed 27 June 1356; vacated 14 April 1371.
Attested twenty-three writs, the earliest 25 Nov. 1363, the latest 23 Jan. 1370.
Numbers: 8, 9, 12, 13, 16, 22, 42, 49, 51, 61, 64, 72, 75, 76, 77, 84, 86, 99, 100, 111, 114, 115, 117.

Witchingham (Wychyngham), William de, third justice, appointed 29 Oct. 1365, his last term was Trinity, 1377.
Attested one writ, 18 June 1374.
Number: 180.

EXCHEQUER

Allerthorp, Lawrence, auditor of the exchequer c.1366–75, baron appointed 27 Nov. 1375; reappointed 26 June 1377; second baron appointed 2 Nov. 1387; reappointed 12 May 1389, 30 Sept. 1399; paid until Michaelmas 1400; treasurer 31 May 1401 – 27 Feb. 1402. Died 21 July 1406.
Attested one writ, 5 Dec. 1394.
Number: 457

Asty, Henry, serjeant at law, chief baron appointed 12 Nov. 1375; reappointed 26 June 1377; third justice of Common Pleas, 6 Dec. 1380 to Easter term 1383.
Attested five writs, the earliest 12 Feb. 1376, the latest 13 Nov. 1379.
Numbers: 187, 189, 192, 199, 207.

Brantingham (Brantyngham), Thomas de, bishop of Exeter, treasurer, 27 June 1369 – 27 March 1371, 19 July 1377 – 1 Feb. 1381, 4 May – 20 Aug. 1389.
Attested two writs, 16 Jan. 1370 and 12 Dec. 1377.
Numbers: 116, 198

Cary, John, chief baron appointed 5 Nov. 1386; removed from office 1 Feb. 1388.[2]
Attested nine writs, the earliest 14 Feb. 1387, the latest 28 Jan. 1388.
Numbers: 321, 322, 326, 332, 333, 342, 343, 344, 346

Cassy, John, serjeant at law, chief baron appointed 12 May 1389; reappointed 30 Sept. 1399; dead by June 1400.
Attested twenty-two writs, the earliest 31 May 1389, the latest 10 May 1397.
Numbers: 361, 362, 367, 368, 369, 370, 372, 374, 375, 376, 377, 381, 384, 385, 399, 408, 448, 466, 473, 474, 493, 497.

Greystock, Henry de, baron, appointed 6 Oct. 1356; his last term was Easter 1365.
Attested three writs, 6 and 20 June and 12 July 1364.
Numbers: 15, 18, 19.

Lodelowe, Thomas de, second baron appointed 15 April 1365; chief baron appointed 20 Oct. 1365; his last term was Michaelmas 1373; dead by 26 Feb. 1374.
Attested ninety-three writs, the earliest 10 Dec. 1365, the latest 23 Nov. 1372.
Numbers: 28, 29, 30, 31, 32, 33, 34, 35, 36, 37, 38, 40, 45, 46, 47, 52, 53, 54, 55, 56, 57, 59, 60, 62, 63, 65, 66, 67, 68, 69, 70, 71, 74, 78, 79, 80, 81, 82, 83, 85, 87, 89, 92, 93, 94, 95, 96, 97, 98, 101, 102, 104, 105, 106, 107, 108, 109, 110, 112,

---

[2]   And imprisoned in the Tower, *The Westminster Chronicle 1381–1394*, ed. L.C. Hector and Barbara F. Harvey (Oxford, 1982), p. 307.

113, 118, 119, 120, 121, 122, 123, 124, 125, 126, 128, 129, 130, 131, 132, 135, 136, 137, 138, 139, 140, 143, 147, 148, 149, 150, 151, 153, 158, 161, 165, 167, 172, 173.

Plesyngton, Robert de, chief baron appointed 6 Dec. 1380; discharged 4 Nov. 1386; died 27 Sept. 1393.
Attested twenty-seven writs, the earliest 12 Dec. 1383, the latest 23 Nov. 1386.
Numbers: 218, 222, 227, 228, 229, 237, 238, 245, 259, 260, 261, 262, 266, 269, 270, 284, 285, 286, 291, 292, 295, 297, 302, 303, 304, 309, 310.

Skipwith (Skypwyth), William de, justice of Common Pleas 1359–61; chief baron of the Exchequer appointed 25 June 1361, a post from which he was deprived for 'enormous unfaithfulness' in 1365, though soon restored to office; 1370 chief justice of the Pleas following the king's lieutenant in Ireland;[3] later a justice of the Common Pleas, 8 Oct. 1376 to Hilary term 1388.
Attested eleven writs, the earliest 4 July 1363, the latest 16 Oct. 1365.
4, 5, 6, 7, 10, 11, 14, 21, 25, 26, 27.

Tauk, William,[4] serjeant at law; chief baron appointed 3 Feb. 1374; died 14 July 1375.
Attested three writs, dated 9, 14 Feb. and 18 June 1374.
Numbers: 178, 179, 181.

ITINERANT JUSTICES

Cavendish (Cavendissh), John, chief justice king's bench, appointed 5 July 1372; murdered during the Peasant's Revolt on 14 June 1381.
Attested three writs dated Lincoln 3 March 1373, Westminster 18 June 1374, Northampton 27 Nov. 1380.
Numbers: 152, 185, 218.

Fulthorpe, Roger de, fifth justice of the common bench, appointed 28 Nov. 1374; removed from office 1 Feb. 1388.[5]
Attested two writs, Northampton 7 Dec. 1386, Northampton 16 July 1387.
Numbers: 308, 329.

Ingelby, Thomas de, justice of king's bench from 25 June 1361; his last term was Michaelmas 1377.
Attested four writs, Northampton 24 July 1364, Westminster 28 Oct. 1366, Westminster 27 Nov. 1366, Westminster 11 June 1369.
Numbers: 17, 48, 58, 91.

Thirnyng, William. See above under common bench.
Attested four writs, all dated at Lincoln: 3 March and 28 July 1396, 6 March 1397, 4 March 1398.
Numbers: 506, 507, 508, 509.

---

3 Tout, *Chapters*, III.259 and n. 2
4 See also J.B. Post, 'The Tauk Family in the 14th and 15th Centuries', *Sussex Archaeological Collections* 111 (1973). I am grateful to Professor W.M. Ormrod for this reference.
5 *Westminster Chronicle*, p. 307.

KING'S BENCH

Knyvet, John, chief justice, appointed 29 Oct. 1365 until 5 July 1372 when he became chancellor.
Attested three writs, dated 12 Nov. 1366, 20 May and 10 July 1367,
Numbers: 39, 41, 50.

INDEX OF PERSONS AND PLACES

All references are to sections unless otherwise indicated; roman numerals refer to page numbers in the introduction. Unidentifed place-names are given in *italics*.

Abbreviations used in the index.

INDEX OF SUBECTS

All references are to sections unless otherwise indicated; roman numerals refer to page numbers in the introduction.